A GUIDE TO FORTRAN IV PROGRAMMING

SECOND EDITION
DANIEL D. McCRACKEN
JOHN WILEY & SONS, INC.
NEW YORK LONDON SYDNEY TORONTO

A GUIDE TO FORTRAN IV PROGRAMMING

To John Backus

This book was set in Zenith
by York Graphic Services,
Inc., and printed and bound
by Semline Inc. The designer
was Jerome B. Wilke; the
drawings were done by the
Wiley Illustration Department. The editor was Beverly
D. Nerenberg. Joan E. Rosen-
berg supervised production.
Cover art prepared by
Thomas J. Huston

Library of Congress Cataloging in Publication Data:

McCracken, Daniel D.
A guide to Fortran IV programming.

1. FORTRAN (Computer program language) I. Title.
II. Title: Fortran IV programming.

QA76.73.F25M3 1972   001.6'424   72-4745
ISBN 0-471-58281-6

Printed in the United States of America

10 9 8 7 6 5 4 3

PREFACE

This book is written for the person who wishes to gain a rapid grasp of the use of computers and of Fortran in the solution of problems in such fields as science, engineering, statistics, education, and business. The essentials of Fortran IV are presented here in a form that can be mastered in a few hours of careful reading and computer use. For the reader who wishes a fuller understanding, some of the more challenging exercises and term problem suggestions provide an opportunity to deepen one's comprehension.

There is a certain leaning toward what might be called "technical" applications as distinguished from things like payroll and accounts receivable, but the business administration student will find the examples and exercises meaningful. Calculus is not required for study of the text.

It is anticipated that the book will be helpful in a variety of learning situations.

1. It can be used as the text for a course in computer programming. Some schools teach only the rudiments of Fortran programming in a first course, which may carry one credit or possibly none. Other schools use the first programming course as a way of introducing the students to other languages as well as Fortran, or include some applications, or perhaps cover some basic notions of numerical mathematics. In such cases the course might carry two or three credits. Either way, students are expected to run programs on a computer, which is strongly recommended as the best way to learn the subject. The book has been organized to facilitate getting the students on the machine as early as possible in the course, which all instructors agree is desirable. If the compiler being used permits input and output without the use of FORMAT statements, which is also highly desirable, the instructor will find no difficulty in skipping over a few pages of material in the first chapter and telling the students how to write FORMATless programs.

2. It can be used as the text for a supplement to some other course. Covering the fundamentals of Fortran will take only a few hours and the time required will ordinarily be more than recovered by improved learning of the primary subject matter. One common combination, for students in science or engineering, is Fortran and numerical methods, or Fortran and a sampling of computer applications, or Fortran and some other programming language. The presentation is suited to many such combinations, with an appropriate selection of exercises. Courses in statistics or business management, for example, can readily be built around the text.

3. Students in an industrial course in Fortran programming will find the book useful as an elaboration of the necessarily rather terse descriptions contained in most Fortran reference manuals and as a guide to the many ways in which Fortran can be applied to the solution of realistic problems.

4. The book is suitable for individual study in school or industry.

For all types of usage the value of the book is enhanced by the inclusion of a large number of graded exercises, with answers to a selected set given at the back of the book and answers to all others in a *Teacher's Manual*. These exercises induce thorough mastery of the fundamentals and provide an insight into methods and applications that often go considerably beyond those presented in the body of the text.

Of particular importance are the 14 case studies and the text-processing program shown in Excursion I, which show Fortran in use in the context of meaningful examples. They demonstrate how to go about setting up a program, emphasizing the concept of an algorithm. They also show how programs work by reproducing actual computer output from representative test runs. One case study is the medium for an introduction to program checkout, and several present nonnumerical applications to convey the concept that a computer is an *information* processor rather than just a *number* processor.

The Fortran IV language presented here is in conformity with the language defined in the American National Standard document USAS X3.9-1966, "FORTRAN," approved March 7, 1966. Most actual Fortran implementations go somewhat beyond the Standard, and many of the most useful and widely adopted of these extensions are presented in the text; these extensions are always carefully noted as such when introduced. In the interest of clarity no attempt has been made to point out the many detailed ways in which actual implementations deviate from the language described in this book; it is assumed that any reader writing programs for an actual implementation will have available an appropriate reference manual, together with a brief summary of any necessary job control language cards for running under an operating system.

The preparation of this second edition has been guided by the following intentions. First, the aspects of the first edition that students and instructors found useful have been kept largely intact. For instance, the order of presentation of the major topics has not been altered, and the exercises in the first edition have been carried over with only minor modifications. Second, the presentation has been brought completely up to date. (At the time of the publication of the first edition, the Standard had not yet been adopted, and many changes have occurred in the computing field in other ways as well.) For example, there is as much coverage of operating systems—both batch and time sharing—as the beginning reader needs to know. Third, a good deal of new material has been added. All chapters have new exercises, especially in Chapters 5 and 6, by which point the reader knows enough about programming to be able to tackle really meaningful problems. There is an extended case study on time sharing (Excursion I), a discussion of the crucial topic of data entry and validation (Excursion II), an essay on writing readable programs to facilitate program proving and documentation (Excursion III), and a brief monograph on how to write Fortran programs that are efficient in execution (Excursion IV). Finally, full recognition has been given to the importance of WATFOR and WATFIV in greatly improving the effectiveness of computing in an educational environment (and, indeed, everywhere).

For the many users who will be taking advantage of WATFOR or WATFIV, Appendix 4 contains a summary of the language differences and a complete listing of the diagnostic error messages for both WATFOR and WATFIV. Throughout the entire text are indications of the ways in which the reader using WATFOR or WATFIV will find his task simplified.

As outlined more fully in the *Teacher's Manual,* the instructor will ordinarily wish to supply students with a two- or three-page handout giving the necessary details of how to run a program at a particular installation. This will cover such matters as the format of the JOB card, how to submit decks or sign on to the time-sharing system, and the like. One section of this handout should specify how to write READ and WRITE statements for the first third or half of the course, if some simplified input/output system is available.

Students should be aware of the existence and value of the samples of statements at the back of the book, after the index. Once the fundamentals have been mastered, it is surprising how great a percentage of the day-to-day questions about statement punctuation and other such matters can be answered most quickly by reference to samples.

Daniel D. McCracken
Ossining, New York
May 1972

ACKNOWLEDGMENTS

One of the pleasures of authorship is the privilege of working with talented and interesting colleagues. I am delighted to acknowledge my debts to the following people.

George W. Armerding of Capital Data Systems, Los Angeles, Mrs. Joyce Fodor of the University of Wisconsin, and Mrs. Susan Jaedecke of the University of Denver have been my primary reviewers. They have read the entire book at least twice, making a truly astonishing number of suggestions for improvement and catching a great many slips of one kind and another. I am happy to give them all the credit they deserve, while reserving to myself responsibility for whatever flaws remain. Mr. Armerding's contribution includes, as well, extremely helpful discussions of how the revision should be done. My debt to him is difficult to convey, perhaps, to someone who has not written a book.

The cover design is "Mobius Curves" by computer artist Thomas J. Huston, and is provided by the courtesy of COMPUTRA, Box 608, Upland, Indiana, and the Taylor University Computing Center.

The WATFOR and WATFIV error messages reproduced in Appendix 4 were graciously supplied by J. Wesley Graham and Mrs. Sandra J. Ward of the University of Waterloo, Canada.

Gerald M. Weinberg, of the State University of New York, Binghamton, George W. Armerding, above, and D. Chris Larson, Telex Computer Products, Inc., all contributed to or wrote parts of the Excursions.

Mrs. Ursula Connor and Douglas B. Kuhn, of National CSS, Inc., were of great assistance in the preparation and running of the programs presented in the text. All programs were tested and the output prepared using the facilities of National CSS.

Robert R. Fenichel of the Massachusetts General Hospital supplied a number of the more interesting examples and term problem suggestions, as credited in the text, and proofread several sections of the manuscript.

Mrs. Phyllis Dennen typed the entire manuscript and otherwise served faithfully as a tolerant and understanding secretary.

The following people assisted in a variety of ways too numerous to try to detail, either in the planning of the book or in the preparation of some of the material, especially the Excursions and exercises:

Edmund C. Berkeley, Berkeley Enterprises, Inc.
Miss Christine Braun, The University of Toronto, Canada
John W. Carr, III, The University of Pennsylvania
Kern W. Dickman, The University of Illinois
William S. Dorn, The University of Denver
Patrick D. Fischer, The University of Waterloo, Canada
H. George Friedman, Jr., The University of Illinois
Charles J. Gibbons, The University of Nebraska, Omaha
C. C. Gotlieb, The University of Toronto, Canada
David Gries, Cornell University
Thomas A. Keenan, The National Science Foundation
Thomas A. Murrell, The University of Illinois
Jerry L. Ray, The University of Nebraska, Omaha
Thomas J. Schriber, The University of Michigan
John E. Skelton, The University of Denver

Finally, I express my appreciation to all of the wonderfully talented people at Wiley who contributed to the development and production of this book.

D. D. M.

CONTENTS

1 FUNDAMENTALS OF FORTRAN COMPUTATION

1.1 THE USE OF COMPUTERS

Electronic computers are widely used in the solution of the problems of science, engineering, business, and education. This use is based on their ability to operate at great speed, to produce accurate results, to store large quantities of information, and to carry out long and complex sequences of operations without human intervention.

In this book we shall deal with a broad spectrum of problems that might be characterized as "technical," which is meant to distinguish them from the kinds of applications that are usually described as "data processing." The following examples illustrate the kinds of situations that are assumed to be of interest to the readers of this book, where a computer might be used.

☐ The design of a new airplane consumes thousands of hours of computer time in the investigation of the interrelated requirements of structures, aerodynamics, power plants, and control systems as they would operate under various flight conditions. After a prototype has been built, flight testing generates voluminous data that must be processed and analyzed, often employing statistical techniques.

☐ The design of a chemical plant requires calculations of capacities, operating conditions, and yields, under a variety of circumstances. The techniques of operations research often come into play in determining the optimum operating conditions, taking into account economic factors and sometimes demanding very large amounts of computer time.

☐ Weather prediction studies involve large amounts of data and the solution of equations that, although not very difficult in principle, call for vast amounts of calculation.

☐ Statistical studies of the relationships among various factors that affect learning often call upon the computer, ranging from modest computations that a student might do in a research project to nationwide studies involving millions of people.

☐ The communications industry is making increasing use of computers to store, process, and disseminate information. All text for this book, for instance, was processed by a computer that controlled the composition, and the index was prepared by the Fortran program shown in Excursion I.

☐ The investigation of the possible structure of a complex compound in biochemistry could involve a combination of "scientific" computations having to do with binding energies, interatomic distances, and so on, with an elaborate computer program to present the results in a visually meaningful form.

The computer techniques that are involved in applications as diverse as those cited depend to a certain extent on the task, but the person intending to use a computer in any of them would need to know something about the primary subject of how to communicate his intentions to the computer, which is essentially what this book is about. And while we are learning how to talk to the computer, we shall also present small but representative examples of a wide variety of typical computer applications.

1.2 THE STEPS IN SOLVING A PROBLEM WITH A COMPUTER

There is much more to solving a problem with a computer than the part the computer does. It will be instructive to outline the complete process of setting up a representative technical problem for computer solution to see just what the person does and what the computer does.

Problem Identification and Goal Definition

The computer cannot decide for us what we want to do. *We* have to decide what the system under development is supposed to accomplish, what goal or combination of goals it must satisfy, under what conditions it must operate, and what general approach to solving the problem is to be taken. In some applications this step is trivial; in others it may take months or years. In any case, the step clearly demands a full knowledge of the problem; there is usually little the computer can do to help us with this step.

Mathematical Description

In many, although not all, of the kinds of applications we are considering in this book, it is necessary to begin by formulating a mathematical description of the process under study. This can generally be done in a variety of ways; one particular approach must be chosen or a new one developed if no standard method applies. This step, in which the computer does nothing, requires full knowledge of the problem and of any relevant fields of mathematics.

Numerical Analysis

The mathematical formulation of the problem may not be directly translatable to the language of the computer, since the computer can only do arithmetic and make simple quantitative decisions. Differential equations, integrals, and correlation coefficients, to name a few common examples, must be expressed in terms of arithmetic operations. Furthermore, it must be established that any errors inherent in the data or introduced by the computations do not invalidate the results.

This entire branch of modern mathematics is outside the scope of this book. We shall assume that the reader will approach the computer with his problem expressed in terms that are suitable for computer solution. We shall, however, illustrate quite a number of elementary numerical procedures in the examples and case studies in the course of demonstrating various programming concepts.

Algorithm Formulation

The next step is to devise a precise and unambiguous statement of exactly what we want the computer to do in terms of operations of which it is capable. A computer cannot follow the order "solve the equation." It can follow the order "square the number identified by the variable name X2REAL," or, "go back to the beginning if the current value of the variable named EPS is greater than 0.0001," or "divide SUM by N." Furthermore, and very important, the exact sequence of actions must be specified in complete detail, especially all points where the computer is to make a "decision" based on relationships among values in its storage. An unambiguous definition of the actions to be carried out in solving a problem is called an *algorithm*. It might be expressed in English sentences, or in a computer language, or, commonly, in a graphical form called a *flowchart*.

Computer Programming

With the algorithm in hand, that is, knowing exactly what we want to do, the next task is to express the algorithm in a language that the computer can understand. Fortran is one such language. The computer language imposes restrictions of its own in terms of what kinds of orders it can interpret and execute; different languages have different capabilities. Furthermore, the exact form in which our orders to the computer are written is prescribed for each language, and the rules are generally rather inflexible.

The primary objective of this book is to enable the reader to construct a correct Fortran program to solve problems of interest to him.

(Secondary purposes are to show what kinds of applications can usefully be attacked with a computer, to indicate what some of the common algorithmic techniques are, and to demonstrate a sampling of widely used numerical methods.)

Program Checkout

There are so many chances to make mistakes in programming that most programs do not work as intended when first tried. The mistakes must be located and corrected, and the program must be thoroughly tested to prove that it actually does what the writer meant it to do. The computer is used in this step, which ordinarily takes longer than writing the program in the first place.

We shall place considerable emphasis throughout the book on writing programs so as to facilitate the checkout step. The techniques to be suggested will also greatly facilitate the maintenance of programs; all programs that are used over an extended period of time have to be modified periodically as requirements change. Programs that have been written with future maintenance in mind, and otherwise properly documented, are immensely easier to maintain than those where this consideration has been ignored.

Production

Now, finally, the program can be combined with problem data and run. In a typical situation many sets of data are entered into the computer in one run, and answers are produced without human intervention between sets. This step may take from a few seconds to many hours, depending on the problem and the computer.

Interpretation

The results printed by the computer do not always constitute a final answer to the problem. The user of the computer must often now interpret the results to see what they mean in terms of the combinations of goals of the proposed system. It is often necessary to repeat some or all of the preceding steps before the problem is really solved.

Several conclusions may be drawn from this discussion. First, the computer does not, by it-self, solve problems; it only follows exactly the computational procedures given to it. Second, a computer does not relieve the user of the responsibility of planning the work carefully; in fact, the computer demands much more careful planning. The computer is faster and more accurate than a human being, but it cannot decide how to proceed or what to do with the results. Third, a computer does not in any way reduce the need for a full and detailed understanding of the problem area or for a thorough knowledge of the related mathematics.

As we have already suggested, the emphasis in this book is on the programming step. Problem identification, goal definition, and mathematical formulation are in the province of the technical area under consideration, whatever it may be: electrical engineering, physics, statistics, or operations research. Numerical analysis is a branch of modern mathematics in its own right. Program checkout is discussed, but at lesser length; production is ordinarily not the programmer's responsibility; the interpretation of results brings us once again back into the specialized field of the problem area.

We take it, then, that the reader approaches the subject of this book with a full understanding of his problem, and with a realization that he must know exactly what he wants the computer to do. A computer cannot be told, "solve my problem." All it can do, basically, is follow a precisely defined sequence of elementary steps. Readers without prior computer experience may be assured that we shall give many examples of the development of algorithms and of the translation of algorithms into correct Fortran programs. But when the reader approaches a computer with his own problem, he will have to know exactly what it is he wants the machine to do.

1.3 A FORTRAN PROGRAM

A procedure for solving a problem with Fortran consists of a series of *statements,* which are of several types. One type specifies the operations on numbers or other information that are the heart of the procedure. A second calls for input or output, such as reading a data card, printing a line of results, or punching a card of results. Statements of these first two types are executed in the order in which they are written. A third type of statement alters the *flow of control* of statement execution, so that groups of statements can be executed repeatedly or the sequence otherwise changed. The fourth type of statement provides certain information *about* the procedure without itself requiring any computation.

Taken together, all the statements that specify the problem-solving procedure constitute a *source program*. When the source program has been written, it must either be punched into cards and entered into the computer or typed in using a time-sharing terminal. Either way, it is next translated by a Fortran *compiler* or *processor* into an *object program*. This step is required because the computer can actually "understand" only certain *machine instructions* that call for relatively simple operations like adding two numbers, comparing two sets of letters, or carrying out part of the conversion from one number representation to another. The compiler translates our source program statements, which often call for actions much more elaborate than can be carried out by one machine instruction, into suitable sequences of machine instructions. The object program is actually executed by the computer to obtain the results we want.

The word Fortran thus refers both to a language for expressing problem-solving procedures and to a compiler. The Fortran compiler, which is also called a *processor* or *translator,* is itself a large program of computer instructions; the compiler is usually supplied by the computer manufacturer. It was this translation aspect that led to the original meaning of the word Fortran: FORmula TRANslation.

The organization and operation of the computer at the level of machine instructions is a fascinating subject in its own right, but for the person who will be writing programs entirely in Fortran it is largely optional knowledge. Only occasionally will an understanding of how the machine operates enable the Fortran programmer to write better programs. We have accordingly not included a sketch of machine operation in the text.

Fortran has gone through a steady process of evolution since its introduction in the mid-fifties. In this book we shall deal exclusively with what is called Fortran IV (Fortran four), and we shall not cover the differences between For-

tran IV and earlier versions, which were designated Fortran II.

With a few exceptions that will be carefully noted as they occur, we shall confine ourselves to USA Standard Fortran, as defined in standard USAS X3.9-1966, of the American National Standards Institute, Inc. (ANSI), approved in 1966. In the ANSI terminology, which unfortunately has not been widely adopted on this item, "Fortran" means what we call Fortran IV, and "Basic Fortran" is used to describe what we call Fortran II.

Particular versions of Fortran, as implemented by different manufacturers or other organizations, differ from Standard Fortran to various degrees. Some implementations omit features and many provide additional features. We shall take advantage of some of the additional features that are widely used, especially some in WATFOR and WATFIV, which are also available in most IBM System/360 Fortran implementations as well as some of the Fortrans from other manufacturers. We shall also occasionally point out areas in which extensions beyond the standard are commonly made. We shall not otherwise attempt to delineate the variations in Fortran implementations, which unfortunately are numerous. The reader learning Fortran from this book will gain a solid foundation of the core of the language, but it will be essential to have available a reference manual on the particular system being used.

We turn now to a study of the various elements of which statements are composed: constants, variables, operations, expressions, and functions. After a study of these basic language units, we shall learn how to combine them into statements, and we shall then be able to write simple programs.

1.4 CONSTANTS

We begin by considering two of the kinds of numbers that can be used in Fortran: *integer* and *real*.

A Fortran integer is just what it says—a whole number. It may be zero or any positive or negative number of less than, typically, ten decimal digits. The limits on the size of an integer vary from computer to computer. Because integers are restricted to integral values, they are ordinarily used only in special situations, as we shall see later.

Most numbers used in Fortran computations are real. Inside the computer Fortran real numbers are represented in floating point form. This is similar to scientific notation, in which a number is treated as a fraction between 0.1 and 1.0 times a power of 10. The *magnitude* (sign not considered) of the number so represented must be zero or must lie between limits in the range of approximately 10^{-50} to 10^{+50}. Again, the exact limits vary.

A Fortran integer is always an integer in the mathematical sense, whereas a Fortran real number may be an integer or may have a fractional part. Furthermore, Fortran carries out computations on real numbers in such a way that we do not have to be concerned with the location of decimal points. All questions of lining up decimal points before, for example, addition or subtraction are automatically taken care of by the computer.

A Fortran real number is a rational real number in the mathematical sense. Irrational numbers are not permitted; they can only be approximated to some degree of precision. Indeed, not all rational numbers can be represented exactly in Fortran; the simple fraction $\frac{1}{3}$, for instance, can only be approximated as a decimal or binary or hexadecimal fraction.

(Fortran provides another kind of number, called *double precision,* to improve the accuracy of approximation. We shall postpone consideration of this type of number, however, so that we may write a complete program as quickly as possible. For the same reason we postpone discussion of the other two Fortran quantities: complex and logical. These additional types will be taken up in Chapter 3.)

Any number that appears in a statement in explicit form is called a *constant,* whereas a quantity that is given a name and is allowed to vary is a *variable.* For instance, we shall see a little later that the following are arithmetic assignment statements.

```
I = 2

X = A + 12.7
```

Here 2 and 12.7 are constants; *I*, *X*, and *A* are variables.

Fortran distinguishes between integer and real constants by the presence or absence of a decimal point and/or exponent (see below). If the constant does not contain a decimal point and does not contain an exponent, it is taken to be an integer constant. If it contains a decimal point or an exponent or both, it is taken to be a real constant. The two forms are *not* interchangeable because they are ordinarily stored and processed within the computer in quite different ways.

If a constant is positive, it may or may not be preceded by a plus sign, as desired. If it is negative, it must be preceded by a minus sign. The following are acceptable integer constants.

```
0
6
+400
-1234
10000
-2000
```

The following are not acceptable integer constants.

```
12.78          (decimal point not allowed in integer)
-10,000        (comma not allowed)
1234567890000  (too large in most Fortrans)
```

The decimal point in a real constant may appear at the beginning of a number, at the end, or between any two digits. In theory a real constant may have any number of digits, but there are at least three practical restrictions. First, many systems place a restriction on the number of digits permitted, such as eight or twelve. As usual, details vary among different implementations, and the reader must consult a reference manual for his system. Second, some systems use the number of digits as a signal that the constant is double precision: if there are more than, say, seven digits, the constant is taken to be double precision. Sometimes this is of no consequence, but in other cases it can cause serious errors or compiler diagnostic error indications. Finally, there is always the practical consideration that any machine has a limit on the amount of precision that can be carried in a given amount of storage space. If a certain machine provides for 36 binary digits of precision in a real constant, which is the equivalent of about 12 decimal digits, then it makes no sense to write constants with 20 or 30 digits even if the Fortran system permits it, because the computer word cannot hold that much information.

It is possible to follow a real or integer constant by the letter E (for "exponent") and a one- or two-digit positive or negative integer power of 10, by which the number is to be multiplied, to give a real constant. The power of 10 is then called the *exponent* of the constant. This simplifies the writing of very large or very small numbers. The following are acceptable real constants.

```
0.0
0.1
.1
6.0
6.
-20000.0
-0.0002783
+15.083
5.0E-12
-7.E+6
6.215E13
-.1E7
11E2
```

The following are not acceptable real constants.

```
12,345.6     (comma not allowed)
+234         (no decimal point)
1.6E97       (too large in most Fortrans)
5.862E2.5    (exponent part must be an integer)
E+7          (exponent alone not permitted)
```

EXERCISES

*1. Write the following numbers as Fortran real constants.

256   2.56   −43,000 10^{12}
0.000000492   −10 10^{-16}

2. Write the following as Fortran real constants.

16   4.59016   −10,000 10^{17}
0.000006   −1 -10^{-10}

*3. All of the following are unacceptable as real constants. Why?

87,654.3   +987   9.2E+98   7E-9.3

*Answers to starred exercises are given at the back of the book.

4. All of the following are unacceptable as real constants. Why?

−10000   1E-99   2.34-E12   2E5.1

*5. Do the following pairs of real constants represent the same number in each case?

```
16.9         +16.9
23000.       2.3E4
0.000007     .7E-5
1.0          1.
.906E5       906.0E+02
110.0        11E1
```

*6. Some of the following are unacceptable as integer constants. Identify the errors.

+234.   −234   23,400   1E12   100000000000

7. Some of the following are unacceptable as integer constants. Identify the errors.

−16.5   16000   16,000   2.E12.5   0.01

1.5 VARIABLES AND THE NAMES OF VARIABLES

The term *variable* is used in Fortran to denote any quantity that is referred to by name instead of by explicit appearance. A variable is able to take on many values during the execution of a program, whereas a constant is restricted to just one value.

Variables may be integer or real. An integer variable is one that may take on any of the values permitted for an integer constant, namely, zero or any positive or negative integer in the range permitted for the particular version of Fortran being used.

The *name* of an integer variable has one to six letters or digits, the first of which is *I*, *J*, *K*, *L*, *M*, or *N*. (The limit of six letters or digits is typical but may be different in some versions.) Examples of acceptable names of integer variables are: I, KLM, MATRIX, L123, I6M2K, KAPPA. Examples of unacceptable names of integer variables are: J123456 (too many characters), ABC (does not begin with the correct letter), 5M (does not begin with a letter), *J78 (contains a character other than a letter or digit), J34.5 (contains a character other than a letter or digit).

A number of Fortran systems permit the use of the dollar sign as a valid character in a variable name.

A real variable is represented inside the computer in the same form as a real constant, that is, as a fraction times a power of 10 (or other number base). The *name* of a real variable has one to six letters or digits, the first of which is a letter but *not I, J, K, L, M,* or *N*. As might be suspected, Fortran compilers use the first letter of a variable name to determine whether the variable is integer or real. This convention can be overridden, however, with the type statements REAL and INTEGER that we shall consider in Chapter 3. For now, and in any case in the absence of type statements, the distinction between integer and real variable names is made on the basis of the first letter.

Examples of acceptable names of real variables are: AVAR, R5ITX, FRONT, G, F0009, SVECT, AMATRX. Examples of unacceptable names of real variables are: A1234567 (contains too many characters), 8BOX (does not begin with a letter), KJL1 (does not begin with the correct letter), AL,GOL (contains a character other than a letter or a digit).

The assignment of names to the variables appearing in a program is entirely under the control of the programmer. Care must be taken to observe the rule for distinguishing between the names of integer and real variables, but most people learn fairly readily to avoid this pitfall. If the rule is violated, the Fortran compiler will sometimes signal the error, but in many other cases the program as written will make sense although it will not convey the programmer's intentions, and the program will be compiled but will give incorrect results.

It should be noted that the compiler places no significance on names beyond inspecting the first letter to establish whether the variable is integer or real (and not even that, if type statements are used). A name such as B7 specifically does *not* mean *B* times 7, *B* to the seventh power, or B_7. Most programmers assign variable names that simplify recall of the meaning of the variable, which is good programming practice and strongly recommended, but no such meaning is attached by the Fortran system. It should also be noted that every combination of letters and digits is a separate name. Thus the name ABC is not the same as BAC, and A, AB, and ABC are all different and distinct variable names.

*1. Which of the following are acceptable names for integer variables (in the absence of a type statement), which are acceptable names for real variables (in the absence of a type statement), and which are unacceptable names for *any* variable?

```
G       GAMMA     GAMMA421      I      IJK
J79-1   LARGE     R(2)19        BTO7TH
ZSQUARED   ZCUBED    12AT7       2N173
B6700   CDC6600   S/360       IBM360
DELTA   KAPPA     EPSILON     EPSILN
A1.4    A1POINT4  A1P4        AONEP4
FORTRAN ALGOL     PL/1        SNOBOL
```

2. Same as Exercise 1.

```
K       I12G      CAT       X+2      XPLUS2
NEXT    42G       LAST      NUMBER     MU
A*B     X1.4      (X61)     GAMMA81     AI
IA      X12       1X2       XFIFTH    AVER
MEAN    VARIANCE  SIGMA2    KURTOSIS
COBOL   LISP1.5   MAD       JOVIAL
```

1.6 OPERATIONS AND EXPRESSIONS

Fortran provides five basic arithmetic operations: addition, subtraction, multiplication, division, and exponentiation. Each of these operations is represented by a distinct symbol:

Addition	+
Subtraction	−
Multiplication	*
Division	/
Exponentiation	**

Notice that the combination of two asterisks for exponentiation is considered to be one symbol; there is no confusion between ** and * because, as we shall see, it is never correct to write two operation symbols side by side. These are the only mathematical operations for which symbols are provided; any others must be built up from the basic five or computed by using the functions that are discussed later.

A Fortran *expression* is a rule for computing a numerical value. In many cases an expression consists of a single constant, a single variable, or a single function reference (as described in Section 1.7). Two or more of these elements may

FUNDAMENTALS OF FORTRAN COMPUTATION

TABLE 1.1

Expression	Meaning
K	The value of the integer variable K
3.14159	The value of the real constant 3.14159
A + 2.1828	The sum of the value of A and 2.1828
RHO - SIGMA	The difference in the values of RHO and SIGMA
X*Y	The product of the values of X and Y
OMEGA / 6.2832	The quotient of the value of OMEGA and 6.2832
C**2	The value of C raised to the second power
(A + F) / (X + 2.0)	The sum of the values of A and F divided by the sum of the value of X and 2.0
1. / (X**2 + Y**3)	The reciprocal of $(X^2 + Y^3)$

be combined, by using operation symbols and parentheses, to build up more complex expressions. Some examples of expressions and their meanings are given in Table 1.1.

In writing expressions, the programmer must observe certain rules to convey his intentions correctly.

1. Two operation symbols must never appear next to each other. Thus A* −B is not a valid expression, although A*(−B) is.

2. Parentheses must be used to indicate groupings just as in ordinary mathematical notation. Thus $(X + Y)^3$ must be written (X + Y)**3 to convey the correct meaning; X + Y**3 would be a valid expression, but, of course, the meaning is not the same. Again, $A − B + C$ and $A − (B + C)$ are both legitimate expressions, but the meanings are different. Parentheses force the *inner* operation to be done first, as in ordinary mathematical notation.

3. When the hierarchy of operations in an expression is not completely specified by the use of parentheses, the "strength" of the operations is as follows: all exponentiations are performed first, then all multiplications and divisions, and finally all additions and subtractions. Thus these two expressions are equivalent:

(a) A*B + C/D − E**F
(b) (A*B) + (C/D) − (E**F)

4. Within a sequence of consecutive multi-

plications and/or divisions, or additions and/or subtractions, in which the order of the operations is not completely specified by parentheses, the meaning is that of a left-to-right evaluation. Thus the expression A/B*C would be taken to mean $\frac{A}{B} \cdot C$ not $\frac{A}{B \cdot C}$ and $I − J + K$ means $(I − J) + K$, not $I − (J + K)$.

This rule is not universally followed, however, especially in the case of operators that are mathematically associative and/or commutative. Thus, whether the expression A + B + C is evaluated as (A + B) + C or as A + (B + C) will vary from system to system. (See below for an example of how the difference could matter.) However, there is ordinarily no need to go to the trouble of finding out how a particular system is designed to operate, since parentheses can always be used to convey exactly what is intended. Free use of parentheses may occasionally lead to writing more than are absolutely essential, but there is no important penalty for doing so, and considerable grief may be avoided thereby. *When in doubt, parenthesize.*

5. Any expression may be raised to a power that is a positive- or negative-integer quantity, but only a real expression may be raised to a real power. An exponent may itself be any expression of real or integer type. Thus X**(I + 2) is perfectly acceptable. In no case, however, is it permissible to raise a negative value to a real power or to raise zero to the zero power.

6. Integer and real quantities, constants included, must not be *mixed* in the same expression, except that a real quantity may be raised to an integer power.

Many Fortran implementations relax this rule, but taking advantage of the relaxation, to mix integer and real quantities casually, can lead to results that are altogether different from what the programmer intended.

7. Parentheses in an expression indicate grouping. (They also have other uses for entirely different purposes, as we shall see later.) They do *not* imply multiplication. Thus the expression (A + B) (C + D) is incorrect; it should be written (A + B)*(C + D).

Table 1.2 lists some examples of correct and incorrect ways of forming Fortran expressions.

These rules are important for a number of reasons. For one, it is necessary to convey the programmer's intentions correctly. Just as in ordinary mathematical notation, the expression A*(B + C) *must* be written with parentheses. For a second reason, some things are impossible

because of the way the computer and the compiler operate. An integer cannot be raised to a real power because, in general, the result would have a fractional part that cannot be expressed in integer form.

The third reason for following these rules is less obvious: arithmetic operations with fractions of finite length do not obey all the normal rules of mathematics exactly. For an example of what can happen, assume that we are working with an eight-digit decimal system and consider this expression:

$$0.40000000 + 12345678. - 12345677.$$

If this is evaluated from left to right, the result of the addition, to eight figures, is just 12345678; the 0.4 has been lost entirely since retaining it would require a ninth digit position, which would not be available in an eight-digit machine. Then, when the 12345677. is subtracted, the final result is 1.0000000.

Suppose, on the other hand, that the expression had been written

$$0.40000000 + (12345678. - 12345677.)$$

TABLE 1.2

Mathematical Notation	Correct Expression	Incorrect Expression	
$a \cdot b$	A*B	AB	(no operation)
$a \cdot (-b)$	A*(-B) or -A*B	A*-B	(two operations side by side)
$a + 2$	A + 2.0	A + 2	(mixed integer and real)
$-(a + b)$	-(A+B) or -A-B	-A+B or -+A+B	
a^{i+2}	A**(I+2)	A**I + 2	($= a^i + 2$, and is mixed integer and real)
$a^{b+2} \cdot c$	A**(B+2.0)*C	A**B + 2.0*C	($= a^b + 2 \cdot c$)
$\dfrac{a \cdot b}{c \cdot d}$	A*B/(C*D)	A*B/C*D	($= \dfrac{a \cdot b}{c} \cdot d$)
$\left(\dfrac{a + b}{c}\right)^{2.5}$	((A+B)/C)**2.5	(A+B)/C**2.5	($= \dfrac{a + b}{c^{2.5}}$)
$a[x + b(x + c)]$	A*(X+B*(X+C))	A(X+B(X+C))	(missing operators)
$\dfrac{a}{1 + \dfrac{b}{(2.7 + c)}}$	A/(1.0+B/(2.7+C))	A/(1.0+B/2.7+C)	($= \dfrac{a}{1 + \dfrac{b}{2.7} + c}$)

The parentheses force the subtraction to be done first, giving 1.0000000. Now when the 0.40000000 is added, the result is 1.4000000. In other words, in the original form the addition of a small and a large number caused a complete loss of the significance of the small number.

The order of arithmetic operations can lead not only to loss of significance but also to a failure to get any answer, as the following example shows. Suppose we wanted to evaluate the expression A*B/C, in which the values of A, B, and C are all about 10^{40}. The multiplication is done first, as the expression has been written, giving 10^{80}. This is too large for a real variable in many versions of Fortran. The final result after the division, 10^{40}, would be within allowable limits, but the intermediate result is not. Since the computer cannot represent the intermediate result, it would either stop executing the program or give a completely erroneous answer, depending on how the particular computer and compiler are designed to operate.

The simple solution is to use parentheses to force the division to be done first: A*(B/C). The result of the division is a number within the allowable range, and so is the final result.

Integer division raises a special problem of its own. When two integers are divided, the quotient is not usually an integer. Integer division is arranged to *truncate* a quotient having a fractional part to the next smaller integer, which means simply to ignore any fractional part. Thus the result of the integer division 5/3 is 1, not 2 or 1.666667.

As it happens, most calculations do not require integer division, but it might be well to point out the precautions that should be observed if it is needed. Consider the integer expression 5/3*6. Rule 4 says that the division will be done first; thus the truncated result is 1; this is multiplied by 6 to give 6 as the final answer. The result is *not* 10, which we would get from multiplying 5 by 6 and then dividing by 3, or 12, which we would get if the quotient were rounded instead of truncated. On the other hand, if the expression is written as 5*6/3, 6*5/3, 5*(6/3), or (6/3)*5, the result is 10.

All of this applies only to integer arithmetic. Any of the forms in the preceding paragraph, if written with real constants, would give 10.000000 (with perhaps one incorrect digit in the last place; see the next paragraph).

Even in real arithmetic, however, things can happen that might not be expected. Suppose we were to form this sum:

$$1.0/3.0 + 1.0/3.0 + 1.0/3.0$$

The real representation of 1.0/3.0, using floating point decimal fractions, is 0.33333333, to eight digits. The result of the additions, then, is 0.99999999. If we were to write a program that compared this actual sum with the expected result of 1.0000000, the answer, of course, would be "not equal." This might come as something of a shock to the unsuspecting programmer.

These problems are not insuperable, and some of them are not actually so different from things that can happen when working with paper and pencil or desk calculator. With a computer, however, we sometimes have to take special measures to *anticipate* such difficulties, for by the time the computer has begun to run the program we have become bystanders.

EXERCISES

1. Write Fortran expressions corresponding to each of the following mathematical expressions.

*(a) $x + y^3$

(b) $(x + y)^3$

(c) x^4

*(d) $a + \dfrac{b}{c}$

(e) $\dfrac{a + b}{c}$

*(f) $a + \dfrac{b}{c + d}$

(g) $\dfrac{a + b}{c + d}$

*(h) $\left(\dfrac{a + b}{c + d}\right)^2 + x^2$

(i) $\dfrac{a + b}{c + [d/(e + f)]}$

*(j) $1 + x + \dfrac{x^2}{2!} + \dfrac{x^3}{3!}$

*(k) $\left(\dfrac{x}{y}\right)^{g-1}$

(l) $\dfrac{(a/b) - 1}{g[(g/d) - 1]}$

2. Following are a number of mathematical expressions and corresponding Fortran expressions, each of which contains at least one error. Point out the errors and write correct expressions.

(a) $(x + y)^4$ `X + Y**4`

*(b) $\dfrac{x + 2}{y + 4}$ `X + 2.0/Y + 4.0`

(c) $\dfrac{a \cdot b}{c + 2}$ `AB/(C + 2.)`

(d) $-\dfrac{(-x + y - 16)}{y^3}$ `-(-X+Y-16)/Y**3`

*(e) $\left(\dfrac{x + a + \pi}{2z}\right)^2$ `(X+A+3.14)/(2.*Z)**2`

(f) $\left(\dfrac{x}{y}\right)^{n-1}$ `(X/Y)**N - 1`

*(g) $\left(\dfrac{x}{y}\right)^{r-1}$ `(X/Y)**(R-1)`

(h) $\dfrac{a}{b} + \dfrac{c \cdot d}{f \cdot g \cdot h}$ `A/B + CD/FGH`

(i) $(a + b)(c + d)$ `A + B*C + D`

*(j) $a + bx + cx^2 + dx^3$ `A+X*(B+X(C+DX))`
which can be rewritten
$a + x[b + x(c + dx)]$

(k) $\dfrac{1{,}600{,}042x + 10^5}{4{,}309{,}992x + 10^5}$

          `(1,600X+1E5)/(4,309X+1E5)`

(l) $\dfrac{1}{a^2}\left(\dfrac{r}{10}\right)^a$ `1/A**2*(R/10)**A`

1.7 MATHEMATICAL FUNCTIONS

Fortran provides for the use of certain common mathematical functions, such as square root, logarithm, exponential, sine, cosine, arctangent, and absolute value. The exact list of functions available depends on the version of Fortran being used and to a certain extent on the particular computer installation. All Fortran systems have the functions named.

Every function has a preassigned name. Some of those we shall use and their names are given in Table 1.3.

TABLE 1.3

Mathematical Function	Fortran Name
Exponential (base e)	EXP
Natural logarithm (base e)	ALOG
Common logarithm (base 10)	ALOG10
Sine of an angle in radians	SIN
Cosine of an angle in radians	COS
Hyperbolic tangent	TANH
Square root	SQRT
Arctangent; angle computed in radians	ATAN
Absolute value	ABS

In order to make use of a mathematical function, it is necessary only to write its name and follow it with an expression enclosed in parentheses. This directs Fortran to compute the named function of the value represented by the expression in parentheses.

As an example, suppose it is necessary to compute the cosine of an angle named X. This angle must be expressed in radians. Writing COS (X) in a statement will result in the computation of the cosine of the angle. In this example the *argument* of the function is the single variable X. The argument is not limited to a single variable but may in fact be *any* expression, subject to the restriction that in all the mathematical functions in Table 1.3 the argument must be a real quantity and the functional value is computed in real form. If, for example, we wanted the square root of $b^2 - 4ac$, we could simply write SQRT (B**2 − 4.0*A*C).

Appendix 2 contains a complete list of the functions that are ordinarily supplied with any Fortran compiler, including functions that have arguments and/or function values of types other than real. We shall see examples of functions involving double precision and complex values in later chapters.

1.8 ARITHMETIC ASSIGNMENT STATEMENTS

The basic Fortran language elements we have discussed so far have many applications in writing source programs. The most important is computing a new value of a variable, which is done with an *arithmetic assignment statement*.

Its general form is $a = b$, in which a is a variable name written without a sign and b is any expression, as was already described. An arithmetic assignment statement is an order to Fortran to compute the value of the expression on the right and to give that value to the variable named on the left.

The equal sign in an arithmetic assignment statement is not used as it is in ordinary mathematical notation. We are not allowed to write statements such as $Z - RHO = ALPHA + BETA$, in which Z is unknown and the others are known. The only legitimate form of arithmetic assignment statement is one in which the left side of the statement is the name of a single variable, and all variables on the right have previously been assigned values. The precise meaning of the equal sign is then: *replace the value of the variable named on the left with the value of the expression on the right.* Thus the statement $A = B + C$ is an order to form the sum of the values of the variables B and C and to replace the value of the variable A with the sum. The preceding value of A is lost, but the values of the variables B and C are unchanged. It could well be that other parts of the program change the values of B and C during the execution of the program; when we say "the value of the variable B," for instance, we always mean *the value most recently assigned to the variable named B.*

Another example of an arithmetic assignment statement brings out very forcefully the special meaning of the equal sign. A statement such as $N = N + 1$ has the meaning: *replace the value of the variable N with its old value plus 1.* This sort of statement, which is clearly not an equation, finds frequent use.

Although mixed arithmetic is not permitted (or at least not recommended) within an expression, it is possible to convert between integer and real forms by writing an expression of one type on the right and a variable of the other type on the left. If we write an integer expression on the right and a real variable on the left, for instance, all the arithmetic will be done in integers, but the result will be converted to floating-point (real) form before giving the computed value to the variable on the left.

A few examples may help to clarify the uses of arithmetic assignment statements. Suppose the values of A, B, C, D, and X have already been established by preceding statements and that

we need to compute a new value of R from

$$R = \frac{A + BX}{C + DX}$$

The following statement will do what is required.

```
R = (A + B*X) / (C + D*X)
```

None of the variables on the right will be changed by the statement; the previous value of R will be lost.

Suppose we need to compute one of the roots of the quadratic equation $AX^2 + BX + C = 0$. Once again, A, B, and C would have to have been given values by previous assignment statements or by having had values read by using the READ statement described in the next section. This statement would call for the required calculation and would assign the computed value to the variable ROOT1:

```
ROOT1 = (-B+SQRT(B**2-4.0*A*C))/(2.0*A)
```

It might be helpful to review the purposes of the parentheses here. Those enclosing B**2 − 4.0*A*C are required to enclose the argument of the square root function. The parentheses around the numerator in the expression indicate that everything before the slash is to be divided by what follows. The parentheses enclosing the 2.0*A indicate that the A is in the denominator; without this final set the action would be to divide the numerator by 2 and then multiply the entire fraction by A.

A final example shows how the argument of a function can be another function, if desired. Suppose we need to compute the value of V from

$$V = \frac{1}{\cos X} + \log \left| \tan \frac{X}{2} \right|$$

Since not all Fortrans have a function to compute a tangent, we use a trignometric identity:

$$\tan \theta = \frac{\sin \theta}{\cos \theta}$$

The statement to compute V could then be as follows.

```
V=1./COS(X)+ALOG(ABS(SIN(X/2.)/COS(X/2.)))
```

It would be perfectly permissible to use intermediate variables here, perhaps making the computation easier to follow in reading the source program.

```
Y = X/2.0
TAN = SIN(Y) / COS(Y)
ABSVAL = ABS(TAN)
V = 1.0/COS(X) + ALOG(ABSVAL)
```

In a group of statements like this the computer carries out the statements in the order in which they appear. This sequential execution is always followed, unless we explicitly order the computer to follow some other sequence, which we can do with GO TO and IF statements discussed in Chapter 2 on transfer of control.

The examples in Table 1.4 show acceptable arithmetic assignment statements with equivalent mathematical forms. Variable names have been chosen arbitrarily; any other legitimate names would have been just as good. We are assuming, of course, that previous statements have established values of all variables on the right-hand sides.

The examples in Table 1.5 are presented to emphasize the importance of writing expressions and statements in the exact prescribed

format because Fortran demands exact adherence to the rules. Each of the statements in Table 1.5 contains at least one error.

EXERCISES

1. State the value of A or I stored as the result of each of the following arithmetic assignment statements and show whether the result is in integer or real form.

```
*a.   A = 2*6 + 1
*b.   A = 2/3
 c.   A = 2.*6./4.
 d.   I = 2*10/4
*e.   I = 2*(10/4)
*f.   A = 2*(10/4)
 g.   A = 2.*(10./4.)
 h.   A = 2.0*(1.0E1/4.0)
 i.   A = 6.0*1.0/6.0
 j.   A = 6.0*(1.0/6.0)
*k.   A = 1./3. + 1./3. + 1./3. + 1./3.
 l.   A = (4.0)**(3/2)
 m.   A = (4.0)**3./2.
*n.   A = (4.0)**(3./2.)
```

TABLE 1.4

Arithmetic Assignment Statement	Original Formula
`BETA = -1./(2.*X) + A**2/(4.*X**2)`	$\beta = \dfrac{-1}{2x} + \dfrac{a^2}{4x^2}$
`C = 1.112*D*R1*R2/(R1 - R2)`	$C = 1.112D\dfrac{r_1 r_2}{r_1 - r_2}$
`FY = X*(X**2 - Y**2)/(X**2 + Y**2)`	$F_y = x \cdot \dfrac{x^2 - y^2}{x^2 + y^2}$
`Y = (1E-6 + A*X**3)**(2.0/3.0)`	$y = (10^{-6} + ax^3)^{2/3}$
`J = 4*K - 6*K1*K2`	$j = 4K - 6k_1 k_2$
`I = I + 1`	$i_{\text{new}} = i_{\text{old}} + 1$
`K = 12`	$k = 12$
`PI = 3.141593`	$\pi = 3.141593$
`M = 2*M + 10*J`	$m_{\text{new}} = 2m_{\text{old}} + 10j$
`R = COS(X) + X*SIN(X)`	$r = \cos x + x \sin x$
`S = -COS(X)**4 / 4.0`	$s = -\dfrac{\cos^4 x}{4}$
`T = ATAN(1.414214*SIN(X)/COS(X))`	$t = \tan^{-1}(\sqrt{2} \tan x)$

TABLE 1.5

Incorrect Statement	Error
`Y = 2.X + A`	* Missing
`3.14 = X - A`	Left side must be a variable name
`A = ((X + Y)A**2`	Not the same number of right and left parentheses; * missing
`X = 1,624,009.*DELTA`	Commas not permitted in constants
`-J = I**2.`	Integer quantities may not be raised to real powers; variable on left must not be written with a sign
`BX6 = 1./-2.*A**6`	Two operation symbols side-by-side not permitted, even though the minus sign here is not intended to indicate subtraction
`DERIV = N*X**(N-1)`	Mixed integer and real values in the multiplication
`A*X + B = Q`	Left side must be a single variable; should be Q = A*X + B
`FNC = CUBRT(X + Y)`	No cube root function supplied; write FNC = (X + Y)**0.3333333
`SQRT(Z) = Z**0.5`	A function name cannot be used as a variable name; left side must be a variable name

```
*o.    I = 19/4 + 5/4
 p.    A = 19/4 + 5/4
 q.    I = 100*(99/100)
```

2. Each of the following arithmetic assignment statements contains at least one error. Identify them.

```
a.   -V = A + B
b.   4 = I
c.   V - 3.96 = X**1.67
d.   X = (A + 6)**2
e.   A*X**2 + B*X + C
f.   K6 = I**A
g.   Z2 = A*-B + C**4
h.   X = Y + 2.0 = Z + 9.0
i.   R = 16.9X + AB
```

3. Write arithmetic assignment statements to do the following.

* (a) Add 2 to the current value of the variable named BETA; make the sum the new value of a variable named DELTA.

(b) Subtract the value of a variable named B from the value of a variable named A, square the difference, and assign it as the new value of W.

* (c) Square A, add to the square of B, and make the new value of C the square root of the sum.

* (d) A variable named R is to have its present value replaced by the square root of 2.

(e) Multiply THETA by π and store the cosine of the product as the new value of RHO.

(f) Add the values of F and G, divide by the sum of the values of R and S, and square the quotient; assign this result to P.

* (g) Multiply the cosine of two times X by the square root of one-half of X; set Y equal to the result.

* (h) Increase the present value of G by 2 and replace the present value of G with the sum.

(i) Multiply the present value of A by -1.0 and replace the present value of A with the product.

(j) Assign to OMEGA the value of 2π.

(k) Assign to the variable named D a value 1.1 times as great as the present value of the variable named D.

4. Write arithmetic assignment statements to compute the values of the following formulas. Use the letters and names shown for variable names.

* (a) $AREA = 2 \cdot P \cdot R \cdot \sin \dfrac{\pi}{P}$

(b) $CHORD = 2R \sin \dfrac{A}{2}$

*(c) $ARC = 2\sqrt{Y^2 + \dfrac{4X^2}{3}}$

(d) $s = \dfrac{-\cos^4 x}{x}$

*(e) $s = \dfrac{-\cos^{p+1} x}{p + 1}$

*(f) $g = \dfrac{1}{2}\log\dfrac{1 + \sin x}{1 - \sin x}$

(g) $R = \dfrac{\sin^3 x \cos^2 x}{5} + \dfrac{2}{15}\sin^3 x$

(h) $D = \log |\sec x + \tan x|$

*(i) $e = x \arctan\dfrac{x}{a} - \dfrac{a}{2}\log(a^2 + x^2)$

(j) $f = -\dfrac{\pi}{2}\log|x| + \dfrac{a}{x} - \dfrac{a^3}{9x^3}$

(k) $Z = -\dfrac{1}{\sqrt{x^2 - a^2}} - \dfrac{2a^2}{3(\sqrt{x^2 - a^2})^3}$

*(l) $Q = \left(\dfrac{2}{\pi x}\right)^{1/2}\sin x$

(m) $B = \dfrac{e^{x/\sqrt{2}}\cos(\sqrt{x/2} + \pi/8)}{\sqrt{2\pi x}}$

*(n) $Y = (2\pi)^{1/2}x^{x+1}e^{-x}$

(o) $t = a \cdot e^{-\sqrt{w/2p} \cdot x}$

5. A sample, X, with a mean of M and a standard deviation of S can be transformed into a sample, Z, with mean zero and standard deviation 1 by applying to each sample value X the transformation

$$Z = \dfrac{X - M}{S}$$

The transformed sample can be converted to a sample with mean 500 and standard deviation 100 by applying the further transformation

$$T = 100Z + 500$$

Given the variables X, AM (the mean), and S, write assignment statements to compute and store Z and T.

6. If a wheel of radius a rolls along a straight line, a particle on its circumference describes a cycloid, as sketched. The parametric equations of the cycloid are

$$x = a(\theta + \sin\theta)$$
$$y = a(1 + \cos\theta)$$

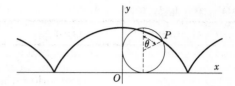

where θ is the angle that the particle makes at the center with the highest point of the circle. Given A and THETA, compute X and Y.

*7. If the lengths of the sides of a triangle are given by the values of the variables A, B, and C, then the area of the triangle can be computed from

$$AREA = \sqrt{S(S - A)(S - B)(S - C)}$$

where

$$S = \dfrac{A + B + C}{2}$$

Write two statements that compute S and AREA, given A, B, and C.

*8. If λ is the mean arrival rate of customers requiring service at a window and μ is the mean rate at which customers can be serviced, then the probability that the queue is of length n is

$$P_n = \left(\dfrac{\lambda}{\mu}\right)^n\left(1 - \dfrac{\lambda}{\mu}\right), \text{ if } \dfrac{\lambda}{\mu} < 1$$

Given XLMBDA and XMU, both real variables, and N, an integer variable, write the assignment statement to compute the probability and assign it to the real variable named PN.

9. Given the variables of Exercise 8, write the assignment statement to compute the mean length of the queue and assign it to AVERN, using the formula

$$\bar{n} = \dfrac{\lambda/\mu}{1 - \lambda/\mu}, \text{ if } \dfrac{\lambda}{\mu} < 1$$

1.9 INPUT AND OUTPUT

If a problem is to be executed on the computer only once, all data can be entered with the program in the form of constants in statements. This is seldom done, however; programs are usually set up to read problem data from cards or some other source external to the computer at the time the program is executed, and constants are used only for quantities that really are constant. The same program can then carry out the computation on as many sets of data as desired.

Fortran provides a great deal of power and flexibility in the reading of data and the printing of results. The experienced programmer needs this power and flexibility, since much of the total programming task revolves around input and output. For our purposes now we need only the minimum that will permit us to write complete programs. We present here accordingly a small subset of the total Fortran input/output capability. Various other facets of the subject are introduced in subsequent chapters, and in Chapter 6 we present a complete summary; Chapter 6 is organized to be suitable for reference.

Readers using WATFOR or WATFIV have a significant advantage at this point because they can begin writing meaningful programs with even less preliminary material on input and output than we shall present here. This is a major advantage of these languages for learning programming. Such readers may wish to skip or skim most of the material on the FORMAT statement that follows, since they will probably use the READ and PRINT statements without

formatting information instead of the READ and WRITE statements as we shall use them.

What we need to know about input and output now can be presented with a simple example. Consider the data card in Figure 1.1. The punches on this card represent four numbers. The first is punched in columns 1 to 6; it is to be read into the computer and is to become the value of an integer variable named *J*. The next number is punched in columns 7 to 13; it is to become the value of an integer variable named *K*. The third number, in columns 14 to 19, is to become the value of a real variable named *X*. The last number, columns 20 to 28, is to become the value of a real variable named *Y*.

We note that a plus sign may be punched or not, as desired.

The vertical lines drawn on the card in Figure 1.1 are only for our convenience in studying the card; the computer "sees" only the punches.

In order to read this card in Fortran, we must execute a READ statement that names the four variables that are to receive values in the same order as the values are punched on the card, and we also reference a FORMAT statement that describes to the program how the data values are punched. The READ-FORMAT combination might be as follows.

```
      READ (5, 123) J, K, X, Y
  123 FORMAT (I6, I7, F6.0, F9.0)
```

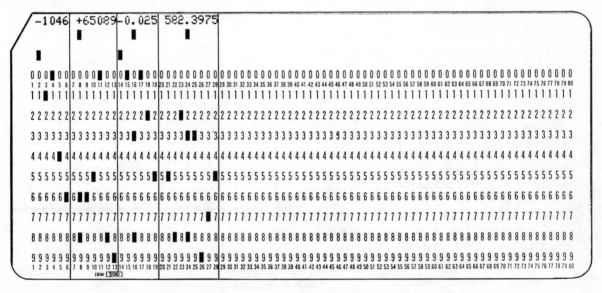

FIGURE 1.1. An example of a data card.

In the READ statement the 5 is the designation of the input unit that reads the data card. In some installations a number other than 5 may be the standard for data input; the reader must determine this for himself.

The 123 refers to the *statement number* written in front of the FORMAT statement. A statement number is simply a cross-referencing device that allows one statement to refer to another; we shall encounter several other examples of the usefulness of statement numbers in later chapters.

The four variable names are listed in the READ statement in the same sequence as the corresponding values are punched on the data card.

This sequence also applies to the *field descriptors* within parentheses in the FORMAT statement, which tell the program how the data values are punched on the card and whether the variables are integer or real. In "I6" the I means that the value on the card is an integer; the 6 means that the card field contains six columns. The correspondence between the *first* card field, the *first* variable name, and the *first* field descriptor is basic; this kind of correspondence is assumed in all input and output statements. The "I7" describes a value that is an integer, which is punched in seven columns. The pattern holds; the *second* value goes with the *second* variable name and the *second* field descriptor.

The F6.0 goes with the third field and the third variable name, X. The F means that the number on the card is the value of a real variable; the 6 means that the card field occupies six columns; the zero has no meaning in this case, although it must still be there. The F9.0 field descriptor describes a card field of nine columns containing the value of a real variable.

For input of values for real variables, we usually punch a decimal point in the card field. If this is done, the corresponding field descriptor can be of the form Fw.0, where w is a number giving the width of the field in card columns.

In summary, the READ statement calls for the reading of the card. The READ statement designates the input unit, a FORMAT statement number, and the names of the variables that are to be read. The FORMAT statement contains field descriptors that describe the data card and distinguish between integer and real variables.

Such a READ statement would ordinarily be executed many times, to read many data cards. The values on the different data cards would not, of course, be all the same, but the arrangement of the fields on the cards would have to be the same; for instance, in every data card read by this READ statement and described by this FORMAT statement the first field must always occupy columns 1 to 6 and contain an integer. Any number that contains fewer than six digits must be punched at the right side of the field, since blanks are interpreted as zeros.

These basic ideas carry over very directly to output. Suppose that we have read this data card and now want to print the four values. Consider these two statements:

```
      WRITE (6, 67) J, K, X, Y
67    FORMAT (I10, I10, F10.4, F12.4)
```

The 6 in the WRITE statement designates the output unit onto which the values of the variables are to be written. The 67 is once again the statement number of a FORMAT statement, although of a different one this time. In this FORMAT statement we have specified that J and K are each to be printed with a total of ten printing positions. This is more space than is required for the values we read; the numbers will be printed at the right of the assigned spaces. In F10.4 we ask for ten printing positions and specify that there shall be four digits to the right of the decimal point. F12.4 asks for 12 printing positions and also four decimals. The result of executing this WRITE statement, assuming the values on the card in Figure 1.1, would be as shown in the first line of Figure 1.2.

The F field descriptor is quite suitable when we know the maximum and minimum sizes of the numbers to be printed. When we cannot anticipate sizes, we turn to the E field descrip-

```
     -1046      65089     -0.0250        582.3975
     -1046      65089     -0.2500000E-01      0.5823975E 03
     -1046      65089     -2.500000E-02       5.823975E 02
```

FIGURE 1.2.   Three ways the values on the sample data card of Figure 1.1 might be printed, under the control of different FORMAT statements.

tor, which puts the number into exponent form, similar to the way we write very large or very small real constants. Consider these statements:

```
      WRITE (6, 1672) J, K, X, Y
1672  FORMAT (I10, I10, E16.7, E16.7)
```

The line printed this time would be as shown in the second line of Figure 1.2. The two integers are printed in the same form as before. In E16.7, the 16 specifies a total of 16 printing positions; the 7 dictates seven decimal places. We see in the printed output there are exponents giving the powers of 10 by which the fractional parts are to be multiplied.

It may be noted that the E field descriptor calls for a form of output in which the fraction is a number between 0.1 and 1.0, times a power of 10. Many people prefer numbers of this sort to be written as a multiplier between 1.0 and 10.0, times a power of 10. This we can call for by writing 1P in front of the field descriptor. The 1P is called a *scale factor;* it says that the fractional part should be multiplied by 10 and the exponent correspondingly decreased by one. We might write

```
     WRITE (6, 9) J, K, X, Y
9    FORMAT (I10, I10, 1PE16.6, 1PE16.6)
```

The output would be as shown in the third line of Figure 1.2.

Whenever several consecutive field descriptors are the same, we are permitted to write a *repeat count* in front of a single field descriptor. We might have written, for instance,

```
      WRITE (6, 1672) J, K, X, Y
1672  FORMAT (2I10, 2E16.7)
```

or

```
     WRITE (6, 9) J, K, X, Y
9    FORMAT (2I10, 1P2E16.6)
```

The printed results would be exactly the same as before.

There is a good deal more to be said about input and output, but this much will let us get started nicely, and permit the reader to proceed to writing and running complete programs as soon as possible. For many simple programs there will be only real data, which can be punched in a fairly standardized form, if desired: make all card fields ten columns wide, use F10.0 field descriptors, and punch an actual

decimal point. For writing such numbers use a field descriptors of 1PE15.6.

For programs having no more than eight values to be read from any one card or written on any one line, all of which are real, the entire FORMAT question can be simplified even further as follows. For input use

```
     READ (5, 1) A, B, C, ...
1    FORMAT (8F10.0)
```

with an appropriate statement number, of course.
For output use

```
     WRITE (6, 2) A, B, C, ...
2    FORMAT (1P8E15.6)
```

Instead of *A, B, C, . . . ,* you would, of course, write the names of the actual variables in your program. If there is more than one READ or more than one WRITE in your program, you need not—and in fact must not—repeat the associated FORMAT statement, at least not using the same statement number; a given FORMAT can be referenced by any number of READs or WRITEs.

Most programs will have many FORMAT statements, all different, but each must have a unique statement number. In fact, it is an error for any statement number to be duplicated.

If your system permits free-format input, things are a bit simpler yet. The standardized FORMATs just given can still be used, but the punching need not conform to the field descriptors except that in some cases the actual field width must not exceed what was specified in the FORMAT. Instead, the input is simply punched as one pleases, with the successive data fields separated by blanks or commas, making it unnecessary to count card columns.

This is particularly convenient in running Fortran programs in a time-sharing environment, where the data values are entered from a typewriter-like console. This question of the way programs are actually entered into the computer and executed is considered in Section 1.12 and in Excursion I.

EXERCISES

In each of the following exercises data values are to be read, the values used in a computation, and the results printed. The data values are to be printed with the results for easy reference. Assume that each data value is punched in 10 columns; use an 8F10.0 field descriptor with all READ statements and a 1P8E15.6 field descriptor for all WRITE statements.

*1. READ: a, b, c
Evaluate:

$$F = \frac{1 + a}{1 + [b/(c + 6)]}$$

WRITE: a, b, c, F

2. READ: s, x
Evaluate:

$$g = (12.7 - x)^{s+2}$$

WRITE: s, x, g

3. READ: x, y
Evaluate:

$$h = \frac{x \cos^4 x}{2y}$$

WRITE: x, y, h

*4. READ: a, b, c
Evaluate:

$$X1 = \frac{-b + \sqrt{b^2 - 4ac}}{2a}$$

$$X2 = \frac{-b - \sqrt{b^2 - 4ac}}{2a}$$

WRITE: a, b, c, $X1$, $X2$

5. READ: a, b, c, x
Evaluate:

$$r = \frac{b \cdot c}{12}\left[6x^2\left(1 - \frac{x}{a}\right) + b^2\left(1 - \frac{x}{a}\right)^3\right]$$

WRITE: a, b, c, x, r

*6. READ: a, e, h, p
Evaluate:

$$x = \frac{e \cdot h \cdot P}{(\sin a)[(h^4/16) + h^2 p^2]}$$

WRITE: a, e, h, p, x

*7. READ: a, x, s
Evaluate:

$$y = \sqrt{x^2 - a^2}$$

$$z = \frac{x \cdot s}{2} - \frac{a^2}{2} \log |x + s|$$

WRITE: a, x, s, y, z

8. READ: ET, ES, RG, ROPT, RIN
Evaluate:

$$F = \cfrac{1}{1 - \cfrac{1 + \left(\dfrac{RG}{ROPT}\right)^2}{\left(\dfrac{ET}{ES}\right)^2\left(1 + \dfrac{RG}{RIN}\right)^2}}$$

WRITE: ET, ES, RG, ROPT, RIN, and F

9. Add appropriate READ, WRITE, and FORMAT statements to the program segments you wrote for Exercises 5 to 9, page 15.

1.10 THE STOP, PAUSE, AND END STATEMENTS

The STOP statement is used to indicate that we wish to terminate execution of the program and relinquish control of the machine. There is ordinarily at least one STOP in every program; there may be several, as for example, when there are various conditions under which execution can be stopped because of invalid data.

On a very small computer, running without an operating system and without time sharing (see Section 1.12), the STOP statement may actually cause a total termination of object program execution, leaving the machine doing absolutely nothing until the operator takes some action. This mode of operation is increasingly uncommon, however. In the more usual case of running under an operating system, after a STOP is encountered the operating system moves on to whatever program comes next in the job stream. With time sharing, control is returned to the programmer at the time-sharing console.

The PAUSE statement also causes termination of execution of the object program, but does so in such a way that the computer operator can resume execution of the program by taking appropriate action at the computer console. It is also possible to display a very small amount of information to the computer operator by writing it following the word PAUSE.

The PAUSE statement creates a certain amount of awkwardness in running a large machine under an operating system, where there may be many programs executing concurrently. Some installations forbid its use. With time sharing there are often simpler ways to accomplish the same results as the PAUSE permits. For various reasons, then, the PAUSE statement is not often used.

So far we have been talking about the termination of the *object* program. Now we turn to the question of informing the compiler that the physical end of the *source* program has been reached and that no more program statements follow. This need is answered by the END statement, which must be the last statement of every program. By "last," in this case, we mean *physically* or *geographically* last, as distinguished from the STOP statement that is *executed* last when the compiled program is run.

To put it another way, a STOP statement may appear anywhere in the program; there may be more than one, and it is not required that the last statement executed be the last statement on the last page of the program. The END statement, on the other hand, *must* be the very last card when the program is punched on cards (not counting any job control language cards that may follow the program or data cards). There must be only one END card in a program.

If a program does not contain a STOP statement, many compilers will treat the END statement as though it were a combination of STOP and END, in that order.

1.11 WRITING A FORTRAN PROGRAM ON A CODING FORM

A Fortran program is ordinarily written on a form similar to that shown in Figure 1.5 in Section 1.12, with one or more lines for each statement. The information on each line is then punched into a card similar to that shown in Figure 1.6. The complete set of cards constitutes the *source program deck,* which is compiled into an object program of machine instructions by a process that we shall outline shortly.

In a time-sharing system, the program is entered into the computer from a time-sharing terminal, usually with the aid of an editing program, and there is no card deck. We still speak of a source program in this case, but the source program exists as a file on the auxilliary storage of the computer instead of as a deck of cards.

See Excursion I for a discussion of the use of time-sharing terminals and editors.

In order to be able to show sample programs on a standard form, it is necessary to describe the purpose of each of its parts. In this discussion we shall speak of cards and card columns, card input being the more common mode of operation, but the same concepts apply to time sharing, with minor variations in usage and terminology.

The numbers shown above the first line of the coding form stand for the card columns into which the information on the form will be punched. The first field on the form, columns 1 to 5, contains the *statement number,* if any. We have seen one application of the statement number in connection with the FORMAT statement, and in the next chapter we shall see other applications.

Column 1 has another function, that of indicating a *comment line.* If column 1 contains a C, Fortran does not process the information on the card but prints it on a *listing* of the program (a printed version produced during compilation). Free use of comments is strongly encouraged to make the program more easily understandable by other programmers. For that matter, the original programmer will be helped by comments when he returns to a program at a later date after he has forgotten its details.

Column 6 is used to indicate a *continuation* card. If a statement can be punched entirely on one card, column 6 may be left blank or punched with a zero. If more than one card is required for a statement, each card after the first must be punched with some nonzero character in column 6. The first card of a continued statement must still have a zero or blank in column 6.

The statement itself is punched in columns 7 to 72. *Blanks in this field are ignored,* with one specific exception to be discussed later. Blanks may thus be used freely to improve readability. The statement need not begin in column 7. Some programmers, for instance, indent the continuation of a long statement to make it a little clearer that the statement is continued; others like to leave a space on both sides of each operation symbol for readability. A number of other conventions will be introduced at appropriate points and followed consistently, but all such conventions are at the discretion of the programmer.

In any case, it is necessary to indicate clearly to the person who will punch the cards exactly how many spaces are desired at each point. It is for this reason that most Fortran coding forms have a box for each character or a short vertical

Zero	0	The letter O	$\emptyset$
One	1	The letter I	I
Two	2	The letter Z	$\bar{Z}$

FIGURE 1.3. One acceptable way of distinguishing between easily-confused pairs of characters.

line to indicate the character divisions.

Columns 73 to 80 are not processed by Fortran and may be used for any desired card or program identification.

It is essential that the coding forms be filled out with great care and attention to detail. The statements must always be written in the format specified; if a comma is misplaced or omitted, the program will usually not be compiled or it will be compiled incorrectly. At most installations it is required that only capital letters be used and that great care be taken to write certain easily confused characters in a distinctive manner. Various conventions are available for distinguishing between such characters as the letter "O" and zero. One acceptable way to write these characters is shown in Figure 1.3, but local usage varies greatly.

1.12 CASE STUDY 1: ECONOMIC ORDER QUANTITY; RUNNING A PROGRAM WITH OPERATING SYSTEMS AND TIME SHARING

To illustrate the application of some of the ideas presented in this chapter, let us take a very simple program and see how a complete Fortran program to solve it could be worked out.

In inventory control theory, the economic order quantity is defined to be the number of units of an item that a firm should order at one time to minimize the sum of the cost of ordering and the cost of storing the item. In simplest form it is given by

$$EOQ = \sqrt{\frac{2RS}{CI}}$$

where

EOQ = economic order quantity
R = number of units used annually
S = cost of placing one order
C = cost of one unit
I = inventory carrying cost, expressed as a fraction of the value of average inventory

Thus, if a firm uses 8000 units per year of some item that costs $1.00 per unit, if the firm's inventory carrying cost is 20 percent of average inventory, and if it costs $12.50 to place an order, the EOQ would be

$$EOQ = \sqrt{\frac{(2)(8000)(\$12.50)}{(\$1.00)(0.20)}}$$
$$= 1000$$

and the firm should order 1000 at a time.

We are to read values of R, S, C, and I from a card, compute the EOQ, then print the four data values and the answer. The value of R is punched in columns 1 to 10, with a decimal point but without an exponent. The value of S is punched in columns 11 to 20 in the same format, the value of C is in columns 21 to 30, and I is in 31 to 40. Figure 1.4 shows a data card containing the values that were used in the numerical example above.

In assigning variable names we can use R, S, and C just as they appear in the formula, but something must be done about I since it would be incorrectly taken as an integer variable if used as is. We shall use XI instead.

The output is to be written on one line, with all four of the data values and the one result printed in 16 printing positions each, with an exponent.

A program that will do the required computing is shown in Figure 1.5. We note that the statement number of the first FORMAT statement has been written in columns 3 to 5, whereas that of the second FORMAT statement has been written in columns 1 to 3. This demonstrates that statement numbers may be written anywhere in columns 1 to 5 if fewer than five digits. We see repeat counts used in both FORMAT statements, for in this example the four numbers to be read all have the same format and all five numbers to be printed have the same format. The FORMAT statements have been written immediately after their associated input and output statements; this is often done but not required: a FORMAT statement may, in fact, be written anywhere in the program before the END statement. The statement number identifies which FORMAT to use even if it does not immediately follow the statement that refers to it.

In the first FORMAT statement the field descriptor is F10.0. We recall that F means that the input data will be stored inside the computer

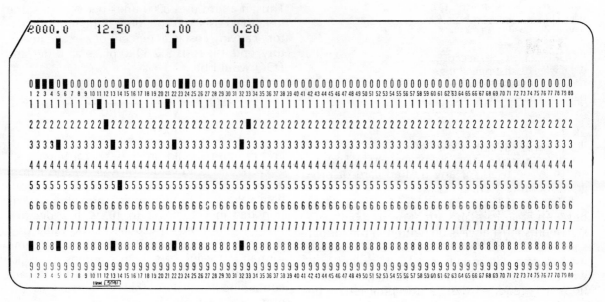

FIGURE 1.4.   An illustrative data card for the program of Figure 1.5. (Case Study 1.)

in real form, that is, as a fraction and exponent. The 10 tells Fortran that we have allocated 10 columns to each number. The zero means that if no decimal points were punched in the data field in the card the numbers in that field would be taken to have zero decimal places. If decimal points are punched the zero has no effect. In the second FORMAT statement the 1P means that the decimal point will be shifted one place to the right and the exponent adjusted accordingly, and the E means that the numbers will be printed with an exponent, indicating the power of 10 by which the fractional part is multiplied. The 16 means that we have allocated 16 printing positions to each number; the 6 means that six decimal places will be printed.

We see that all equal signs and operation symbols have been written with spaces on both sides and that commas in the READ and WRITE statements have been followed by spaces. This was done for readability; it is not required, although recommended. In the programs in this book we shall ordinarily follow this practice, as well as using many explanatory comment cards. Some comment cards are seen to be blank except for the C in column 1; this is done to make the comments easier to read and, in some cases, to make the divisions between parts of the program more obvious.

Most commonly, the program is now punched on cards for entry into the computer. Figure 1.6 shows one of the cards that would be punched from the coding sheet of Figure 1.5. This is not the only way the program might be entered into the machine, however; it is also possible in some installations to type the program directly into the computer using a time-sharing system. We temporarily postpone discussion of the various ways that are available for getting the program into the machine, in order to clarify just what is happening in the compilation and execution process, and the sequence in which the various operations are performed.

The complete story is a little more complicated than it is useful for us to explore at this stage. For our purposes now we can say that a compiler produces an object program made up of machine instructions. That last statement is a condensation of the full story, but the point is that the compilation does *not* include running the object program. In fact, we have a choice of whether to call for compilation only or to ask for compilation followed by execution of the object program, since the two processes take place at separate points in time. It is occasionally useful to ask that the object program be produced as a deck of cards, which is reloaded at later times when the execution of the object program is desired.

FORTRAN CODING FORM

| Punching Instructions | | Page | of |

| Program | Economic Order Quantity | | Graphic | | | | | | Card Form # | | * | Identification | |
| Programmer | D.D. McCracken | Date 2/29/72 | Punch | | | | | | | | | 73 | 80 |

C FOR COMMENT

FORTRAN STATEMENT

```
C CASE STUDY 1
C ECONOMIC ORDER QUANTITY COMPUTATION
C
C
C READ THE DATA VALUES
      READ (5, 100) R, S, C, XI
  100 FORMAT (4F10.0)
C
C COMPUTE THE ECONOMIC ORDER QUANTITY
      EOQ = SQRT(2.0 * R * S / (C * XI))
C
C WRITE A LINE CONTAINING DATA AND RESULT
      WRITE (6, 110) R, S, C, XI, EOQ
  110 FORMAT (1P5E16.6)
      STOP
      END
```

* A standard card form, IBM electro 888157, is available for punching source statements from this form.

FIGURE 1.5. A program to find an economic order quantity, after reading the necessary data. (Case Study 1.)

One of the products of the compilation process is thus an object program, in some form. Another output can be a *program listing,* which shows the source program as it was entered into the machine. Figure 1.7 shows the listing of our program. This becomes the primary program documentation. The original coding sheets are often discarded at this point, since the listing is easier to read and since it represents exactly what went into the computer, which, sadly, sometimes has to be distinguished from what we *meant* to enter into the computer.

Figure 1.8 summarizes the complete process. We write a Fortran program on a coding form and enter it into the computer by one of the methods to be described next. We tell the computing system to compile our program and leave the object program in storage ready to be executed, placing it on disk or tape for later execution, or possibly punching it out as a deck of cards. At a later time—perhaps immediately, perhaps next week—we ask for the object program to be executed. It then takes control of the machine and does the things we asked for when we wrote the Fortran source program, except that it is the translated machine-language object program that is now in charge. These actions ordinarily include the reading of data and the writing of results.

Figure 1.9 shows the line of results produced when the object program produced from the source program of Figure 1.5 was executed.

To describe the actions taken to enter the program into the computer, call for compilation,

FUNDAMENTALS OF FORTRAN COMPUTATION

23

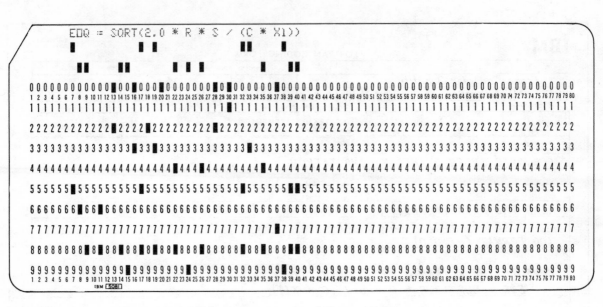

FIGURE 1.6. A source program card from the program of Figure 1.5. (Case Study 1.)

and execute the object program, we need to distinguish three modes of computer operation: batch operating systems, time sharing, and stand-alone.

Most commonly today, the computer is run under the control of an *operating system*. This is a master control program that brings in jobs from input devices, allocates the resources that each job needs (main storage, tapes, and so on), schedules the running of each job (often several jobs are running concurrently), controls the input and output that each job calls for, and

```
C CASE STUDY 1
C ECONOMIC ORDER QUANTITY COMPUTATION
C
C
C READ THE DATA VALUES
      READ (5, 100) R, S, C, XI
  100 FORMAT (4F10.0)
C
C COMPUTE THE ECONOMIC ORDER QUANTITY
      EOQ = SQRT(2.0 * R * S / (C * XI))
C
C WRITE A LINE CONTAINING DATA AND RESULT
      WRITE (6, 110) R, S, C, XI, EOQ
  110   FORMAT (1P5E16.6)
      STOP
      END
```

FIGURE 1.7. The listing produced by the computer as one output of the compilation of the program of Figure 1.5. (Case Study 1.)

finally terminates the job when it is finished, deallocating resources. An operating system makes possible efficiencies of computer operation that could not be approached if all the actions were to be initiated and controlled by human operators. Furthermore, great flexibility is provided in the way of changing, for example, the input and output devices, the amount of main storage allocated, or the scheduling priority, when the same job is run at different times under different conditions.

The Fortran programmer ordinarily comes into closest contact with an operating system when he is required to specify the characteristics of his input and output devices and files. We shall accordingly devote considerable space to the subject in Chapter 6 on input and output. All we need to know now is that when a Fortran program is run under an operating system, the source program deck must be preceded and followed by a few cards that are generally called *job control language* (JCL) cards. These give accounting information and programmer identification, establish priority, specify whether the object program is to be executed, state where the data is to be found, and so on. The exact details depend on the operating system and the particular installation, so that it will be impossible to give complete details that would be accurate for every reader. You must obtain from

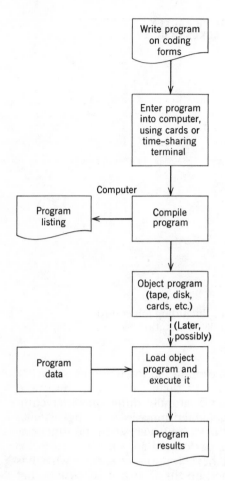

FIGURE 1.8. Schematic representation of the complete process of writing, compiling, and executing a Fortran program.

The flowchart contains the following boxes:
- Write program on coding forms
- Enter program into computer, using cards or time–sharing terminal
- Computer
- Program listing
- Compile program
- Object program (tape, disk, cards, etc.)
- (Later, possibly)
- Program data
- Load object program and execute it
- Program results

Figure 1.10 shows a listing of the complete deck for this case study as it was submitted to the computer center for execution. The lines that begin with two slashes (//) are *job control language* (JCL) lines. The first two lines contain the JOB statement; the X at the end of the first line signals a continuation onto the second line. Every job deck must begin with a JOB card, and it will usually contain the programmer's name and some accounting information, but that's just about as much as we can say with complete generality: details vary with the installation. The particular JOB statement shown here would presumably not be acceptable at any other installation anywhere, except the one where this program was run.

All we can say, therefore, is that you will have to have a JOB card, and that it will probably contain at a minimum your name and account number. You must obtain from your instructor or installation manager the details of what is required and the form in which it has to be punched.

The next line contains the EXEC (for execute) statement. The statement itself has been given a name (STEP1), which in this case is not important. FORTGCLG is the name of a *cataloged procedure* that will be called to carry out all the detailed actions of compiling our program, linking together all the various program segments that we have called into play, and executing the combined program. The details of these actions are of no concern to us.

Now comes a DD statement (for Data Definition). The name (FORT.SYSIN) is important. The asterisk means that the source program cards follow this card.

After all the source program cards we find another DD card, this time for a different step in the cataloged procedure, and again the name (GO.SYSIN) has to be as shown. This card tells the operating system that the program data comes next. In our case the program data consists of just one card, and after that we find a *null statement*, which consists simply of two slashes in columns 1 and 2.

This may sound more complicated than it is.

your instructor or your installation manager a description of the JCL's required to do common operations at your shop.

As an indication of what is involved, however, in one of the most widely used systems, we can show a typical complete deck for our economic order quantity program as it might be run on the full-scale operating system for the IBM System/360, which is called simply the System/360 Operating System, or OS 360.

```
8.000000E 03     1.250000E 01     1.000000E 00     2.000000E-01     1.000000E 03
```

FIGURE 1.9. The line of output produced by the program of Figure 1.5, when run with the data shown in Figure 1.4. (Case Study 1.)

```
//FCS10S       JOB  (MCRACKEN,DAN,FJCL-YES,ACCT-FIV,X00A-MCRACKEN,        X
//    X00B-MCRACKEN,X00D-MCRACKEN,X001-MCRACKEN),DDMCCRACKEN,MSGLEVEL=1
//STEP1        EXEC FORTGCLG
//FORT.SYSIN  DD *
C CASE STUDY 1
C ECONOMIC ORDER QUANTITY COMPUTATION
C
C
C READ THE DATA VALUES
      READ (5, 100) R, S, C, XI
  100 FORMAT (4F10.0)
C
C COMPUTE THE ECONOMIC ORDER QUANTITY
      EOQ = SQRT(2.0 * R * S / (C * XI))
C
C WRITE A LINE CONTAINING DATA AND RESULT
      WRITE (6, 110) R, S, C, XI, EOQ
  110    FORMAT (1P5E16.6)
         STOP
         END
//GO.SYSIN      DD *
8000.0    12.50     1.00      0.20
//
```

FIGURE 1.10.   A listing of the complete deck of the program of Figure 1.5, including job control language (JCL) cards for running the program under the IBM System 360 Operating System. (Case Study 1.)

The reader will discover that the whole procedure is quite routine:

1. In front of your source program deck, place a JOB card, an EXEC card, and a DD * card. It is quite possible that you will be using a different cataloged procedure, which means that your EXEC card will name something other than FORTGCLG. If you are using WATFOR, for instance, the EXEC card will say EXEC WATFOR. Again, it is possible that your DD * card will have some other name on it than FORT.SYSIN.

2. At the end of the source program deck, place another DD * card, although the name will not be the same as the earlier one. Now add your data. If there is no data, omit the DD * card.

3. Put a null card at the end of the deck. (This may not be absolutely required at some installations, or you may be instructed to punch /* instead of //.)

In other words, your typical deck makeup will look like this:
```
// JOB
// EXEC
//DD *
Source program
//DD *
Data
//
```

Not every computer in the world uses OS 360, much as IBM might like to have it that way, and the details will naturally differ on other computers. The general outline is surprisingly similar on other systems, however, since the functions that must be performed are similar.

Once you have found out exactly what has to be punched on the five or six JCL cards that you will typically need, you can add them to a deck in a completely routine fashion that takes only a matter of minutes.

Needless to say, that is not the whole story on operating systems, some of which have cost hundreds of millions of dollars to produce. Our sole purpose at this stage is to convince the reader that there is nothing to be frightened of, and that getting his first program run need not be excessively traumatic. The universal experience of large numbers of instructors and classes is that most of what we have presented in this chapter will not really make much sense until the reader has run a couple of programs himself, and we have accordingly tried to make it possible to get that first program running as early in the game as possible.

WATFOR and WATFIV run under an operating system, with special measures taken to achieve speed in carrying out the various operations, sometimes at the expense of speed of execution of the object programs. Since WATFOR and WATFIV are most commonly used in educational situations and for program checkout, the latter is a negligible consideration. The object program is placed directly in main storage as soon as it has been compiled, and it is executed immediately. In fact, no provision is made for saving the object program at all, contrary to all the other systems we have discussed. A WATFOR or WATFIV program must be recompiled every time it is used. For the purposes for which the system was devised and considering the extremely fast compile times, this is no serious penalty.

The second possibility for getting our program into the machine is that a *time-sharing* system can be used. This means that the program is entered through a typewriter-like *terminal* connected to the computer by a telephone line. One computer can handle many terminals simultaneously, since the speed of typing is so very much slower than the speed of the machine. (On the system used to run many of the programs in this book, the computer can do roughly 100,000 additions in the interval between typing two characters. As a matter of fact, it is fairly common for a single computer to be running programs in the *batch mode* just described, under an operating system, *and* servicing a few dozen time-sharing terminals.)

In time sharing, once we connect the terminal to the computer, make the appropriate telephone (or other) connections, and *sign on* properly to establish that we are authorized to use the machine, we can type the program into a computer storage area reserved for us in the machine. When the program has been entered and any typing errors have been corrected, we instruct the system to compile the program by typing an appropriate command. If there are errors, we are notified immediately and can correct them on the spot. When we order the object program to be run, the system will either accept input data directly from the terminal or we can instruct it to obtain data from computer files that we would previously have entered. The output can go either to the terminal, back to computer files, or perhaps be printed at the computer center on a line printer and mailed to us.

Excursion I shows a terminal session on the system used to prepare many of the programs

for this book. In fact, the major program demonstrated there is the one that was used to prepare the index for the book.

Finally, there are smaller computers that do not use an operating system, batch or time sharing, but run in *stand-alone* mode. (Prior to about 1960 this was the usual way to run almost all computers.) In this case, the machine is devoted to exactly one job at a time, and nothing whatever is done between jobs. In such a situation we would take our deck to the computer room and either the programmer himself or (more commonly for the larger machines) a computer operator would enter it into the machine, after loading the compiler from tape or disk. During the compilation our work would ordinarily be tying up the complete resources of the system, whether fully utilizing them or not. We might place data cards behind the deck, so that if the compilation was successful the object program could be immediately executed. Once our job was done, the operator or the next user would take over the machine for whatever was to be done next.

It is generally economical to run only the smallest computers in this mode. Among the small computers, however, there is an increasing number of minicomputers, which are deliberately made small precisely so that the user *can* have one all to himself, which has advantages, too. Not all such machines have Fortran IV compilers available, however.

As of the time of writing (1972), perhaps 80 percent of all Fortran programs are run under batch operating systems, with 10 percent each on time-sharing and stand-alone systems. The present trend is for time sharing to grow at the expense of both of the others.

EXERCISES

Add STOP and END statements to the programs you wrote for Exercises 1 to 9, pages 18–19, choose data values, and run the programs. You will, of course, need to get the necessary information on how to use the batch operating system or interactive time-sharing system at your installation, which will be provided by your instructor or your installation manager.

2 TRANSFER OF CONTROL

2.1 INTRODUCTION

In the brief programming examples in Chapter 1 it was tacitly assumed that Fortran statements are executed sequentially, in the order written. However, we shall often want to execute statements in some order other than the normal one-after-the-other sequence. Sometimes we shall return to the beginning of a program to execute it again with different data, or we may branch around a section of the program, depending on the values of computed intermediate results.

In this chapter we shall explore some of the Fortran language elements available for making transfers of control, and we shall also look into a number of examples that illustrate the use of these language elements and of computers generally.

2.2 THE GO TO STATEMENT

The GO TO statement provides a means of *transferring control* to some statement other than the next one in sequence. The statement takes the form

GO TO n

where n is the statement number of another statement in the program. When such a GO TO statement is encountered, the next statement executed will be the one having the specified statement number n. This other statement is allowed to be any executable statement in the program, either before or after the GO TO statement itself.

We have already had brief contact with statement numbers in connection with the FORMAT statement. We saw that a statement number is merely an identification of a statement, so that statements elsewhere in the program may refer to it.

A statement number is an unsigned number of five decimal digits or fewer; it is written in columns 1 to 5 of the Fortran coding form and punched in columns 1 to 5 of the statement card. No two statements may have the same number, but there is no requirement that every statement be numbered. Furthermore, there is no sequencing implied by the statement numbers. The first numbered statement need not bear the number 1, and statement numbers need not be assigned in an unbroken sequence or even in an ascending sequence. To emphasize this point, an acceptable sequence of statement numbers would be 500, 7, 9936, 9935, 9937, 201, and 258. Interspersed between the statements having these numbers could be others having no statement numbers. In short, statement numbers provide a cross reference when one statement must refer to another. They serve no other purpose.

In order to make it easier to locate statements in a long program, it is advisable to assign statement numbers in ascending sequence. Since statement numbers are sometimes assigned after later statements have been given numbers, it is a good idea to assign statement numbers initially by tens. Then if it is found necessary to transfer to a statement that was not initially numbered, it can be given an intermediate number and all statement numbers will still be in ascending sequence. We shall adopt a few other conventions regarding statement numbers that will be introduced at appropriate points.

2.3 THE ARITHMETIC IF STATEMENT

The simple GO TO statement causes an *unconditional* transfer of control to the statement having the statement number written after the GO TO. That is, execution of the transfer does not depend on any condition of the data, status of the machine, or anything else. The unconditional GO TO is important, but by itself it would permit little work to be done. We must also be able to transfer *if* some condition is met during program execution. This is the function of the arithmetic and logical IF statements.

The arithmetic IF statement has the form

$$\text{IF (e) } n_1, n_2, n_3$$

in which e stands for any arithmetic expression and n_1, n_2, and n_3 are statement numbers. The operation of the statement is as follows: if the value of the expression within parentheses is negative, the statement having the statement number n_1 is executed next; if the value of the expression is zero, statement n_2 is executed next; and if the expression is positive, n_3 is executed next.

For a simple example of the use of the arithmetic IF statement, consider the following formula:

$$Q = \begin{cases} -\dfrac{\pi}{2} & \text{if } a < 0 \\[2mm] 0 & \text{if } a = 0 \\[2mm] \dfrac{\pi}{2} & \text{if } a > 0 \end{cases}$$

Suppose now that we are doing a problem in which it is necessary to select the appropriate value for Q, assuming that A has already been given a value by a previous statement (not shown). The program segment of Figure 2.1 will do this.

```
      IF (A) 40, 50, 60
40    Q = -1.570796
      GO TO 70
50    Q = 0.0
      GO TO 70
60    Q = 1.570796
70
```

FIGURE 2.1. A program segment illustrating the use of the arithmetic IF statement to make a three-way transfer of control. Other statements would precede and follow this segment.

The arithmetic IF statement calls for an examination of the value of the variable A. If the value of this variable at the time the IF is executed is negative, statement 40 will be executed next. This calls for Q to be set equal to -1.570796, which is an approximation to $-\pi/2$. After that we find the statement GO TO 70; statement 70 is the next statement after this program segment, whatever it might be. If the GO TO 70 were not there, the program would automatically go on in sequence to statement 50, in which Q would be set equal to zero; this, of course, would not be what we want. In other words, the GO TO 70 statement skips around the other parts of the program to statement 70, in which the value of Q would presumably be used. If the value of A is found to be zero, the IF statement causes a transfer to statement 50, in which Q is set equal to zero and once again we transfer to the continuation of the program. If the value of A is found to be positive, the IF statement causes a transfer of control to statement 60 in which Q is set equal to $\pi/2$, and we then go on immediately to the next statement.

Most programs are run many times with different sets of data. As this arithmetic IF statement is encountered in different runs, the paths taken would vary as the value of A varies. In other words, the "decision" here is made each time the IF statement is executed in the object program.

For another example of the use of the arithmetic IF statement, suppose we are required to compute y as a function of x by one of two formulas:

$$y = 0.5x + 0.95 \text{ if } x \leq 2.1$$
$$y = 0.7x + 0.53 \text{ if } x > 2.1$$

This computation may be carried out by the

```
      IF (X - 2.1) 30, 30, 40
30    Y = 0.5 * X + 0.95
      GO TO 50
40    Y = 0.7 * X + 0.53
50
```

FIGURE 2.2.   Another illustration of the use of the arithmetic IF statement, this time to make a two-way transfer of control.

program segment shown in Figure 2.2. The branch of the IF statement taken depends on the value of the expression $x - 2.1$. If $x - 2.1$ is negative, x is less than 2.1 and we transfer to statement 30, which computes y according to the appropriate formula for that case. If x is equal to 2.1, we also reach the same formula, as required in the problem statement. If $x - 2.1$ is positive, then x is greater than 2.1 and we go to statement 40, which computes y according to the appropriate formula. Whatever appears at 50 could use the value of y that has now been computed—by whichever method.

2.4 THE COMPUTED GO TO STATEMENT

The arithmetic IF statement provides us with a three-way test on the value of an arithmetic expression. The computed GO TO extends the range of the Fortran language providing an n-way branch based on the value of an integer variable.

The statement has the general form

$$\text{GO TO } (n_1, n_2, \ldots, n_m), i$$

In this statement i must be an integer variable written without a sign, and $n_1, n_2, \ldots, n_m$ must be statement numbers of statements elsewhere in the program. If the value of the variable i at the time this statement is executed is j, then control is transferred to the statement with the statement number n_j. For instance, suppose we have written the statement

```
GO TO (4, 600, 13, 9, 526), IAC
```

If the value of the variable IAC is 1, then control will be transformed to statement number 4; if it is 2, to statement 600; if it is 3, to statement 13; and so on. The value of the integer variable must be in the range of 1 to m, where m denotes how many statement numbers there are in pa-

rentheses. If it is not in this range, the results are not predictable; in other words, we do not know in general what the program will do.

As an example of one kind of calculation that can be done with the computed GO TO statement, consider another problem. We are required at a certain point in a program to compute the value of one of the first five Legendre polynomials, which are defined as follows.

$$P_0(x) = 1$$
$$P_1(x) = x$$
$$P_2(x) = \frac{3}{2}x^2 - \frac{1}{2}$$
$$P_3(x) = \frac{5}{2}x^3 - \frac{3}{2}x$$
$$P_4(x) = \frac{35}{8}x^4 - \frac{15}{4}x^2 + \frac{3}{8}$$

We assume that x has previously been computed and that a value between zero and four has been given to an integer variable named LEG. It is the value of LEG that determines which of the five Legendre polynomials must be computed: if LEG = 0, we are to compute $P_0(x)$; if LEG = 1, we are to compute $P_1(x)$, and so on. We cannot use the computed GO TO directly because of the restriction that the value of the integer variable must not be less than 1. Therefore a new variable named LEGP1 ("LEG plus 1") will be calculated by adding 1 to LEG. The value of this new variable falls in the range of 1 to 5 instead of 0 to 4. A program for carrying out this computation is shown in Figure 2.3. P is the value of whichever Legendre polynomial is computed.

```
      LEGP1 = LEG + 1
      GO TO (60, 70, 80, 90, 100), LEGP1
60    P = 1.0
      GO TO 110
70    P = X
      GO TO 110
80    P = 1.5*X**2 - 0.5
      GO TO 110
90    P = 2.5*X**3 - 1.5*X
      GO TO 110
100   P = 4.375*X**4 - 3.75*X**2 + 0.375
110
```

FIGURE 2.3.   A program segment using the computed GO TO statement to select one of five formulas, depending on the value of an integer variable.

2.5 THE LOGICAL IF STATEMENT

The final tool for transfer of control that we shall consider in this chapter is the logical IF statement, which has the general form

IF (e) S

where e is a *logical expression* and S is any other statement except another logical IF or a DO (discussed in Chapter 5). The simplest form of logical expression is one that asks a question about two arithmetic expressions. Is x greater than or equal to 12? Is l equal to $n - 1$? We write such *relational expressions* by using any of the following six *relational operators*:

Relational Operator	Meaning
.LT.	Less than
.LE.	Less than or equal to
.EQ.	Equal to
.NE.	Not equal to
.GT.	Greater than
.GE.	Greater than or equal to

The periods in these relational operators are required to distinguish them from other Fortran language elements with which they appear in a program.

The action of the logical IF is as follows: if the logical expression is true, statement S is executed; if the logical expression is false, statement S is not executed. Either way, the next statement executed is the one following the logical IF, unless S was a GO TO and the expression was true.

To see a simple example of the use of logical IF, let us return to an earlier example:

$$y = 0.5x + 0.95 \text{ if } x \le 2.1$$
$$y = 0.7x + 0.53 \text{ if } x > 2.1$$

This calculation can be done with two logical IF statements:

```
IF (X .LE. 2.1) Y = 0.5 * X + 0.95
IF (X .GT. 2.1) Y = 0.7 * X + 0.53
```

If x is less than or equal to (.LE.) 2.1, the statement $Y = 0.5*X + 0.95$ will be executed, which is the correct formula for computing y in that case. If x is greater than (.GT.) 2.1, the statement

in the first IF will not be executed, but the statement in the second IF will be.

It may occur to some readers to wonder why a condition is needed on the second statement: if x is not less than or equal to 2.1, it surely must be greater—there are no other possibilities. Why not write

```
IF (X .LE. 2.1) Y = 0.5 * X + 0.95
Y = 0.7 * X + 0.53
```

The difficulty, of course, is that the second statement would *always* be executed, even when the answer on the first IF had been "yes." Thus y would first be computed from the first formula and then recomputed from the second. The second result would destroy the first, and we would not have the correct value for y.

On the other hand, if the two statements were reversed, things would work out perfectly well. y would always first be calculated by the formula appropriate for a value of x greater than 2.1, and then recomputed if in fact the value of x turned out to be less than or equal to 2.1. This is an acceptable programming technique, and one that we shall utilize from time to time.

The power of the logical IF is considerably increased by the combination of several relational expressions with the *logical operators* .AND., .OR., and .NOT.. We can write, for instance,

```
IF (X .GE. Y .AND. N .LT. 9) GO TO 90
```

This says that if *both* conditions are met, the GO TO should be executed, but if either of the conditions is not satisfied, the GO TO will not be executed, and the next statement in sequence will be taken.

For the sake of added clarity, in this book we shall ordinarily show such *compound conditions* on as many lines as there are simple conditions, using continuation lines, and indent conditions as necessary to align them vertically. For instance, we would write the last IF statement this way:

```
     IF (          X .GE. Y
    1        .AND. N .LT. 9 ) GO TO 90
```

The extra spaces before and after the parentheses enclosing the logical expression are also simply for added clarity.

The .OR. operator is "satisfied" if *either or both* of the expressions it joins are true. The

.NOT. operator reverses the truth value of the expression it modifies. For instance, the logical IF statement

```
IF ( .NOT. (X .LT. 12.0) ) R = X + 3.1
```

has the same effect

```
IF ( X .GE. 12.0 ) R = X + 3.1
```

because "not less than" means the same thing as "greater than or equal to."

In the expression .NOT. (X .LT. 12.0) the parentheses are required to inform the compiler that the .NOT. modifies the entire relational expression. Under certain circumstances the meaning would otherwise be ambiguous.

We shall see several examples of the use of the various forms of the logical IF in the case studies at the end of this chapter. The use of the logical operators .AND., .OR., and .NOT. will be studied more thoroughly in the next chapter in the discussion of logical variables.

Experience shows that it is easier to understand a complex program and to prove that it operates as intended if logical IF statements are used in preference to arithmetic IFs, and if the use of all types of GO TO statements is minimized. We shall ordinarily make heavy use of the logical IF and almost no use of the arithmetic IF or the computed GO TO. We shall see in Chapter 5 on the DO statement a convenient way to eliminate many of the usages of the GO TO statement.

2.6 FLOWCHARTS

An important tool of programming is the *flowchart,* which allows the programmer to plan the sequence of operations in a program before writing it. In any problem that is even moderately complex the interrelationships within it are difficult to keep clearly in mind without some visual representation. A flowchart provides this visual assistance. It also greatly facilitates communication between programmers and is a valuable part of the documentation of a program.

A flowchart consists of a set of boxes, the shapes of which by convention indicate the nature of the operations described in the boxes, along with connecting lines and arrows that show the "flow of control" between the various operations.

For our purposes here, the notation, which is quite simple, contains the following symbols.

A rectangle indicates any <u>processing operation</u> except a decision.

A diamond indicates a <u>decision.</u> The lines leaving the box are labeled with the decision results that cause each path to be followed.

A parallelogram indicates an <u>imput</u> or <u>output</u> operation.

An oval indicates the <u>beginning</u> or <u>ending point</u> of the program.

A small circle indicates a <u>connection</u> between two points in a flowchart, where a connecting line would be too clumsy.

Arrows indicate the direction of <u>flow</u> through the flowchart; every line should have an arrow on it.

These symbols are consistent with the American National Standard ANSI X3.5-1970, "Flowchart Symbols and Their Usage in Information Processing," approved September 1, 1970, by the American National Standards Institute (ANSI).

To illustrate how a flowchart may be used, we shall work out another problem involving IF statements. Suppose we are required to read a value of x, perform certain checking on x, and compute a value of y according to the following step function:

$$y = \begin{cases} 8.72 \text{ if } 0.0 \leq x < 10.9 \\ 16.19 \text{ if } 10.9 \leq x < 21.6 \\ 24.07 \text{ if } 21.6 \leq x < 50.0 \end{cases}$$

The values of *x* and *y* are then to be printed. If $x < 0.0$ or $x \geq 50.0$, we are to stop without computing *y* or printing *x* and *y*.

A flowchart of a procedure for doing this job is shown in Figure 2.4. This flowchart has been drawn with some consideration for its implementation in Fortran terms. For instance, the first decision box actually will require two comparisons, which we shall do with a logical IF containing an .OR.. If we did not have the logi-

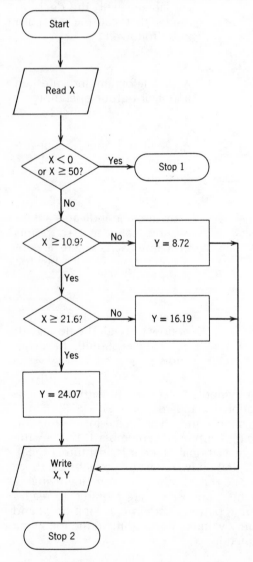

FIGURE 2.4. A flowchart of a method for evaluating a step function. The corresponding program is shown in Figure 2.5.

```
C READ THE VALUE OF X
        READ (5, 10) X
10   FORMAT (F10.0)
C
C CHECK FOR X OUT OF RANGE
        IF (        X .LT. 0.0
1         .OR. X .GE. 50.0 ) STOP 1
C
C SEE IF X IS OUTSIDE FIRST INTERVAL
        IF ( X .GE. 10.9 ) GO TO 20
C
C IT IS NOT; ASSIGN Y AND JUMP TO WRITE
        Y = 8.72
        GO TO 40
C
C SEE IF X IS OUTSIDE SECOND INTERVAL
20   IF ( X .GE. 21.6 ) GO TO 30
C
C IT IS NOT; ASSIGN Y AND JUMP TO WRITE
        Y = 16.19
        GO TO 40
C
C IF WE GET HERE, X IS IN LAST INTERVAL
30   Y = 24.07
C
C WRITE X AND Y
40   WRITE (6, 50) X, Y
50   FORMAT (1P2E16.6)
        STOP 2
        END
```

FIGURE 2.5. A program for the step function evaluation flowcharted in Figure 2.4.

cal IF available, it would be necessary to combine two arithmetic IF statements to accomplish the same thing, which is entirely possible, of course.

A program corresponding to the flowchart of Figure 2.4 is shown in Figure 2.5. We begin by reading the value of *x*, after which comes the FORMAT statement. A FORMAT statement is said to be *nonexecutable,* and it is allowed to appear almost anywhere in the program. Next is a logical IF to test for an out-of-range *x* value. Another logical IF branches to the third test if *x* is greater than or equal to 10.9; if this branch is not taken, then *x* must be less than 10.9, so we set *y* equal to 8.72 as required and transfer to the WRITE statement. Another IF checks *x* against 21.6, after which we set *y* equal to 16.19 or 24.07, whichever is correct.

There is never just one way to write a program, and seldom is it even true that one way is clearly better than all other possibilities. Figure 2.6 presents another program that does the same processing as the program in Figure 2.5,

```
C READ THE VALUE OF X
      READ (5, 10) X
   10 FORMAT (F10.0)
C
C CHECK FOR X OUT OF RANGE
      IF (      X .LT. 0.0
   1      .OR. X .GE. 50.0 ) STOP 1
C
C TEST X AND ASSIGN CORRECT Y
      IF (      X .LT. 10.9 ) Y = 8.72
      IF (      X .GE. 10.9
   1      .AND. X .LT. 21.6 ) Y = 16.19
      IF (      X .GE. 21.6 ) Y = 24.07
C
C WRITE X AND Y
      WRITE (6, 50) X, Y
   50 FORMAT (1P2E16.6)
      STOP 2
      END
```

FIGURE 2.6. Another version of the program for evaluation of the step function evaluation flowcharted in Figure 2.4, this time using no GO TO statements.

although it carries it out in a slightly different manner than suggested by the flowchart of Figure 2.4. The new version uses no GO TO statements at all, but instead arranges logical IFs in such a manner that exactly one of them will be satisfied. The net result is a program containing fewer statements than the other one, and using statement numbers only to identify FORMAT statements. The new version may in some cases take slightly longer to execute, but probably not by much, and it is easier to understand. Perhaps more important, it is probably easier to check for accuracy, a problem which, in larger programs, can take on overriding importance.

Additional flowcharts will be found in the case studies.

2.7 CASE STUDY 2: CURRENT IN AN AC CIRCUIT

This case study is a realistic application of the GO TO and IF statements in carrying out the same basic computations on several different sets of data values.

Suppose that we are required to compute the current flowing in an alternating current (ac) circuit that contains resistance, capacitance, and inductance in series.* The current in the circuit is given by

$$I = \frac{E}{\sqrt{R^2 + [2\pi f L - 1/(2\pi f C)]^2}}$$

where I = current, amperes
E = voltage, volts
R = resistance, ohms
L = inductance, henrys
C = capacitance, farads
f = frequency, hertz

We shall assume that the purpose of the computation is to provide the data for drawing a graph of the relation between current and frequency. Therefore we shall arrange to read in fixed values of voltage, resistance, inductance, and capacitance, and then a series of values of frequency. We shall print each frequency with the current at that frequency.

We wish to write a program that will process any number of frequency cards without knowing in advance how many there may be in a given run. To accomplish this we shall specify that the last data card will be a *sentinel* consisting of a negative frequency. It could never actually be necessary to compute the current for a negative frequency. We choose our sentinel so that it may safely be used without danger of confusion with actual data. After reading each frequency card, we need only use an IF to determine whether it is the sentinel. If it is not, we simply proceed with the computation. After printing each result we return to read another frequency card, knowing that eventually a negative number will turn up and that the IF statement will cause a STOP to terminate program execution.

The sequence of operations can be visualized more clearly with the help of a flowchart, as shown in Figure 2.7. We first read the values of the four parameters that do not change: voltage,

*The examples used in case studies and elsewhere are taken from various areas of the application of computers. As outlined at the beginning of the book, the *complete* process of problem solution requires a full understanding of the subject matter and of the formulation of the problem. We are assuming, however, that the preliminary steps have been completed. The reader is therefore *not* required to know how the formulas are derived or, for that matter, what they mean. The emphasis is on programming; it should not matter very much if a particular example is taken from an unfamiliar area.

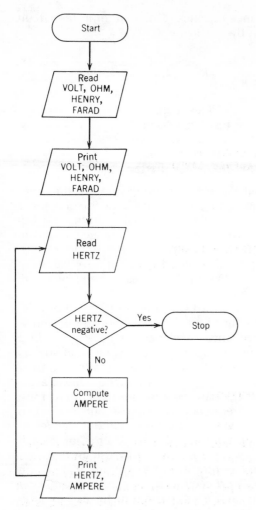

FIGURE 2.7. A flowchart of an ac circuit calculation. (Case Study 2.)

resistance, inductance, and capacitance. These quantities are identified in the flowchart by the symbols that will be used in the program, making it easier to compare the flowchart and the program. After reading the four parameters we immediately print them, since the printed output would otherwise be of limited value; the behavior of the circuit depends entirely on these four numbers.

The initial steps of reading and printing the parameters will not be repeated; all of the following steps will be carried out for each frequency card. In order to be able to read new frequency cards as long as more remain, without reading the fixed parameters again, we make the reading of a frequency card a separate box (and

a separate statement in the program). Immediately after reading a frequency card we check to see whether it is a sentinel (negative frequency) and stop the execution of the program if it is. Naturally this should not happen after reading the *first* frequency card, and it may appear pointless to test for the possibility the first time. The point to remember is that we are now in a section of the program that will be repeated an unknown number of times; there may be one frequency card or a hundred. This being the case, we *do* need to test for a sentinel every time except the first. Arranging to avoid the test the first time would be more trouble and more time-consuming in the computer than making the test the first time also.

If the frequency card is not a sentinel, we reach the box that calls for the computation of the current (AMPERE). This will be a long statement in the program; we have not shown the formula in the box, although it would not be incorrect flowcharting practice to do so. After computing the current we print the frequency and the corresponding current and return to read another frequency card.

The program, as diagrammed here, will continue to read frequency cards, to compute and print the current, and then return to read another card, until it "gets out of the loop" by discovering a sentinel card.

With the process precisely defined by a well-understood flowchart, the program in Figure 2.8 is fairly easy to write and to understand.

In setting up the program we do run into a minor difficulty. The symbols in the formula are not acceptable as variable names, since I and L would represent integer variables, and we want all the variables to be real. This is often a problem; we must always be on guard to avoid unintentionally mixing integer and real computations. One solution to this problem is to prefix the unacceptable variable names with some letter that will make them real, which is perfectly satisfactory. Or, by using simple techniques to be discussed in Chapter 3, we could designate I and L as real, overriding the naming convention. We shall follow a different approach: since the units in which the variables are expressed all happen to begin with the proper letters for real variables, we shall use the unit names as variable names.

It will be noted that the first two lines of the program are comment lines that identify the

```
C CASE STUDY 2
C CURRENT IN AN AC CIRCUIT
C
C
C READ VALUES OF THE 4 PARAMETERS
C (THIS FIRST READ IS EXECUTED ONLY ONCE)
      READ (5, 100) VOLT, OHM, HENRY, FARAD
C
C WRITE THE 4 PARAMETERS FOR IDENTIFICATION
      WRITE (6, 110) VOLT, OHM, HENRY, FARAD
C
C READ A VALUE OF FREQUENCY, IN HERTZ (CYCLES PER SECOND)
C (THIS SECOND READ IS EXECUTED ONCE FOR EACH FREQUENCY CARD)
   10 READ (5, 100) HERTZ
C
C TEST FOR SENTINEL
      IF ( HERTZ .LT. 0.0 ) STOP
C
C COMPUTE THE CURRENT FROM THE FORMULA
      AMPERE = VOLT / SQRT(OHM**2 + (6.283185 * HERTZ * HENRY
     1  - 1.0 / (6.283185 * HERTZ * FARAD))**2)
C
C WRITE FREQUENCY AND CURRENT
      WRITE (6, 110) HERTZ, AMPERE
C
C GO BACK FOR ANOTHER FREQUENCY CARD
      GO TO 10
  100 FORMAT (4F10.0)
  110 FORMAT (1P4E16.6)
      END
```

FIGURE 2.8. A program for an ac circuit calculation, corresponding to the flowchart of Figure 2.7. (Case Study 2.)

program, and that comment lines interspersed throughout explain its various points. Heavy use of comments for these purposes is strongly recommended.

Statement numbers have been given to the FORMAT statements and to the one statement that is referred to by the GO TO. Notice that the assignment statement has been written on two lines by use of a continuation line.

The GO TO statement specifies that after the frequency and the computed value of the current have been printed, control should return to the second READ statement, which has been given the statement number 10, to repeat the whole process.

The first FORMAT statement is used with two different READ statements, even though the first reads four values and the second only one. We shall explore the precise rules for this sort of thing in Chapter 6; for now we can say that if the same field descriptors are desired, there is no problem as long as a READ statement never names more variables than there are field descriptors in the associated FORMAT. (This latter

is actually legal also, but it has a special action.) In the second FORMAT statement notice the use of the scale factor (the 1P) to shift the decimal point to a position between the first and second digits. The exponent is automatically adjusted to reflect the change.

Notice also that both FORMAT statements have been placed at the end of the program. We shall ordinarily do this whenever a FORMAT is referred to by more than one READ or WRITE, but this is strictly a matter of individual preferences.

This program was run with a data card that gave the parameters as 10 volts, 1000 ohms, 0.1 henry, and 0.00000005 farad ($= 0.05$ mF). The frequency cards ranged from 1000 to 3500 hertz in steps of 100 hertz. The output is shown in Figure 2.9. Notice that what was entered as 0.1 has been printed as 9.999996E-02. The problem here is that the computer used, the IBM 360, represents real numbers in a hexadecimal form in which the precision is the equivalent of slightly fewer than seven decimal digits; decimal 0.1 cannot be represented exactly in this number

```
1.000000E 01      1.000000E 03      9.999996E-02      5.000000E-08
1.000000E 03      3.644950E-03
1.100000E 03      4.134011E-03
1.200000E 03      4.660144E-03
1.300000E 03      5.225275E-03
1.400000E 03      5.828913E-03
1.500000E 03      6.466519E-03
1.600000E 03      7.127400E-03
1.700000E 03      7.792424E-03
1.800000E 03      8.432589E-03
1.900000E 03      9.009905E-03
2.000000E 03      9.482328E-03
2.100000E 03      9.812735E-03
2.200000E 03      9.979222E-03
2.300000E 03      9.981338E-03
2.400000E 03      9.838954E-03
2.500000E 03      9.584691E-03
2.600000E 03      9.254605E-03
2.700000E 03      8.881118E-03
2.800000E 03      8.489624E-03
2.900000E 03      8.098021E-03
3.000000E 03      7.717818E-03
3.100000E 03      7.355720E-03
3.200000E 03      7.015079E-03
3.300000E 03      6.697092E-03
3.400000E 03      6.401606E-03
3.500000E 03      6.127693E-03
```

FIGURE 2.9.   The output of the program of Figure 2.8. (Case Study 2.)

system. The other numbers on the first line are either mathematical integers, which can be represented exactly in floating hexadecimal if they are not too large, or fractions that happen to have accurate floating hexadecimal representations since they involve powers of 2. This sort of annoyance is unavoidable in any computer. A simple solution in this case would be to use an output FORMAT field descriptor of 1P4E16.5, that is, specify one less decimal place. The number would then be rounded off to the correct value (1.00000E-01) in the output conversion process. (This only works, of course, if the output routines do round; on a few compilers they do not.)

(For the engineers: When $2\pi fL = 1/(2\pi fC)$, the term in parentheses in the radical is zero and the circuit is said to be *resonant*. In the printout of Figure 2.9 a broad resonance peak around the resonant frequency of about 2250 hertz is evident.)

2.8 CASE STUDY 3: COLUMN DESIGN

A designer wishes to obtain data for plotting a curve of the safe loading of a certain type of load-bearing column as a function of the slim-

ness ratio of the column. He has selected from a handbook two empirical formulas that give the safe loading in two ranges of the slimness ratio.

$$S = \begin{cases} 17{,}000 - 0.485R^2 & \text{for } R < 120 \\ \dfrac{18{,}000}{1 + (R^2/18{,}000)} & \text{for } R \geq 120 \end{cases}$$

where S = safe loading, pounds per square inch
  R = slimness ratio, dimensionless

The safe loading is to be calculated for slimness ratios of 20 to 200 in steps of 5.

Planning an algorithm to produce the desired output can be approached by breaking it down into three decisions:

1. How to choose between the two formulas, given a value of R. This is fairly easy: use an IF statement to compare the size of R against 120 and choose one of two arithmetic statements to apply the appropriate formula.

2. How to run through the required values of R. This can be handled in a number of ways. Perhaps the easiest is to start R at 20, compute S, then add 5 to R, compute a new value of S, and so on, each time around testing to see whether R has reached 200. This method will not require the reading of data cards, which makes the program a bit simpler, but it does mean that to run it for any values of R other than those "built into" it would require a program change. We are buying simplicity at the cost of inflexibility—a common tradeoff.

3. How to present the results, taking into account the accuracy expected. The accuracy of the computed results is almost completely dominated by the question of the accuracy of the approximation formulas. The handbook from which they were taken is silent on accuracy (a not uncommon situation), but we can draw some conclusions from the fact that the constants are given to only two or three significant figures. Furthermore, mechanical design formulas of this kind usually include a safety factor, so that extreme precision is clearly not indicated.

We shall see, however, that there *is* an accuracy problem in getting the successive values of R for values of the increment in R other than the one stated. We shall return to this question later.

It appears that if we presented the results as integers, we should be providing more significant figures than could possibly mean anything. In fact, we should probably be much closer to reality if we printed three or four significant figures, multiplied by a power of 10—which is exactly what we can do using the E field specification.

A flowchart is shown in Figure 2.10. We begin by setting R equal to 20 to get our starting value, in a step that is not repeated. Then we must test to see whether R is more or less than 120—which seems pointless, since we just set it equal to 20. The reason, as in Case Study 2, is that we are now in a part of the program that will be repeated many times as R increases. There is no way to say to a computer, "Be sensible: use the first formula until R reaches 120." We must provide an e*xplicit* test on the value of *R every time.*

The decision box takes us to one of the two formulas to compute S, after either of which we print the values of R and S. (It is a good idea, incidentally, to print both the computed function value *and* the argument. If we were to print only the computed result, anyone using the output would have to figure out for himself the R value corresponding to each value of S.)

Now we ask whether R is greater than or

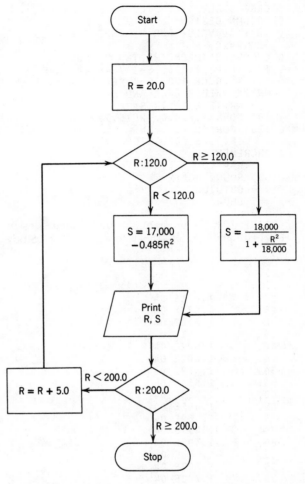

FIGURE 2.10. A flowchart of a column design calculation. (Case Study 3.)

equal to 200. If it is, we have just computed the last line of the output and we accordingly stop. If not, we add five to it and go around again. One would think that R could never be greater than 200 at this point; if it were, we should already have left the loop the time before. This is indeed true *with the numbers used here.* We shall return to this point shortly.

The Fortran program is shown in Figure 2.11. If the flowchart has been clearly understood, it should not be too much trouble to follow the program. The FORMAT statement provides a review of two of the most common field specifications. In F10.0 the *F* means that the number will be printed in fixed format (without an exponent), the 10 means that 10 printing positions will be allotted to the number, and the zero

```
C CASE STUDY 3
C COLUMN DESIGN
C INITIAL VALUE FOR R - NOT REPEATED
      R=20.
C CHOOSE BETWEEN THE TWO FORMULAS
   10 IF(R.LT.120.)S=1.7E4-.485*R*R
      IF(R.GE.120.)S=1.8E4/(1.+R*R/1.8E4)
C WRITE VALUES OF R AND S
      WRITE(6,101)R,S
  101 FORMAT(F10.0,1PE15.3)
C TEST FOR COMPLETION
      IF(R.GE.200.)STOP
C INCREMENT R
      R=R+5.
C GO AROUND AGAIN
      GOTO10
      END
```

FIGURE 2.11. A program for the column design calculation flowcharted in Figure 2.10. (Case Study 3.)

20.	1.681E 04
25.	1.670E 04
30.	1.656E 04
35.	1.641E 04
40.	1.622E 04
45.	1.602E 04
50.	1.579E 04
55.	1.553E 04
60.	1.525E 04
65.	1.495E 04
70.	1.462E 04
75.	1.427E 04
80.	1.390E 04
85.	1.350E 04
90.	1.307E 04
95.	1.262E 04
100.	1.215E 04
105.	1.165E 04
110.	1.113E 04
115.	1.059E 04
120.	1.000E 04
125.	9.636E 03
130.	9.284E 03
135.	8.944E 03
140.	8.617E 03
145.	8.302E 03
150.	8.000E 03
155.	7.710E 03
160.	7.431E 03
165.	7.164E 03
170.	6.908E 03
175.	6.663E 03
180.	6.429E 03
185.	6.204E 03
190.	5.989E 03
195.	5.783E 03
200.	5.586E 03

FIGURE 2.12. The output of the program of Figure 2.11. (Case Study 3.)

means that there will be no digits after the decimal point. In 1PE15.3 the 1P means shifting the decimal point to the more familiar position between the first and second digits, the E means floating point form (with an exponent), the 15

195.0840	5.780E 03
195.1840	5.776E 03
195.2840	5.772E 03
195.3839	5.768E 03
195.4839	5.764E 03
195.5839	5.760E 03
195.6839	5.756E 03
195.7839	5.752E 03
195.8839	5.748E 03
195.9839	5.744E 03
196.0839	5.740E 03
196.1839	5.736E 03
196.2839	5.732E 03
196.3839	5.728E 03
196.4838	5.724E 03
196.5838	5.720E 03
196.6838	5.716E 03
196.7838	5.712E 03
196.8838	5.708E 03
196.9838	5.704E 03
197.0838	5.700E 03
197.1838	5.696E 03
197.2838	5.692E 03
197.3838	5.688E 03
197.4837	5.684E 03
197.5837	5.680E 03
197.6837	5.676E 03
197.7837	5.672E 03
197.8837	5.669E 03
197.9837	5.665E 03
198.0837	5.661E 03
198.1837	5.657E 03
198.2837	5.653E 03
198.3837	5.649E 03
198.4837	5.645E 03
198.5836	5.641E 03
198.6836	5.637E 03
198.7836	5.633E 03
198.8836	5.629E 03
198.9836	5.626E 03
199.0836	5.622E 03
199.1836	5.618E 03
199.2836	5.614E 03
199.3836	5.610E 03
199.4836	5.606E 03
199.5836	5.602E 03
199.6835	5.598E 03
199.7835	5.595E 03
199.8835	5.591E 03
199.9835	5.587E 03
200.0835	5.583E 03

FIGURE 2.13. The last few lines of the output of the program of Figure 2.11, modified to use an interval of 0.1 and print more digits of R.

means 15 printing positions, and the 3 means three decimal places.

This program has been written in a more compact style than will ordinarily be used, to demonstrate that matters of spacing in writing programs are at the discretion of the programmer, and that intelligent spacing conventions do make programs easier to read.

The output is shown in Figure 2.12.

Let us now return to the question of the accuracy in the method of incrementing R. Suppose we ask that S be printed for all values of R from 20 to 200 in steps of 0.1. To do this we simply change the constant in $R = R + 5$. to make it read $R = R + 0.1$. While we are changing the program, let us also change the FORMAT statement so that we can get seven digits in R. These will be needed to see what is happening. The last few lines of the output this time are shown in Figure 2.13.

What has happened? Why is the last value of R not 200? The answer once again has to do with the nondecimal representation of decimal fractions. This program was also run on an IBM 360. The difference between the machine representation of 0.1 and the true value is only about $3 \cdot 10^{-8}$, but this small error accumulates in the hundreds of times that 0.1 is added to R in the program. Furthermore, the process of shifting to align decimal points (hexadecimal points, actually, in this case) in the addition amplifies the error.

If we had required R to be *exactly* 200 in order to get out of the loop, we would naturally never have achieved the equality.

This particular problem would not arise in a decimal computer, since decimal 0.1 obviously has an exact representation in such a machine. The problem is nevertheless fairly common, since there are relatively few decimal computers.

The best solution is to make the addition of the increment either in integers, which are exact, or in some real number that has an exact

```
C CASE STUDY 3
C COLUMN DESIGN - MODIFIED VERSION
C
C
C TENR IS ALWAYS A WHOLE NUMBER IN THIS VERSION, AND WHOLE NUMBERS
C OF THIS SIZE ARE REPRESENTED EXACTLY IN THE COMPUTER USED.
C THEREFORE, ERRORS DO NOT ACCUMULATE.   TENR IS DIVIDED BY 10 TO
C GET THE VALUE OF R.
C
C
C GIVE TENR ITS INITIAL VALUE - THIS STATEMENT IS NOT REPEATED
      TENR = 200.0
C
C DIVIDE BY 10.0 TO GET VALUE OF R - PROGRAM REPEATS FROM HERE
   10 R = TENR / 10.0
C
C CHOOSE BETWEEN THE TWO FORMULAS
      IF ( R .LT. 120.0 ) S = 1.7E4 - 0.485 * R * R
      IF ( R .GE. 120.0 ) S = 1.8E4 / (1.0 + R * R / 1.8E4)
C
C WRITE VALUES OF R AND S
      WRITE (6, 101) R, S
  101   FORMAT (F10.4, 1PE15.3)
C
C TEST FOR COMPLETION
      IF ( R .GE. 200.0 ) STOP
C
C INCREMENT TENR
      TENR = TENR + 1.0
C
C GO AROUND AGAIN
      GO TO 10
      END
```

FIGURE 2.14.   The program of Figure 2.11 revised to use an interval of 0.1 and with a modified method of incrementing R. (Case Study 3.)

195.0000	5.783E 03
195.1000	5.779E 03
195.2000	5.775E 03
195.3000	5.771E 03
195.4000	5.767E 03
195.5000	5.763E 03
195.6000	5.759E 03
195.7000	5.755E 03
195.8000	5.751E 03
195.9000	5.747E 03
196.0000	5.743E 03
196.1000	5.739E 03
196.2000	5.735E 03
196.3000	5.731E 03
196.4000	5.727E 03
196.5000	5.723E 03
196.6000	5.719E 03
196.7000	5.715E 03
196.8000	5.711E 03
196.9000	5.707E 03
197.0000	5.703E 03
197.1000	5.699E 03
197.2000	5.695E 03
197.3000	5.691E 03
197.4000	5.688E 03
197.5000	5.684E 03
197.6000	5.680E 03
197.7000	5.676E 03
197.8000	5.672E 03
197.9000	5.668E 03
198.0000	5.664E 03
198.1000	5.660E 03
198.2000	5.656E 03
198.3000	5.652E 03
198.4000	5.648E 03
198.5000	5.644E 03
198.6000	5.640E 03
198.7000	5.637E 03
198.8000	5.633E 03
198.9000	5.629E 03
199.0000	5.625E 03
199.1000	5.621E 03
199.2000	5.617E 03
199.3000	5.613E 03
199.4000	5.609E 03
199.5000	5.606E 03
199.6000	5.602E 03
199.7000	5.598E 03
199.8000	5.594E 03
199.9000	5.590E 03
200.0000	5.586E 03

FIGURE 2.15. The output of the program of Figure 2.14. (Case Study 3.)

representation. As it happens, the floating point (Fortran real) representation of a mathematical integer (whole number) is exact in almost all systems. What we can do, therefore, is to work with a variable called, say, TENR, which is ten times the value of R. This eliminates the decimal fraction that caused the problem. To this we add

1.0 each time, getting an exact sum. Then before going into the computation we divide TENR by 10.0 to get R. This division will give a result that is seldom exactly correct, *but this error is very small, and, more important, does not accumulate.*

The revised program is shown in Figure 2.14. The last few lines of output this time are given in Figure 2.15.

2.9 CASE STUDY 4: THE NEWTON- RAPHSON METHOD, PROGRAM CHECKOUT

In this case study we shall use the Newton-Raphson method, one of the most common numerical techniques, for finding a root of an equation and for introducing methods of *checking out* a program to remove its errors and to ensure accuracy.

Given a function of x, $F(x) = 0$, the Newton-Raphson method says that, subject to certain conditions, if x_i is an approximation to a root, a better approximation is given by

$$x_{i+1} = x_i - \frac{F(x_i)}{F'(x_i)}$$

where the prime denotes the derivative.*

For instance, suppose we have the function $F(x) = x^2 - 25$. As a first approximation to the root, take $x_0 = 2$. Since $F'(x) = 2x$, a better approximation can be found from

$$x_1 = x_0 - \frac{x_0^2 - 25}{2x_0} = 2 - \frac{4 - 25}{4} = 7.25$$

This is called an *iteration* formula. Continuing in the same way, now substituting 7.25 into the same formula, and so on, we get a succession of approximations:

---

*Readers who do not know calculus must refuse to be intimidated by this formula! If you don't know what a derivative is, you wouldn't be able to understand the proof of why this formula works and you won't be able to apply it to other problems—but you can still understand this case study. Just take it on faith that this method does provide a way to find a *root* of an equation (a value of x that makes the equation true), and read the case study for what it has to say about program checkout.

You have now encountered the most advanced mathematics in the text, other than in some of the optional exercises.

$x_0 = 2$
$x_1 = 7.25$
$x_2 = 5.35$
$x_3 = 5.0114$
$x_4 = 5.00001$
$x_5 = 5.0000000$

The approximation can be made as accurate as we please by continuing the process. One root of the original equation is indeed 5, the positive square root of the constant term.

The Newton-Raphson method is readily adapted to computer use. In fact, some variation of the scheme just sketched is actually used for finding square roots. Let us try it on a more interesting equation:

$$F(x) = \cosh x + \cos x - 3 = 0$$

We find that

$$F'(x) = \sinh x - \sin x$$

so the iteration formula is

$$x_{i+1} = x_i - \frac{\cosh x_i + \cos x_i - 3}{\sinh x_i - \sin x_i}$$

We shall have to compute the hyperbolic sine and cosine from exponentials, since not all Fortrans have built-in functions for evaluating them:

$$\cosh x = \frac{e^x + e^{-x}}{2}$$

$$\sinh x = \frac{e^x - e^{-x}}{2}$$

Figure 2.16 is a flowchart of the basic computational scheme. We begin by assigning a value to X, which becomes our "previous" approximation. In the iteration formula we wrote x_i. The subscript is not necessary; we only need two different variables, one for the "old" value of X and another for the "new" value. We write XNEW for the new and compute it from the iteration formula. Because it will be interesting to see the succession of approximations, we now write out the value of XNEW. Ordinarily we would do this only at the conclusion, when the root has been found.

Next comes the test for convergence: Are the last two approximations the same, to within 10^{-6}? This question has to be asked in terms of the absolute value of the difference between X and XNEW because we do not know, in general,

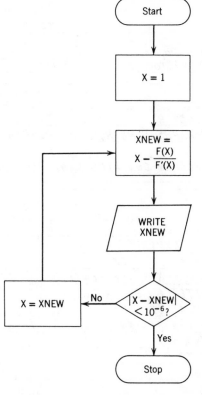

FIGURE 2.16. A flowchart of the Newton-Raphson method for finding the root of an equation $F(x) = 0$. (Case Study 4.)

whether the convergence will be from above or below. If the process has not converged, we set X = XNEW, which makes the just-computed value the "old" value the next time around, and return to compute another XNEW.

The program shown in Figure 2.17 contains quite a number of deliberate errors. After noting a few features of the program, we shall trace through the steps we might follow in discovering and correcting the various kinds of errors. To simplify this discussion, all statements have been given statement numbers.

Statement 2 assigns the value of e^x to the variable EX. This will be used twice in the formula, and it is wasteful of time to go through the function evaluation twice. Statement 3 assigns the value of e^{-x} to EMX, since e^x and e^{-x} are reciprocals. Division is also faster than function evaluation. (*In this program* the time savings could not be detected with a stopwatch, but the principle is valid.) The iteration formula in

```
IBM                                                          Form X28-7327-4
                                                            Printed in U.S.A.
                        FORTRAN CODING FORM

                                Punching Instructions          Page    of
Program  Newton-Raphson        Graphic              Card Form #    *   Identification
Programmer  D.D. McCracken   Date 3/1/72  Punch                      73        80

C FOR COMMENT
STATEMENT                      FORTRAN STATEMENT
NUMBER

C CASE STUDY 4
C NEWTON-RAPHSON METHOD -- PROGRAM CHECKOUT
C
C THIS PROGRAM CONTAINS MANY DELIBERATE ERRORS
C --- ------- -------- ---- ---------- ------
C
C
     1  X = 1.0
     2  EX = EXP(X)
     3  EMX = 1.0 / EX
     4  XNEW = X + ((EX+EMX)/2 + COS(X) -3.) /((EX-EMX)2. - SINE(X)
     5  WRITE (6, 6,) XNEW
     6  FORMAT (F6.10)
     7  IF ( ABS(X-XNEW) .LESS. /E-6 ) END
     8  XNEW = X
     9  GO TO 2
    10  STOP

* A standard card form, IBM electro 888157, is available for punching source statements from this form.
```

FIGURE 2.17.   A program for the Newton-Raphson method for finding the root of an equation, corresponding to the flowchart of Figure 2.16. (Case Study 4.) *This program contains many deliberate errors.*

statement 4 is routine, as is the WRITE statement.

The IF statement uses the absolute value function ABS to eliminate any minus sign in the difference between X and XNEW. Statements 8 and 9 are unexceptional.

There are a great many ways to make mistakes in a program. One of the easiest is in punching the program cards or typing the program at a terminal. If the programmer punches cards himself, he may make mistakes because he is not experienced at operating the card punch. If they are punched by a cardpunch operator, there is the danger of misreading handwriting. Either way, much time can be saved in the long run by checking the deck carefully before trying to compile it.

One common way to prove the accuracy of card punching is to *verify* the deck with a *verifier*. This machine has the same general appearance as a card punch but only examines the punching. A second operator strikes the same keys, but all that happens is that the holes in the cards are matched to see if they correspond to the keys struck by the verifier operator. If not, a red light signals the discrepancy.

In the time-sharing case it is not usually economical to enter a program twice and use the computer to make a comparison, although it can be done. More common practice is simply to call for the program to be printed out and make a careful check of it. It definitely is worthwhile to get a clean copy for the checking, rather than checking from the terminal printout produced as the program was typed in, since the process of correcting typing errors will ordinarily have caused the original printout to be fairly hard to read.

With a punched card deck a listing can be produced using a *tabulator*. Figure 2.18 shows the listing of the program of Figure 2.17. In fact, this listing was produced on a time-sharing terminal, but a tabulator listing would not appear greatly different, and the checking we can do is the same. Study discloses three errors in typing the program.

Statement 2 starts in the wrong position, because of incorrect use of the tab key. If there were no statement number this would not really matter, since blanks to the right of column 6 are almost always ignored, but placing a statement number other than in columns 1 to 5 would cause trouble. In statement 4 there is an equals sign where a plus sign was meant; this is easy to do because the two symbols appear on the same key on the terminal used to enter the program. Finally, FORMAT has been misspelled. We correct these errors, checking each correction most carefully to be sure that the correction process has not introduced new errors, which happens all too frequently.

A study of this listing of the program will no doubt reveal to the careful reader many of the deliberate errors also. This is generally true. *Desk-checking* of the program listing before compiling is usually a good investment of the programmer's time as well as a saving of some wasted computer time. Let us pretend that we have not seen these other errors, so that we may

learn how they can be detected later in the process.

Now we try to compile. All Fortran compilers include some degree of diagnostic checking for statements that are *syntactically* illegal; that is, statements that do not follow the rules for forming a statement, no matter what they might mean. Fortran cannot determine whether we wrote what we meant to, in general, but it can sometimes establish without question that a statement is illegal. The degree of checking in the various Fortran systems varies widely.

In our case there are four diagnostic error messages when we attempt to compile, as shown in Figure 2.19. The syntax error indication on statement 4 is not altogether explicit, although the dollar sign printed as a pointer in the line below the statement indicates that the problem might be something missing at the end of the statement. Indeed, a closing right parenthesis is missing. The illegal F6.10 field specification is pointed out clearly, as is the LESS where there should be LT, and the absence of an END statement.

There are still some fairly serious errors in this program, some of which are detectable by the computer. However, not all of the checking is done by any one part of the compiling and loading system. The errors that were discovered during this stage were bad enough to disable compilation, and further steps were not attempted. When we correct the errors pointed out in the first attempt at compilation and try again, we get two further error indications. First is a warning (not shown) to the effect that an

```
C CASE STUDY 4
C NEWTON-RAPHSON METHOD -- PROGRAM CHECKOUT
C
C THIS PROGRAM CONTAINS MANY DELIBERATE ERRORS
C ---- ------- -------- ---- ---------- ------
C
C
      1 X = 1.0
       2 EX = EXP(X)
      3 EMX = 1.0 / X
      4 XNEW = X + ((EX+EMX)/2. = COS(X) - 3.)/((EX-EMX)/2. - SINE(X)
      5 WRITE (6, 6,) XNEW
      6 FROMAT (F6.10)
      7 IF ( ABS(X - XNEW) .LESS. 1E-6 ) END
      8 XNEW = X
      9 GO TO 2
     10 STOP
```

FIGURE 2.18. Listing of the program produced from the coding sheet of Figure 2.17. (Case Study 4.)

```
0004      4 XNEW = X + ((EX+EMX)/2. + COS(X) - 3.)/((EX-EMX)/2. - SINE(X)
                                                                              $
01)   IEY013I SYNTAX
0006      6 FORMAT (F6.10)
                        $
01)   IEY010I SIZE
0007      7 IF ( ABS(X - XNEW) .LESS. 1E-6 ) END
                                       $
01)   IEY013I SYNTAX
0010     10 STOP
            $
01)   IEY015I NO END CARD
```

FIGURE 2.19.   An error listing produced by the compiler from the program of Figure 2.18, after correcting some of the errors. (Case Study 4.)

END statement is not supposed to have a statement number. This, however, did not disable compilation. Second is a notice that SINE is an undefined name. We should have written SIN, of course, but the system didn't know that, and searched several extensive libraries looking for something with the name SINE. If by coincidence there had been a function with that name in any of the libraries, the system would have tried to use it, which might have produced thoroughly confusing results. If the programmer is lucky, that kind of error leads to illegal usage of the unintended function and a diagnostic message of some kind. If he is unlucky, the unintended function may be completely legal, but may produce incorrect results. Once again, the programmer can be lucky or unlucky. If he is lucky, the incorrect results will be wildly wrong, and he will notice the error in checking a test case. If he is unlucky, the incorrect results will be fairly close on the test cases, and he may be years discovering the error.

Once again we correct the errors uncovered by the compiler and try to compile. This time there are no error messages, and the program runs. But the output consists of a great many identical lines: 32.987549, double spaced. The double spacing is the result of something we have not yet covered—but that's life, too: what you don't know *can* hurt you. Because of problems we have yet to clear up, the actual computed result was −32.987549. This fills the ten printing positions we allocated. But the *first* printing position on a line is used to control line spacing, and a zero designates double spacing. The manual on this system does not say what a minus sign will do, but evidently the machine took it to be equivalent to a zero for this purpose. The carriage control character is not printed, so we have the further confusion that

what was printed was not the actual value in the machine.

However, we have enough to go on to know that something is seriously amiss. The value is rather far from what we might have expected, and worse, the endless repetition of that same value means we are not converging. (Running under time sharing has a big advantage here. When we see a process that is in an endless loop it is a simple matter on most systems to press a button or some combination of buttons to interrupt the operation. On a batch system it is possible to print out a great many pages of identical useless values, unless the operating system imposes some limit on the computer time and/or output.)

After another round of checking we discover that in statement 4 there is a plus sign where there should be a minus, and we notice that statement 8 is backwards: it should be X = XNEW, not XNEW = X. While we are correcting these errors we should insert an *iteration counter* to guarantee that if the process does not converge—for whatever reason—it will stop after a reasonable number of iterations, say 20. The corrected program is shown in Figure 2.20.

This program still contains one error, a thoroughly unintentional one, which took the author over an hour to find—even though correct variations of this program have appeared in three previous books! This is admitted, ruefully, in the hope that the reader will believe that programming errors do creep into almost everybody's work, and that careful checking really is an essential part of the task of programming.

(A program that runs correctly the first time it is tried is called a *gold-star program*. Producing such a program is something that most programmers never experience, with the exception of extremely small and unrealistic exercises.

```
C CASE STUDY 4
C NEWTON-RAPHSON METHOD -- PROGRAM CHECKOUT
C
C REVISED VERSION -- ERRORS REMOVED AND AN ITERATION COUNTER INCLUDED
C
C
    1 X = 1.0
C
C N IS A COUNT OF THE NUMBER OF ITERATIONS
      N = 1
    2 EX = EXP(X)
    3 EMX = 1.0 / X
    4 XNEW = X - ((EX+EMX)/2. + COS(X) - 3.)/((EX-EMX)/2. - SIN(X))
    5 WRITE (6, 6,) XNEW
    6 FORMAT (F10.6)
C
C THE IF STATEMENT NOW INCLUDES A TEST OF THE ITERATION COUNTER
    7 IF (       ABS(X - XNEW) .LT. 1E-6
    1       .OR. N .GT. 20 ) STOP
C
C INCREMENT ITERATION COUNTER
      N = N + 1
    8 X = XNEW
    9 GO TO 2
      END
```

FIGURE 2.20. A supposedly correct version of the program for the Newton-Raphson method, which contains one unintentional error. (Case Study 4.)

This is true of good programmers as well as bad; the ability to write gold-star programs is most distinctly *not* a reliable test of whether a person is a good programmer. The vast majority of programs of realistic size do not work 100 percent correctly until they have been exercised extensively under realistic operating conditions—if ever.)

The last remaining error, which most readers have no doubt already long since caught, is that statement 3 should be EMX = 1.0/EX, not EMX = 1.0/X. This is possibly the most insidious kind of error: something clearly wrong, but close enough that in proofreading you "see" what you know *ought* to be there instead of what actually *is* there.

The final corrected version is shown in Figure 2.21, and the output in Figure 2.22. We see that convergence to the root is quite rapid, which is characteristic of the Newton-Raphson method as long as the function is reasonably well-behaved.

(Actually, there is still one syntactic error in this program, the extra comma in the WRITE. This was not diagnosed by the compiler, and evidently caused no trouble.)

Most programs either do not compile the first time or, if they do, they produce incorrect answers. Experienced programmers expect to have

to spend time on program checkout and they plan accordingly. We may conclude this brief introduction to the subject of program checkout with a few suggestions on how to go about it.

1. Checkout is usually facilitated if values of intermediate variables are available. Generally we insert extra WRITE statements to get the values, then remove the cards and recompile when checkout is completed. In time sharing it is a simple matter to edit out the extra statements after checkout is complete.

2. Time spent in desk-checking a program will shorten the total time the programmer must spend on checkout and it will also save computer time. This should be done both before and after the program cards are punched or the program entered.

3. Accomplish as much as you can with each computer run. Resist the almost overwhelming temptation to rush back to the machine after finding each error.

4. Never assume that a program is correct just because the compiler detects no errors.

5. If the answers do not come out the way you expected, there is no point in running the program again—unchanged—to see if it was the machine's fault. It wasn't.

6. When you resubmit a program to try to

```
C CASE STUDY 4
C NEWTON-RAPHSON METHOD -- PROGRAM CHECKOUT
C
C REVISED VERSION -- ERRORS REMOVED AND AN ITERATION COUNTER INCLUDED
C
C
    1 X = 1.0
C
C N IS A COUNT OF THE NUMBER OF ITERATIONS
      N = 1
    2 EX = EXP(X)
    3 EMX = 1.0 / EX
    4 XNEW = X - ((EX+EMX)/2. + COS(X) - 3.)/((EX-EMX)/2. - SIN(X))
    5 WRITE (6, 6,) XNEW
    6 FORMAT (F10.6)
C
C THE IF STATEMENT NOW INCLUDES A TEST OF THE ITERATION COUNTER
    7 IF (      ABS(X - XNEW) .LT. 1E-6
   1      .OR. N .GT. 20 ) STOP
C
C INCREMENT ITERATION COUNTER
      N = N + 1
    8 X = XNEW
    9 GO TO 2
      END
```

FIGURE 2.21.   The final correct version of the program for the Newton-Raphson method. (Case Study 4.)

locate the errors, *always* insert lots of temporary WRITE statements to get the values of intermediate variables. Failure to do so will ordinarily mean a complete waste of the next computer run.

7. When in doubt about exactly how to write a statement, *look it up.*

8. Proofread every line of your program, and all sample data cards. Be especially certain that the arithmetic assignment statements really do represent what you meant to write.

9. If the diagnostic error messages make no sense to you, probably something you wrote made no sense to the computer. Running the program again without changes will produce another set of identical meaningless messages.

10. The final test of a program is comparison with hand calculations of test cases. In choosing test values, try to select values that bring all

```
3.746588
2.947446
2.348739
1.995280
1.871751
1.858076
1.857921
1.857921
```

FIGURE 2.22.   The output of the program of Figure 2.21. (Case Study 4.)

parts of the program into operation. Be sure to try erroneous values to check out whatever error-detection routines you have provided. (One good check is to put in some cards punched with random digits, to make sure that bad data really is rejected.) It is also important to guard against unintentional use of special cases that do not properly test the program. For instance, if a compiler permits mixed mode expressions but all your test values are whole numbers, an error caused by erroneous use of the mixed-mode feature could go undetected.

11. Program checkout is not a contest between you and the machine. Machine errors these days are extremely rare, and errors in the compilers and operating systems, although slightly more common, are very unlikely to be the cause of your troubles. The probability is very great that the trouble is something you wrote, which either was not what you meant to write or was written wrongly through misunderstanding of the required format. The proper attitude is that if you are clever enough, you can get the machine to help you find the problem.*

*This list is approximately twice as long as the corresponding list in the first edition of the book. The additions are to be credited primarily to Mrs. Joyce Fodor of the University of Wisconsin and Mrs. Susan Jaedecke of the University of Denver, both of whom have extensive experience in helping beginning programmers with program checkout.

1. In each of the following you are to draw a flowchart of the decisions required and to write statements to carry out the actions. You may regard these actions as small parts of larger programs; that is, you may assume that previous statements have given values to all variables and you need not write input and output statements.

*(a) If a is greater than b, set x equal to 16.9, but if a is less than or equal to b, set x equal to 56.9.

(b) If rho + theta $< 10^{-6}$, transfer to the statement numbered 156; otherwise go to next statement.

*(c) If rho + theta $< 10^{-6}$, transfer to statement 156; otherwise transfer to statement 762.

*(d) Place whichever of the variables x and y is algebraically larger in BIG.

(e) Place whichever of the variables x, y, and z is algebraically largest in BIG3. (This can be done with only two IF statements. Establish which of x and y is larger, place it in a temporary location, and then compare this number with z to find the largest of the three.)

(f) The variables named r and s may be positive or negative. Place the one that is larger *in absolute value* in BIGAB.

*(g) An angle named THETA is known to be positive and less than 30 radians. Subtract 2π from THETA as many times as necessary to reduce it to an angle less than 2π; leave the reduced angle in THETA.

*(h) If g and h are both negative, set SIGNS equal to. -1; if both are positive, set SIGNS to $+1$; if they have different signs, set SIGNS to zero.

(i) $Y1$, $Y2$, and $Y3$ are the ordinates of three points on a curve. If $Y2$ is a *local maximum*, that is if $Y2 > Y1$ and $Y2 > Y3$, transfer to statement 456; otherwise transfer to statement 567.

*(j) If $a < 0$ and $b > 0$, or if $c = 0$, set OMEGA equal to cos $(x + 1.2)$; otherwise go to next statement.

(k) If $i = 1$ and $R < S$, transfer to statement 261; if $i = 1$ and $R \geq S$, transfer to statement 275; if $i \neq 1$, transfer to statement 927.

*(l) If $N = 1, 2$, or 8, transfer to statement 250; if $N = 3$ or 7, transfer to statement 251; if $N = 4, 5, 6$, transfer to statement 252. You may assume that N is not less than 1 nor greater than 8.

(m) Same as l, except STOP if it is not true that $1 \leq N \leq 8$.

*(n) If $0.999 \leq x \leq 1.001$, STOP; otherwise transfer to statement 639. Do this in two ways:
   (1) With a logical IF having two relations combined with an .AND..
   (2) With a logical IF having only one test, using the absolute value function.

*(o) XREAL and XIMAG are the real and imaginary parts of a complex number. Set SQUARE equal to 1 if XREAL and XIMAG are both less than 1 in absolute value; otherwise do nothing.

(p) Set CIRCLE equal to 1 if

$$\sqrt{XREAL^2 + XIMAG^2} \leq 1;$$

otherwise go to next statement.

(q) Set DIAMND equal to 1 if the point with coordinates XREAL and XIMAG lies within a square of side $\sqrt{2}$ with its corners on the coordinate axes.

2. In the following exercises you are to draw a flowchart and write a complete program, including input and output. You may use F10.0 field specifications for all input and 1PE15.6 for all output.

*(a) Read the value of ANNERN; print ANNERN and compute and print TAX according to the following table:

ANNERN (annual earnings)	TAX
Less than $2000	Zero
$2000 or more but less than $5000	2% of the amount over $2000
$5000 or more	$60 plus 5% of the amount over $5000

(b) GROSS is an employee's earnings for the year; DEPEND is the number of dependents he claims. Multiply DEPEND by 675.00, subtract the product from GROSS, and place the difference in TAXABL. However, if this difference is negative, place zero in TAXABL.

*(c) Y is to be computed as a function of X according to

$$Y = 16.7X + 9.2X^2 - 1.02X^3$$

There will be no data to read; compute and print both X and Y for X values from 1.0 to 9.9 in steps of 0.1. You may assume for this exercise that you are working with a decimal computer, so that adding 0.1 to X repeatedly will eventually give 9.9 *exactly*.

*(d) Same as (c) but your computer is binary. Since the binary representation of decimal 0.1 is a nonterminating fraction, there is no guarantee that adding the binary representation of 0.1 to X repeatedly will give 9.9 *exactly*. Therefore, if you were to start X at 1.0, add 0.1 each time around, and each time test X against 9.9, the odds are you would not get exact equality and thus go past 9.9. In fact, you might never get out of the loop. Write a program to solve this problem by letting an integer variable run from 10 to 99; convert to real, then divide by 10. Use the result as the independent variable.

(e) Y is to be computed as a function of X according to the formula

$$Y = \sqrt{1 + X} + \frac{\cos 2X}{1 + \sqrt{X}}$$

for a number of equally spaced values of X. Three numbers are to be read from a card: XINIT, XINC, and XFIN. XINIT, we assume, is less than XFIN; XINC is positive. Y is to be computed and printed initially for $X =$ XINIT. Then X is to be incremented by XINC, and Y is to be computed and printed for this new value of X, and so on, until Y has been computed for the largest value of X not exceeding XFIN. (The phrase "the largest value of X not exceeding XFIN" lets us ignore the problem presented in the last two exercises. However, this formulation does mean that if the data is set up with the intention of terminating the process with X exactly equal to XFIN it may not do so.)

3. In the following exercises the emphasis is on trying to devise decision processes rather than on computations. Draw a flowchart or describe your method in words. Write a program if you wish. The methods you devise must be *capable* of implementation in Fortran, even if you do not write programs. (Some of them are quite difficult.)

(a) Given four line segments that supposedly form a square as sketched in Figure 2.23, compute the value of CLOSRE, the distance of the end of L_4 from the origin. You may not take advantage of any particular orientation of the square. If the error of closure is less than 1 percent of the sum of the lengths of the four sides and no side is zero, set the variable OK to 1; otherwise set OK to zero.

(b) Given two times, both expressed in hours and minutes since midnight, such as 0145, 1130, or 2350, you are guaranteed that $h_1 m_1$, the first time, is earlier than $h_2 m_2$, the second time, and that they are less than 24 hours apart. You are *not* guaranteed that they are in the same day: for instance, 2350 before midnight is earlier than 0200 after midnight of the same night. Compute the difference between the two times in minutes.

(c) Suppose that the squares of a tic-tac-toe game are numbered as shown in Figure 2.24 and that you are given N1, N2, and N3, the numbers of three squares. Assume that $N1 < N2 < N3$. If the three squares so designated lie in a line, set LINE to 1; otherwise set LINE to zero. Can you suggest a way to renumber the squares that would greatly simplify the test?

(d) A certain parlor game requires the determination of the number of common letters in two five-letter words, neither of which has any duplicated letters. For instance, there are no common letters in BLACK and WHITE; one common letter in BLACK and MAUVE, and five common letters in NAILS and SNAIL. Outline a method of computing in DUPE the number of common letters.

(e) You are given 10 pairs of $x - y$ values, representing coordinate points on a bubble-chamber photograph. Devise a way to decide whether the track is circular and, if so, to compute its radius of curvature. There should be an allowance for

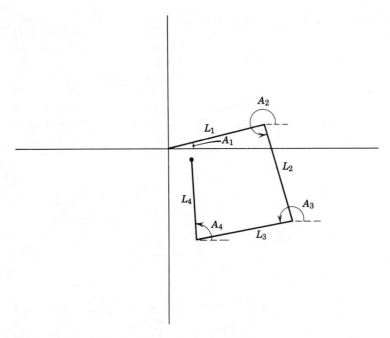

FIGURE 2.23. One possible figure to be analyzed in Exercise 3a.

experimental error; that is, your test must not ask that the points represent a circular arc *exactly*.

(f) Devise an approximation process to find a value of x for which $\cosh x = 3 - \cos x$.

(g) Devise an approximation process to find a value of x for which

$$\cos x + \sqrt{4.28 - x^2} = x^2 + 5.32.$$

(h) For each of two aircraft you are given the speed, altitude, direction, and position. If the altitudes vary by at least 1000 ft., do nothing else. If the altitudes vary by less than 1000 ft. and the flight paths intersect within a half hour, determine whether at any time the two aircraft are within 10 minutes flying time of each other.

(i) A checkerboard is placed on a coordinate system, as shown in Figure 2.25. The

1	2	3
4	5	6
7	8	9

FIGURE 2.24. The numbering scheme for the tic-tac-toe problem in Exercise 3c.

equations of two lines are determined by four numbers a, b, c, d in

$$y = ax + b$$
$$y = cx + d$$

If the two lines intersect anywhere on the board, produce the square number. If they do not intersect, determine whether at any point on the board they pass through adjacent squares.

(j) Suppose you have discovered that your Fortran system contains a function

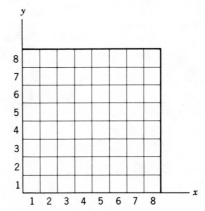

FIGURE 2.25. The numbering system for the checkerboard used in Exercise 3i.

named F. You know nothing about it, except that if you write a statement such as

$$Y = F(X)$$

where X has already been given a value, a value is stored for Y. Devise a test to establish whether F is a continuous function of X over the range (0, 5). (You will have to arrange a suitable modification of the usual definition of continuity to allow for the fact that Fortran "real" numbers are only rational fractions in the mathematical sense. By *mathematical* definitions, no function of any sort in a digital computer is ever continuous.)

3 DOUBLE-PRECISION, COMPLEX, AND LOGICAL VARIABLES

3.1 INTRODUCTION

So far we have dealt with real and integer quantities and have used the IJKLMN naming convention for distinguishing between them. In this chapter we shall learn first how to override the naming convention, for example, allowing ABC to be the name of an integer variable and IM the name of a real variable. Most of the chapter is devoted to studying three other types of variables, double precision, complex, and logical, all of which simplify or make possible various kinds of useful and interesting processing and which we shall investigate in three case studies.

This material will not be of equal importance for all readers. Complex variables arise most commonly in certain engineering applications and logical variables usually only in fairly special situations. All readers should be aware of the type statements and have a general idea what double precision operations are about, but not all will need to understand complex or logical operations completely. Skimming is in order, as applications and interests dictate, but all readers should at least look over Section 3.2 on type statements and Sections 3.3 and 3.4 on double precision operations.

3.2 TYPE STATEMENTS

A *type statement* consists of one of the declarations INTEGER, REAL, DOUBLE PRECISION, COMPLEX, LOGICAL, or EXTERNAL, followed by as many variable names as necessary, separated by commas. For instance, we might write the following type statements in a program:

```
REAL J
INTEGER B
INTEGER K, ABC, ROOTS
REAL MATRIX, NUMBER, X
DOUBLE PRECISION DENOM, PREVX, TERM, N
COMPLEX T, N1, N2, D1
LOGICAL A1, A2, K
EXTERNAL COS, MULT
```

The variable K could have been omitted from the INTEGER statement and X from the REAL statement without effect; these names are already identified as integer and real, respectively, by their first letters. On the other hand, there is no harm in such "unnecessary" inclusions in type statements, and some programmers make a point of naming every variable in a type statement. This helps to guard against failure to give a correct type to a variable whose name does not agree with the naming convention. (An electrical engineer's habit and training is to use *I* for current and *L* for inductance, for instance. If he makes the point of putting all variable names in type statements, he will be less likely to overlook the necessity of naming *I* and *L* in a REAL statement.)

In contrast, variables that are to be considered as double precision, complex, or logical *must* be named in suitable type statements; otherwise they are taken to be real or integer, according to the naming convention.

Many Fortran systems provide an IMPLICIT statement, making it possible to designate all variables having specified initial letters as being of a certain type. We might write, for instance,

```
IMPLICIT COMPLEX(C, W-Z), REAL(I)
```

which would mean that all variable names in the program beginning with the letters C, W, X, Y, or Z are to be taken as complex variables and all variables beginning with I are real. This facility, if available in a given system, can be a significant time and effort saver in certain situations. Notice that the standard naming convention operates as though we had specified

```
IMPLICIT REAL(A-H, O-Z), INTEGER(I-N)
```

In a number of systems there are alternative forms for storage of certain variable types. In the IBM System/360, for example, it is possible to store an integer variable in either two or four "bytes" of storage, a byte consisting of eight binary digits. In such systems a type statement may be written with the number of bytes specified. For instance, we may write

```
INTEGER*2 I, M, P23
```

to indicate that the three named variables should be assigned to two-byte locations instead of the normal four. This would ordinarily be done only when large arrays of storage are needed in which each individual data item is short.

In systems where this facility is provided, we may also write REAL*8 as an alternative to DOUBLE PRECISION.

The EXTERNAL statement is mentioned here only for completeness, since it is considered to be a type statement. However, we shall not consider it until Chapter 7 in functions and subroutines. At that time we shall also learn that the five type specifications can be applied to functions as well as to variables.

For the rest of this chapter we shall study the three new types of quantity, double precision, complex, and logical.

3.3 DOUBLE-PRECISION CONSTANTS, VARIABLES, AND OPERATIONS

A double-precision number is one that is represented and used more or less like a real number but has more digits. Sometimes there are twice as many digits, as suggested by the name double precision, but this is not always the case. It would probably be safe to say *at least* twice as many digits; one important computer has about $2\frac{1}{3}$ times as many in a double-precision float-ing-point number as in a single-precision number.

This extra precision in the representation of numbers is most commonly needed to guard against the effect of rounding error in computations that involve long sequences of arithmetic or operations combining very large and very small numbers in addition or subtraction. We shall examine some examples later.

A double-precision constant is written in exponent form, but with a D instead of an E. The following are acceptable double-precision constants.

```
1.5D0
5.0D4
5.0D-4
1.23456789023456D0
```

In many Fortran systems a long number such as the last may be written without the exponent because constants containing a decimal point and more than some specified number of digits are taken to be double precision. In Fortran for the Burroughs 6000 series machines, for instance, any constant with more than twelve digits is taken to be double precision; in the IBM System/360 series, more than seven digits signifies double precision. This can occasionally cause unexpected results or compiler diagnostics. If we write, for instance,

```
SQRT(3.14159265 * X)
```

in 360 Fortran, we get a diagnostic stating that the type of the function (real) does not match the type of its argument, which is forced to be double precision because we wrote the approximation to π with more than seven digits.

Arithmetic expressions are formed in double precision according to the same rules governing hierarchy of operators that apply to real expressions.

The only question we need to investigate in this area is that of combining double-precision quantities with real (single-precision) quantities in an arithmetic expression. This is explicitly permitted and always gives a double-precision result, which means that simple constants need not be written in double-precision form. In fact, double-precision constants are needed only if they really have more digits than can be expressed with a real constant, or as arguments of double precision functions.

It is permissible to have an integer, a real, or

a double-precision variable on the left side of an arithmetic assignment statement and an expression on the right of some other type. All arithmetic is done according to the type of expression on the right, and the result is converted according to the type of variable on the left.

Appendix 1 contains tables showing the permissible combinations of integer, real, and double-precision values.

The following examples are all acceptable uses of double-precision quantities, assuming that R1, R2, etc., are all real variables, D1, D2, etc., are double-precision and I1, I2, etc., are integer variables.

```
D1 = D2*D3 + (D4 - 8756.7865432D0)/D5
D1 = 4.0*D2 - D3/1.1D0
D1 = R1 + D1 + R2
R1 = (D1*D2 - D3*D4) / (D1*D5 - D3*D6)
D1 = R1 + 2.0
D1 = (I1 - 8)*I2
I1 = R1 + D1
D1 = D2**2
```

Observe in the second example that the Fortran compiler will be able to determine by the context that D1, D2, and D3 are the names of variables, but that D0 is a double-precision exponent. It may be noted that in this same example there is a point to making 1.1D0 a double-precision constant: in a binary computer, 1.1 has no exact representation of any length, but the double-length constant would be a closer approximation. On the other hand, 4.0, being a whole number, is represented exactly in almost all floating-point systems, so that there is no loss of accuracy in using it as a real (single-length) constant.

Fortran double-precision functions are provided for a number of mathematical functions. For convenience in remembering, the names of all functions with double-precision function values begin with D. Appendix 2 summarizes the most common functions involving double-precision values. Most of them, as noted, take one or more double-precision arguments and furnish a double-precision function value, but certain special purpose functions do not follow the pattern. For instance, the function SNGL ("Single") takes a double-precision argument and supplies as the function value the real representation of the most significant part of the argument.

Input and output of double-precision quantities is handled with D, a new field descrip-

tor. D-conversion is the same as E-conversion, except that (1) the list variable associated with such a field descriptor should be double-precision, (2) there can be more digits (17 is typical), and (3) D is used for the exponent indicator rather than E. It is also permissible to write out double-precision values using the F field descriptor, simply by providing space for more digits.

3.4 CASE STUDY 5: ERROR ANALYSIS IN A DOUBLE-PRECISION SINE ROUTINE

The Taylor series for the sine

$$\sin x = x - \frac{x^3}{3!} + \frac{x^5}{5!} - \frac{x^7}{7!} + \cdots$$

is usually described as valid for any finite angle, and the truncation error committed by stopping the summation after a finite number of terms is said to be less in absolute value than the first term neglected. These statements would be true *if there were some way to keep an infinite number of digits in each arithmetic result*. Actually, the series is useless for large values of x.

In this case study we shall investigate why this happens in an attempt to understand the need for double-precision quantities even when the final results are much less accurate than the number of digits carried in program variables.

We shall write a program to evaluate the series directly; that is, we shall start with the first term and continue to compute terms until we find one that is less in absolute values than, say, 10^{-8}. The sum of the series then ought to be within 10^{-8} of the correct value of the sine.

The program requires a stratagem to avoid producing intermediate results too large to be represented in the computer. The largest angle we shall consider will be about 70 radians; if we were to try to raise 70 to the large powers that will be required, we should greatly exceed the sizes permitted of real and double-precision variables in all but a few Fortran systems. Therefore, we shall take another approach, that of computing each term from the preceding term. The recursion relation is not complicated. Having the first term, x, we can get the next term by multiplying by $-x^2$ and dividing by 2×3. Having the second term, we can get the third by multiplying by $-x^2$ and dividing by 4×5.

In short, given any term, we can get the next one by multiplying by $-x^2$ and dividing by the product of the next two integers.

A flowchart of the algorithm is shown in Figure 3.1. The first action is to print a line of column headings at the top of a new sheet of paper in the printer, using techniques that we shall explore after describing the rest of the flowchart. The first action after that is the reading of a card containing an angle in degrees. The procedure will be to read cards repeatedly, computing and printing the sine of the angle on each, until reaching a *sentinel card* containing an angle of zero. This will signal the end of the deck.

After reading an angle, we begin by converting it to radians, which is done by dividing by $180/\pi$; the result is called X. Now we need to get the recursion process started. We shall continually be adding a new term to a sum that will eventually become the sine when enough terms have been computed. To get started we set this sum equal to X; the first term computed by the recursion relation will be $-x^3/3!$. Thus the preceding term is initially X. To get the successive integers (mathematical integers, not Fortran integers!) we start a variable named DENOM at 3.0. To avoid recomputing x^2 repeatedly, we compute it once before entering the loop, giving it the name XSQ.

Getting a new term is a simple matter of multiplying the preceding term by $-$XSQ and dividing by the product of DENOM and DENOM-1.0. This new term replaces the preceding term and is added to the sum. We are now ready to find out whether enough terms have been computed. We ask whether the absolute value of the term just computed is less than 10^{-8}. If it is, we are ready to print the result and go back to read another card. If not, the value of DENOM must be incremented by 2.0 before returning to compute another term.

Besides printing the value of the sine computed by this method, it might be interesting to use the sine routine supplied with the Fortran system to compute it also. This is done just before printing.

The program shown in Figure 3.2 carries out the actions of this algorithm with all numbers in single-precision form. The only feature of this program that involves any new programming concepts is the printing of the heading line at the beginning.

We see that the WRITE statement names no

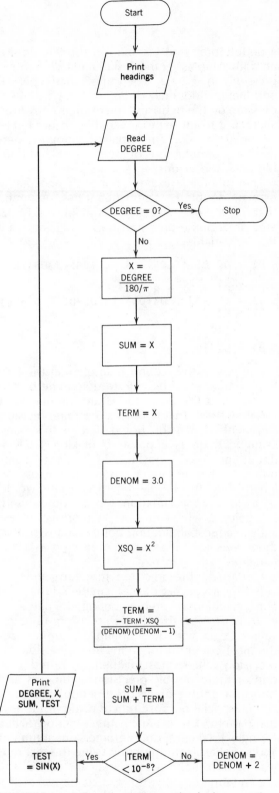

FIGURE 3.1. A flowchart of a method of computing a sine from the Taylor series. (Case Study 5.)

```
C CASE STUDY 5
C COMPUTATION OF SINE FROM TAYLOR'S SERIES
C
C SINGLE PRECISION VERSION
C
C
C WRITE COLUMN HEADINGS
      WRITE (6, 100)
 100  FORMAT (1H1, 7H DEGREE, 10X, 1HX, 9X, 29HSERIES-SINE    FUNCTION-
     1SINE//)
C
C READ A VALUE OF THE ANGLE
  10  READ (5, 110) DEGREE
 110  FORMAT (F10.0)
C
C TEST FOR END-OF-DECK SENTINEL
      IF ( DEGREE .EQ. 0.0 ) STOP
C
C CONVERT FROM DEGREES TO RADIANS
      X = DEGREE / 57.29578
C
C SET UP INITIAL VALUES
      SUM = X
      TERM = X
      DENOM = 3.0
      XSQ = X**2
C
C COMPUTE NEW TERM FROM PREVIOUS TERM
  20  TERM = - TERM * XSQ / (DENOM * (DENOM - 1.0))
C
C GET SUM OF TERMS SO FAR
      SUM = SUM + TERM
C
C TEST FOR CONVERGENCE
      IF ( ABS(TERM) .LT. 1.0E-8 ) GO TO 30
C
C PREPARE TO GO AROUND AGAIN
      DENOM = DENOM + 2.0
      GO TO 20
C
C GET VALUE FROM SUPPLIED SINE ROUTINE FOR COMPARISON
  30  TEST = SIN(X)
C
C PRINT RESULTS
      WRITE (6, 120) DEGREE, X, SUM, TEST
 120  FORMAT (1H , F6.0, 3F16.7)
C
C GO TO READ ANOTHER ANGLE
      GO TO 10
      END
```

FIGURE 3.2. A program for computing a sine, corresponding to the flowchart of Figure 3.1.
(Case Study 5.)

variables, which means that whatever is printed will have to come from FORMAT statement. The first field descriptor in the FORMAT brings up two new factors.

First is the fact that the first character of each line sent to the printer is not actually printed at all but is used to control spacing of the printed lines, according to the following scheme. If the first character is a blank, normal single spacing occurs. We have always to this point simply arranged the first number printed so that the first character in its field was a blank, with the exception of the error condition in the checkout phase of Case Study 4. If the first character is a zero, double spacing is called for. If it is a one, the paper is moved to the top of the next page before printing. Finally, a plus sign specifies that the paper should not be moved at all, which can be used, for instance, to produce underlining.

We can introduce the desired spacing control character in several ways in most systems. One way that will always work is to use a *Hollerith field descriptor,* which consists of an integer denoting the number of characters, the letter H, and the characters to be sent to the output device. To call for a skip to the top of the next page we have written

```
1H1
```

Alternatively, in most Fortran systems we could enclose the 1 in quotation marks or some other delimiter character, writing, for instance,

```
'1'
```

Finally, in the case of the blank for single spacing, we can use a new field descriptor, the X. Here, when we write nX, the next n spaces in the line are filled with blanks. Thus, if the first field descriptor in the FORMAT statement for a line to be printed is 1X, we are defining single spacing.

Finally, in the way of new FORMAT features, we introduce the slash(/). This instructs the system that the FORMAT refers to more than one line (or card, or whatever). In our case, we shall place two slashes at the end of the line; since no other field descriptors are associated with the two new lines that are thus indicated, we simply produce two blank lines. This is done to separate the heading line from the numerical output below it.

Putting all this together, we see in the FORMAT statement numbered 100 and the WRITE before it the following features. The WRITE names no variables; the only things printed will therefore come from the FORMAT statement. We have written 1H1 to get a skip to the top of the next sheet of paper before printing the heading. Now we begin to produce the characters that are desired in the heading line. When we write

```
7H DEGREE
```

we are calling for seven characters to be placed in the line, beginning at the left; the seven characters are a blank and the letters of the word

DEGREE. The blank here *is* significant; this is the one and only place in a Fortran program where blanks mean anything to the compiler. Next we call for ten blanks with the 10X, then the letter X and nine more blanks. Now we want 29 characters for the next two headings and the five blanks between them. All this runs past position 72 in the line, so we are forced to use a continuation line. It would have been possible, of course, to produce these two column headings with two separate H field specifications and a 5X; the choice is largely a matter of whim, in this case. Finally, there are two slashes, calling for two blank lines.

All this may sound more complicated than it is. In practice, setting up the FORMAT statements to produce output identification is not difficult and is definitely recommended. We shall routinely provide such identification from now on. Chapter 6 contains another view of the material in this section, organized to be suitable for reference.

Figure 3.3 shows the output produced when this program was run with a set of input values, all of which are ±30° plus or minus multiples of 360°. The absolute value of the result in every case should therefore be $\frac{1}{2}$. The entry for 30° is exactly correct, which is almost accidental; we would have been content with an error of one or two units in the last place. The entry for 390° is barely tolerable, that for 750° quite poor, and for 1110° and larger angles we get nonsensical results. The entries that consist of asterisks indicate values that were too large to be contained in the space available.

Let us consider the successive values of TERM and SUM for some representative values of the angle to try to get some insight into what has caused these drastically wrong results in a method that is taught in most calculus classes as involving no such difficulties.

Using a modified version of the program, not shown, we arrange to print out the values of DENOM, TERM, and SUM, in that order, just after the statement

```
SUM = SUM + TERM
```

Figure 3.4 presents the output of the modified program for an angle of 30°. The first term is not shown there, but since the first value of both TERM and SUM is just X, we know from Figure 3.3 that the value is 0.5235988. The second term is then −0.0239256, which, added to

DEGREE	X	SERIES-SINE	FUNCTION-SINE
30.	0.5235988	0.5000000	0.4999999
390.	6.8067837	0.5000133	0.4999996
750.	13.0899696	0.5055103	0.5000001
1110.	19.3731537	-11.2978935	0.4999991
1470.	25.6563263	891.7993164	0.4999881
1830.	31.9395142	639408.0000000	0.4999903
2190.	38.2227020	****************	0.4999925
2550.	44.5058899	****************	0.4999948
2910.	50.7890778	****************	0.4999970
-30.	-0.5235988	-0.5000000	-0.4999999
-390.	-6.8067837	-0.5000133	-0.4999996

FIGURE 3.3. The output of the program of Figure 3.2 for representative values of the angle. The rows of asterisks designate values that were too large to print in the space available. (Case Study 5.)

the previous value of SUM, gives 0.4996742, as we see. For this small angle, the series converges rapidly, and the fifth term in the series is evidently already less than 10^{-8} in absolute value. The error in this case is zero, which is indeed less than 10^{-8}; no problems.

Figure 3.5 reproduces the output of the modified program for an angle of 1110°, where there are very serious problems. The primary culprit is the discrepancy between the size of the largest terms in the series and the limited precision of a single-precision number. Observe the term where DENOM was 19, for instance. The computer has printed 15 digits in the value for TERM, but all the digits to the right of the decimal point are zero—which is suspicious to say the least. In fact, this program was run on an IBM 360, where a single-precision (real) number is represented in six hexadecimal digits, which can contain as much information as slightly fewer than seven decimal digits. Not only the zeros in this number, but the right-most digit 6 as well, are all nonsignificant.

This means that there is no hope of ever getting an accurate value for the sine, since a correct value for the function must, of course, be

DENOM	TERM	SUM
3.	-0.0239246	0.4996742
5.	0.0003280	0.5000021
7.	-0.0000021	0.5000000
9.	0.0000000	0.5000000

FIGURE 3.4. The second, third, fourth, and fifth terms of the Taylor series for the sine of 30°. The first term of the series is 0.5235988. (Case Study 5.)

less than one—and here we have terms that are uncertain within a margin of at least ten! Furthermore, we note that the value for SUM is uncertain by a similar amount; earlier terms,

DENOM	TERM	SUM
3.	-1211.8515625	-1192.4782715
5.	22741.5312500	21549.0507813
7.	-203222.0000000	-181672.9375000
9.	1059347.0000000	877674.0625000
11.	-3614480.0000000	-2736805.0000000
13.	8696041.0000000	5959236.0000000
15.	-15541847.0000000	-9582611.0000000
17.	21445376.0000000	11862765.0000000
19.	-23534656.0000000	-11671891.0000000
21.	21030944.0000000	9359053.0000000
23.	-15599421.0000000	-6240368.0000000
25.	9757921.0000000	3517553.0000000
27.	-5216996.0000000	-1699443.0000000
29.	2411375.0000000	711932.0000000
31.	-973155.0625000	-261223.0625000
33.	345874.3750000	84651.3125000
35.	-109086.6875000	-24435.3750000
37.	30737.4531250	6302.0781250
39.	-7784.3046875	-1482.2265625
41.	1781.4609375	299.2343750
43.	-370.2189941	-70.9846191
45.	70.1768188	-0.8078003
47.	-12.1825523	-12.9903526
49.	1.9440212	-11.0463314
51.	-0.2861285	-11.3324594
53.	0.0389657	-11.2934933
55.	-0.0049241	-11.2984171
57.	0.0005790	-11.2978373
59.	-0.0000635	-11.2979002
61.	0.0000065	-11.2978935
63.	-0.0000006	-11.2978935
65.	0.0000001	-11.2978935
67.	-0.0000000	-11.2978935

FIGURE 3.5. The second and following terms of the Taylor series for the sine of 1110°. (Case Study 5.)

such as the first, which was 19.3731537, have had their influence on SUM destroyed in the process of lining up decimal points in addition. (Not all of the digits of a number like 19.3731537 are dependable, either, but *some* of them are. The good have been lost with the bad!)

Eventually, we get back to terms that are small enough to have accurate representations to eight decimal places—but by then it is too late because prior uncertainties hold over to destroy the accuracy.

If we really wanted to compute sines, we obviously would not proceed in this manner. Since the sine function is periodic with a period

```
C CASE STUDY 5
C COMPUTATION OF SINE FROM TAYLOR'S SERIES
C
C DOUBLE PRECISION VERSION
C
C
      DOUBLE PRECISION X, TERM, SUM, XSQ, DENOM, TEST, DEGREE
C
C WRITE COLUMN HEADINGS
      WRITE (6, 100)
 100  FORMAT('1 DEGREE',14X,'X',16X,'SERIES-SINE',11X,'FUNCTION-SINE'//)
C
C READ A VALUE OF THE ANGLE
 10   READ (5, 110) DEGREE
 110  FORMAT (D23.16)
C
C TEST FOR END-OF-DECK SENTINEL
      IF ( DEGREE .EQ. 0.0D0 ) STOP
C
C CONVERT FROM DEGREES TO RADIANS
      X = DEGREE / (180.0/3.1415926535897932)
C
C SET UP INITIAL VALUES
      SUM = X
      TERM = X
      DENOM = 3.0
      XSQ = X**2
C
C COMPUTE NEW TERM FROM PREVIOUS TERM
 20   TERM = - TERM * XSQ / (DENOM * (DENOM - 1.0))
C
C GET SUM OF TERMS SO FAR
      SUM = SUM + TERM
C
C TEST FOR CONVERGENCE
      IF ( DABS(TERM) .LT. 1.0D-17 ) GO TO 30
C
C PREPARE TO GO AROUND AGAIN
      DENOM = DENOM + 2.0
      GO TO 20
C
C GET VALUE FROM SUPPLIED DP SINE ROUTINE FOR COMPARISON
 30   TEST = DSIN(X)
C
C PRINT RESULTS
      WRITE (6, 120) DEGREE, X, SUM, TEST
 120  FORMAT (1X, F8.0, 3F23.14)
C
C GO TO READ ANOTHER ANGLE
      GO TO 10
      END
```

FIGURE 3.6. A double precision version of the program of Figure 3.2 for finding the sine of an angle from the Taylor series. (Case Study 5.)

of 2π, it is a simple matter to reduce any angle to a value less than 2π, below which our method is seen to be almost tolerable. It is not much added effort to reduce any angle to one that is equivalent, except possibly for a sign reversal, and which is less than $\pi/2$; the method is entirely adequate for such angles, and the correct sign can be restored.

However, there are often situations where such alternatives are not readily available. Let us proceed with our example to see what can be accomplished with double precision as an attempt to deal with the problem. Figure 3.6 presents our program modified to use double-precision quantities in most places, permitting us to examine some typical double-precision programming examples.

The DOUBLE PRECISION statement has been placed at the beginning of the program, prior to any other appearances of the variables named in it.

The heading line will be different this time, since more space is allowed for the longer double-precision values. In modifying the FORMAT statement, we have used quoted literals in place of the H field descriptors to demonstrate how this would look. In the systems where this feature is available, its use makes it unnecessary to count the characters in the literal—an operation that causes many errors. (If the count in an nH descriptor is wrong, it usually creates an error in interpreting the following field descriptor.)

In the READ statement we ask for a double-precision value, which is associated with a D field descriptor in the FORMAT statement. The field width of 23 allows space for a sign, 1 digit before the decimal, the decimal point, 16 digits after the decimal, and a 4-position exponent. We are not restricted, however, to entering data values in exactly this form. Using this same FORMAT, numbers can also be punched in F format (without an exponent); the exponent can be either E or D; as long as the exponent, if there is one, is punched at the right side of the field, the rest of the number need not occupy the full 23 columns. Finally, if the program is run using any type of free-field input, such as WATFOR or WATFIV and many other batch processors and almost all time-sharing systems, the number need only occupy as many positions as required as long as it is followed by a delimiter (comma or space, usually).

In the IF statement that checks for a zero-degree sentinel we compare DEGREE with a double-precision zero, but a single-precision (real) value would also have been acceptable. It is not permitted, however, to mix real and integer, or double precision and integer, in a comparison.

The statement that converts from degrees to radians shows something that we ordinarily avoid, at least in heavily used program segments: a division of one constant by another, which should be made with a desk calculator beforehand—but desk calculators that do 17-digit arithmetic are not readily available. If this program were to be run a great many times, it might be worthwhile to make a preliminary run to get the conversion constant.*

We observe occasional instances of the mixing of real and double-precision quantities, which, we have noted, is permitted. In each case where it is done here, the real quantity is a mathematical integer, which has an exact single-precision representation in the computer being used. The convergence criterion has been changed to 10^{-17}. Notice the function DSIN for getting the double-precision sine.

The FORMAT statement used in writing the output demonstrates that it is permissible to use the F field specification with double precision quantities, simply providing more room if the added digits are desired.

Figure 3.7 shows the output of this program run with the same values for the angle as before. Figure 3.8 shows the output when the field specification in the output FORMAT statement was changed to 1P3D23.14. We see that the additional precision has indeed alleviated the problem. The value for 1110°, where before we got meaningless results, now has nine correct digits. The algorithm does not break down completely until 2190°, by which time the single-precision version was telling us that the sine was something in excess of 10^8.

Still, even double precision does not indefinitely avoid the problems of limited precision. The algorithm does eventually break down, just as before. The example was chosen deliberately

*Finding tables to give constants to many places can be a problem also. This program was initially written during a visit to Chicago forced by a snowstorm. Most motels do not carry π to 16 decimals, so it was originally computed in the program by writing 4.0*DATAN(1.0D0). This statement was modified in the version displayed.

DEGREE	X	SERIES-SINE	FUNCTION-SINE
30.	0.52359877559830	0.50000000000000	0.50000000000000
390.	6.80678408277789	0.50000000000000	0.50000000000000
750.	13.08996938995747	0.50000000000036	0.50000000000000
1110.	19.37315469713706	0.50000000016191	0.50000000000000
1470.	25.65634000431664	0.49999865780756	0.50000000000000
1830.	31.93952531149623	0.50012945598551	0.50000000000000
2190.	38.22271061867582	0.76348214126836	0.50000000000000
2550.	44.50589592585540	158.59741983818510	0.50000000000000
2910.	50.78908123303499	-4670.64707745315400	0.50000000000000
3270.	57.07226654021458	-6243271.74036605500000	0.50000000000000
3630.	63.35545184739416	*********************	0.50000000000000
3990.	69.63863715457375	*********************	0.50000000000000
-30.	-0.52359877559830	-0.50000000000000	-0.50000000000000
-390.	-6.80678408277789	-0.50000000000000	-0.50000000000000

FIGURE 3.7. The output of the program of Figure 3.6 run with a series of representative values for the angle. (Case Study 5.)

to try to make this point: double precision is often a big help in reducing numerical difficulties caused by the limited precision of number representation—but it is not a panacea, and it is not a substitute for proper problem analysis. It is *not* possible to keep out of trouble by putting a DOUBLE PRECISION statement at the beginning of every program.

Naturally, the behavior of this algorithm depends heavily on the form of number representation used by the computer on which the program is run. The program of Figure 3.6 was also run on a Control Data Corporation CDC 6600, which, having been designed specifically for large-scale scientific calculations, has a somewhat longer word length than the IBM 360. A double-precision word in the CDC 6600

contains the equivalent of about 24 decimal digits, and the double precision program gives a result for 2190° that is correct to about 12 digits; the process does not break down completely until 3990°. These results go considerably beyond what we were able to achieve with the 360.

3.5 COMPLEX CONSTANTS, VARIABLES, AND EXPRESSIONS

A complex quantity in Fortran is an ordered pair of Fortran real quantities, the first representing the real part of the complex number and the second the imaginary part. We are able to write constants that represent complex numbers; we

DEGREE	X	SERIES-SINE	FUNCTION-SINE
30.	5.23598775598299D-01	5.00000000000000D-01	5.00000000000000D-01
390.	6.80678408277789D 00	5.00000000000005D-01	5.00000000000000D-01
750.	1.30899693899575D 01	5.00000000000361D-01	4.99999999999998D-01
1110.	1.93731546971371D 01	5.00000000161913D-01	4.99999999999998D-01
1470.	2.56563400043166D 01	4.99998657807555D-01	4.99999999999998D-01
1830.	3.19395253114962D 01	5.00129455985512D-01	4.99999999999998D-01
2190.	3.82227106186758D 01	7.63482141268363D-01	4.99999999999996D-01
2550.	4.45058959258554D 01	1.58597419838185D 02	4.99999999999996D-01
2910.	5.07890812330350D 01	-4.67064707745315D 03	4.99999999999996D-01
3270.	5.70722665402146D 01	-6.24327174036606D 06	4.99999999999996D-01
3630.	6.33554518473942D 01	-1.35443587047316D 09	4.99999999999996D-01
3990.	6.96386371545738D 01	1.18836954575115D 13	4.99999999999996D-01
-30.	-5.23598775598299D-01	-5.00000000000000D-01	-5.00000000000000D-01
-390.	-6.80678408277789D 00	-5.00000000000005D-01	-5.00000000000000D-01

FIGURE 3.8. The output of the program of Figure 3.6 when the output format statement was changed to use a field descriptor of 1P3D23.14. (Case Study 5.)

can specify, using a COMPLEX type statement, that a variable represents the real and imaginary parts of a complex number; we can do arithmetic on complex numbers; we have functions available for carrying out various mathematical operations on complex quantities. The capability provided by Fortran complex operations is a great savings in programming effort in certain problems.

A complex constant consists of a pair of real constants enclosed in parentheses and separated by a comma. The following are examples of complex constants and their meanings:

```
(2.0, 3.0)        2.0 + 3.0i
(2.E5, 2.5E4)     200,000 + 25,000i
(1.075, -0.653)   1.075 − 0.653i
(1.0, 0.0)        1.0 (pure real)
(0.0, 5.0)        5.0i (pure imaginary)
```

A Fortran complex variable is one that has been declared to be complex in a COMPLEX statement. The initial-letter naming convention has no application here because a variable is never considered to be complex unless it has been so declared; there are no restrictions on the initial letter. A complex variable is stored within the computer as two real quantities.

The five familiar arithmetic operations are all defined for operations on complex quantities, although, of course, the computer must do all the manipulations necessary to separate the complex operations into actions on the real and imaginary parts. For reference, these may be reviewed:

$$(a + bi) + (c + di) = (a + c) + (b + d)i$$
$$(a + bi) − (c + di) = (a − c) + (b − d)i$$
$$(a + bi)*(c + di) = (ac − bd) + (ad + bc)i$$
$$(a + bi)/(c + di) = \frac{(ac + bd)}{c^2 + d^2} + \frac{(bc − ad)}{c^2 + d^2}i$$
$$(a + bi)**n$$

A meaning has not been shown for exponentiation because the method of raising a complex number to a power in the computer depends on the size of the exponent. For small powers, an actual multiplication is used. For larger powers, the number may be converted to polar form and use made of De Moivre's formula.*

---

*A complex number $a + bi$ can be converted to the form $\rho(\cos\theta + i\sin\theta)$ in which $\rho = \sqrt{a^2 + b^2}$ is called the absolute value and $\theta = \tan^{-1}b/a$ is called the amplitude. Then

A complex quantity can be raised to an integer power only; it cannot be raised to a power that is a real or complex number (using the Fortran operator **, that is; the operations are, of course, defined mathematically and can be done in Fortran with functions).

Fortran provides functions for computing the exponential function, logarithm, sine, cosine, and square root of a complex number. The argument and function values are both complex in these cases. The complex absolute value function supplies a real value from a complex argument. The first letter of all complex-valued functions has been made C for ease in remembering. The list may be found in Appendix 2.†

The complex square root function CSQRT again applies De Moivre's formula.

Four other functions that are provided for manipulating complex variables find heavy use. REAL supplies the real part of its complex argument; AIMAG supplies the imaginary part of its complex argument, both as a Fortran real number. The function CMPLX takes two real argument expressions, separated by commas, and supplies as the function value the complex number composed of the two values. For instance, we could write

```
Z = CMPLX(A, B)
```

A and B would have to be Fortran real variables and Z a Fortran complex variable. The result of the statement would be to assign the value of A as the real part of Z, and B as its imaginary part. Since the arguments can be any real-valued expressions, we might also write

```
Z2 = CMPLX(0.0, 4.0*OMEGA + 3.56)
```

This would create in Z2 the pure imaginary number with the value given by the expression.

De Moivre's theorem states that $(a + bi)^n = \rho^n(\cos n\theta + i\sin n\theta)$.

†For reference, here are the definitions of these functions in terms of separate operations on their real and imaginary parts.

$$CABS(a + bi) = \sqrt{a^2 + b^2}$$
$$CEXP(a + bi) = e^a(\cos b + i\sin b)$$
$$CLOG(a + bi) = \frac{1}{2}\log(a^2 + b^2) + i\tan^{-1}b/a$$
$$CSIN(a + bi) = \sin a\frac{e^b + e^{-b}}{2} + i\cos a\frac{e^b − e^{-b}}{2}$$
$$CCOS(a + bi) = \cos a\frac{e^b + e^{-b}}{2} − i\sin a\frac{e^b − e^{-b}}{2}$$

DOUBLE-PRECISION, COMPLEX, AND LOGICAL VARIABLES

The function CONJG takes a complex argument and supplies the complex conjugate of the number as the function value:

```
CONJG(a + bi) = (a - bi)
```

Input and output of complex numbers is fairly simple. Whenever a complex variable appears in the list of a READ or WRITE statement, Fortran expects to transmit two real values and to find two corresponding field descriptors in the FORMAT statement. For instance, if H is real and Z is complex, we could write

```
      WRITE (6, 100) H, Z
100   FORMAT (F10.0, F10.3, F12.5)
```

The F10.0 would be associated with the value of H, the F10.3 with the real part of Z, and the F12.5 with the imaginary part of Z.

Complex and real Fortran quantities may be mixed in an expression. When this is done, the Fortran reals are taken to be pure real numbers, mathematically; the result is always a complex number. Thus, if Z has been declared to be complex, we may write such expressions as 4.0∗Z or Z − H, where H is a Fortran real number. No other mixing is permitted except that a complex quantity may be raised to an integer power. Specifically, complex and double precision quantities may not be combined in an expression, and a complex quantity may not be raised to a real power. If the latter operation is needed, it must be done with the complex exponential and logarithm functions, using the relation

$$a^b = \text{CEXP (B∗CLOG (A))}$$

(Some systems, including some of the IBM System/360 compilers, provide for double-precision complex operations using the type specification COMPLEX∗16.)

Figure 3.9 is a simple illustrative program showing several arithmetic statements and some functions. The program reads values of two complex variables named A and B and prints various arithmetic combinations of the two and functions of A. The READ statement lists A and B, with a FORMAT statement having four field descriptors. The output FORMAT statement includes H field descriptors to provide line identifications. The values of A and B that were read were $1.0 + 2.0i$ and $3.0 + 4.0i$ throughout. (The i is not punched on the card. All we punch on the card are the two values representing the real and imaginary parts of the complex number.) The output is shown in Figure 3.10.

3.6 CASE STUDY 6: A SERVOMECHANISM FREQUENCY RESPONSE PLOT

The following case study uses Fortran complex variables in a practical engineering problem.

The transfer function of a certain servomechanism is given by

$$T(j\omega) = \frac{K(1 + j0.4\omega)(1 + j0.2\omega)}{j\omega(1 + j2.5\omega)(1 + j1.43\omega)(1 + j0.02\omega)^2}$$

where ω = angular frequency, radians/second
$j = \sqrt{-1}*$
T = transfer function
K = amplification factor

Without attempting to show the complete theory, we may characterize a transfer function as follows. Consider a "black box" with two input terminals and two output terminals. An input signal with a given frequency is applied to the input; the signal appears at the output, multiplied by the magnitude (absolute value, in the complex variables sense) of the transfer function, with its phase shifted by the phase angle (amplitude) of the transfer function.

The transfer function will in general be a complex number. If we indicate the transfer function as $T(j\omega) = a + bi$, the situation can be restated a little more simply. The magnitude of the input signal appears at the output multiplied by $\sqrt{a^2 + b^2}$ and with its phase shifted by an angle $\theta = \arctan b/a$. Both effects depend strongly on the frequency of the input signal. We shall develop a program, therefore, to show how the servomechanism represented by the transfer function responds to different frequencies. This information is important in designing the servomechanism for stability, among other things.

The program is set up to operate as follows. We wish to read a value of K along with initial and final values of ω and an increment by which

---

*In mathematics the symbol for $\sqrt{-1}$ is, of course, i. In electrical engineering i is used for current; j is written for $\sqrt{-1}$.

```
C ILLUSTRATIONS OF OPERATIONS ON COMPLEX NUMBERS
C
C
      COMPLEX A, B, Z, R
C
C DATA CARD FOR THE FOLLOWING READ CONTAINS A = 1 + 2I AND B = 3 + 4I
      READ (5, 100) A, B
  100 FORMAT (4F10.0)
      Z = A + B
      WRITE (6, 101) Z
  101 FORMAT (15H1ADDITION        , 2F10.5)
C
      Z = A * B
      WRITE (6, 102) Z
  102 FORMAT (15H0MULTIPLICATION, 2F10.5)
C
      Z = CEXP(A)
      WRITE (6, 103) Z
  103 FORMAT (15H0EXPONENTIAL     , 2F10.5)
C
      Z = CSQRT(A)
      WRITE (6, 104) Z
  104 FORMAT (15H0SQUARE ROOT    , 2F10.5)
C
      Z = 2.0 * A + (10.0, 20.0)
      WRITE (6, 105) Z
  105 FORMAT (15H0EXAMPLE 5       , 2F10.5)
C
      R = CMPLX(1.0, 1.0)
      Z = A - R
      WRITE (6, 106) Z
  106 FORMAT (15H0EXAMPLE 6       , 2F10.5)
      STOP
      END
```

FIGURE 3.9. A program illustrating some selected operations on Fortran complex variables.

ω should be multiplied to obtain successive points. For each value of ω we are to print the real and imaginary parts of the transfer function, the magnitude, and the phase angle.

A flowchart is shown in Figure 3.11. We begin by reading the data and immediately make two rudimentary validity checks. Data that cannot pass these tests would give meaningless results.

ADDITION	4.00000	6.00000
MULTIPLICATION	-5.00000	10.00000
EXPONENTIAL	-1.13120	2.47173
SQUARE ROOT	1.27202	0.78615
EXAMPLE 5	12.00000	24.00000
EXAMPLE 6	0.0	1.00000

FIGURE 3.10. The output of the program of Figure 3.9.

The probable cause would be either a card-punching error or a misunderstanding of the required format or sequence of the data. In a more realistic situation we would print the offending data along with an explanatory comment rather than just stopping. (At some convenient time the reader should look at Excursion II for a more complete discussion of the topic of data validation.)

After printing some heading material, including the value of the amplification factor, we enter the computation loop proper. We begin by setting ω equal to the starting value that has been read, compute the four output numbers, and print them. After incrementing ω we ask whether the new value is greater than the specified final value of ω and stop if it is; otherwise we return to compute the new point.

In the program of Figure 3.12 we begin with the type statements. The REAL statement includes the names of the four variables (FIRST,

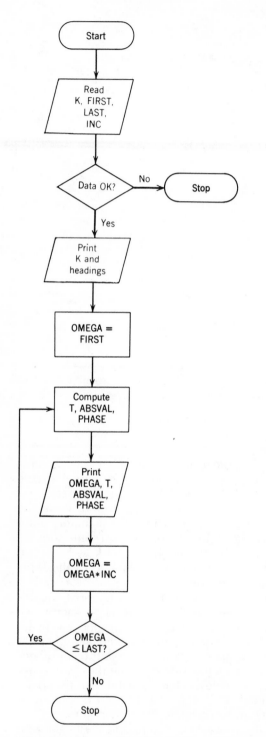

```
        ┌──────────┐
        │  Start   │
        └──────────┘
             │
         ┌───────┐
        / Read    /
       /  K, FIRST /
      /   LAST,    /
     /    INC     /
    └───────────┘
             │
         ◇ Data OK? ◇ ──No──► ( Stop )
             │
            Yes
             │
        ┌────────┐
       /  Print   /
      /  K and    /
     /  headings  /
    └────────────┘
             │
     ┌──────────────┐
     │   OMEGA =    │
     │    FIRST     │
     └──────────────┘
             │
     ┌──────────────┐
     │  Compute     │
     │  T, ABSVAL,  │
     │   PHASE      │
     └──────────────┘
             │
       ┌──────────┐
      /  Print     /
     /  OMEGA, T,   /
    /   ABSVAL,     /
   /    PHASE       /
  └────────────────┘
             │
     ┌──────────────┐
     │   OMEGA =    │
     │  OMEGA*INC   │
     └──────────────┘
             │
        ◇  OMEGA   ◇ ──Yes──► (back to Compute)
        ◇ ≤ LAST?  ◇
             │
            No
             │
        ( Stop )
```

FIGURE 3.11. A flowchart of a servomechanism frequency response plot calculation. (Case Study 6.)

ABSVAL, OMEGA, and PHASE) that would be regarded as real by default even if they were not mentioned in the REAL statement.

There are no new concepts in the printing of the heading material, but we see some of the concepts that were introduced in Case Study 5 applied in different ways. The first WRITE produces a page heading at the top of a new page, then uses a carriage control character of zero to get double spacing before the next heading line. This next line contains both characters taken from the H field descriptor of the FORMAT and a data value. After printing this line we use slashes to call for two blank lines and then to produce the column headings followed by two more blank lines. With this one WRITE-FORMAT pair we have thus produced a page skip, three lines of printing, and five blank lines.

The computation loop begins at statement 10, where we see the CMPLX function used to assemble the real and imaginary parts of N1, the first complex factor in the numerator of the transfer function. The six statements at 10 and following would, of course, make no sense if the variables had not been declared to be complex. D1 is the $j\omega$ factor in the denominator. Pure imaginaries like this must be set up as complex numbers, whereas pure reals can simply be written as Fortran reals. We see this in the statement for computing T: K, which was declared to be REAL, is multiplied by N1, N2, and so on, which are complex. We are explicitly permitted to do this kind of mixing.

T is a complex number. We are able to print its real and imaginary parts simply by naming it in the WRITE statement and putting two field descriptors in the associated FORMAT. The absolute value is found with the CABS function. The phase is a little more complicated. Mathematically, the arctangent is a many-valued function: there are infinitely many angles having the same tangent. The Fortran arctangent function must therefore be written under some assumption of the range of angles that will be regarded as the principal values. The function ATAN accepts a single argument and provides an angle as the result in the range of $-\pi/2$ to $+\pi/2$. The function ATAN2 accepts two arguments, which are taken to be, respectively, the ordinate and abscissa of a point in any one of the four quadrants. The function provides the arctangent of the quotient of the first argument divided by the second; the result is in the range of $-\pi$ to $+\pi$.

```
C CASE STUDY 6
C COMPUTATION OF A SERVOMECHANISM FREQUENCY RESPONSE
C    USING FORTRAN COMPLEX OPERATIONS
C
C
      REAL K, FIRST, LAST, INC, OMEGA, ABSVAL, PHASE
      COMPLEX T, N1, N2, D1, D2, D3, D4
C
C READ PARAMETERS
      READ (5, 100) K, FIRST, LAST, INC
 100  FORMAT (4F10.0)
C
C CHECK INPUT FOR VALIDITY
      IF (      (FIRST .GE. LAST)
     1    .OR. (INC   .LE. 1.0) )  STOP
C
C WRITE VALUE OF AMPLIFICATION FACTOR AND COLUMN HEADINGS
      WRITE (6, 200) K
 200  FORMAT ('1', 20X, 'SERVOMECHANISM FREQUENCY RESPONSE DATA'/
     1   '0', '     AMPLIFICATION FACTOR = ', 1PE12.5///8X,
     2   'OMEGA       T REAL          T IMAG       ABS VALUE        PHASE'//)
C
C SET FREQUENCY TO STARTING VALUE
      OMEGA = FIRST
C
C SET UP COMPLEX FACTORS, USING THE CMPLX FUNCTION TO CONVERT FROM
C   THE FORM OF TWO FORTRAN REAL NUMBERS, REPRESENTING THE REAL AND
C   IMAGINARY PARTS OF THE COMPLEX NUMBER, TO THE FORM OF ONE FORTRAN
C   COMPLEX NUMBER.
 10   N1 = CMPLX(1.0, 0.4 * OMEGA)
      N2 = CMPLX(1.0, 0.2 * OMEGA)
      D1 = CMPLX(0.0, OMEGA)
      D2 = CMPLX(1.0, 2.5 * OMEGA)
      D3 = CMPLX(1.0, 1.43 * OMEGA)
      D4 = CMPLX(1.0, 0.02 * OMEGA)
C
C COMPUTE TRANSFER FUNCTION
      T = K * N1 * N2 / (D1 * D2 * D3 * D4**2)
C
C GET COMPLEX ABSOLUTE VALUE
      ABSVAL = CABS(T)
C
C USE TWO-ARGUMENT ARCTANGENT FUNCTION TO GET PHASE ANGLE
C ANGLE IS RETURNED IN RADIANS -- CONVERT TO DEGREES
      PHASE = 57.29578 * ATAN2(AIMAG(T), REAL(T))
      WRITE (6, 300) OMEGA, T, ABSVAL, PHASE
C
C NOTE THAT T IS COMPLEX, REQUIRING TWO ASSOCIATED FIELD DESCRIPTORS
 300  FORMAT (1X, 1P5E14.4)
C
C INCREMENT OMEGA
      OMEGA = INC * OMEGA
C
C TEST FOR COMPLETION, AND GO AROUND AGAIN IF NOT FINISHED
      IF ( OMEGA .LE. LAST ) GO TO 10
      STOP
      END
```

FIGURE 3.12. A program for a servomechanism frequency response plot calculation, corresponding to the flowchart of Figure 3.11. (Case Study 6.)

The difference between the two types of arctangent function is that the two arguments of ATAN2 carry quadrant information.

The result, for either function, is an angle in radians. We convert to degrees by multiplying by $180/\pi$.

We now write the five required numbers, increment ω, and return to compute another point if ω is less than or equal to LAST.

This program was run with suitable input values. The output is shown in Figure 3.13. (For readers with engineering background and interests, we notice that for frequencies out through about 20 radians/sec the input signals are amplified, but after that they are attenuated. The phase angle starts out near $-90°$, moves to nearly $-180°$, moves across the real axis to values a little less than $+180°$, then back down again, and back up again. This behavior for larger frequencies would be of considerable interest to a servomechanism designer.)

3.7 LOGICAL CONSTANTS, VARIABLES, AND EXPRESSIONS

A Fortran logical quantity is one that can take on only the values "true" and "false."

A *logical constant* is either of the following:

```
.TRUE.
.FALSE.
```

A *logical variable* is a variable that has been declared in a LOGICAL type statement. As with double precision and complex variables, there is no initial-letter naming convention, since a variable is never assumed to be the logical type unless it has appeared in a LOGICAL statement. A logical variable can take on only the values .TRUE. and .FALSE..

A *logical assignment statement* has the form

$$a = b$$

in which a is a logical variable and b is a logical expression.

A logical expression, as we have already seen many times in connection with the logical IF statement, may be a relational expression, such as I .EQ. 20. Thus if L1, L2, and so on, are logical variables, we may write logical assignment statements like these:

```
L1 = .TRUE.
L2 = .FALSE.
L3 = A .GT. 25.0
L4 = I .EQ. 0
L5 = L6
```

The first two are the logical equivalent of statements of the form

$$variable = constant$$

L3 would be set to .TRUE. if the value of the real variable A is greater than 25.0, and to .FALSE. if A is less than or equal to 25.0. Likewise, L4 would be set to .TRUE. if the value of I were in fact zero and to .FALSE. otherwise. L5 would be set to the same truth value as L6 currently has.

We have seen that a *relational expression* is one that compares integer, real, or double-precision values by using the relational operators .LT., .LE., .EQ., .NE., .GT., and .GE.. A *logical expression* combines logical values and/or relational expressions by using the *logical operators* .AND., .OR., and .NOT.. Thus we can write logical assignment statements like these:

```
L1 = D .LT. EPS .OR. ITER .GT. 20
L2 = D .GE. EPS .AND. ITER .LE. 20
L3 = BIG .GT. TOLER .OR. SWITCH
```

L1 would be given the value .TRUE. if *either* or *both* of the relations were true, and .FALSE. otherwise. L2 would be given the value .TRUE. if and only if *both* relations were true, and false otherwise. L3 would be given the value .TRUE. if the relation were satisfied, if the logical variable SWITCH were true, or both.

The logical operator .NOT. reverses the truth value of the expression it operates on. For instance, consider this statement:

```
L = A .GT. B .AND. .NOT. SWITCH
```

If SWITCH is true, .NOT. SWITCH is false, and if SWITCH is false, .NOT. SWITCH is true. Thus *L* would be given the value .TRUE. if the value of *A* were greater than the value of *B and* the value of SWITCH were .FALSE..

In the absence of parentheses, the hierarchy of logical operators is .NOT., .AND., and .OR.. For instance, take this expression, in which all variables are logical:

```
L = A.AND.B .OR. C.AND..NOT.D.AND.E
```

The .NOT. D is performed first, then the three .AND.s, then the .OR.. It is very much better to

SERVOMECHANISM FREQUENCY RESPONSE DATA

AMPLIFICATION FACTOR = 9.00000E 02

OMEGA	T REAL	T IMAG	ABS VALUE	PHASE
2.0000E-02	-3.0236E 03	-4.4825E 04	4.4927E 04	-9.3859E 01
2.5000E-02	-3.0183E 03	-3.5782E 04	3.5909E 04	-9.4822E 01
3.1250E-02	-3.0101E 03	-2.8528E 04	2.8687E 04	-9.6023E 01
3.9062E-02	-2.9974E 03	-2.2702E 04	2.2899E 04	-9.7522E 01
4.8828E-02	-2.9777E 03	-1.8012E 04	1.8256E 04	-9.9387E 01
6.1035E-02	-2.9473E 03	-1.4225E 04	1.4527E 04	-1.0171E 02
7.6294E-02	-2.9010E 03	-1.1155E 04	1.1526E 04	-1.0458E 02
9.5367E-02	-2.8310E 03	-8.6526E 03	9.1039E 03	-1.0812E 02
1.1921E-01	-2.7272E 03	-6.6013E 03	7.1425E 03	-1.1245E 02
1.4901E-01	-2.5775E 03	-4.9127E 03	5.5478E 03	-1.1768E 02
1.8626E-01	-2.3699E 03	-3.5246E 03	4.2473E 03	-1.2392E 02
2.3283E-01	-2.0976E 03	-2.3991E 03	3.1868E 03	-1.3116E 02
2.9104E-01	-1.7658E 03	-1.5171E 03	2.3280E 03	-1.3933E 02
3.6380E-01	-1.3975E 03	-8.6770E 02	1.6450E 03	-1.4816E 02
4.5475E-01	-1.0312E 03	-4.3271E 02	1.1183E 03	-1.5724E 02
5.6843E-01	-7.0793E 02	-1.7677E 02	7.2967E 02	-1.6598E 02
7.1054E-01	-4.5486E 02	-4.9786E 01	4.5758E 02	-1.7375E 02
8.8818E-01	-2.7736E 02	-2.7065E-01	2.7736E 02	-1.7994E 02
1.1102E 00	-1.6365E 02	1.1616E 01	1.6406E 02	1.7594E 02
1.3878E 00	-9.5371E 01	9.7046E 00	9.5864E 01	1.7419E 02
1.7347E 00	-5.5858E 01	5.0283E 00	5.6084E 01	1.7486E 02
2.1684E 00	-3.3256E 01	1.3113E 00	3.3282E 01	1.7774E 02
2.7105E 00	-2.0240E 01	-8.5927E-01	2.0258E 01	-1.7757E 02
3.3881E 00	-1.2615E 01	-1.8497E 00	1.2750E 01	-1.7166E 02
4.2351E 00	-8.0561E 00	-2.1286E 00	8.3325E 00	-1.6520E 02
5.2939E 00	-5.2776E 00	-2.0381E 00	5.6575E 00	-1.5888E 02
6.6174E 00	-3.5556E 00	-1.7839E 00	3.9780E 00	-1.5336E 02
8.2718E 00	-2.4720E 00	-1.4763E 00	2.8793E 00	-1.4915E 02
1.0340E 01	-1.7784E 00	-1.1690E 00	2.1282E 00	-1.4668E 02
1.2925E 01	-1.3232E 00	-8.8535E-01	1.5921E 00	-1.4621E 02
1.6156E 01	-1.0117E 00	-6.3441E-01	1.1942E 00	-1.4791E 02
2.0195E 01	-7.8401E-01	-4.1982E-01	8.8934E-01	-1.5183E 02
2.5243E 01	-6.0331E-01	-2.4448E-01	6.5096E-01	-1.5794E 02
3.1554E 01	-4.4979E-01	-1.1174E-01	4.6346E-01	-1.6605E 02
3.9443E 01	-3.1698E-01	-2.3326E-02	3.1783E-01	-1.7579E 02
4.9304E 01	-2.0702E-01	2.3999E-02	2.0841E-01	1.7339E 02
6.1629E 01	-1.2398E-01	3.9887E-02	1.3024E-01	1.6217E 02
7.7037E 01	-6.8088E-02	3.7407E-02	7.7687E-02	1.5122E 02
9.6296E 01	-3.4608E-02	2.7951E-02	4.4486E-02	1.4107E 02
1.2037E 02	-1.6515E-02	1.8297E-02	2.4647E-02	1.3207E 02
1.5046E 02	-7.5117E-03	1.1000E-02	1.3320E-02	1.2433E 02
1.8808E 02	-3.3009E-03	6.2539E-03	7.0715E-03	1.1783E 02
2.3510E 02	-1.4163E-03	3.4271E-03	3.7082E-03	1.1245E 02
2.9387E 02	-5.9797E-04	1.8334E-03	1.9284E-03	1.0806E 02
3.6734E 02	-2.4980E-04	9.6562E-04	9.9740E-04	1.0450E 02
4.5917E 02	-1.0362E-04	5.0346E-04	5.1402E-04	1.0163E 02
5.7397E 02	-4.2793E-05	2.6080E-04	2.6428E-04	9.9318E 01
7.1746E 02	-1.7620E-05	1.3453E-04	1.3568E-04	9.7462E 01
8.9682E 02	-7.2416E-06	6.9210E-05	6.9588E-05	9.5973E 01

FIGURE 3.13. The output of the program of Figure 3.12. (Case Study 6.)

use extra parentheses, however, than to rely on these rules, if there is any doubt whatever as to the effect.

The .AND. .NOT. and .OR. .NOT. combinations are the only ones in which two operators may appear side by side.

Parentheses may be used to dictate a meaning other than that implied in the hierarchy of operators. For instance, we may write

```
L = A.AND.(B.OR.C).AND..NOT.(D.OR.E)
```

Most Fortran systems provide for input and output of logical values by use of the L field descriptor. This is of the form Lw, where w specifies the number of columns or printing positions. On input the first letter in the card field must be *T* or *F*, which may be followed by any other characters. Thus it is possible, if we wish, to use the field descriptor L5 and punch TRUE or FALSE. On output a *T* or *F* is printed at the right side of the w printing positions.

Logical variables may be used for a variety of purposes. We shall see in Case Study 7 how they can be valuable when the problem actually does require processing of variables that are permitted to take on only two values, as in digital computer circuits. But logical variables are valuable in many other circumstances as well.

One common use of logical variables is to "save" the result of a decision to avoid having to repeat the test on which it is based. Consider the following simple example.

In Chapter 2 we defined a function of x

$$y = 0.5x + 0.95 \text{ if } x \leq 2.1$$
$$y = 0.7x + 0.53 \text{ if } x > 2.1$$

This computation can be written in a compact and easily understood form:

```
LOGICAL FIRST
FIRST = X .LE. 2.1
IF (       FIRST ) Y = 0.5*X + 0.95
IF ( .NOT. FIRST ) Y = 0.7*X + 0.53
```

Obviously it can also be written in many other ways, but this way is about as easy to follow as any and about as fast. The speed is based on the fact that a test of a logical variable can be done very quickly by the computer.

Suppose that we have values of X and Y, which represent a point in Cartesian coordinates. We wish to set Q (for quadrant) equal to the number of the quadrant in which the point lies.

```
LOGICAL XPOS, YPOS
INTEGER Q
XPOS = X .GT. 0.0
YPOS = Y .GT. 0.0
IF (       XPOS .AND.       YPOS) Q = 1
IF (.NOT. XPOS .AND.       YPOS) Q = 2
IF (.NOT. XPOS .AND. .NOT. YPOS) Q = 3
IF (       XPOS .AND. .NOT. YPOS) Q = 4
```

In this case the logical variables make it unnecessary either to repeat the determination of the signs of X and Y or to go into a complicated series of GO TO statements. (We have not worried here about points on the axes. With suitable

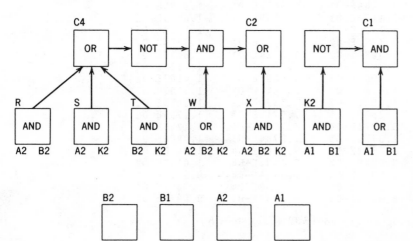

FIGURE 3.14.   The arrangement of the input binary digits (B_2, B_1, A_2, and A_1) and the logical operations leading to the sum (C_4, C_2, and C_1) in one "logical design" of a binary adder. (Case Study 7.)

agreements about the conventions needed, this aspect could easily be handled differently.)

Another example of the usefulness of logical variables would be a calculation in which a certain factor would be included or omitted from a formula. The program could be set up to read a value of a logical variable and then used to determine the course of the calculation.

3.8 CASE STUDY 7: LOGICAL DESIGN OF A BINARY ADDER

Digital computers are built from thousands of individual logical elements, each of which is able to take on one of just two states, depending on some logical function of its inputs. In this case study we begin with four logical variables named B2, B1, A2, and A1, which are to represent two binary numbers, B and A, of two digits each. From these, using formulas representing computer logical elements, we are to produce the three digits C4, C2, and C1 of the sum. We visualize the arrangement of the digits as

$$\begin{array}{r} A2 \quad A1 \\ + \quad B2 \quad B1 \\ \hline C4 \quad C2 \quad C1 \end{array}$$

As an example,

$$\begin{array}{r} 01 \\ +11 \\ \hline 100 \end{array}$$

We shall be working with logical variables that have truth values only; a digit of one will be represented by .TRUE., zero by .FALSE.. We shall generate all 16 possible combinations of the four binary digits for a complete test of the adder circuit.

The circuit is shown in schematic form in Figure 3.14. The four digits are represented by boxes at the bottom. All the other boxes stand for logical elements, the nature of which is stated in the box. Boxes representing values to which a name is given in the program have the name shown at the top left. In the middle row, inputs are shown below the boxes; in the top row inputs are marked by arrows.

This diagram presents the logical design of the adder in graphic form. For instance, the units digit of the sum (C1) is seen to be 1 if either A1 *or* B1 is 1 *and* it is *not* true that both A1 *and*

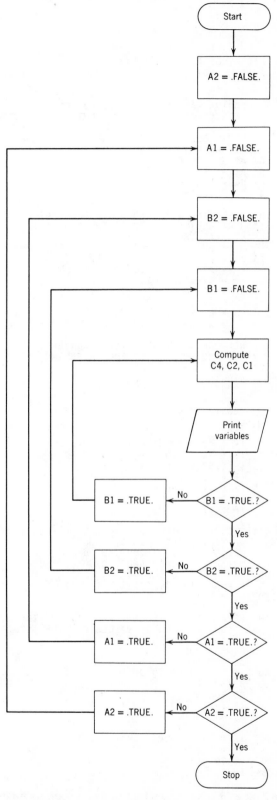

FIGURE 3.15. A flowchart of a method of testing the logical design of a binary adder. (Case Study 7.)

```
C CASE STUDY 7
C LOGICAL DESIGN INVESTIGATION OF A BINARY ADDER
C
C
      LOGICAL A1, A2, B1, B2, K2, C1, C2, C4, R, S, T, W, X
      INTEGER A1OUT, A2OUT, B1OUT, B2OUT, C1OUT, C2OUT, C4OUT
C
C THE NEXT FOUR STATEMENTS ARE PART OF THE SCHEME FOR OBTAINING ALL
C   COMBINATIONS OF VALUES FOR THE FOUR INPUT VARIABLES.
   10 A2 = .FALSE.
   20 A1 = .FALSE.
   30 B2 = .FALSE.
   40 B1 = .FALSE.
C
C THE NEXT NINE STATEMENTS ARE ALL LOGICAL ASSIGNMENT STATEMENTS,
C   COMPUTING THE VALUES OF THE SUM DIGITS.
   50 K2 = A1 .AND. B1
      C1 = .NOT. K2 .AND. (A1 .OR. B1)
      X  = A2 .AND. B2 .AND. K2
      W  = A2 .OR. B2 .OR. K2
      T  = B2 .AND. K2
      S  = A2 .AND. K2
      R  = A2 .AND. B2
      C4 = R .OR. S .OR. T
      C2 = X .OR. (W .AND..NOT. C4)
C
C THE NEXT GROUP OF STATEMENTS CONVERTS FROM LOGICAL VALUES TO
C   ZEROS AND ONES, ZERO FOR FALSE AND ONE FOR TRUE, FOR OUTPUT.
      A2OUT = 0
      A1OUT = 0
      B2OUT = 0
      B1OUT = 0
      C4OUT = 0
      C2OUT = 0
      C1OUT = 0
      IF ( A2 ) A2OUT = 1
      IF ( A1 ) A1OUT = 1
      IF ( B2 ) B2OUT = 1
      IF ( B1 ) B1OUT = 1
      IF ( C4 ) C4OUT = 1
      IF ( C2 ) C2OUT = 1
      IF ( C1 ) C1OUT = 1
C
C WRITE OUTPUT, WITH SPACING AND H-FIELD TEXT
      WRITE (6, 100) A2OUT, A1OUT
      WRITE (6, 110) B2OUT, B1OUT
      WRITE (6, 120) C4OUT, C2OUT, C1OUT
  100 FORMAT ('   ', 2I2)
  110 FORMAT ('+ +', 2I2/'   _____')
  120 FORMAT (' ', 3I2/)
C
C THE REMAINING STATEMENTS ARE PART OF THE SCHEME FOR OBTAINING
C   ALL COMBINATIONS OF VALUES FOR THE INPUT VARIABLES.
      IF ( B1 ) GO TO 60
      B1 = .TRUE.
      GO TO 50
   60 IF ( B2 ) GO TO 70
      B2 = .TRUE.
      GO TO 40
   70 IF ( A1 ) GO TO 80
      A1 = .TRUE.
      GO TO 30
   80 IF ( A2 ) STOP
      A2 = .TRUE.
      GO TO 20
      END
```

FIGURE 3.16.   A program for testing the logical design of a binary adder. (Case Study 7.)

B1 are 1. The second digit (C2) is 1 if either all three K2 (the carry from position 1), A2, and B2 are 1 or any one of them, but not two, is 1. C4 is 1 if any two or more of K2, A2, and B2 are 1.

The logical assignment statements to evaluate the various expressions here will be shown shortly. First, we should look at the flowchart of Figure 3.15, which shows how we shall work through the 16 combinations of values of B2, B1, A2, and A1. This scheme uses a nest of loops. The result is that B1 alternates between true and false, B2 is false twice, then true twice, then false twice, and so on.

The type declarations and the first four logical assignment statements in the program of Figure 3.16 present no difficulties. In the statement for C1 we see the need for parentheses. The intention, as written, is to evaluate the expression in the following sequence:

1. .NOT. K2
2. A1 .OR. B1
3. .AND. of the above.

Without the parentheses, the sequence would be

1. .NOT. K2
2. .NOT. K2 .AND. A1
3. .OR. of the above.

The two expressions (with and without parentheses) do not mean the same thing, just as $-A*(B + C)$ and $-A*B + C$ do not mean the same thing.

In the next statement X will be set to .TRUE. only if all three of the variables are true.

In the statement in which C2 is computed the parentheses make the intention clear but are not actually required; the sequence of evaluation and the meaning would be the same without them.

After computing C2, we are ready to print the results. This could be done with the L field specifications, giving T's and F's. We prefer, however, to make the printout more attractive by making it look like what it represents: binary additions. To this end we convert each logical variable to an integer variable, in which zero stands for false and 1 stands for true. This translation is accomplished by first setting all seven of the output variables to zero and then setting

```
  0 0
+ 0 0
  0 0 0

  0 0
+ 0 1
  0 0 1

  0 0
+ 1 0
  0 1 0

  0 0
+ 1 1
  0 1 1

  0 1
+ 0 0
  0 0 1

  0 1
+ 0 1
  0 1 0

  0 1
+ 1 0
  0 1 1

  0 1
+ 1 1
  1 0 0

  1 0
+ 0 0
  0 1 0

  1 0
+ 0 1
  0 1 1

  1 0
+ 1 0
  1 0 0

  1 0
+ 1 1
  1 0 1

  1 1
+ 0 0
  0 1 1

  1 1
+ 0 1
  1 0 0

  1 1
+ 1 0
  1 0 1

  1 1
+ 1 1
  1 1 0
```

FIGURE 3.17. The output of the program of Figure 3.16. The 16 triplets can be read as exercises in binary addition. (Case Study 7.)

to 1 any that correspond to logical values of .TRUE..

Three WRITE statements are used with slightly elaborate FORMAT statements, to make the output look like exercises in binary addition. Bear in mind that the first character in each line is the carriage control character. In the first FORMAT (100) we thus have a blank for single spacing, followed by two blanks that will be inserted in the line. In FORMAT 110 we have a plus sign to suppress spacing after the printing of the line, then a blank and another plus sign. The second plus sign will be printed. After a slash to start a new line we have a blank for single spacing, then underlines that will be printed. Finally the last FORMAT calls for single spacing followed by an extra line after printing.

If this seems like more trouble than it is worth to you at this stage, forget it; you are probably right. We shall take up input and output again in Chapter 6, where these matters will be covered again.

The testing that comes after the output closely follows the logic of the flowchart.

The output from the program is shown in Figure 3.17. We see that, viewed as exercises in binary addition, all 16 cases give correct results, and we conclude that the adder design (and the program) is correct.

We hasten to point out that this is by no means the only way to set up a binary adder. In fact, this one is a copy of a system that may be used to demonstrate to elementary school children how computers work. Seventeen children, arranged as in Figure 3.14, but spread out so that each logical element can see his inputs, and with each child holding a card defining his logical operation, will function beautifully.

EXERCISES

Note. Throughout these exercises variable names beginning with R, I, D, C, and L should be assumed to be real, integer, double-precision, complex, and logical, respectively.

1. State the value stored by each of the following assignment statements:

(a) C1 = 2.0*(1.0, 2.0)
(b) C2 = (2.0, 0.0)(1.0, 2.0)
(c) C3 = (2.0, 3.0)**2
*(d) C4 = CMPLX(1.0 + 4.0, 4.0**2)
(e) C5 = CMPLX(REAL((1.0, 2.0)),
        AIMAG((3.0, 4.0)))
(f) R1 = CABS((3.0, 4.0))
*(g) R2 = AIMAG((4.0, 0.0)
        *(1.0, 3.0))*2.0
(h) R3 = AIMAG((4.0, 0.0)
        *(1.0, 3.0)*2.0)
(i) R4 = SQRT(REAL(C6)**2
        + AIMAG(C6)**2)/CABS(C6)
(j) C6 = CEXP((0.0, 3.1415927))
        + (1.0, 0.0)

2. Do the following pairs of logical expressions have the same truth values?

*(a) L1 .AND. L2 .OR. L3
    (L1 .AND. L2) .OR. L3
(b) L1 .AND. L2 .OR. L3
    L1 .AND. (L2 .OR. L3)
*(c) L1 .AND. L2 .OR. L3 .AND. L4
    (L1 .AND. L2) .OR. (L3 .AND. L4)
(d) .NOT. L1 .AND. L2
    .NOT. (L1 .AND. L2)
*(e) .NOT. (L1 .OR. L2)
    .NOT. L1 .AND. .NOT. L2
*(f) L1 .AND. L2 .AND. L3 .AND. 1 .EQ. 2
    L4 .AND. .NOT. L4
(g) L1 .AND. L2 .OR. A .LT. B .OR. A .GE. B
    L3 .OR. .NOT. L3

3. Are the mixtures of data types in the following expressions permitted?

*(a) D2 = D1*4.0
(b) D2 = D1*4
(c) D2 = D1**4
(d) C1 = R1(4.0, 5.0)
(e) L1 = R1 .GE. D1 .OR. D3 .LT. 1.E-11
*(f) IF (D1 .EQ. 0) R2 = I1*I2/I3
(g) L1 = R1 .GE. C1 .AND. I1 .LT. 10
*(h) L1 = C1 .GT. C2
(i) L1 = C1 .EQ. C2
*(j) L1 = CABS(C1) .GE. CABS(C2)
(k) L1 = ABS(REAL(C1)
        − AIMAG(C1)) .LT. 1.E-2
*(l) L2 = 4.0*D1 .LT. 2.0
        + R1 .AND. I1 .LE. 9 .AND. L1
(m) L3 = R1 .NE. R2 .OR.
        L1 .AND. .NOT. L2
*(n) L1 = R1 .EQ. R2
(o) R1 = L1 .OR. L2
*(p) R1 = I1 + 6
(q) D1 = I1 + 5

(r) $I1 = R1**2$
* (s) $I1 = D1**3$
(t) $D2 = 2.0/D1 + R1 - I1$
(u) $L1 = L1 .OR. L2$

4. Consider the following system of equations:

$$140679x + 556685y = 146710$$
$$81152x + 321129y = 84631$$

Write two programs to solve this system, using Cramer's rule (see page 78, Chapter 4), in one program using real variables and in the other, double precision. (It is assumed that your computer has real numbers with about 6 to 8 decimal digits of significance). Why should there be a difference in the results, when the data can be represented exactly with single precision (real) variables?

5. Write a program, using double precision throughout, to compute the values of D1 and D2 from

$$D1 = (A + \sin B - 10^9)*C$$
$$D2 = (A - 10^9 + \sin B)*C$$

The data card read by the program should enter the following values:

A: 1.0D9
B: 2.0D0
C: 1.0D7

Why the difference in the two results? Are not the two formulas equivalent, since addition is commutative?

*6. Write a program, using complex variables throughout, to solve two simultaneous equations in two unknowns.

$$(2 + 3i)x + (4 - 2i)y = (5 - 3i)$$
$$(4 + i)x + (-2 + 3i)y = (2 + 13i)$$

The solution is $x = 1 + i$, $y = 2 - i$.

7. Write a program, using complex variables throughout, to solve the quadratic equation

$$ax^2 + bx + c = 0$$

where a, b, and c are complex. Use the formula

$$x = \frac{-b \pm \sqrt{b^2 - 4ac}}{2a}$$

Run the program with a data card that specifies

$$a = 1 + i$$
$$b = 2 + 3i$$
$$c = -7 + i$$

Run again, this time with a card that gives

$$a = 2$$
$$b = 3$$
$$c = -12$$

(Read them as complex numbers (i.e., as $2 + 0i$, etc., and use the program without change.)

*8. Write a program, using complex variables throughout, to compute and print z and e^z for a succession of values along a vertical line through $(1,0)$, such as $1 - 5i$, $1 - 4i$, $1 - 3i, \ldots, 1 + 4i, 1 + 5i$. This will demonstrate how the complex exponential function maps a vertical line.

9. Write a program, using complex variables throughout, to compute and print z and e^z for a succession of values along a 45° line through the origin: $-5 - 5i$, $-4 - 4i, \ldots, 4 + 4i, 5 + 5i$.

10. Write a program, using complex variables throughout, to compute and print z and e^z for 20 points equally spaced along the arc of a circle with the center at the origin and radius 1.

11. Write a program, using complex variables throughout, that reads a value of z, then computes and prints $a = \cos^2 z + \sin^2 z$. Make up a series of data cards and run the program as a demonstration that $\cos^2 z + \sin^2 z = 1$ holds with complex variables.

*12. Write a program, using complex variables throughout, to read z and c, then compute and print $A = z^c = \exp(c \log z)$. Use the program to demonstrate that $(-i)^i = e^{\pi/2}$.

13. Write a program to demonstrate that $\log 3 - \pi i$, $\log 3 + \pi i$, $\log 3 + 3\pi i$, and $\log 3 + 5\pi i$ are all solutions of $e^z + 3 = 0$.

14. Modify the program of Figure 3.12 to compute the following transfer function instead of the one given:

$$T(j\omega) = \frac{100}{j\omega(1 + 0.25j\omega)(1 + 0.0625j\omega)}$$

15. Modify the program of Figure 3.12 to compute the following transfer function in-

stead of the one given:

$$T(j\omega) = \cfrac{1260}{j\omega(1 + 0.25j\omega)\,(1 + 0.001j\omega) + \cfrac{20(j\omega)^4}{(1 + 0.5j\omega)\,(1 + 0.4j\omega)}}$$

16. Modify the program of Figure 3.16 so that C1, C2, and C4 can be computed without the use of intermediate variables, using the following formulas:

   C1 = A1 .AND. .NOT. B1 .OR. .NOT. A1 .AND. B1
   C2 = (A2 .AND. .NOT. B2 .OR. .NOT. A2 .AND. B2) .AND. (.NOT. A1 .OR. .NOT. B1) .OR. A1 .AND. B1 .AND. (.NOT. A2 .AND. .NOT. B2 .OR. A2 .AND. B2)
   C4 = A1 .AND. B1 .AND. B2 .OR. A1 .AND. B1 .AND. A2 .OR. A2 .AND. B2

17. Case Study 7 can be done entirely without logical variables. Let the values of A1, A2, etc., be zero or 1 instead of false or true. Then write statements of the following sort:

   IF (K2 .EQ. 0 .AND. (A1 .EQ. 1 .OR. B1 .EQ. 1)) C1 = 1

   Modify the program along these lines and run it to see if it gives identical results.

18. The author's United States Social Security number is of the form aaa-bb-cccc. If we call the number formed from the first three digits A, that formed from the second two B, and that formed from the last four C, and write the quadratic equation $Ax^2 + Bx + C = 0$, the roots are $-0.020561 \pm 1.7200i$. Find the author's Social Security number, bearing in mind that A, B, and C must be integers. The answer appears elsewhere in the book.

19. Visualize a friend who studied algebra somewhere in his education but didn't really get much out of it. Suppose you wanted to show him what is meant by the "elegance" of the equation

$$e^{i\pi} + 1 = 0$$

which combines the five most fundamental entities in mathematics in one beautifully simple equation. Can you think of any way you could use a computer program to help in the demonstration?

4 SUBSCRIPTED VARIABLES

4.1 INTRODUCTION

The Fortran techniques that we have discussed so far permit a great deal of useful computing to be done, but they do not provide us with much power in dealing with certain problems that occur frequently. In particular, we need better methods of handling large arrays of related data, such as those found in simultaneous equations and many other applications. In this chapter we shall investigate the use of subscripted variables, which make it possible to refer to a complete array of data by one generic name. Subscripted variables are useful in themselves, as we shall see in a case study, and they take on added power in conjunction with the DO statement, which we shall investigate in Chapter 5.

4.2 DEFINITIONS

Subscripted variables permit us to represent many quantities with one variable name. A particular quantity is indicated by writing a subscript (or subscripts) in parentheses after the name. The complete set of quantities is called an *array,* and the individual quantities are called *elements*. A subscripted variable in Fortran may have one, two, or three subscripts, and it then represents a one-, two-, or three-dimensional array, respectively. (When used in this connection, "one-dimensional" refers to the number of *subscripts,* not to the number of

elements: a one-dimensional array can have many elements, and it would be permissible for a three-dimensional array to have only one element.)

The first element of a one-dimensional array is element number 1, the second is element number 2, and so on up to the number of elements in the array. In mathematical notation we might write $x_1, x_2, x_3, \ldots, x_{19}, x_{20}$; in Fortran subscript notation we write X(1), X(2), X(3), . . . , X(19), X(20). We must always number elements consecutively, starting with 1.

A two-dimensional array may be thought of as composed of horizontal rows and vertical columns. The first of the two subscripts then refers to the *row number,* running from one up to the number of rows, and the second refers to the *column number,* running from one to the number of columns. For instance, an array of two rows and three columns might be shown in mathematical notation as

$$a_{1,1} \quad a_{1,2} \quad a_{1,3}$$
$$a_{2,1} \quad a_{2,2} \quad a_{2,3}$$

In Fortran subscript notation, the elements would be written A(1,1), A(1,2), A(1,3), A(2,1), A(2,2), and A(2,3). We note that the subscripts are separated by commas.

A three-dimensional array may be viewed as composed of planes, each of which contains rows and columns. The interpretation, however, depends somewhat on the purpose of the computation; other interpretations are possible.

Some versions of Fortran allow more than three subscripts; seven are permitted in several systems, and some systems set no limit.

The name of a subscripted variable is formed in the same way as the name of a nonsubscripted variable. If the name is not mentioned in a type statement, the array is assumed to consist entirely of integer elements or entirely of real elements, depending on the initial letter. If the name is mentioned in a DOUBLE PRECISION, COMPLEX, or LOGICAL statement, the elements are assumed to be entirely of the one kind. To emphasize: the elements of any given array must *all* be of one kind. An array, for instance, cannot consist partly of real and partly of integer elements.

4.3 EXAMPLES OF THE SUBSCRIPT NOTATION

Suppose that the ordinates of five points on a curve are represented by the five elements of a one-dimensional array named Y. The five elements are then Y(1), Y(2), Y(3), Y(4), and Y(5). If we wanted to get the average of the first three values and assign the average as the new value of a variable named AVER1, we could write:

```
AVER1 = ( Y(1) + Y(2) + Y(3) ) / 3.0
```

If we wanted to replace the second point by the average of the first three points, we would write:

```
Y(2) = ( Y(1) + Y(2) + Y(3) ) / 3.0
```

If the spacing between the *x* values corresponding to these *y* values is *h* and we want to compute the area under the curve according to the trapezoidal rule, we could write:

```
  TRAP = 0.5 * H *
1 (Y(1) + 2.*(Y(2)+Y(3)+Y(4)) + Y(5))
```

Observe that we have shown the statement on two lines to fit the column size of this book; the "1" at the beginning of the second line denotes the continuation. If we want to place in BIG either Y(1) or Y(5), whichever is larger, we can place Y(1) in BIG and then replace it with Y(5) if the latter actually is larger, using these two statements:

```
BIG = Y(1)
IF ( Y(5) .GT. Y(1) ) BIG = Y(5)
```

For another example of the subscript notation consider the problem of solving two simultaneous equations in two unknowns. To emphasize the similarity of subscripted variables with mathematical notation we may write the system of equations completely in mathematical subscript form.

$$a_{1,1}x_1 + a_{1,2}x_2 = b_1$$
$$a_{2,1}x_1 + a_{2,2}x_2 = b_2$$

This problem can conveniently be set up with a one-dimensional array of two elements for the constant terms b_1 and b_2 and another for unknowns x_1 and x_2, which we shall compute. The coefficients (*a*'s) are the four elements of a two-dimensional array of two rows and two columns.

The solution of such a small system of equations can be computed conveniently by Cramer's rule, according to which

$$x_1 = \frac{b_1 a_{2,2} - b_2 a_{1,2}}{a_{1,1} a_{2,2} - a_{2,1} a_{1,2}}$$

$$x_2 = \frac{b_2 a_{1,1} - b_1 a_{2,1}}{a_{1,1} a_{2,2} - a_{2,1} a_{1,2}}$$

A program segment to evaluate these formulas is:

```
DENOM = A(1,1)*A(2,2) - A(2,1)*A(1,2)
IF ( ABS(DENOM) .LT. 1E-5 ) STOP
X(1) = (B(1)*A(2,2)-B(2)*A(1,2))/DENOM
X(2) = (B(2)*A(1,1)-B(1)*A(2,1))/DENOM
```

The computation of the denominator is done in a preliminary statement to avoid having the computer repeat the arithmetic. After that we make a test on the size of the denominator to determine whether it is close to zero. If it is exactly zero, there is either no solution or an infinity of solutions, depending on the constant terms. Either way, this formulation does not apply, and if we tried to use it we would be dividing by zero. This would give an error indication in most computers. We have tested for a small divisor instead of specifically for zero because rounding errors could give a nonzero denominator even when there is a possibility of trouble.

The test we have used here would not be suitable if the value of the denominator could properly be very large or very small. If the variables were such that the correct values of the numerator and denominator were both in the range of 10^{-8}, the test we have used would clearly not give a proper indication of the course of the calculation. On the other hand, if the values were properly in the 10^6 range, our test would also tell us very little.

The solution in such a case would be to use a test of the size of the denominator *in relation* to the numerator. We might decide, for instance, that if the numerator is more than 10^6 times larger than the denominator in absolute value, we should stop. The program could be appropriately rewritten. A similar observation applies to several programs in other chapters.

4.4 MOTIVATIONS FOR THE USE OF SUBSCRIPTED VARIABLES

The foregoing examples show the fundamental ideas of the subscript notation, but they do not really indicate the power of the technique. After all, there is nothing in the examples that could not be done just as conveniently by giving each element a separate name. Why then are subscripted variables such an important feature of Fortran?

The reason is that the subscripts themselves may be variables or certain types of expressions, which means that we can set up a program to perform a basic computation and then make the same computation on many different values by changing the value of the subscripting variable.

Suppose, for example, that we need to compute the sum of the squares of 20 numbers, x_1 to x_{20}, stored in the computer. We could, of course, give them 20 different names and set up a long arithmetic statement to compute the sum of their squares, but this would be tedious, cumbersome, inflexible, and error-prone. Instead, we set up the 20 numbers as the elements of a one-dimensional array, which we shall call X. Now, any of the 20 numbers can be referenced by the name X(I), and we arrange for I to take on all the values from 1 to 20.

In the usual mathematic notation

$$SUMSQ = \sum_{i=1}^{20} x_i{}^2$$

The computation can be done with the following program segment:

```
      SUMSQ = 0.0
      I = 1
  180 SUMSQ = SUMSQ + X(I)**2
      I = I + 1
      IF (I .LE. 20) GO TO 180
```

We first set SUMSQ equal to zero so that we may use a single expression to compute each of the intermediate sums. Then I is made 1, so that when statement 180 is first executed we get the first element from the array of values. Then 1 is added to I and a test is made to determine whether all of the values have been processed. Notice that when the IF shows that $I = 20$ we must still go back once more because I is incremented *before the test*.

Statement 180 and the two following it are executed exactly 20 times to give the sum of the squares of the 20 elements of the array. We shall see in Chapter 5 that this program can be made even simpler by use of a DO statement.

4.5 THE DIMENSION STATEMENT AND OTHER INFORMATION

When subscripted variables are used in a program, certain information about them must be supplied to the Fortran compiler.

1. Which variables are subscripted?
2. How many subscripts are there for each subscripted variable?
3. What is the maximum size of each subscript?

These questions are answered by the DIMENSION statement. Every subscripted variable in a program must be mentioned in a DIMENSION statement,* and this statement must appear before the first occurrence of the variable in the program. A common practice is to give the dimension information for all subscripted variables in DIMENSION statements at the beginning of the program. One DIMENSION statement may mention any number of variables, and there may be any number of DIMENSION statements.

The DIMENSION statement takes the form

DIMENSION V, V, V, . . .

where the V's stand for variable names followed by parentheses enclosing one, two, or three unsigned integer constants that give the maximum size of each subscript. When Fortran

---

*Or it must be mentioned in a COMMON statement that includes dimension information, as we shall see in Chapter 7, or in a type statement.

processes a DIMENSION statement, it sets aside enough storage locations to contain arrays of the sizes specified by the information in the statement. Thus, if a program contains the statement

```
DIMENSION X(20), A(3, 10), K(2, 2, 5)
```

the Fortran compiler will assign 20 storage locations to the one-dimensional array named X; 30 (i.e., 3×10) to the two-dimensional array A; and 20 (i.e., $2 \times 2 \times 5$) to the three-dimensional array K. If any of these variables had been named in a DOUBLE PRECISION or COMPLEX statement, twice as much storage would have been assigned to each. The extra storage is automatically taken into account in all usage of the subscripts; the programmer need give no thought to the extra storage required.

It is the programmer's responsibility to write the program so that no subscript is ever larger than the maximum size that he has specified for the subscript in the DIMENSION statement. Furthermore, subscripts must never be smaller than 1; zero and negative subscripts are not permitted. If these restrictions are violated, the source program will in some cases be rejected by the compiler. In other cases, in which the illegal subscripts are developed only at execution time, the program will be compiled but will give incorrect results when executed.

The DIMENSION statement is said to be *nonexecutable;* that is, it provides information to the Fortran compiler but does not by itself cause any processing actions in the object program. It is also described as a *specification* statement, since it conveys information about the program.

The ANSI standard requires that all specification statements appear prior to the first executable statement in a program. Many systems relax this requirement, perhaps requiring only that a specification statement such as a DIMENSION appear prior to the occurrence in an executable statement of any variable named in it. Even when this additional flexibility is permitted, however, following the standard is advisable. Not only does it improve transferability, if programs have to be recompiled on a compiler that requires following the standard, but it is better documentation practice. Placing all the specification statements together at the beginning of the program makes it much easier to understand how a program is intended to operate and

makes it less likely that specifications will be overlooked.

Subscripted variables, with a few exceptions noted later, may appear in any place in which a nonsubscripted variable may be written. For a simple example, consider the READ statement that might be used to read in the data for the simultaneous equations example in Section 4.3. The DIMENSION, READ, and FORMAT statements for that problem could be

```
      DIMENSION A(2, 2), B(2), X(2)
      READ (5, 100) A(1,1), A(2,1),
     1   A(1,2), A(2,2), B(1), B(2)
100   FORMAT (6F10.0)
```

When a READ statement is written with the elements indicated in this explicit form, the elements may be entered in any sequence desired. The programmer may choose, for instance, to write

```
   READ (5, 100) A(1,1), A(1,2), B(1),
  1              A(2,1), A(2,2), B(2)
```

The data naturally would have to be punched on the data card in the corresponding order.

We may occasionally want to deal with the elements of an array *without* explicitly naming them all. It is permissible to use an input or output statement in which the name of the array is written without any subscripts; this will cause reading or writing of the entire array. Thus we could follow the DIMENSION statement in the example above with

```
   READ (5, 100) A, B
```

to read all the elements of the two arrays.

It is necessary, of course, in such a case to have a convention regarding the sequence of the elements, since we are not specifying the sequence we require. The sequence in which the elements must appear on a card read by an input statement without subscripts or the order in which they will be printed by an output statement without subscripts is as follows. For one-dimensional arrays the elements are taken in sequence, starting with the element corresponding to the subscript 1 and proceeding to the largest subscript as defined in the DIMENSION statement. For two-dimensional arrays the elements are taken in such a manner that the first subscript varies most rapidly. Thus the statements

```
   DIMENSION R(2,3)
   READ (5, 100) R
```

would require that the elements be punched in the sequence R(1,1), R(2,1), R(1,2), R(2,2), R(1,3), R(2,3). To summarize: the elements of a two-dimensional array are taken in *column-order*. For three-dimensional arrays the elements are taken in such a manner that the first subscript varies most rapidly and the last varies least rapidly.

It is not always advisable to take advantage of the ability to read arrays without subscripting, however. In most practical applications it is unwise to arrange the program so that it reads cards that do not contain any identification of the data contained on them. That is, it is much better to punch on each card some kind of definite identification of the data items, such as the element number. If data cards contain only the data values themselves, it is far too easy to get the cards out of order, or to omit one data item, or to commit any of dozens of other possible errors in data preparation. Many of the errors, which unfortunately occur all too frequently, will not be detected unless considerable effort has been put into writing the program so that it checks the validity of the data.

We shall explore some rudimentary ways to arrange such checking in Case Study 8 at the end of the chapter and elsewhere. A more complete discussion may be found in Excursion II.

4.6 ALLOWABLE FORMS OF SUBSCRIPTS

So far we have seen that subscripts may be integer constants or integer variables. Three other forms of subscript are permitted in ANSI Fortran. If I stands for a nonsubscripted integer variable and L and L' are integer constants, all of the allowable subscript forms are as follows.

General Form	Example
I	J12
L	3
I $\pm$ L	K + 29
L*I	2*LIMIT
L*I $\pm$ L'	3*LAST$-$7

The value of a subscript expression is determined each time the subscripted variable is used in the program. The value must never be less than 1 nor greater than the maximum specified in a DIMENSION statement, and a variable

in a subscript expression must not itself be subscripted.

Most Fortran systems permit a subscript expression to be *any* expression, rather than the limited forms specified in the ANSI standard. In some cases the restricted forms will lead to more efficient programs, however, even when the more general style is permitted. One particular convenience, when it is permitted, is for a variable in a subscript expression to be itself a subscripted variable. One example of the usefulness of such a flexibility is sketched in Exercise 19 in Chapter 5.

The most common use of subscripted variables is in carrying out the same basic computation on a set of related values. We shall see examples in the following case studies.

4.7 CASE STUDY 8: USING SUBSCRIPTS IN COMPUTING MEANS, STANDARD DEVIATIONS, AND A CORRELATION COEFFICIENT

In descriptive statistics the mean and standard deviation are widely used to characterize a distribution, and the coefficient of correlation is used to describe a certain relationship between two distributions.

If we are given a collection of N values of x, $x_1, x_2, x_3, \ldots, x_N$, the *mean* of the distribution is defined as

$$\text{Mean}_x = \frac{\sum\limits_{i=1}^{N} x_i}{N}$$

and the standard deviation can be computed from

$$\text{Standard deviation}_x = \frac{\sqrt{N \sum\limits_{i=1}^{N} x_i{}^2 - \left(\sum\limits_{i=1}^{N} x_i \right)^2}}{N}$$

(Readers familiar with statistics will realize that these measures can be computed in other ways that are more convenient or more accurate in certain situations, and that we are generally presenting the subject in a highly simplified fashion to make it useful as a vehicle for studying the use of subscripting, whether or not the reader knows statistics.)

Now, if we have a second distribution y, also with N values, $y_1, y_2, y_3, \ldots, y_N$, its mean and standard deviation can be computed in the same way as before. For the two distributions, the coefficient of correlation between them can be computed from

$$r = \frac{N \sum\limits_{i=1}^{N} x_i y_i - \sum\limits_{i=1}^{N} x_i \sum\limits_{i=1}^{N} y_i}{\sqrt{N \sum\limits_{i=1}^{N} x_i^2 - \left(\sum\limits_{i=1}^{N} x_i \right)^2} \sqrt{N \sum\limits_{i=1}^{N} y_i^2 - \left(\sum\limits_{i=1}^{N} y_i \right)^2}}$$

Loosely speaking, the coefficient of correlation can be thought of as a measure of the degree to which the dispersion of the values in one distribution around its mean can be explained in terms of the dispersion of the values of the other distribution around its mean.

We wish to develop a program to read x values and y values from a deck of cards, to compute the mean and standard deviation for both distributions, and then to perform a check on the reliability of the data before proceeding to compute the correlation coefficient. The check is based on the idea that if a value deviates greatly from the mean of the distribution of which it is a member, there is a certain likelihood that it is erroneous. If the mean of a distribution of 100 numbers is 250, but one of the numbers is 2000, that value is very possibly in error because of some mistake in collecting, transcribing, or punching the data. Accordingly, we wish to discard such values, provided there are not too many of them, before computing the final means, standard deviations, and the correlation coefficient.

But how much is "too far" from the mean? If all but one of the 100 values in the example just cited fell between 240 and 260, then a value of 300 would probably be erroneous, but if the values ranged between 50 and 800, a value of 300 would be perfectly acceptable. What we shall do is to use the computed standard deviation to judge what is acceptable deviation from the mean. We know that for a *normal* (bell-shaped) distribution, about 99.7 percent of the values will fall within three standard deviations on either side of the mean. Now, if the data contains an erroneous value, we know already that the sample (including that point) is *not* normally distributed, but on the assumption that the errors we shall catch this way will be the big blunders—like missing decimal points that make values wrong by a factor of 10^4—we can still sometimes make worthwhile use of such a test.

At any rate, the program is to be devised so that after computing the *tentative* mean and standard deviation for each distribution we discard any value that is more than 3.0 times the standard deviation from its mean. We then recompute the mean and standard deviation, using only the good points, and then compute the correlation coefficient. However, we are not willing to rely on data that has very many error points that have to be discarded, and we shall not carry out the calculations if more than 3 percent of the data points are bad.

We have now essentially stated the computational task, but we do not yet have an algorithm because we have not specified in complete and unambiguous detail how all of the actions are to be carried out. We now turn to a flowchart to continue the process of making the definition of the task successively more precise.

To guard against the danger that any reader might think that flowcharts like those ordinarily displayed in this book spring complete—without erasures—from the forehead of a programmer, we pause to show, in greatly reduced form since it is not really readable anyway, approximately the second version of the author's flowchart for this procedure. See Figure 4.1. Even if it were readable, this one is not complete or accurate. The author's habit is to bring the flowchart to the point where it is useful as a guide to programming, then switch to writing the program. There is, for most programmers, an unavoidable interaction between flowcharting and programming, making it necessary to redraw the flowchart in any event, no matter how carefully it might have been prepared. With the program all completed and tested, the flowchart shown in Figure 4.2 was drawn. It may as well be admitted further that the details of how the boxes and arrows were laid out were influenced by a desire to make the flowchart and the program "look alike," especially in terms of how GO TO's transfer around program segments.

Some programmers never draw flowcharts; others draw them only under extreme pressure from their supervisors. Some never write a line of code until a complete flowchart exists, and after the program is done they do not have to revise the flowchart; others claim to work this way or wish they could. Programmers differ to a remarkable degree in how they make use of flowcharts if left to their own devices. We believe that flowcharts are helpful to the programmer himself if the program logic is even

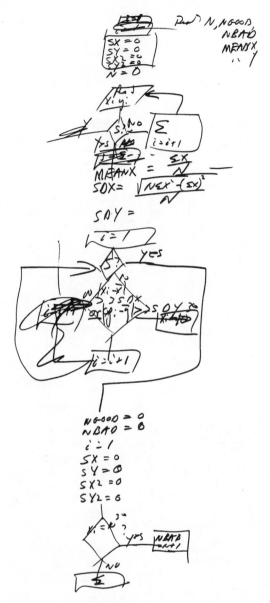

FIGURE 4.1. A highly preliminary sketch of a flow-chart for calculating means, standard deviations, and a correlation coefficient. See Figure 4.2 for the final version. (Case Study 8.)

A variable I will be used in the program as a subscript to identify the data point we are currently working with; X(I) and Y(I), where I may vary between one and the number of values in each distribution, will be an associated pair of numbers, one from each distribution. We set I equal to 1 before starting to read cards. We also initialize to zero, five variables named SUMX, SUMY, SUMXSQ, SUMYSQ, and SUMXY that will be used to accumulate the sums we need for the computations. Then we set a card counter variable named N to zero and enter the card reading loop.

We read a card and immediately ask whether it is a sentinel, which we take to be any value greater than 10^8. If not, we add the appropriate functions of the two data values (x_i, y_i, x_i^2, y_i^2, and $x_i y_i$) to the appropriate sums, increment the subscript, and add one to the card counter and return to read another card. When we detect the sentinel we compute the two means and standard deviations and prepare to check the data points by setting our index back to one and setting a count variable named NBAD of bad data points to zero.

The decision box that says "Good point?" will become, in the program, a logical IF statement having two conditions combined by an AND. Each condition will ask whether a data point is more than 3.0 times the standard deviation from the mean; if both x_i and y_i are less than that far away from their means, we skip around a program segment that, in effect, discards the data point. This discarding is done by subtracting from the five sums the proper functions of x_i and y_i. (We shall return to this procedure below; it can cause trouble.) We also add one to a count of bad data points, increment the subscript variable, and check to see whether we have yet tested all the data points. If not, we go back.

If we have checked them all, we now ask whether the number of bad data points exceeds 3 percent of the total number of data points, and give up if so after printing an error message that states how many bad data points were found. (In real life we would probably list the bad data points themselves, as well. We do so in later programs.)

If the number of bad data points is sufficiently small, we subtract NBAD from the previous count of the number of data points, N, recompute the means and standard deviations, and compute the correlation coefficient. Naturally,

mildly complex, and that they are *always* helpful, if well drawn, to anyone else who must try to understand a program later. In other words, they are necessary documentation whether or not the original programmer finds them helpful.

This important digression completed, we may return to the flowchart to see what the program is to do.

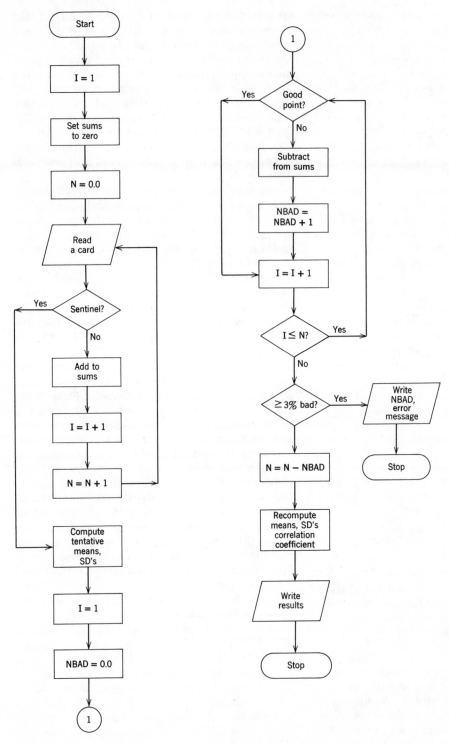

FIGURE 4.2.   A flowchart of a procedure for finding the means and standard deviations of two distributions and the coefficient of correlation between them. (Case Study 8.)

if there were *no* bad data points, we are needlessly repeating part of the computation; if it were thought worth the saving of computer time it would achieve, we could easily test for this possibility and take it into account. The results are written, with identifications, and we are finished.

When a flowchart and a program correspond as closely as those of Figures 4.2 and 4.3 and the flowchart has been studied carefully, there is not too much more to be said about the program. The DIMENSION statement has been written to allow for a maximum of 200 data points; it would be a good idea to check as the cards are being read to see that no more than that many appear because reading values into positions 201 and beyond can cause fabulous foul-ups. Most of the variable names are quite descriptive of what they stand for in this case (and effort to make this the case is definitely recommended). Notice following statement 40 that I has been converted to real form before making the comparison with N. Some compilers will accept real-integer comparisons, but not all. Notice in FORMAT statement 300 that slashes have been used to separate successive lines. Also, the scale factor (the "1P" in 1PE14.6) has not been repeated; we shall learn in Chapter 6 that once a scale factor has been given, it applies to all succeeding field descriptors in the same FORMAT statement.

Figure 4.4 shows the output when the program was run with a set of nine data points consisting, for both x and y distributions, of the integers from 1 to 9. Figure 4.5 is the output when the data points were, writing them as *x-y* pairs, (1,9), (2,8), (3,7), . . . , (8,2), (9,1). We see that the correlation coefficient this time is minus 1, where before it was plus 1. Figure 4.6 is the output when the data consisted of the height and weight of 9 men between the ages of 25 and 29, as shown in Table 4.1. Next, Figure 4.7 presents the output when the data consisted of heights in inches of 100 fathers and their grown sons.* These results are unexceptional, but consider Figure 4.8, where the data points were exactly the same except that one point was added, for which $x = y = 59999$. This was well

beyond the 3.0 standard deviations away from the tentative means, so that the point was discarded and the statistics recomputed. Why then the change of about 10 percent in the standard deviation of the x distribution, and smaller changes in the other values?

The answer, as so often in such matters, lies in the limited precision of representation of real numbers. When 59999 is squared, we get 3599880001. That is more digits than can be represented in a real number on the IBM 360, on which the program was run, so we lose the 1 at the end—but that is not the main problem. The trouble is that when a number like $72^2 = 5184$ is added to something of this size, digits are discarded in lining up the decimal points (hexadecimal points, actually, of course). When 3599880001 is later subtracted back off, the lost digits of 5184 and other such numbers cannot be recovered. The situation is thus quite similar to that in Case Study 5 on the computation of the sine of an angle, except that it is even easier to see here.

It is particularly simple to prove that this is the trouble, and the only trouble, by rerunning the program with SUMXSQ, SUMYSQ, and SUMXY specified as double precision. Nothing else needs to be double precision—not SUMX or SUMY, or any of the data, or any of the computed results. When this is done, the standard deviation is computed to be the same number, exactly, whether the 59999 data point is present or not.

This sort of problem is just one small sample of the reason why no one who actually wants to do statistical calculations should *ever* write his own programs to do so! The proper approach is to use packages of subroutines written and tested by someone else who specializes in

*The example is taken from Alexandra I. Forsythe, Thomas A. Keenan, Elliott I. Organick, and Warren Stenberg, *Computer Science: A First Course,* New York, Wiley, 1969, p. 359.

TABLE 4.1

Height	Weight
72	174
68	152
66	154
74	180
62	135
70	161
64	140
76	174
64	157

```
C CASE STUDY 8
C MEANS, STANDARD DEVIATIONS, AND CORRELATION COEFFICIENT
C FOR TWO DISTRIBUTIONS READ FROM CARDS
C
C THE INPUT DATA APPEARS ON A DECK OF CARDS.  EACH CARD CONTAINS AN
C X VALUE IN COLUMNS 1-10 AND ITS ASSOCIATED Y VALUE IN 11-20.
C CARDS ARE READ UNTIL DETECTING AN X-VALUE GREATER THAN 1E+08,
C WHICH IS USED AS AN END-OF-DECK SENTINEL.
C
C SUMMATIONS ARE MADE AS CARDS ARE READ.  MEANS AND STANDARD
C DEVIATIONS ARE THEN COMPUTED FOR BOTH DISTRIBUTIONS, AND BOTH ARE
C CHECKED FOR VALUES GREATER THAN 3.0 STANDARD DEVIATIONS AWAY
C FROM THE MEAN.  ANY SUCH VALUES ARE DISCARDED, AND UNLESS MORE
C THAN 3 PER CENT OF THE VALUES WERE THUS DISCARDED, THE MEANS
C AND STANDARD DEVIATIONS ARE RECOMPUTED USING ONLY THE GOOD
C DATA POINTS.  THE COEFFICIENT OF CORRELATION BETWEEN THE TWO
C DISTRIBUTIONS IS THEN COMPUTED AND THE VARIOUS VALUES PRINTED.
C
C
C
      DIMENSION X(200), Y(200)
      REAL N, NBAD, MEANX, MEANY
C
C INITIALIZE DATA POINT INDEX (I), VARIOUS SUMMATION VARIABLES,
C AND DATA POINT COUNTER.
      I = 1
      SUMX = 0.0
      SUMY = 0.0
      SUMXSQ = 0.0
      SUMYSQ = 0.0
      SUMXY = 0.0
      N = 0.0
C
C READ A CARD
  10  READ (5, 100) X(I), Y(I)
 100  FORMAT (2F10.0)
C
C WAS THIS A SENTINEL?
      IF ( ABS(X(I)) .GT. 1E8 ) GO TO 20
C
C NO -- FORM SUMS, INCREMENT INDEX, AND COUNT THE DATA POINT
      SUMX = SUMX + X(I)
      SUMY = SUMY + Y(I)
      SUMXSQ = SUMXSQ + X(I)**2
      SUMYSQ = SUMYSQ + Y(I)**2
      SUMXY = SUMXY + X(I) * Y(I)
      I = I + 1
      N = N + 1.0
      GO TO 10
C
C COMPUTE TENTATIVE DISTRIBUTION MEANS AND STANDARD DEVIATIONS
  20  MEANX = SUMX / N
      MEANY = SUMY / N
      SDEVX = SQRT(N*SUMXSQ - SUMX**2) / N
      SDEVY = SQRT(N*SUMYSQ - SUMY**2) / N
C
C INITIALIZE FOR CHECKING DATA
      I = 1
      NBAD = 0.0
```

FIGURE 4.3. A program for finding means, standard deviations, and a correlation coefficient, corresponding to the flowchart of Figure 4.2. (Case Study 8.)

```
C
C CHECK ALL DATA POINTS, SUBTRACTING OFF BAD ONES FROM SUMS
   30  IF (        ABS(X(I) - MEANX) .LE. 3.0*SDEVX
      1     .AND. ABS(Y(I) - MEANY) .LE. 3.0*SDEVY ) GO TO 40
C
C IF WE GET HERE, THE DATA POINT WAS BAD -- SUBTRACT IT AND COUNT IT
       SUMX = SUMX - X(I)
       SUMY = SUMY - Y(I)
       SUMXSQ = SUMXSQ - X(I)**2
       SUMYSQ = SUMYSQ - Y(I)**2
       SUMXY = SUMXY - X(I) * Y(I)
       NBAD = NBAD + 1.0
C
C INCREMENT INDEX AND CHECK FOR COMPLETION OF LIST
   40  I = I + 1
       AI = I
       IF ( AI .LE. N ) GO TO 30
C
C CHECK WHETHER THERE WERE TOO MANY ERRORS
C PRINT COMMENT AND STOP IF SO
       IF ( NBAD .LT. 0.03 * N ) GO TO 50
       WRITE (6, 200) NBAD
  200  FORMAT (1X, F5.0, '   ERRORS FOUND -- JOB ABORTED')
       STOP
C
C SUBTRACT NUMBER OF BAD POINTS FROM N
   50  N = N - NBAD
C
C COMPUTE ALL VALUES
       MEANX = SUMX / N
       MEANY = SUMY / N
       XFACTR = SQRT(N*SUMXSQ - SUMX**2)
       YFACTR = SQRT(N*SUMYSQ - SUMY**2)
       SDEVX = XFACTR / N
       SDEVY = YFACTR / N
       CORRLN = (N*SUMXY - SUMX*SUMY) / (XFACTR*YFACTR)
C
C WRITE OUTPUT
       WRITE (6, 300) N, MEANX, MEANY, SDEVX, SDEVY, CORRLN
  300  FORMAT (1X, 'NUMBER OF GOOD DATA POINTS = ', F5.0/
      1    'MEAN OF X DISTRIBUTION = ', 1PE14.6/
      2    'MEAN OF Y DISTRIBUTION = ', E14.6/
      3    'STANDARD DEVIATION OF X DISTRIBUTION = ', E14.6/
      4    'STANDARD DEVIATION OF Y DISTRIBUTION = ', E14.6/
      5    'COEFFICIENT OF CORRELATION = ', E14.6)
       STOP
       END
```

FIGURE 4.3. (Cont.)

that kind of work. We shall consider these in Chapter 7 on Fortran subprograms.

The goal, after all, is to get some work done quickly, inexpensively, and accurately—although those subgoals are sometimes in conflict. It will almost never be advisable for a person who wants to do statistical calculations to write his own programs. We chose the example because it is a realistic application of subscripting, and because it permitted us to illustrate how programs work and how they can get messed up—things that a statistician (or anybody else) needs to know about in using programs written by others.

```
NUMBER OF GOOD DATA POINTS =     9.
MEAN OF X DISTRIBUTION =   5.000000E 00
MEAN OF Y DISTRIBUTION =   5.000000E 00
STANDARD DEVIATION OF X DISTRIBUTION =    2.581988E 00
STANDARD DEVIATION OF Y DISTRIBUTION =    2.581988E 00
COEFFICIENT OF CORRELATION =   1.000000E 00
```

FIGURE 4.4.   The output of the program of Figure 4.3 when run with two identical distributions. (Case Study 8.)

```
NUMBER OF GOOD DATA POINTS =     9.
MEAN OF X DISTRIBUTION =   5.000000E 00
MEAN OF Y DISTRIBUTION =   5.000000E 00
STANDARD DEVIATION OF X DISTRIBUTION =    2.581988E 00
STANDARD DEVIATION OF Y DISTRIBUTION =    2.581988E 00
COEFFICIENT OF CORRELATION =  -1.000000E 00
```

FIGURE 4.5.   The output of the program of Figure 4.3 when run with two distributions that were identical except that the second was in reverse order of the first. (Case Study 8.)

```
NUMBER OF GOOD DATA POINTS =     9.
MEAN OF X DISTRIBUTION =   6.844444E 01
MEAN OF Y DISTRIBUTION =   1.585555E 02
STANDARD DEVIATION OF X DISTRIBUTION =    4.597369E 00
STANDARD DEVIATION OF Y DISTRIBUTION =    1.456107E 01
COEFFICIENT OF CORRELATION =   9.125199E-01
```

FIGURE 4.6.   The output of the program of Figure 4.3 when run with two distributions giving the height and weight of nine men. (Case Study 8.)

```
NUMBER OF GOOD DATA POINTS = 100.
MEAN OF X DISTRIBUTION =   7.336914E 01
MEAN OF Y DISTRIBUTION =   7.366539E 01
STANDARD DEVIATION OF X DISTRIBUTION =    3.657102E 00
STANDARD DEVIATION OF Y DISTRIBUTION =    3.432084E 00
COEFFICIENT OF CORRELATION =   6.559863E-01
```

FIGURE 4.7.   The output of the program of Figure 4.3 when run with two distributions giving the height in inches of 100 fathers and their grown sons. (Case Study 8.)

```
NUMBER OF GOOD DATA POINTS = 100.
MEAN OF X DISTRIBUTION =   7.336874E 01
MEAN OF Y DISTRIBUTION =   7.366499E 01
STANDARD DEVIATION OF X DISTRIBUTION =    3.308655E 00
STANDARD DEVIATION OF Y DISTRIBUTION =    3.302846E 00
COEFFICIENT OF CORRELATION =   6.525637E-01
```

FIGURE 4.8.   The output of the program of Figure 4.3 when run with the same distribution as those used to produce Figure 4.7, except that one highly erroneous data point was added. The validity test in the program rejected this point; see text for discussion of the differences in the results. (Case Study 8.)

EXERCISES

Note. Include an appropriate DIMENSION statement in each program segment for these exercises, realizing, of course, that in a complete program each subscripted variable is mentioned only once in a DIMENSION statement, usually at the beginning of the program.

*1. A one-dimensional array named *A* contains ten elements. Write separate program segments to accomplish the following:

(a) Place the product of the first and second elements in PROD.
(b) Replace the third element by the average of the first, third, and fifth elements.
(c) If the last element is zero or positive, do nothing, but if it is negative, replace it by its absolute value.
(d) Replace every element in the array by its absolute value, using a loop.

2. A one-dimensional array named *B* contains 20 elements. Write separate program segments to accomplish the following:

(a) Divide the fourth element by the sum of the fifth and sixth elements, and place the result in *ABC*.
(b) Replace the last four elements by zero, without using a loop.
(c) If the tenth element is greater than TEST, replace the tenth element by the average of the ninth and eleventh elements.
(d) Double every element in the array, using a loop.

*3. A two-dimensional array named XYZ2 contains three rows and four columns. Write separate program segments to accomplish the following:

(a) Place the sum of the elements in the third column in RST.
(b) Replace the first row by the second row, without using a loop.
(c) Replace each element in the third row by the sum of the corresponding elements from the first and second rows, using a loop.

4. A two-dimensional array named XYZ3 contains four rows and three columns. Write separate program segments to accomplish the following:

(a) Replace all the elements in the fourth row by zeros.
(b) If the product of the first element in the first row, the second element in the second row, and the third element in the third row is less than 10^{-5} in absolute value, place a zero in DET.
(c) Replace each element in the second column by the average of the corresponding elements in the first and third columns.

*5. A three-dimensional array named PUPILS contains information about the pupil population of a certain school district, organized as follows. The first subscript distinguishes between boys and girls: 1 for girls, 2 for boys. The second subscript indicates the grade level, from 1 to 12. The third subscript is related to the year: 1 stands for 1968, 2 for 1969, 3 for 1970, 4 for 1971, and 5 for 1972. Thus, the element designated by PUPILS(2, 6, 3) contains the enrollment for this school system of sixth grade boys in 1970. Write program segments to accomplish the following:

(a) Compute and store in D1 the total number of fifth graders in 1969.
(b) Using one loop, place in E1971 the total enrollment for the system in 1971.
(c) Place in BIG the number of boys or the number of girls, whichever is larger, in the twelfth grade in 1972.
(d) A one-dimensional array named SUM71 contains 12 elements. For each grade, I, place in SUM71(I) the total enrollment, boys and girls, in grade I for 1971, using a loop.

6. A three-dimensional array named SALES contains information about the current year's sales of the Ajax Company, organized as follows. The first subscript describes the division: 1 stands for the Bolt Division, 2 for Nuts, 3 for Washers, 4 for Gadgets, and 5 for Widgets. The second subscript relates to product number, of which each division has exactly 20. The third tells what kind of information about a division's product is contained in an element: 1 stands for year-to-date sales in

SUBSCRIPTED VARIABLES

89

dollars, 2 for the year-to-date sales in units, and 3 for the average sale price in the previous year. Thus, SALES(3, 7, 1) would give the dollar amount of the sales for the Washer Division's product number 7, and SALES(3, 7, 2) would tell how many of that product have been sold. Write program segments to carry out the following:

(a) Compute and place in AV the average sale price so far this year of Gadget number 13.

(b) Place in SALES (2, K, 3) the average sale price so far this year of the Nut Division's product number K, for all products, using a loop.

(c) Place in DOLLAR the total dollar sales of Widgets.

(d) Place in NUTS the average number of units sold, for all products of the Nut Division.

*7. Suppose that the coordinates of a point in three-dimensional space are given by the three elements of a one-dimensional array named X. (Notice the different uses of the word dimension: the elements of a one-dimensional array are being used as the coordinates of a point in three-dimensional space!) Write a statement to compute the distance of the point from the origin, which is given by the square root of the sum of the squares of the coordinates.

8. If the coordinates of a point in space are x_1, x_2, and x_3, the direction cosines of the line from the origin to the point are given by

$$CA = \frac{x_1}{\sqrt{x_1^2 + x_2^2 + x_3^2}}$$

$$CB = \frac{x_2}{\sqrt{x_1^2 + x_2^2 + x_3^2}}$$

$$CC = \frac{x_3}{\sqrt{x_1^2 + x_2^2 + x_3^2}}$$

Write statements to compute these three numbers, assuming that the coordinates are the elements of a one-dimensional array named X.

*9. Given two arrays named A and B, both two-dimensional, write statements to compute the elements of another two-dimensional array named C from the fol-

lowing equations. The maximum value of all subscripts is 2.

$$c_{11} = a_{11}b_{11} + a_{12}b_{21}$$
$$c_{12} = a_{11}b_{12} + a_{12}b_{22}$$
$$c_{21} = a_{21}b_{11} + a_{22}b_{21}$$
$$c_{22} = a_{21}b_{12} + a_{22}b_{22}$$

Readers familiar with matrix notation will recognize the multiplication of two 2×2 matrices.

10. Given a two-dimensional array named R, the elements of which are to be viewed as the elements of a 3×3 determinant, write a statement to compute the value of the determinant by any method you know. The value of the determinant should be named DET.

*11. Two one-dimensional arrays named A and B each contain 30 elements. Compute

$$D = \left[\sum_{i=1}^{30} (A_i - B_i)^2 \right]^{1/2}$$

Write a program segment to perform the calculation.

*12. If we have a list of tabular values represented by a one-dimensional array, then the first differences of the list are formed by subtracting each element except the last from the element immediately following it. Suppose we have a one-dimensional array named X that contains 50 elements. Compute the 49 elements of another array named DX from

$$DX(I) = X(I + 1) - X(I)$$
$$I = 1, 2, \ldots, 49$$

Write a program segment to perform this calculation.

13. Suppose we have a one-dimensional array named Y that contains 32 elements; these are to be regarded as the 32 ordinates of an experimental curve at equally spaced abscissas. Assuming that a value has already been given to H, compute the integral of the curve represented approximately by the Y values from

$$TRAP = \frac{H}{2}(Y_1 + 2Y_2 + 2Y_3 + \cdots$$
$$+ 2Y_{31} + Y_{32})$$

14. A two-dimensional array named AMATR

contains 10 rows and 10 columns. A one-dimensional array named DIAG contains 10 elements. Write a program segment to compute the elements of DIAG from the formula

$$DIAG(I) = AMATR(I,I)$$
$$I = 1, 2, \ldots, 10$$

*15. Given a one-dimensional array named Y, with 50 elements, and numbers U and I, write a statement to compute the value of S from the following equation, written in ordinary mathematical subscript notation.

$$S = y_i + u\frac{y_{i+1} - y_{i-1}}{2}$$
$$+ \frac{u^2}{2}(y_{i+1} - 2y_i + y_{i-1})$$

This is called *Stirling's interpolation formula* (through second differences), and may be described as follows: we have three points of a curve: (x_{i-1}, y_{i-1}), (x_i, y_i), and (x_{i+1}, y_{i+1}), such that $x_{i+1} - x_i = x_i - x_{i-1} = h$, and a value of x. We write $u = (x - x_i)/h$. Then the formula stated gives the interpolated value of y corresponding to x, found by passing a quadratic through the three given points.

16. Using the assumptions of Exercise 15, write a statement to compute the value of T from the following equation:

$$T = y_i + u(y_{i+1} - y_i)$$
$$+ \frac{u(u - 1)(y_{i+2} - y_{i+1} - y_i + y_{i-1})}{4}$$
$$+ \frac{(u - \frac{1}{2})u(u - 1)(y_{i+2} - 3y_{i+1} + 3y_i - y_{i-1})}{6}$$

This is called *Bessel's interpolation formula* (through third differences). With the notation used in Exercise 15, it finds a value of y corresponding to x by passing a cubic through the four given points. The arrangement of the differences is somewhat different from that in Stirling's formula, however.

*17. Given two one-dimensional arrays named A and B, of seven elements each, suppose that the seven elements of A are punched on one card and the seven elements of B are punched on another card. Each element value is punched in 10 columns in a form suitable for reading with an F10.0

field descriptor. Write a program to read the cards, then compute and print the value ANORM from

$$ANORM = \sqrt{\sum_{i=1}^{7} a_i b_i}$$

Use a 1PE20.7 field specification for ANORM.

18. Using the assumptions of Exercise 17, write a program to read the data cards and then carry out the following procedure. If every $a_i > b_i$, for $i = 1, 2, \ldots, 7$, print an integer 1; if this condition is not satisfied, print a zero.

*19. Rewrite the program segment for Exercise 11 to use double-precision variables for the arrays.

20. Rewrite the program segment for Exercise 16 to use double-precision variables for the arrays.

*21. COMPLX is a one-dimensional array containing 30 complex numbers. Write statements to form the sum of the absolute values of the 30 elements, using the CABS function.

22. With assumptions as in Exercise 21, write statements to form the sum of all the imaginary parts of the 30 elements of COMPLX, but include in the sum only those imaginary parts that are positive.

*23. A one-dimensional array named TRUTH contains 40 truth values. Write a program to place in TRUE the count of the number of elements of TRUTH that are .TRUE., and in FALSE the count of the number of elements that are .FALSE.. Notice that TRUE is a legitimate variable name; .TRUE., with periods, is a logical constant.

24. A one-dimensional array named COMPLX contains 30 elements. A two-dimensional array of logical variables named QUAD contains 30 rows and 4 columns. For all 30 values of I, if the point represented by COMPLX(I) lies in quadrant J, make QUAD(I, J) .TRUE. and the other three elements in row I of QUAD .FALSE..

25. Refer to Exercise 3d in Chapter 2. Suppose that WORD1 and WORD2 are one-dimensional arrays, each containing 5 alphanumeric variables of one letter each. (See Chapter 6 for a further discussion of alphanumeric variables.) Compare each letter of

WORD1 with each letter of WORD2 and place in DUPE the number of letters the two words have in common.

*26. Given two sets of numbers u_i and v_i, each consisting of the integers from 1 to n in some order, which are the rank orderings of two other sets of numbers x_i and y_i, then the rank difference coefficient of correlation between the sets x and y is

$$\rho = 1 - \frac{6 \sum\limits_{i=1}^{N} (u_i - v_i)^2}{n(n^2 - 1)}$$

Given two one-dimensional arrays named U and V that are rank orderings, each containing 14 elements, compute the rank-order coefficient of correlation and store it in RHO. Use a loop to compute the sum of the squares of the differences.

27. Extend the program written for Exercise 26 as follows. U and V contain 100 elements each, all but the first N of which are zero. You must determine what N is by inspecting the entries in either U or V in sequence from the first until finding one that is zero, counting as you go. The value of N thus computed by your program can be used in the formula. Write a program segment to do this, containing *one* loop that does the inspecting, the counting, and the summing of the squares of the differences. You may assume that U and V do have the same number of elements, that is, that there are no errors in the data, and, if it is any help, that there are at least two elements in each array.

28. From the definition of the rank orderings in Exercise 26, it should be that $\Sigma(u_i - v_i) = 0$. Modify the loop in the program of Exercise 27 so that it forms this sum as well as the sum of the squares of the differences. Then after the completion of the loop insert a test to determine whether the sum of the differences is zero. If it is not, print an error comment and stop, without computing or printing the coefficient of correlation.

5 THE DO STATEMENT

5.1 INTRODUCTION

The DO statement is one of the most powerful and most widely used features of the Fortran language. This statement makes it possible to execute a section of a program repeatedly, with automatic changes in the value of an integer variable between repetitions. Coupled with subscripted variables, the DO statement provides a simple way to perform calculations that would be a great deal more difficult otherwise. In view of the importance of the topic, we shall study its application in a variety of examples, including two case studies.

5.2 FUNDAMENTALS AND DEFINITIONS

The DO statement may be written in either of these forms:

$$\text{DO } n \; i = m_1, m_2$$

or

$$\text{DO } n \; i = m_1, m_2, m_3$$

In this statement n must be a statement number, i must be a nonsubscripted integer variable, written without a sign, and m_1, m_2, and m_3 must each be either an unsigned integer constant or a nonsubscripted unsigned integer variable. If m_3 is not stated, as in the first form of the statement, it is understood to be 1.

The action of the DO statement is as follows. The statements following the DO, up to and including the one with the statement number n, are executed repeatedly. They are executed first with $i = m_1$; before each succeeding repetition i is increased by m_3; repeated execution continues until the statements have been executed with i equal to the largest value that does not exceed m_2.

To illustrate how the DO statement works and how it may be used, let us consider again the problem stated in connection with subscripting on page 79, where we wished to form the sum of the squares of the 20 elements of the array named X and store that sum in SUMSQ. We recall that the program segment to do the job without the DO statement was:

```
      DIMENSION X(20)
      SUMSQ = 0.0
      I = 1
180   SUMSQ = SUMSQ + X(I)**2
      I = I + 1
      IF (I .LE. 20) GO TO 180
```

With the DO statement, we would write:

```
      DIMENSION X(20)
      SUMSQ = 0.0
      DO 180 I = 1, 20
180   SUMSQ = SUMSQ + X(I)**2
```

The DIMENSION statement must appear somewhere in the program to establish X as a one-dimensional array having 20 elements. (We realize that a segment such as this would ordinarily be part of a larger program, and that the DIMENSION statement would usually appear somewhere near the beginning of the program.) We first set the sum location to zero, then go

93

into the DO statement. This says, in our case, to execute repeatedly all the statements following the DO, down to and including the one numbered 180. There is, of course, only one statement in this range, and statement 180 itself is the program segment that is repeatedly executed. Statement 180 is carried out first with $I = 1$, so that the first time through we get x_1^2 in SUMSQ since the latter was cleared to zero before entering the loop. Then I is increased by 1 and the new value is tested against 20, as specified in the DO statement; since I is still less than or equal to 20, the range of the DO is executed again. This time, when statement 180 is executed (with $I = 2$), x_2^2 is added to the x_1^2 that was placed in SUMSQ the first time around. Again I is incremented by 1 and the new value is checked to see if it is less than or equal to 20, and so on. This process continues until statement 180 has been executed with $I = 20$. Now, when I is incremented to 21, the test will show that the new value of I is *not* less than or equal to 20, and control passes on to the statement after 180, whatever that might be.

It is instructive to realize that this process is very similar to the sequence of operations followed in the version written without using the DO statement. In fact, precisely the same flowchart would describe the actions of both, as demonstrated in Figure 5.1.

We may generalize this flowchart slightly to demonstrate graphically what the actions are in any simple DO. Figure 5.2 may be regarded as a definition of what the DO statement calls for in the kind of situation we are discussing. It is worth noting that after *i* has been set to its initial value, the statements following the DO are immediately executed once before any testing of *i* against the specified final value. If, for some reason, intentional or not, the final value (m_2) is *less* than the initial value (m_1)—which we might think would logically cause *no* executions of the statements following the DO—there will nevertheless be one execution of them.

For another example of a DO statement, suppose we have a one-dimensional array called DATA1 that contains 21 elements. We wish to form the sum of all the odd-numbered elements and to place the sum in a location that we shall call SUM. The program segment could be:

```
        SUM = 0.0
        DO 500 K = 1, 21, 2
  500   SUM = SUM + DATA1(K)
```

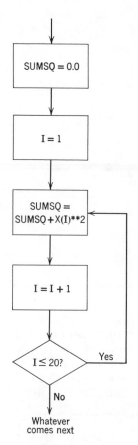

FIGURE 5.1. A flowchart depicting the actions taken in forming the sum of the squares of the 20 elements of an array named X. This same flowchart applies to the program segments written with and without the use of the DO statement.

We assume that these three statements are a small part of a larger program and that elsewhere in the program there is a DIMENSION statement that establishes DATA1 as a one-dimensional array with 21 elements. The DO statement, in this case, says to execute the statement numbered 500 with K equal to 1, 3, 5, . . . , 17, 19, 21. The first time statement 500 is executed the value of the variable SUM is zero, so that the net effect is to move the first element of DATA1 to SUM. The second time it is executed the effect is to add to this the value of the third element of DATA1, and so on. When it has been executed with K equal to 21, which adds in the last element, control passes to the statement following statement 500.

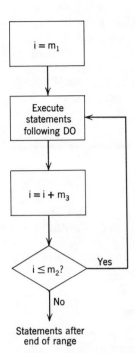

FIGURE 5.2. A flowchart of the actions taken as a result of a simple DO statement.

5.3 FURTHER DEFINITIONS

Before proceeding to more examples we present a few definitions that will make it easier to talk about the DO statement.

The *range* of a DO statement is the set of repeatedly executed statements. In short, it consists of the statements beginning with the one immediately following the DO and continuing up to and including the one whose statement number is given in the DO. The integer variable i in the general form of the DO statement is called its *index*. Throughout the execution of the range i is available for any purpose permitted for an integer variable. We have seen how it may be used as a subscript and we shall see later how it can be applied in other ways.

There are two ways by which control can transfer outside the range of a DO. The *normal exit* occurs when the DO is *satisfied*, that is, at the completion of the number of executions of the range as specified by the *indexing parameters* m_1, m_2, and m_3. When this happens, as we have seen, control passes to the statement following that named in the DO. The second

method by which control can get outside the range of a DO is by execution of a GO TO or IF statement that is within the range. This can happen when we wish to specify in the DO parameters the *maximum* number of executions of the range but to set up tests within the range to determine the *actual* number of executions needed for a specific case.

When control is transferred outside the range of a DO *before* the DO is satisfied, the index i is available for any purpose permitted for an integer variable. This can be quite valuable. After a normal exit, however, i is *not* available, that is, its value is not defined and you *cannot* assume that it has some specific value, such as m_2, or $m_2 + m_3$. This is no serious inconvenience in practice.

To examine another way in which the index of a DO may be used within the range, consider the following example. In a problem involving combinations we are required to form M! (M factorial), which is the product of all integers from 1 through M; the value of M has been determined earlier in the program. M is an integer variable and we wish to obtain the factorial in real form. The program segment below does the necessary computation and places the product in a location called FACTRL.

```
    FACTRL = 1.0
    DO 6 I = 2, M
    AI = I
6   FACTRL = FACTRL * AI
```

We first set FACTRL equal to 1.0 and then go into the DO loop, asking for the range to be executed with I equal to all values from 2 to M. To use the index I in a computation of real variables without mixing integer and real modes, we execute the statement AI = I, which calls for the conversion of I to real form, assuming the real-integer naming convention. The first time statement 6 is executed the effect is to multiply 1.0 by 2.0 (since FACTRL has been started at 1.0) and to store the product in FACTRL. The next time this product is multiplied by 3.0 and the new product is stored back in FACTRL. The process continues until the two statements in the range have been executed with I equal to M.

Implicit in this formulation is the assumption that M is at least 2. If M could be 1, the DO statement would ask for the range to be executed with I equal to all values from 2 up to

1, which, of course, is impossible. This would result in the erroneous value FACTRL = 2.0, since the range would be executed once before testing the index. If M were equal to 2, the program would not get into trouble: the two statements in the range would be executed exactly once, which would be correct, and control would pass to the statement following 6.

This example shows that it is important to be sure that the range of a DO is executed precisely the correct number of times. Experience reveals that it is all too easy to make mistakes on this point, especially by calling for one too few or one too many repetitions. A good way to check is to ask, "What would the parameters have to be if the range were to be executed *once?*" Based on this question, it is usually not too difficult to decide whether the actual situation is properly handled.

The DO statement can often be used effectively to run through a set of values of an independent variable. In Case Study 5, for instance, we computed the sine of a series of angles: 30°, 390°, 750°, and so on up to 3990°. It was indicated in Figure 3.6 that these angles were read from cards; the same arguments could have been generated more simply by a DO statement, as is shown in Figure 5.3. The index of a DO statement must be an integer variable; we have used K. In the computation the angle is a double-precision variable, called DEGREE in Figure 3.6. Therefore the first operation after the DO is an assignment statement:

```
DEGREE = K
```

With DEGREE having been declared to be double precision, this statement calls for a conversion from integer to double precision. The body of the computation is as before. The end of the range is the WRITE statement that prints the results.

For a second example of this kind of use of the DO statement, consider the modification of the program of Case Study 3, Figure 2.14. In the modified program we needed to run through all values of *S* from 20.0 to 200.0, in steps of 0.1. Here we cannot use the value of the DO index directly, since it must be an integer variable and we need steps of 0.1. This is only a minor difficulty, however, since we can write

```
DO 40 I = 200, 2000
S = I
S = S / 10.0
```

These steps are placed before the body of the computation; statement 40 would be the WRITE statement that prints the results. The DO index will run through the values 200 to 2000 in steps of 1. After conversion to Fortran real form and division by 10.0, S will therefore run through the values 20.0 to 200.0 in steps of 0.1.

5.4 RULES GOVERNING THE USE OF THE DO STATEMENT

A great deal of flexibility is permitted in the use of the DO statement so long as certain rules are observed. We shall state all of these rules together and later illustrate the situations that some of them cover.

Rule 1

It is permissible for the range of one DO (which we call the *outer* DO) to contain one or more other DOs (which we call the *inner* DOs). The DO statements are then said to be *nested*. When this occurs, it is required that all statements in the range of an inner DO also be in the range of the outer DOs. This does not prohibit the ranges of two or more DO's from ending with the same statement, but it does prohibit a situation in which the range of an inner DO extends past the end of the range of an outer DO. In other words, the inner DO must be completely contained within the outer DO.

A simple example is provided by the common chore of clearing a two-dimensional array to zeros. Often we wish to place data only in the nonzero elements of an array, making it necessary to clear the entire array. Suppose, for a concrete example, that we have a 20 by 30 array named AMATRX to clear. The following three-statement segment will do the job:

```
    DO 12 I = 1, 20
    DO 12 J = 1, 30
12  AMATRX(I, J) = 0.0
```

Both DO statements refer to the same ending statement, but the two do not have the same range, since the range of the first DO includes the second DO. This means that after I has been set equal to 1 by the first DO, the second DO will cause J to run through all of the specified 30 values of J. When the second DO has been

```
C CASE STUDY 5
C COMPUTATION OF SINE FROM TAYLOR'S SERIES
C
C DOUBLE PRECISION VERSION
C
C MODIFIED TO USE A DO STATEMENT TO GENERATE VALUES OF THE ANGLE
C
C
      DOUBLE PRECISION X, TERM, SUM, XSQ, DENOM, TEST, DEGREE
C
C WRITE COLUMN HEADINGS
      WRITE (6, 100)
 100  FORMAT('1 DEGREE',14X,'X',16X,'SERIES-SINE',11X,'FUNCTION-SINE'//)
C
C THE FOLLOWING DO GENERATES THE SAME VALUES OF 'DEGREE'
C AS WERE READ FROM CARDS TO PRODUCE THE OUTPUT IN FIG. 3.7,
C WITH THE EXCEPTION OF THE LAST TWO NEGATIVE VALUES.
      DO 40 K = 30, 3990, 360
C
C CONVERT FROM INTEGER TO DOUBLE PRECISION FORM
      DEGREE = K
C
C CONVERT FROM DEGREES TO RADIANS
      X = DEGREE / (180.0/3.1415926535897932)
C
C SET UP INITIAL VALUES
      SUM = X
      TERM = X
      DENOM = 3.0
      XSQ = X**2
C
C COMPUTE NEW TERM FROM PREVIOUS TERM
 20   TERM = - TERM * XSQ / (DENOM * (DENOM - 1.0))
C
C GET SUM OF TERMS SO FAR
      SUM = SUM + TERM
C
C TEST FOR CONVERGENCE
      IF ( DABS(TERM) .LT. 1.0D-17 ) GO TO 30
C
C PREPARE TO GO AROUND AGAIN
         DENOM = DENOM + 2.0
         GO TO 20
C
C GET VALUE FROM SUPPLIED DP SINE ROUTINE FOR COMPARISON
 30   TEST = DSIN(X)
C
C PRINT RESULTS
 40   WRITE (6, 120) DEGREE, X, SUM, TEST
      STOP
 120  FORMAT (1X, F8.0, 3F23.14)
      END
```

FIGURE 5.3. The program of Figure 3.6, modified to use a DO statement to replace the reading of the data.

satisfied, the index of the first is incremented and tested; when the range of the first DO is now executed with I = 2, the second DO once again causes J to run through all of the values from 1 to 30, and so on.

The following segment exhibits a violation of this rule.

```
        DO 400 K = 1, 20
        DO 500 L = 2, 7
 400    A(K) = B(L)
 500    C(L) = L + 6
```

The range of the inner DO extends past the end of the range of the outer DO, which is not permitted.

Rule 2

The last statement in the range of a DO must not be a GO TO in any form, nor an arithmetic IF, RETURN (discussed in Chapter 7), STOP, PAUSE, or DO statement. Neither can it be a logical IF containing any of these. These statements, with the exception of the RETURN, may be used freely anywhere else in the range. The CONTINUE statement, described later, is provided for situations that would otherwise violate this rule.

Rule 3

No statement within the range of a DO may redefine or otherwise alter any of the indexing parameters of that DO; that is, it is not permitted within the range of a DO to change the values of i, m_1, m_2, or m_3. These numbers may still be used in any way that does not alter their values.

Rule 4

Control, with one exception, must not transfer into the range of a DO from any statement outside its range. Thus it is expressly prohibited to use a GO TO or an IF statement to transfer into the range of a DO without first executing the DO itself. This rule *does* prohibit a transfer from the range of an outer DO into the range of an inner DO, but it *does not* prohibit a transfer out of the range of an inner DO into the range of the outer DO that contains it. The latter is permissible because from the standpoint of the outer DO the transfer is entirely within its range. Some illustrations of the application of this rule are provided in Figure 5.4. The brackets here represent the ranges of DO's and the arrows represent transfers of control. Transfers 2, 3, and 4 are acceptable, since 2 and 3 are transfers from the range of an inner DO into the range of an outer DO and 4 is a transfer entirely within the range of a single DO. Transfers 1, 5, and 6 all represent transfers into the range of a DO from outside its range.

The one exception to the rule prohibiting transfers into the range of a DO from outside its range is this: it is permissible to transfer control completely outside the nest to which a DO belongs, to perform a series of calculations that makes no changes in any of the indexing parameters (i, m_1, m_2, m_3) in the nest, and then to

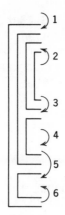

FIGURE 5.4. Some examples of permissible nests of DOs and some correct and incorrect transfers of control. Transfers 2, 3, and 4 are permissible; 1, 5, and 6 are not.

transfer back to the range of the same DO from which transfer was originally made. The restriction on the exit and reentry transfer location may be stated another way: no DO and no statement that is the last statement in the range of a DO may lie, logically speaking, between the exit and reentry points.

CONTINUE is a dummy statement that causes no action when the object program is executed. It merely satisfies the rule that the last statement in the range of a DO must not be one that can cause transfer of control. It is also used to provide a statement to which an IF can transfer when the computations in the range of a DO have been completed. This is necessary because a transfer within the range of a DO is not permitted to return to the DO itself, unless, of course, it really is intended to start the execution of the DO from the beginning again, which would be unusual.

It is altogether legal to use the CONTINUE statement as the end of the range of *any* DO, even if the construction would be legal without it, for the sake of clarity. In fact, we shall ordinarily do just that in the examples in the rest of the book.

This will be done, in most cases, in conjunction with a convention on the indentation of the statements in the range of a DO. In many programs it is not uncommon to have a large number of DO statements, many of them nested, leading to difficulty in understanding the intended functioning of the program and in proving its correctness. Anything we can do to clarify the intended structure of the program is of benefit both as documentation and as an aid to checkout.

Toward this end we shall write most programs according to the following conventions. Every DO statement will refer to a CONTINUE as the end of its range; in the case of nested DO's, each DO will refer to a separate CONTINUE. All the statements within the range of a DO, with the exception of the CONTINUE, will be indented at least three spaces from the DO. This last rule will apply to each DO in a nest, leading to a stepped appearance that will help to make the nested structure clear.

As an example, consider the following puzzle problem, taken from *Computer Science: A First Course*,* and referred to by the authors as "The Stickler Problem": Find all the three-digit numbers that are equal to the sum of the cubes of their digits. This is a "good" computer problem in the sense that if you really want to know the answer, it is hard to do without a computer and easy with one. (A "bad" computer problem is one that can be solved better or more easily without a computer, even though a computer can do it.) The computational task is simply to run through all three-digit numbers, making the specified test on each. Arranging to obtain the 900 different three-digit numbers having a nonzero first digit is easily carried out with a nest of three DO statements, as seen in Figure 5.5. The hundred's digit must run through the values from one to nine, whereas the ten's and unit's digits need to run through all the values from zero to nine. Since a Fortran DO index cannot be less than one, we set up the ten's and unit's loops to go from one to ten, then subtract one from the indices before using them in the test. The output, consisting of the four numbers that are the answer to the puzzle, is also shown in Figure 5.5.

Notice the way the appearance of the problem exhibits its structure, with each DO referring to a CONTINUE that is lined up under it. Naturally, in a simple problem like this one, the value of the typographical convention is minimal—but most realistic programs run more like

a dozen pages (at least) than a dozen lines. Anything we can do to assist in the process of ferreting out errors is worthwhile.

This program was run on a time-sharing system, and the system commands and responses have been left in the output shown in Figure 5.5. Each time the system asked for a command, it printed the time of day in hours, minutes, and seconds. The command "print stickler fortran" consists of the command word "print," the file name "stickler," under which the source program was stored, and the file type, "fortran." After printing the program, the system typed the time of day, after which the command "fortran" was issued, with the program name "stickler," causing compilation and the storage of an object program. We next asked that the object program be loaded, and instructed the system to start executing it; these two operations could also have been called for with the equivalent single command "run." The system typed the word "EXECUTION" to indicate where in the complete process it was, then ran the program, which produced the output shown.

We hasten to point out that the elapsed times here do not represent full usage of the computer for this one function. The total time used by the central processing unit (CPU) in carrying out all of the operations shown here was 1.12 seconds.

5.5 EXAMPLES OF THE USE OF THE DO STATEMENT

Since the DO statement is so powerful and since it is so heavily used in most Fortran programs, we shall give some additional examples of its use.

We shall suppose for a first example that the input to a certain program consists of a series of experimentally measured values. Each point in the experiment consists of an *x* value and a *y* value, corresponding to the abscissa and ordinate of a point on a graph. The data points were gathered and entered into the computer in random order; that is, we know that the first *x* value goes with the first *y* value, the second *x* value goes with the second *y* value, and so on, but we cannot assume that the first *x* is the smallest of the *x* values. For the purposes of the calculations that are to be done later in the program, it is necessary to rearrange the data points in

*Alexandra I. Forsythe, Thomas A. Keenan, Elliott I. Organick, and Warren Stenberg, *Computer Science: A First Course*, New York, Wiley, 1969, pp. 172-175.

```
14.55.22 print stickler fortran

C THE STICKLER PROBLEM -- FROM
C FORSYTHE, KEENAN, ORGANICK, AND STENBERG, FORTRAN LANGUAGE
C SUPPLEMENT, PAGE 112
C
C FINDING THREE-DIGIT NUMBERS THAT ARE EQUAL TO THE SUM
C   OF THE CUBES OF THEIR DIGITS
C
C
      INTEGER H, T, U, TM1, UM1
      DO 30 H = 1, 9
         DO 20 T = 1, 10
            DO 10 U = 1, 10
               TM1 = T - 1
               UM1 = U - 1
               IF (100*H + 10*TM1 + UM1 .EQ. H**3 + TM1**3 + UM1**3)
     1            WRITE (6, 100) H, TM1, UM1
 10            CONTINUE
 20         CONTINUE
 30      CONTINUE
         STOP
100      FORMAT (3I15)
         END


14.56.07 fortran stickler

14.56.29 load stickler

14.56.37 start stickler
EXECUTION:
       1            5            3
       3            7            0
       3            7            1
       4            0            7

14.56.42
```

FIGURE 5.5.   A program using three nested DO statements to find all three-digit numbers that are equal to the sum of the cubes of their digits. See the text for discussion of the time-sharing commands shown in lower case letters.

storage so that the first x value *is* the smallest and that the second x value is the next larger, and so on. In other words, we must order the data points into ascending sequence on the x values. In computing terminology, this operation is called *sorting*.

We shall assume that the x values as they were originally read (that is, in scrambled order) are the elements of an array named X and that there are 25 of them. The y values are the 25 elements of another array called Y.

The Fortran program to rearrange these data points into ascending sequence of the x values involves a nest of two DO loops. We shall show the development of the program by displaying a simplified version of the inner loop before writing the full program. This simplified loop will place the smallest x value in the first position of the x array. This can be done by the following process. First compare the first and second x values in the original array. If X(1) is smaller than or equal to X(2), leave them as they are; but if X(1) is larger than X(2), interchange these two values within the array. Having inspected the first and second elements and interchanged them if necessary to get the smaller in X(1), we compare X(1) and X(3) and interchange them if X(1) is larger. What is in X(1) as we make this second comparison may well be the value that was originally in X(2), but that does not matter. Similarly, we compare X(1) and X(4), X(1) and X(5), and so on, each time interchanging if necessary to get the smaller in X(1). This process guarantees that the smallest x value in the entire array will finally be in X(1), wherever it may have been to begin with. Remembering that to each element of X there corresponds an element of Y, we naturally carry out the same interchange operations on the Y array as we do on the X array, but there is no testing of the Y array values.

To interchange two values from the array in storage, we follow a three-step process: (1) move the first value to a temporary location that we shall call TEMP; (2) move the second value to the location originally occupied by the first; (3) move the first value, now in TEMP, to the location originally occupied by the second.

A program to carry out all of the steps of this process is shown below. We are assuming that the data values have been read in by an earlier part of the program, and we are not showing the statements that complete the rearrangement or use of the data values. Elsewhere in the program there would have to be a DIMENSION X(25), Y(25) statement.

```
      DO 30 J = 2, 25
         IF ( X(1) .LE. X(J) ) GO TO 30
            TEMP = X(1)
            X(1) = X(J)
            X(J) = TEMP
            TEMP = Y(1)
            Y(1) = Y(J)
            Y(J) = TEMP
   30 CONTINUE
```

The program illustrates a number of points worth noting. We see another example of a DO loop in which the index does not start with 1. We see an example of the use of the CONTINUE statement. In this case it is required because if the IF statement shows that X(1) is already less than or equal to the other x value with which we are comparing it, a transfer of control must be made to skip around the six statements that interchange elements in the X and Y arrays. What we want to do in such a case is simply to repeat the whole process with the index J increased by 1. As we have already noted, however, it is not possible to transfer control back to the DO. This would result in starting the DO loop again with J equal to 2—which is not what we want. Therefore we transfer control to the CONTINUE, which has been identified in the DO statement as the last line of the range.

In reading this program, it is well to recall the meaning of an arithmetic assignment statement: the value of the variable on the left side of the

equal sign is replaced by the value of the expression on the right. Thus a statement such as

```
      X(1) = X(J)
```

means that the number identified by the subscripted variable name X(J) is to be moved to the location for the number identified by the name X(1). The value in the location for X(J) is unchanged.

In the data as described earlier there may or may not be two equal x values. As the program has been written, it does not matter; if they are equal, there is no point in exchanging them, and we simply transfer control down to the CONTINUE and go around the loop again.

When this loop has been completed (when the DO is satisfied), we are guaranteed that the data points have been rearranged so that the smallest x value is in X(1) and the corresponding y value is in Y(1). What we would like to do next is to get the next larger x value in X(2). This can be done by comparing X(2) with X(3), then with X(4), X(5), and so on, interchanging when necessary. After that we would like to get the next larger element in X(3). We would similarly like to get the successively larger values in X(4), X(5), and so on.

It appears that what we need to do for the complete program is to make variables of all subscripts that appear as 1's in the first version of the program above. The subscript will then select the element to be compared with all following elements (interchanging if necessary). This subscript, which we shall call I, will start at 1 and run to 24. The subscript that appears as J above will still be J, but it will have to start at one more than the value of the I subscript and run to 25. All of this is easily done with another DO statement that controls the I subscript. This is the outer DO. There is one complication, however. The inner DO must specify that the J subscript will start at one more than I. Looking back at the definition of the DO statement, we see that each indexing parameter must be either an integer constant or a single integer variable. It is *not* permitted, unfortunately, in most Fortrans, to write a statement such as

```
      DO 30 J = I + 1, 25
```

To avoid this restriction, we simply insert a statement that computes the value of a variable IP1, which is always one more than the value of I. The complete program to arrange the data points in sequence is thus:

```
        DO 40 I = 1, 24
            IP1 = I + 1
            DO 30 J = IP1, 25
                IF (X(I) .LE. X(J)) GO TO 30
                    TEMP = X(I)
                    X(I) = X(J)
                    X(J) = TEMP
                    TEMP = Y(I)
                    Y(I) = Y(J)
                    Y(J) = TEMP
    30      CONTINUE
    40  CONTINUE
```

This technique is by no means the most efficient sorting method available. It is presented here only as an interesting application of the

DO statement. See Exercises 19 and 20 for a sample of other techniques.

Let us extend this program segment into a complete program by adding input and output statements. We shall then be able to observe the program in action on sample data. While we are completing the program, we can make one change that will permit a useful flexibility in the number of data points. The final program is shown in Figure 5.6.

The DIMENSION statement specifies that the X and Y arrays both have 25 elements, but we set up the program to read a value for N, the *actual* number of data values that we shall read into each array. The element positions defined by the DIMENSION statement but not loaded with data in a particular run of the program will

```
C A SORTING PROGRAM
C
C THE PROGRAM IS SET UP WITH EACH ARRAY HOLDING A MAXIMUM OF 25 ELEMENTS
C THE ACTUAL NUMBER OF ELEMENTS IN EACH ARRAY IS DETERMINED BY
C   A PARAMETER, N,  READ AT EXECUTION TIME
C
C
      INTEGER X, Y
      DIMENSION X(25), Y(25)
C
C READ N, THE NUMBER OF ELEMENTS TO BE READ INTO EACH ARRAY
      READ (5, 100) N
C
C READ THE ELEMENTS INTO THE ARRAYS
      DO 10 K = 1, N
          READ (5, 100) X(K), Y(K)
   10 CONTINUE
C
C THE SORTING ROUTINE BEGINS HERE
      NM1 = N - 1
      DO 40 I = 1, NM1
          IP1 = I + 1
          DO 30 J = IP1, N
              IF ( X(I) .LE. X(J) ) GO TO 20
                  TEMP = X(I)
                  X(I) = X(J)
                  X(J) = TEMP
                  TEMP = Y(I)
                  Y(I) = Y(J)
                  Y(J) = TEMP
   20         WRITE (6, 200) (X(K), K = 1, N)
              WRITE (6, 200) (Y(K), K = 1, N)
   30     CONTINUE
   40 CONTINUE
      STOP
  100 FORMAT (2I5)
  200 FORMAT (1X, 25I5)
      END
```

FIGURE 5.6.   A program to sort the elements of two arrays named X and Y into ascending sequence on the X values.

simply not be used. The arrays have been specified as INTEGER to simplify sample input and output. The first READ gets the value of N, and all remaining loops that formerly referred to 25 will now refer to N. The loop for reading data, for instance, executes a READ statement N times, each time reading an $x - y$ pair from a data card. When all the data cards have been read, we go into the main sorting loop, which is just as it was before except that loops run from 1 to $N - 1$ instead of from 1 to 24, and from $I + 1$ to N instead of from $I + 1$ to 25.

So that it will be possible to watch the sorting process in operation, we have inserted two WRITE statements in the sorting loop, one for each array. Each WRITE statement employs a programming feature that we shall explore more fully in the next chapter on input and output, but that is not hard to follow: an *implied DO*, as it is called, to get just the first N elements of each array.

Figure 5.7 shows the program in action, so to speak. It was run on a time-sharing system in which all input and output is from a type-writer-like terminal, so that input and output are both displayed. Furthermore, the time-sharing system employed permits free-form input, that is, input values of less than specified field width, separated by commas (or blanks). Thus we see that N was made equal to 4 so that the four pairs of X − Y values were

4	100
3	200
2	300
1	400

In other words, the four data points were in exactly reverse sequence on the x-values.

Since the two WRITE statements appear in the loop *after* the interchange, the first output we see refers to the arrays as they stood following one interchange, and we see that the first two elements of each array have indeed been exchanged. The reader will find it instructive to follow through the complete sorting process.

Studying the operation of a program on a small but representative set of data is one excellent way of making sure we understand how the program works, and, in the process, making sure it does what we meant it to do.

Figure 5.8 shows the input and output for another run of this program, this time with $N = 6$ and the data points in random order.

```
4,
4,100,
3,200,
2,300,
1,400,
     3       4       2       1
   200     100     300     400
     2       4       3       1
   300     100     200     400
     1       4       3       2
   400     100     200     300
     1       3       4       2
   400     200     100     300
     1       2       4       3
   400     300     100     200
     1       2       3       4
   400     300     200     100
```

FIGURE 5.7. The input and output for the program of Figure 5.6 when run under a time-sharing system.

Notice that whenever two successive pairs of X and Y arrays are identical, it means that no interchange was required on that execution of the loop.

To illustrate a slightly different type of DO loop, let us now make some further assumptions about the purpose of the program just written. Suppose that the 25 data points that have been read and now arranged into ascending sequence on the x values lie on a curve and that we are required to find the area under the curve; that is, to find the definite integral of the curve represented approximately by these points. If we now make the further assumption that the distance between successive x values is equal to a constant value h, the approximate integral given by the trapezoidal rule is

$$\text{AREA} = \frac{h}{2}(y_1 + 2y_2 + 2y_3 + \cdots$$
$$+ 2y_{23} + 2y_{24} + y_{25})$$

A DO loop may conveniently be used to form the sum of the y values with subscripts of 2 to 24. Having done so, we can multiply this sum by 2, add the first and last y values, and multiply by $h/2$.

```
      SUM = 0.0
      DO 50 I = 2, 24
   50 SUM = SUM + Y(I)
      H = X(2) - X(1)
      AREA = 0.5*H*(Y(1)+2.0*SUM+Y(25))
```

This program segment would follow statement 40 of the program segment shown in Figure 5.6. It includes the computation of h on

```
6,
4,100,
6,200,
2,300,
1,400,
5,500,
3,600,
         4     6     2     1     5     3
       100   200   300   400   500   600
         2     6     4     1     5     3
       300   200   100   400   500   600
         1     6     4     2     5     3
       400   200   100   300   500   600
         1     6     4     2     5     3
       400   200   100   300   500   600
         1     6     4     2     5     3
       400   200   100   300   500   600
         1     4     6     2     5     3
       400   100   200   300   500   600
         1     2     6     4     5     3
       400   300   200   100   500   600
         1     2     6     4     5     3
       400   300   200   100   500   600
         1     2     6     4     5     3
       400   300   200   100   500   600
         1     2     4     6     5     3
       400   300   100   200   500   600
         1     2     4     6     5     3
       400   300   100   200   500   600
         1     2     3     6     5     4
       400   300   600   200   500   100
         1     2     3     5     6     4
       400   300   600   500   200   100
         1     2     3     4     6     5
       400   300   600   500   100   200
         1     2     3     4     5     6
       400   300   600   100   500   200
```

FIGURE 5.8.   A different set of input and output for
the program of Figure 5.6, also run under a time-
sharing system.

the assumption that it is the interval between
any two x values. If, in fact, the x values are not
equally spaced, the program naturally gives an
incorrect result. If it were required that the program be able to handle unequally spaced x
values, the numerical integration method would
have to be modified.

Simpson's rule, another method for numerical
integration, with the subscripting scheme we are
using, is

$$\text{AREA} = \frac{h}{3}(y_1 + 4y_2 + 2y_3 + 4y_4 + 2y_5 + \cdots$$
$$+ 2y_{23} + 4y_{24} + y_{25})$$

A program to evaluate this formula will be a
little more complex because of the alternating

coefficients of 2 and 4. One way to handle the
problem is to set up two DO loops and to accumulate separately the sums of the y's corresponding to the two coefficients.

```
      EVEN = 0.0
      DO 47 I = 2, 24, 2
 47   EVEN = EVEN + Y(I)
      ODD = 0.0
      DO 48 I = 3, 23, 2
 48   ODD = ODD + Y(I)
      H = X(2) - X(1)
      AREA = (H/3.0)*( Y(1) + 4.0*EVEN
     1    + 2.0*ODD + Y(25) )
```

The computation may also be done with only
one DO loop, which saves a little time in the
running of the object program, if we proceed
as follows. Suppose we set up an index that runs
from 2 to 22 in steps of 2. Such an index always
references an element that should be multiplied
by 4; one plus that index references an element
that should be multiplied by 2. The Y(24) element must be added in separately because there
are more even elements than odd.

```
      ODD = 0.0
      EVEN = 0.0
      DO 51 I = 2, 22, 2
          EVEN = EVEN + Y(I)
          ODD = ODD + Y(I+1)
 51   CONTINUE
      H = X(2) - X(1)
      AREA = (H/3.0)*( Y(1)
     1    + 4.0*(EVEN + Y(24))
     2    + 2.0*ODD + Y(25) )
```

Flexibility in the manner of writing subscripts
is very useful here. It is not possible to form the
sum of the y values with one DO loop unless
some such subscripting arrangement is used.

It may be noted that we have written these
integration formulas with the subscripts starting
at 1, whereas it is conventional to write them
with the subscripts starting at zero. This was
done to make it easier to describe the problem,
since we recall that a Fortran subscript must
always be positive and nonzero.

It is possible to program formulas that have
zero and negative subscripts, but it is somewhat
more effort than it is worth to us at this point.
(It may be noted that some Fortran systems, or
languages similar to Fortran, do permit zero and
negative subscripts.)

5.6 CASE STUDY 9: DAMPED OSCILLATION

This case study, which in its physical situation is closely related to Case Study 2, provides a simple example of a DO loop not involving subscripting.

The current flowing in a series circuit containing resistance, inductance, and an initially charged capacitor, but no voltage source, is given by

$$i = i_m e^{-Rt/2L} \sin 2\pi f_1 t$$

where

$$i_m = \frac{2\pi f_0^2 Q}{f_1}$$

$$f_0 = \frac{1}{2\pi}\sqrt{\frac{1}{LC}}$$

$$f_1 = \frac{1}{2\pi}\sqrt{\frac{1}{LC} - \frac{R^2}{4L^2}}$$

and i = current flowing at time t, amperes
i_m = maximum current, amperes
R = resistance, ohms
t = time since closing switch, seconds
L = inductance, henrys
f_0 = frequency of undamped circuit ($R = 0$), hertz
f_1 = frequency of damped circuit, hertz
C = capacitance, farads
Q = initial charge on capacitor, coulombs

We wish to compute a number of points on the curve of instantaneous current versus time in order to draw a graph. One of the inputs to the program, along with the physical parameters, will be an integer giving the number of cycles of the curve desired (CYCLES) and another number giving the number of points per cycle to be computed (NPERCY).

The program is shown in Figure 5.9. We begin with type declarations, which in this case are a definite convenience: electrical engineers write i for current, and with the REAL statement to override the naming convention we can do the same.

The first processing action in the program is to compute two numerical factors that appear in several places later in the program. It is, of course, possible to compute these with a desk calculator in advance, but this way is less open

to misunderstanding and takes a negligible amount of computer time.

After reading the data, and printing it and column headings, we make some elementary checks on its validity, which is always a good idea. Three of the values are tested to be sure that they are positive and nonzero, and a check is made whether R^2 is less than or equal to $4L/C$. (The formulation here does not apply if R^2 is greater than $4L/C$.)

We compute F0 and F1, the undamped and damped frequencies, as intermediate variables to save time in the loop later. Having F0 we can get the time interval DELTAT. The scheme is to have NPERCY points in each cycle at the undamped frequency. One cycle at a frequency of F0 cycles per sec. (hertz) takes 1/F0 sec. In order to get NPERCY points in one such cycle, the time interval between points should be 1/(NPERCY*F0). C1 and C2 are further intermediate variables.

The total number of points is the number per cycle, NPERCY, times the number of cycles, CYCLES. This product becomes the value of LIMIT, which we then use as the final value in the DO statement that follows. The DO statement here is used only to count the number of repetitions. The incrementing of T is done within this loop;

In the FORMAT statement associated with writing the output values, we have used a scale factor with an F field descriptor, something not seen before. When used with an E field descriptor, a scale factor moves the decimal point *and* causes a corresponding adjustment of the exponent, so that the value printed is the same but represented differently. Here we actually change the value, which is what we desire: instead of seconds and amperes, we want milliseconds (ms) and milliamperes (ma).

Figure 5.10 shows the output from the program when run with suitable data. CYCLES was 3 and NPERCY was 20.

5.7 CASE STUDY 10: THE GAUSS-SEIDEL METHOD FOR SOLVING SIMULTANEOUS EQUATIONS

In this case study we shall see DO statements applied in a way that is very common, in connection with subscripting in arrays. The application is a standard numerical technique.

```
C CASE STUDY 9
C DAMPED OSCILLATION
C
C
      REAL I, IM, Q, R, C, L, F0, F1, C1, C2, T, DELTAT, TEMP
      INTEGER CYCLES, NPERCY, LIMIT
C
C COMPUTE COMMONLY-USED FACTORS
      TWOPI = 2.0 * 3.141593
      REC2PI = 1.0 / TWOPI
C
C READ PARAMETERS
      READ (5, 100) Q, R, C, L, CYCLES, NPERCY
 100  FORMAT (4F10.0, 2I2)
C
C PRINT PARAMETERS, WITH IDENTIFICATION, AND COLUMN HEADINGS
      WRITE (6, 200) Q, R, C, L
 200  FORMAT ('1', 'INITIAL CHARGE = ', F10.6, '   COULOMB'/
     1   1X, 'RESISTANCE      = ', F7.3, '      OHM'/
     2   1X, 'CAPACITANCE     = ', F10.6, '   FARAD'/
     3   1X, 'INDUCTANCE      = ', F7.3, '        HENRY'///
     4   1X, 9X, 'TIME      CURRENT'/' ', 10X, 'MS', 11X, 'MA'//)
C
C CHECK FOR INVALID DATA
      IF (         (Q        .LE. 0.0      )
     1      .OR. (CYCLES .LE. 0       )
     2      .OR. (NPERCY .LE. 0       )
     3      .OR. (R**2    .GT. 4.0*L/C) ) STOP
C
C COMPUTE INTERMEDIATE VARIABLES
      F0 = REC2PI / SQRT(L * C)
      F1 = REC2PI * SQRT(1.0/(L*C) - R**2/(4.0*L**2))
      TEMP = NPERCY
      DELTAT = 1.0 / (TEMP * F0)
      IM = TWOPI * F0**2 * Q / F1
      C1 = R / (2.0 * L)
      C2 = TWOPI * F1
C
C START T AT ZERO BEFORE ENTERING LOOP
      T = 0.0
C
C COMPUTE THE NUMBER OF POINTS NEEDED
      LIMIT = CYCLES * NPERCY
C
C COMPUTING LOOP - DO USED FOR COUNTING THE NUMBER OF EXECUTIONS
      DO 10 J = 1, LIMIT
         I = IM * EXP(-C1 * T) * SIN(C2 * T)
         WRITE (6, 300) T, I
         T = T + DELTAT
  10  CONTINUE
      STOP
 300  FORMAT (' ', 6X, 3PF8.3, F12.3)
      END
```

FIGURE 5.9. A program for computing the instantaneous current flowing in a circuit containing a resistor, an inductor, and an initially charged capacitor. (Case Study 9.)

```
INITIAL CHARGE    =    0.000010    COULOMB
RESISTANCE        =    1.000       OHM
CAPACITANCE       =    0.000010    FARAD
INDUCTANCE        =    0.002       HENRY


       TIME              CURRENT
       MS                  MA


       0.0                0.0
       0.044             21.610
       0.089             40.653
       0.133             55.342
       0.178             64.351
       0.222             66.932
       0.267             62.977
       0.311             53.013
       0.355             38.135
       0.400             19.892
       0.444              0.125
       0.489            -19.221
       0.533            -36.280
       0.578            -49.453
       0.622            -57.549
       0.666            -59.896
       0.711            -56.393
       0.755            -47.508
       0.800            -34.218
       0.844            -17.909
       0.889             -0.223
       0.933             17.095
       0.977             32.378
       1.022             44.190
       1.066             51.466
       1.111             53.599
       1.155             50.496
       1.200             42.574
       1.244             30.704
       1.288             16.122
       1.333              0.300
       1.377            -15.203
       1.422            -28.895
       1.466            -39.488
       1.511            -46.025
       1.555            -47.964
       1.599            -45.216
       1.644            -38.152
       1.688            -27.550
       1.733            -14.513
       1.777             -0.358
       1.822             13.521
       1.866             25.786
       1.910             35.285
       1.955             41.160
       1.999             42.921
       2.044             40.488
       2.088             34.189
       2.133             24.719
       2.177             13.064
       2.221              0.400
       2.266            -12.024
       2.310            -23.011
       2.355            -31.529
       2.399            -36.808
       2.444            -38.408
       2.488            -36.254
       2.532            -30.638
       2.577            -22.180
       2.621            -11.760
```

FIGURE 5.10. The output of the program of Figure 4.9 when run with the values shown. This shows three cycles with 20 points per cycle. Compare with Figures 6.6–6.8. (Case Study 9.)

Let us state the method in terms of a system of three simultaneous equations in three unknowns.

$$a_{11}x_1 + a_{12}x_2 + a_{13}x_3 = a_{14}$$
$$a_{21}x_1 + a_{22}x_2 + a_{23}x_3 = a_{24}$$
$$a_{31}x_1 + a_{32}x_2 + a_{33}x_3 = a_{34}$$

Suppose we make guesses at the values of x_2 and x_3—it doesn't matter whether they are good guesses; zeros will work. Then we solve the first equation for x_1, writing a prime to indicate that this is a new approximation:

$$x'_1 = \frac{a_{14} - a_{12}x_2 - a_{13}x_3}{a_{11}}$$

Now using this new value for x_1 and the initial guess at x_3, we solve the second equation for x_2:

$$x'_2 = \frac{a_{24} - a_{21}x'_1 - a_{23}x_3}{a_{22}}$$

Finally, using the new approximations to x_1 and x_2, we solve the third equation for x_3:

$$x'_3 = \frac{a_{34} - a_{31}x'_1 - a_{32}x'_2}{a_{33}}$$

This process of computing a new value for each of the variables constitutes one *iteration*. Now we perform another iteration, always using the most recently computed value of each variable. If the system of equations satisfies certain conditions that we shall state shortly, the approximations will eventually converge to a solution of the system, regardless of the initial guesses used.

A *sufficient* condition for convergence is that the main diagonal coefficient in each row should dominate the other coefficients in that row, which means that

$$|a_{ii}| > \sum_{j \neq i} |a_{ij}| \quad \begin{array}{l} i = 1, 2, \ldots, n \\ n = \text{number of equations} \end{array}$$

We emphasize that this condition is *sufficient*. *Necessary* conditions are considerably less stringent but, unfortunately, are beyond the scope of this book. In other words, there are systems of equations in which the main diagonal terms do not all dominate their rows, yet the Gauss-Seidel iteration method, as it is called, still converges to a solution. See Figures 5.14 and

5.16 for examples of the convergence and non-convergence of small systems.

We shall write a program that will apply the Gauss-Seidel method to a system of equations of any size up to 80 equations. The program will include the reading of the coefficients and constant terms, of which there could be a total of 6480 in the largest case. The program will perform a certain amount of data validation as the input is read. A test for convergence will determine when to stop making successive iterations and there will be a maximum number of iterations permitted; the convergence criterion and the maximum number of iterations to be permitted will be read as data, along with the numbers defining the system of equations. Zeros will be used for starting guesses.

Figure 5.11 is a flowchart of the method that will be followed. The first action to be taken is to clear the arrays holding the coefficients and the unknowns. Clearing the X array to zeros establishes the starting guesses, and clearing the A array makes it unnecessary to provide data cards for elements that are zero. This clearing will involve two DO statements, which we could naturally flowchart in detail; however, complete and agonizing detail on something so simple is not always required in a flowchart. The next action is to read N, MAXIT (the maximum number of iterations to be permitted), EPSLON (the convergence criterion), and BIGGST (a maximum size to be permitted of any coefficient, as a validity check). Then we compute N + 1 to avoid computing it repeatedly in the loops, set an error count to zero, and compute the maximum number of data cards that there can legitimately be. This will be N^2 for the coefficients, N for the constant terms (which are stored in the same array in this formulation), and one for the sentinel card that contains a 99 where the row number normally appears on the data card, to signal the end of the data. If more than this many cards are read without detecting the sentinel, something is wrong, and we shall stop program execution.

Now we come to the reading, and here we introduce a new flowchart symbol to try to simplify the presentation of the actions involved in the DO statement. The American National Standards Institute (ANSI) flowcharting standard does not suggest a form for this operation, presumably because languages differ so greatly,

and what could be convenient in Fortran might not be much help to people using the other languages. The form adopted here is that used in *Computer Science: A First Course*.*

It will be seen that the condensed representation places the initialization, incrementing, and testing of the DO index all in one rectangular box that is divided into three portions. We are to understand that after setting the index equal to its initial value in the small box in the upper left, the range is immediately executed, without any testing. Every time the range has been executed we return to the incrementing box in the lower left and then move to the testing box on the right.

This first DO is used only to count the number of cards that are read, so that we can stop if there are too many (which would possibly indicate that the value of N was wrong). After reading a card we check whether the indicated row number is 99 and if it is not we carry out the validity checks that we have suggested by the phrase "Valid data?" without detailing them. The checks will consist of determining that the row and column numbers are not out of range and that the data value is no larger than BIGGST. If the data is acceptable, we store it in the correct place in the array and go back for more. If it is not, we write an error message that will identify the data for correction, and add one to the count of bad cards, NERROR. Upon detecting the sentinel (99), we immediately check whether NERROR is zero; if it is, there were no data errors and we can get to work. Otherwise we write an error message and stop.

The first operation in the second part of the flowchart, the DO that is reached at connector 1, is to set up a count of the number of iterations, which establishes MAXIT as the maximum number to be permitted. If the process does not converge to a solution in MAXIT iterations, we write an error message and stop.

Within each iteration the first operation is to set a variable named RESID to zero. RESID, the name of which is meant to stand for "residual," is set up to hold the absolute value of the largest difference between an old value of a variable and a newly computed value. When

---

*Alexandra I. Forsythe, Thomas A. Keenan, Elliott I. Organick, and Warren Stenberg, *Computer Science: A First Course*, New York, Wiley, 1969.

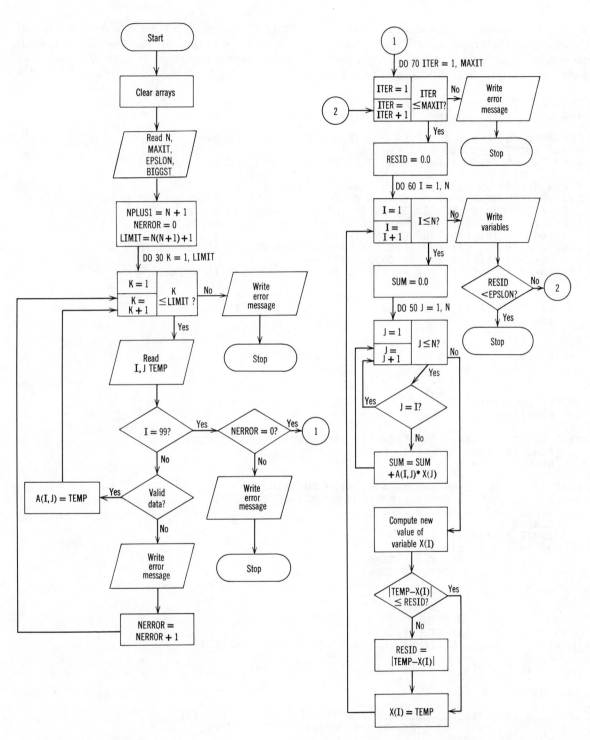

FIGURE 5.11.   A flowchart of a method for solving a system of simultaneous equations by the Gauss-Seidel method. See text for a description of the flowchart symbol used to represent the actions of a DO statement. (Case Study 10.)

this largest difference is less than EPSLON (for "epsilon") we shall have arrived at two successive sets of approximations to the unknowns, where no two values differ by more than EPSLON. The next DO controls an index named I, which picks out an equation. Within each equation, we now need to form the sum of all terms of the form A(I, J)*X(J) except that for

```
C CASE STUDY 10
C THE GAUSS-SEIDEL METHOD FOR SOLVING SIMULTANEOUS EQUATIONS
C
C THE PROGRAM SOLVES A SYSTEM OF N EQUATIONS IN N UNKNOWNS.
C N MAY NOT EXCEED 80; N IS READ AS INPUT.
C ONLY THE NON-ZERO ELEMENTS NEED BE ENTERED, ONE ELEMENT PER DATA
C    CARD, WITH ROW AND COLUMN NUMBERS ON EACH CARD.
C A ROW NUMBER OF 99 ACTS AS AN END-OF-DATA SENTINEL.
C THE PROGRAM READS THE FOLLOWING PARAMETERS PRIOR TO ENTERING THE DATA
C    N -- THE NUMBER OF EQUATIONS IN THE SYSTEM FOR THIS RUN
C    MAXIT -- THE MAXIMUM NUMBER OF ITERATIONS TO BE PERMITTED
C    EPSLON -- THE CONVERGENCE CRITERION
C    BIGGST -- THE MAXIMUM SIZE (IN ABSOLUTE VALUE) TO BE PERMITTED
C        OF ANY COEFFICIENT OR CONSTANT TERM
C ALL INPUT IS CHECKED FOR VALIDITY, EVEN IF AN ERROR IS FOUND.
C
C
        DIMENSION A(80, 81), X(80)
        LOGICAL OK
C
C CLEAR ARRAYS
        DO 20 I = 1, 80
            X(I) = 0.0
            DO 10 J = 1, 81
                A(I, J) = 0.0
   10       CONTINUE
   20   CONTINUE
C
C READ CONTROL PARAMETERS DESCRIBED IN INTRODUCTORY COMMENTS
        READ (5, 100) N, MAXIT, EPSLON, BIGGST
        NPLUS1 = N + 1
C
C READ THE ELEMENTS OF THE ARRAYS, WITH CHECKING
C DO LOOP IS USED TO CONTROL MAXIMUM NUMBER OF ELEMENTS
C FIRST SET ERROR COUNT TO ZERO
        NERROR = 0
        LIMIT = N*NPLUS1 + 1
        DO 30 K = 1, LIMIT
            READ (5, 100) I, J, TEMP
            IF ( I .EQ. 99 ) GO TO 41
            OK = .TRUE.
            IF (      (I .LT. 1)
   1            .OR. (I .GT. N)
   2            .OR. (J .LT. 1)
   3            .OR. (J .GT. NPLUS1)
   4            .OR. (ABS(TEMP) .GT. BIGGST) ) OK = .FALSE.
            IF (      OK ) A(I, J) = TEMP
            IF ( .NOT. OK ) WRITE (6, 110) I, J, TEMP
            IF ( .NOT. OK ) NERROR = NERROR + 1
   30   CONTINUE
C
C IF DO IS SATISFIED, THERE WERE TOO MANY DATA CARDS FOR THE
C    VALUE OF N THAT WAS SPECIFIED -- WRITE ERROR COMMENT
        WRITE (6, 120)
        STOP
```

FIGURE 5.12. A program for solving a system of simultaneous equations by the Gauss-Seidel method, corresponding to the flowchart of Figure 5.11. (Case Study 10.)

```
C
C ALL DATA CARDS HAVE BEEN READ -- CHECK ERROR COUNT AND STOP IF ANY
   41  IF ( NERROR .NE. 0 ) WRITE (6, 130) NERROR
       IF ( NERROR .NE. 0 ) STOP
C
C      BEGIN ITERATION SCHEME -- DO LOOP COUNTS THE NUMBER OF ITERATIONS
       DO 70 ITER = 1, MAXIT
C
C          ... NEXT STATEMENT IS EXECUTED ONCE PER SWEEP OF THE SYSTEM
           RESID = 0.0
C
C          ... INDEX I SELECTS A ROW
           DO 60 I = 1, N
C
C              ... NEXT STATEMENT IS EXECUTED ONCE PER ROW
               SUM = 0.0
C
C              ... GET SUM OF TERMS IN ROW I, NOT INCLUDING DIAGONAL TERM
               DO 50 J = 1, N
                   IF ( J .NE. I ) SUM = SUM + A(I,J)*X(J)
   50          CONTINUE
C
C              ... COMPUTE THE NEW APPROXIMATION TO VARIABLE X(I)
               TEMP = (A(I, NPLUS1) - SUM) / A(I,I)
C
C              ... AT THE END OF A SWEEP OF ALL EQUATIONS, THE FOLLOWING
C              ... STATEMENT WILL HAVE PUT LARGEST RESIDUAL IN RESID
               IF ( ABS(TEMP - X(I)) .GT. RESID ) RESID = ABS(TEMP - X(I))
C
C              ... STORE NEW APPROXIMATION TO VARIABLE X(I)
               X(I) = TEMP
   60      CONTINUE
C
C          ... ONE SWEEP HAS NOW BEEN COMPLETED --  PRINT VARIABLES
           WRITE (6, 140) (X(K), K = 1, N)
C
C          ... IF LARGEST RESIDUAL LESS THAN EPSLON, PROCESS HAS CONVERGED
           IF ( RESID .LT. EPSLON ) STOP
   70  CONTINUE
C
C IF THIS OUTER DO IS EVER SATISFIED, MORE THAN MAXIT ITERATIONS WOULD
C    BE NEEDED FOR CONVERGENCE -- WRITE ERROR COMMENT AND GIVE UP
       WRITE (6, 150) MAXIT
       STOP
C
C
  100  FORMAT (2I2, 2F10.0)
  110  FORMAT (1X, 'ERROR IN CARD WITH I = ',I2,', J = ',I2,
      1    ', VALUE = ', 1PE14.6)
  120  FORMAT ('0', 'DECK CONTAINED TOO MANY CARDS')
  130  FORMAT ('0', 'ERRORS FOUND IN ', I4, '  DATA CARDS - JOB ABORTED')
  140  FORMAT ('0', 8F12.5)
  150  FORMAT ('0', 'PROCESS DID NOT CONVERGE IN', I4, ' ITERATIONS')
       END
```

FIGURE 5.12. (Cont.)

which I = J, that is, all except the main diagonal term. When this sum has been formed, we are ready to compute a new approximation to a variable, check whether the difference between the new and old values is greater than RESID and place it in RESID if so, store the new value in the location for the variable, and go to the next row. When all N rows have been dealt with we have computed new values for all N variables. To observe the convergence of the process we shall print all the approximations; in a realistic application we would probably want only the final results. Now, finally, we make the test for convergence and go back for a complete new iteration if we have not converged.

Once again, most of the work of understanding an algorithm is over when the flowchart has been assimilated, assuming that the logic of the program and the logic of the flowchart really are equivalent. We need only point out a few features of the program shown in Figure 5.12, primarily things that were not presented in complete detail in the flowchart.

Observe that the reading of data is done with a statement

```
READ (5, 100) I, J, TEMP
```

and that only after making the rudimentary validity checks do we have

```
A(I, J) = TEMP
```

Why not write the READ statement in the first place as

```
READ (5, 100) I, J, A(I, J)
```

and avoid the later statement? This seems so plausible that the author and nobody knows how many thousands of other programmers have done it in this kind of program, only to waste some minutes or hours trying to figure out a diagnostic message reading something like "address exception at 12D49." The problem is that when we reach the sentinel, or in the case of any row or column number that is erroneously out of range, we are referring to an array location that does not exist. When this happens the system will come up with some kind of storage address that either destroys a part of our program or data, or gets outside the part of memory assigned to us. In the latter case, and assuming that the computer has memory protection as most machines do, we are summarily thrown off the machine, possibly with some cryptic error comment.

Observe that we have used a logical variable named OK to store the result of the test as to whether the data point is valid. This was done to simplify the three logical IF statements that carry out the actions that are appropriate to each outcome of the test. Naturally, the program could be set up to do the same actions without the logical variable or the three logical IFs, using GO TOs. The choice is up to the programmer; in this text we are urging the point of view that this way is easier to understand and thus less likely to be in error.

The rest of the program follows the flowchart quite closely, and, with careful study, should be clear. One excellent way to study such a flowchart and program is to take a sample system that is small enough to be manageable but large enough to be representative (four or five equations, in this case), and follow the program or the flowchart in terms of the example.

Figure 5.13 displays a system of seven equations that meets the sufficient conditions for convergence of the Gauss-Seidel method, and in Figure 5.14 we see the output of the program when it was run with a deck defining this system. The convergence criterion used was EPSLON = 0.00002.

In Figure 5.15 we have the output when a test deck containing many deliberate errors was run, and in Figure 5.16 we have the output when the program was tried with this system:

$$4x_1 + 3x_2 + 2x_3 = 4$$
$$4x_1 + 8x_2 - 4x_3 = -24$$
$$3x_1 - 3x_2 + 7x_3 = 30$$

This system does have a solution ($x_1 = 1$, $x_2 = -2$, $x_3 = 3$), but the main diagonal term in the first equation is not greater than the sum of the absolute values of the other terms in that equation, and the method diverges.

In actual use, the Gauss-Seidel method would always be used with techniques to accelerate the convergence, along the lines sketched in Exercise 29. With a proper choice of the acceleration factor, the method may become convergent when applied to a system such as this one.

In Figure 5.17 we have 11 successive approximations to the solution of a heat distribution problem in the interior of a rectangular plate. The field descriptor in FORMAT statement 140 was modified to get the 12 numbers all on one line. Problems of this sort, except very much larger, are typical applications of simultaneous equations and of digital computers. Since the coefficients barely meet the criterion for convergence of the Gauss-Seidel method, acceleration is often particularly valuable.

12.418 X_1	−1.061 X_2	2.669 X_3	4.361 X_4	−0.119 X_5	−1.209 X_6	−0.500 X_7 = 8.262
−1.501 X_1	19.832 X_2	0.694 X_3	−4.816 X_4	2.274 X_5	2.001 X_6	−1.909 X_7 = −33.818
2.308 X_1	1.728 X_2	−15.165 X_3	−2.023 X_4	1.104 X_5	2.107 X_6	−1.000 X_7 = −52.673
3.359 X_1	−0.913 X_2	−6.441 X_3	27.864 X_4	3.737 X_5	−4.375 X_6	−2.375 X_7 = −97.284
−1.562 X_1	1.168 X_2	−2.004 X_3	1.818 X_4	9.490 X_5	0.401 X_6	−1.073 X_7 = 20.351
1.174 X_1	7.318 X_2	−2.278 X_3	−0.143 X_4	−9.835 X_5	−31.670 X_6	4.114 X_7 = 149.919
0.109 X_1	−1.313 X_2	−0.900 X_3	−1.972 X_4	−3.514 X_5	−1.107 X_6	12.094 X_7 = 81.653

FIGURE 5.13. A system of seven simultaneous equations to be solved by the Gauss-Seidel method, using the program in Figure 5.12. (Case Study 10.)

0.66532	−1.65487	3.38602	−2.84311	3.71733	−6.47663	6.84153
0.47516	−1.59238	2.66309	−3.91757	4.77873	−5.85327	6.98649
1.08991	−1.95212	3.01331	−3.95463	4.99529	−5.98706	7.01259
0.98702	−1.98998	2.99374	−3.99582	4.99538	−5.99466	7.00057
1.00123	−1.99862	3.00015	−3.99856	4.99962	−5.99946	7.00032
0.99964	−1.99966	2.99982	−3.99982	4.99984	−5.99983	7.00002
1.00002	−1.99994	3.00000	−3.99995	4.99998	−5.99998	7.00001
0.99999	−1.99999	2.99999	−3.99999	4.99999	−5.99999	7.00000
1.00000	−2.00000	3.00000	−4.00000	4.99999	−6.00000	7.00000

FIGURE 5.14. The output of the program of Figure 5.12 when run using the data of Figure 5.13. The nine lines are the nine successive iterates to the values of the seven variables. (Case Study 10.)

```
ERROR IN CARD WITH I =  0, J =  2, VALUE =  -1.061000E 00
ERROR IN CARD WITH I =  6, J =  3, VALUE =   2.669000E 00
ERROR IN CARD WITH I =  1, J =  0, VALUE =   4.360999E 00
ERROR IN CARD WITH I =  1, J =  9, VALUE =  -1.190000E-01
ERROR IN CARD WITH I =  2, J =  1, VALUE =   3.315010E 02
ERROR IN CARD WITH I =  0, J =  0, VALUE =  -8.448999E 00
ERROR IN CARD WITH I =  8, J =  5, VALUE =  -3.303099E 01
ERROR IN CARD WITH I =  4, J =  8, VALUE =  -7.069089E 02

ERRORS FOUND IN   8  DATA CARDS - JOB ABORTED
```

FIGURE 5.15. The use of the program of Figure 5.12 when run with a set of intentionally erroneous data cards. (Case Study 10.)

```
1.00000     -3.50000     2.35714

2.44643     -3.04464     1.93240

2.31728     -3.19244     1.92441

2.43213     -3.25386     1.84886

2.51596     -3.33355     1.77878

2.61077     -3.41599     1.70282

2.71059     -3.50389     1.62237

2.81673     -3.59718     1.53690

2.92944     -3.69627     1.44613

3.04914     -3.80150     1.34973
```

PROCESS DID NOT CONVERGE IN 10 ITERATIONS

FIGURE 5.16.   The output of the program of Figure 5.12
when run with a system of equations that does have a
solution but does not meet the conditions for convergence of the Gauss-Seidel method. (Case Study 10.)

3.500	2.625	2.156	2.539	1.875	1.344	0.875	1.354	0.969	0.578	0.363	0.679
4.625	3.781	3.299	3.163	2.734	2.203	1.805	1.912	1.328	0.974	0.864	0.944
5.129	4.408	3.844	3.439	3.165	2.768	2.347	2.182	1.535	1.292	1.146	1.082
5.393	4.751	4.134	3.579	3.424	3.114	2.644	2.326	1.679	1.485	1.303	1.157
5.544	4.948	4.293	3.655	3.584	3.314	2.809	2.405	1.767	1.596	1.391	1.199
5.633	5.060	4.381	3.697	3.679	3.429	2.901	2.449	1.819	1.660	1.440	1.222
5.685	5.124	4.430	3.720	3.733	3.495	2.954	2.474	1.848	1.696	1.468	1.235
5.714	5.160	4.458	3.733	3.764	3.532	2.983	2.488	1.865	1.716	1.484	1.243
5.731	5.180	4.474	3.741	3.782	3.553	3.000	2.496	1.875	1.728	1.493	1.247
5.741	5.192	4.483	3.745	3.792	3.565	3.009	2.500	1.880	1.734	1.498	1.249
5.746	5.199	4.488	3.747	3.798	3.572	3.014	2.503	1.883	1.738	1.501	1.251

FIGURE 5.17.   The output of the program of Figure 5.12 when run with data giving the temperatures at
points on the edges of a rectangular plate; these approximations represent temperatures in the interior of
the plate. MAXIT and EPSLOM were both changed for this run as was FORMAT statement 140.

*1. Two one-dimensional arrays named A and B each contain 30 elements. Write a program segment using a DO statement to compute

$$D = \left(\sum_{i=1}^{30} (A_i - B_i)^2 \right)^{1/2}$$

2. Given a one-dimensional array named X that contains 50 elements, write a program segment using a DO statement to compute the 49 elements of another array, named DX, from

$$DX(I) = X(I + 1) - X(I)$$
$$I = 1, 2, \ldots, 49$$

3. A two-dimensional array named AMATR contains 10 rows and 10 columns. A one-dimensional array named DIAG contains 10 elements. Write a program segment to compute the elements of DIAG from

$$DIAG(I) = AMATR(I, I)$$
$$I = 1, 2, \ldots, 10$$

*4. A one-dimensional array named M contains 20 integers. Write a program segment using a DO statement to replace each element by itself, multiplied by its element number. In other words, replace m_i by $i \cdot m_i$, $i = 1, 2, \ldots, 20$.

*5. Two one-dimensional arrays named R and S have 40 elements each. The number of elements containing valid data is given by the value of a previously computed integer variable M. Compute the first M elements of any array named T, which also has 40 elements, according to

$$T(i) = R(i) + S(i)$$
$$i = 1, 2, \ldots, M$$

If R, S, and T are thought of as vectors, this is the operation of vector addition.

6. Two one-dimensional arrays, A and B, have 18 elements each. N is an integer, the value of which does not exceed 18. Compute

$$C = \sum_{k=1}^{N} A_k B_k$$

If A and B are thought of as vectors, then C is their scalar (or inner) product.

*7. A one-dimensional array named F contains 50 elements. Each of the first M elements, except the first and Mth, is to be replaced by

$$F_i = \frac{F_{i-1} + F_i + F_{i+1}}{3}$$

This is an example of techniques for *smoothing* experimental data to reduce the effect of random errors.

*8. A one-dimensional array named B contains 50 elements. Place the largest of these elements in BIGB and the element number of BIGB in NBIGB.

9. Two one-dimensional arrays named X and Y contain 50 elements each. A variable named XS is known to be equal to one of the elements in X. If $XS = X_i$, place Y_i in YS.

This kind of *table search* has a wide variety of applications, such as finding a value in a table of electric utility rates from a rate code or finding the numerical code corresponding to an alphabetic name.

*10. A two-dimensional array A contains 15 rows and 15 columns. A one-dimensional array X contains 15 elements. Compute the 15 elements of a one-dimensional array B according to

$$B_i = \sum_{j=1}^{15} A_{ij} X_j \qquad i = 1, 2, \ldots, 15$$

This can be viewed as multiplication of a matrix and a vector.

11. Three two-dimensional arrays A, B, and C have 15 rows and 15 columns each. Given the arrays A and B, compute the elements of C from

$$C_{ij} = \sum_{k=1}^{15} A_{ik} B_{kj} \qquad i, j = 1, 2, \ldots, 15$$

This is matrix multiplication.

*12. A two-dimensional array named RST has 20 rows and 20 columns. Compute the product of the main diagonal elements of RST and store it in DPROD. A main diagonal element is one that has the same row and column number, so that

$$DPROD = \prod_{i=1}^{20} RST(I, I)$$

*13. The formula

$$Y = 41.298\sqrt{1 + x^2} + x^{1/3}e^x$$

is to be evaluated for

$$x = 1.00, 1.01, 1.02, \ldots, 3.00$$

Each $x - y$ pair is to be printed on a separate line, with 1PE20.6 field descriptors. Write a program using a DO loop to carry out this computation.

14. The formula

$$z = \frac{e^{ax} - e^{-ax}}{2}\sin(x + b) + a\log\frac{b + x}{2}$$

is to be evaluated for all combinations of

$$x: 1.0(0.1)2.0$$
$$a: 0.10(0.05)0.80$$
$$b: 1.0(1.0)10.0$$

where x: 1.0(0.1)2.0 means $x = 1.0$, 1.1, 1.2, . . . , 2.0, and so on. For each combination of x, a, and b (there are 1650 combinations) a line giving x, a, b, and z is to be written. Write a program containing three DO loops to carry out this computation.

*15. A solution to the following specialized system of equations is to be found:

$$a_{11}x_1 \qquad\qquad\qquad = b_1$$
$$a_{21}x_1 + a_{22}x_2 \qquad\qquad = b_2$$
$$a_{31}x_1 + a_{32}x_2 + a_{33}x_3 \qquad = b_3$$

$$\cdots\cdots\cdots\cdots\cdots\cdots\cdots\cdots\cdots$$

$$a_{n1}x_1 + a_{n2}x_2 + a_{n3}x_3 + \cdots + a_{nn}x_n = b_n$$

First write a program to solve this system on the assumption that the a's are contained in a two-dimensional array that will have zeros for the missing elements. This is a moderately simple program: first solve for x_1, substitute this result into equation 2, and so on.

The difficulty, from the standpoint of computer solution, is that there is a great deal of wasted space in the array, which uselessly restricts the size of the system that can be solved. Devise a method of storing the coefficients in a *one*-dimensional array and write a program to find the unknowns. Assume that it must be possible to handle a maximum of 100 equations in 100 unknowns. The actual number of equations is given by the value of N.

16. Same as Exercise 15, except that the system of equations is

$$a_{1,1}x_1 + \cdots + a_{1,n-2}x_{n-2} + a_{1,n-1}x_{n-1} + a_{1,n}x_n = a_{1,n+1}$$

$$\cdots\cdots\cdots\cdots\cdots\cdots\cdots\cdots\cdots\cdots\cdots\cdots\cdots\cdots$$

$$a_{n-2,n-2}x_{n-2} + a_{n-2,n-1}x_{n-1} + a_{n-2,n}x_n = a_{n-2,n+1}$$
$$a_{n-1,n-1}x_{n-1} + a_{n-1,n}x_n = a_{n-1,n+1}$$
$$a_{n,n}x_n = a_{n,n+1}$$

Note that it is *not* possible in most Fortrans to write a statement like

```
DO 12 I = N, 1, -1
```

which would be handy here. An equivalent "IF loop" must be written to work backward through the x's. Alternatively we may write

```
DO 12 K = 1, N
I = N - K + 1
```

I is then used as the subscript; it will vary from N downward to 1.

17. Given a two-dimensional array named C, with 10 rows and 11 columns, compare C(1,1) with all other elements in the first column, looking for the element with the largest absolute value; make the value of L equal to the row number of the element in column 1 with the largest value. If at the end of these operations L = 1, do nothing more; otherwise exchange the elements in row 1 with the elements in row L, whatever it is.

18. Rewrite the program of the Case Study 8, Figure 4.3, to use DO statements wherever their use will simplify the programming.

19. Let us assume that it is permissible for a variable in a subscript expression to be itself a subscripted variable. Most Fortran systems do in fact permit this and in those that do not we can readily program it as sketched below. Using this facility, rewrite the sorting program of Figure 5.6 as follows.

We establish a new one-dimensional integer array named NELMNT. At the beginning of the program, we load each element with its element number, so that NELMNT(I) = I. Then during the process of comparing elements in the X array we make two changes. First, whenever it has been established that two elements, call them J and K, should be exchanged, we in fact do nothing at all with the X array elements but instead exchange elements J and K of NELMNT. Second, whenever we wish to refer to an element of X in the testing, the subscript of X becomes the appropriate subscripted value of NELMNT. For instance, the comparison of two elements of X might involve a statement like:

```
   IF ( X(NELMNT(I)) .GT.
 1      X(NELMNT(J)) ) GO TO 20
```

In a Fortran system in which subscript expressions may not contain subscripted variables, we can replace such a statement with a combination of statements having the same effect, such as:

```
 NI = NELMNT(I)
 NJ = NELMNT(J)
 IF ( X(NI) .GT. X(NJ) ) GO TO 20
```

When we have gone through a complete scan of the X array, carrying out all exchanges of the NELMNT array that may be called for, the arrangement of elements of NELMNT will specify the order in which the elements of X and Y should be picked up to place them in ascending sequence on the X values.

In many practical sorting problems the records to be sorted are a great deal longer than two computer words. A technique such as this, which greatly reduces data movement, is then highly advantageous.

20. The method of sorting described in Section 5.5 is only one of many techniques that have been devised for the purpose. One of the disadvantages of the method we displayed is that it takes no advantage of any existing order in the records as they appear at the beginning of the sorting process. If the records are in fact already completely in sequence, the method of Section 5.5 will require exactly as many tests of the X array as any other initial arrangement although there will, of course, be no data interchanges. One method that does take some advantage of initial ordering is called *bubble sorting* and can be described as follows.

We compare the first and second records and exchange if necessary; then we compare the second and third, the third and fourth, always exchanging as necessary, . . . , and finally the N − 1st and Nth.

We call such a complete scan through the file of records a *pass*. A total of at most N − 1 passes through the file will guarantee placing it in an ascending sequence, but it may easily happen that fewer than N − 1 passes will suffice. A very simple way to determine if this has happened is to count the number of interchanges required in each pass; whenever that number turns out to be zero the job is done. If the file was already in exactly correct order we will discover that fact after one pass.

The number of passes required by this method is somewhat sensitive to the details of initial ordering. The worst case, in one sense, is a file which is in correct sequence with the exception that the smallest item is initially at the end of the file. Such a file, which after all does exhibit a great deal of initial ordering, will nevertheless require N passes because that smallest item can only "bubble up" through the file by one position on each pass. This problem is readily alleviated, however, if we make alternate passes through the file in opposite directions. A file like the one just described will then be sorted in three passes regardless of its length. In the first pass the smallest item will move from the Nth position to the N − 1st; in the second pass it will move from the N − 1st position to its correct position at the top; a final pass will be necessary to discover that the process has been completed.

Write a sorting program along the lines of that in Figure 5.6 using bubble sorting, with or without the alternating direction refinement. As a further refinement incorporate the subscripting techniques in Exercise 19.

21. Suppose you have a one-dimensional array named X consisting of 50,000 integers, a great many of which are zeros. For the sake of saving space for long-term storage we wish to *compress* this array by eliminating most of the zeros. One technique for doing this might be as follows. To make this task as simple as possible, we shall assume (unrealistically) that all legitimate data values are either zero or positive. A negative number can therefore be used as a signal that zeros have been eliminated and can

at the same time record a count of the number of consecutive zeros that have been eliminated. There is clearly no point to recording the elimination of just one zero so the scheme would be to leave single zeros alone but replace any string of two or more consecutive zeros by a negative integer stating how many were omitted.

Write two routines, one to pack the array as it originally occurs and the other to unpack it when such a packed file is read. Some means will have to be provided to indicate the length of the compressed array such as an ending sentinel or a total word-count in the first element.

22. One series for inverse sine is

$$\sin^{-1} x = x + \frac{x^3}{2 \cdot 3} + \frac{1 \cdot 3x^5}{2 \cdot 4 \cdot 5}$$
$$+ \frac{1 \cdot 3 \cdot 5x^7}{2 \cdot 4 \cdot 6 \cdot 7} + \cdots$$

This can be evaluated directly, with a loop developing one term at a time, or the series can be rewritten as:

$$\sin^{-1} x$$
$$= x\left(\frac{1}{1} + \frac{1x^2}{2}\left(\frac{1}{3} + \frac{3x^2}{4}\left(\frac{1}{5} + \frac{5x^2}{6}\left(\frac{1}{7} + \cdots\right)\right)\right)\right)$$

To evaluate the rewritten series, which involves very much less arithmetic for the same number of terms, requires determining in advance how many terms are to be computed, since the nested parenthesized expression must be evaluated from the inside out.

Write a program, using a DO loop to generate the integers needed in the nested version, to evaluate this series. Let $x = 0.5$, evaluate the series, and multiply the result by 6.0 to provide an estimate for the value of π.

23. As shipping clerk you are responsible for shipping quantities of products from one location to another as cheaply as possible. Since it is generally less expensive to send 50 items in one large carton than 25 in each of two cartons, the problem is filling the biggest boxes first.

Read cards containing, in any convenient format, the following information:

(a) Stock number (NSTOCK).
(b) Number of items to be shipped (NOITEM).
(c) Maximum number of items that can be contained in the largest-sized box (NSIZE1).
(d) Maximum number of items that can be contained in the middle-sized box (NSIZE2).
(e) Maximum number of items that can be contained in the smallest-sized box (NSIZE3).

It is to be understood that NSIZE1 > NSIZE2 > NSIZE3, and that there may be only one or two sizes of boxes, which will be signalled by NSIZE3 = 0 if there are only two and NSIZE2 = NSIZE3 = 0 if there is only one size.

For each card, write a line containing:

(a) NSTOCK
(b) NUM1 = number of boxes of NSIZE1
(c) NUM2 = number of boxes of NSIZE2
(d) NUM3 = number of boxes of NSIZE3

A negative NSTOCK will signal the end of the deck.

Your program should place as many of the items as possible in the largest box, then place any remaining items in the smallest box in which they will fit.

Since this exercise appears in this chapter, the implication is that a DO statement would be useful in solving it. Could you do it more simply without a DO?

(Suggested by Professor H. George Friedman, Jr., Department of Computer Science, University of Illinois.)

*24. The binomial distribution is given by

$$b(x) = \binom{n}{x} p^x q^{n-x}$$

where

$$\binom{n}{x} = \frac{n!}{x!(n-x)!}$$

n and x are integers, and $p = 1 - q$.

Write a program that, given n, x, and p, computes b. Your program should use DO loops to compute the factorials. Estimate the maximum sizes of n and x that will not cause floating point overflow on your computer.

25. If the mean rate of arrivals at a traffic toll booth is m per time period, then the probability that exactly x arrive during a given time period is given by the Poisson distribution*

$$P(x) = e^{-m}m^x/x!$$

Given values of M and X, both integer variables, write a program segment to compute P. Include a type statement for X. You may assume that M and X are small enough that no term will exceed the size permitted of a real variable in your computer. Use a loop to compute $x!$.

26. Rewrite your program segment for Exercise 25 to remove the assumption that M and X are reasonably small. Now it will be impossible to compute e^{-m}, m^x, and $x!$ separately, because each separately would be outside the size range permitted for a real number in the computer. Try assuming that $m < x$ and rewrite the formula as

$$\frac{e^{-m}\, m^x}{x!}$$
$$= \left(\prod_{i=1}^{20} \frac{e^{-1}m}{i} \right)\left(\frac{m^{x-m}}{(x)(x-1)\cdots(m+1)} \right)$$

$m < x$, both integers. Estimate the maximum sizes for the M and X that would permit this approach to be used in your computer.

27. In Exercise 26, approximate $x!$ from Stirling's formula

$$n! \cong (2\pi)^{1/2}\, n^{n+1/2}\, e^{-n}$$

Take natural logarithms and rearrange to show that

$$P(x) \cong \exp\left\{ (x - m) - \tfrac{1}{2}\log 2\pi x + x \log \frac{m}{x} \right\}$$

Write an assignment statement for this formula. Combine the program segments from these two exercises into a complete program that compares the probability as computed from the two formulas, for a variety of pairs of values of x and m. If the results differ greatly, except for small x, say less than 4 or 5, the problem is in your

program, since Stirling's formula is accurate within 1% for values greater than about 9.

28. Figure 5.18 gives the 1972 United States draft lottery numbers in order from January 1 to December 31, for men born in 1953. Perform the following statistical tests on these 365 numbers.

(If this exercise is to be assigned for a class, some cooperation on the data preparation is very much in order. The most sensible way, if possible in your system, would be to enter the numbers in a disk file from which they could be read by all class members without having to repunch the cards. If this is to be done, your instructor will have to give you the details of one or two additional control cards that will be required in your program deck.)

(a) Perform a rank correlation test between these numbers and the integers from 1 to 365 in order. See Exercise 26, Chapter 4.

(b) Count the number of occurrences of adjacent pairs of numbers that differ by only 1, such as 259 and 258 for January 22 and 23.

(c) Any other tests you know.

29. Observe in the successive iterations of Figure 5.14 that after the first one or two lines each variable approaches its final value from the same direction, slowly arriving at a stable value. With such a convergent system, it can materially speed up the convergence to *accelerate* the process, as follows.

At the point where a new approximation to the ith variable has been computed but not yet stored (we called it x_i'), replace the old value of that variable, x_i, not with x_i' but with $x_i + \omega(x_i' - x_i)$. Assuming that ω is greater than 1.0, this will move the new approximation beyond what it would otherwise have been, in other words, accelerating the convergence.

The Gauss-Seidel method is almost always used with acceleration because the reduction in the number of iterations is almost always worth the trouble, and sometimes results in dramatic savings.

Even more interesting, in some cases, is the fact that a divergent system can sometimes be made to converge by *decelerating*

*See, for instance, C. West Churchman, Russell L. Ackoff, and E. Leonard Arnoff, *Introduction to Operations Research,* New York, Wiley, 1957, pp. 391–402.

Day	No.	Day	No.	Day	No.	Day	No.	Day	No.	Day	No.
1	150	62	220	123	166	184	109	245	17	306	214
2	328	63	47	124	172	185	92	246	226	307	232
3	42	64	266	125	292	186	139	247	356	308	339
4	28	65	1	126	337	187	132	248	354	309	223
5	338	66	2	127	145	188	285	249	173	310	211
6	36	67	153	128	201	189	355	250	144	311	299
7	111	68	321	129	276	190	179	251	97	312	312
8	206	69	331	130	100	191	89	252	364	313	151
9	197	70	239	131	307	192	202	253	217	314	257
10	37	71	44	132	115	193	340	254	334	315	159
11	174	72	244	133	49	194	306	255	43	316	66
12	126	73	117	134	224	195	305	256	229	317	124
13	298	74	152	135	165	196	359	257	353	318	237
14	341	75	94	136	101	197	74	258	235	319	176
15	221	76	363	137	273	198	199	259	225	320	209
16	309	77	357	138	98	199	121	260	189	321	284
17	231	78	358	139	148	200	332	261	289	322	160
18	72	79	262	140	274	201	33	262	228	323	270
19	303	80	300	141	310	202	5	263	141	324	301
20	161	81	317	142	333	203	286	264	123	325	287
21	99	82	22	143	216	204	365	265	268	326	102
22	259	83	71	144	246	205	324	266	296	327	320
23	258	84	65	145	122	206	35	267	236	328	180
24	62	85	24	146	118	207	204	268	291	329	25
25	243	86	181	147	293	208	60	269	29	330	344
26	311	87	45	148	18	209	185	270	248	331	135
27	110	88	21	149	133	210	222	271	70	332	130
28	304	89	213	150	48	211	200	272	196	333	147
29	283	90	326	151	67	212	253	273	184	334	134
30	114	91	12	152	15	213	323	274	215	335	170
31	240	92	108	153	360	214	27	275	128	336	90
32	112	93	104	154	245	215	3	276	103	337	56
33	278	94	280	155	207	216	313	277	79	338	250
34	54	95	254	156	230	217	63	278	86	339	31
35	68	96	88	157	87	218	208	279	41	340	336
36	96	97	163	158	251	219	57	280	129	341	267
37	271	98	50	159	282	220	131	281	157	342	210
38	154	99	234	160	83	221	7	282	116	343	120
39	347	100	272	161	178	222	249	283	342	344	73
40	136	101	350	162	64	223	125	284	319	345	82
41	361	102	23	163	190	224	198	285	171	346	85
42	26	103	169	164	318	225	329	286	269	347	335
43	195	104	81	165	95	226	205	287	14	348	38
44	263	105	343	166	16	227	241	288	277	349	137
45	348	106	119	167	32	228	19	289	59	350	187
46	308	107	183	168	91	229	8	290	177	351	294
47	227	108	242	169	238	230	113	291	192	352	13
48	46	109	158	170	52	231	105	292	167	353	168
49	11	110	314	171	77	232	162	293	352	354	149
50	127	111	4	172	315	233	30	294	288	355	80
51	106	112	264	173	146	234	140	295	191	356	188
52	316	113	279	174	212	235	302	296	193	357	252
53	20	114	362	175	61	236	138	297	256	358	155
54	247	115	255	176	143	237	290	298	9	359	6
55	261	116	233	177	345	238	76	299	78	360	351
56	260	117	265	178	330	239	34	300	325	361	194
57	51	118	55	179	53	240	40	301	327	362	156
58	186	119	93	180	75	241	84	302	349	363	175
59	295	120	69	181	142	242	182	303	346	364	281
60	203	121	58	182	39	243	218	304	10	365	164
61	322	122	275	183	297	244	219	305	107		

FIGURE 5.18   The United States draft lottery numbers for men born in 1953. In each column the number on the left gives the day of the year, numbered consecutively from January 1, onward, and the number on the right gives the selection sequence number for a man born on that date. See Exercise 28.

the process, that is, by using a value of $\omega < 1.0$.

Modify the program of Figure 5.12 to read a value of OMEGA along with the other parameters, and experiment with values of OMEGA to study the effect on convergence rate. It might be interesting, for example, to prepare a plot of the number of iterations required for convergence, as a function of OMEGA, for values of OMEGA from 1.0 to 1.9 in steps of 0.05.

The rate of convergence as a function of ω depends very strongly on the coefficients of the system.

30. Some large modern computers have extensive facilities for *parallel operation* of multiple arithmetic units. A machine might have, say, 64 separate arithmetic units, all operating simultaneously. Various architectures are possible, but we shall assume for this exercise that all of them operate on data contained in the same high-speed data storage.

Such machines are ideally suited for solving systems of simultaneous equations by the Gauss-Seidel method. Indeed, the primary motivation for building such machines has often been the need to solve huge systems of equations arising out of the solution of the partial differential equations of various physical systems, such as weather prediction or thermonuclear reactions.

It must be considered, however, that if many parallel processing elements are working at the same time, each one will be working entirely with *old* values for the variables, whereas our analysis assumed that, as soon as a new value had been computed from one equation, that new value would immediately be used in the next equation to get a new estimate for the next variable. We must expect, therefore, that convergence would require more iterations, although naturally each iteration would be carried out a great deal more rapidly than in a serial processor of the same basic speed.

Revise the program of Figure 5.12 to simulate the operation of a machine with at least as many parallel processing elements as there are equations. You will need another vector for the variables, so that in effect you keep separate the new and old

values; the iteration scheme is carried out always using old values. After each iteration, the "new" values are transferred to the "old" vector before going around again. Try the program out on a variety of systems and compare the number of iterations required for convergence with the number required by the program as shown in the text. Include acceleration, as described in Exercise 29.

31. A great many important computer applications involve logical manipulations of nonnumerical data. As one small sample of the techniques used, let us explore some of the service routines that would be necessary in a chess program. We do not claim that chess playing by computer is in itself important, but that the techniques we can learn are important and that they have broad applicability.

For the benefit of readers who may not be familiar with chess, the following is a brief statement of the rules for the moves of the various pieces.

Each player, black and white, begins the game with 16 pieces: a king, a queen, two bishops, two knights, two rooks (also called castles), and eight pawns. At the start of the game the pieces are arranged as shown in Figure 5.19, in which the abbreviations used are as follows:

K   king
Q   queen
B   bishop
N   knight
R   rook
P   pawn

The (horizontal) rows are called ranks and the (vertical) columns are called files. Figure 5.18 shows the numbering system we shall use for the computer array described later.

The rook may move any distance along a rank or a file.

The bishop may move any distance along a diagonal.

The queen combines the powers of the rook and the bishop, and may thus move any distance in a straight line, along a rank, a file, or a diagonal.

The king may move in any direction also, but only one square at a time.

The knight moves by leaping to the

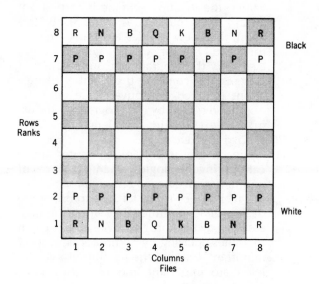

FIGURE 5.19. The arrangement of the pieces at the start of a chess game, together with the scheme for numbering the rows and columns that is used in Exercise 31.

nearest square of opposite color that is not adjacent. The move may also be described as "one over and two the other way," which is hardly precise but perhaps more descriptive. Figure 5.20 shows the eight possible squares to which the knight shown could move.

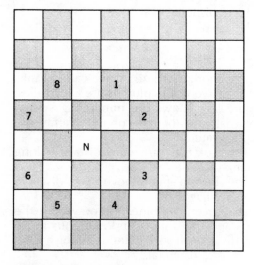

FIGURE 5.20. A schematic representation of the eight possible moves for a knight in the chessboard position shown.

The pawn may move forward and must stay on its original file except when capturing. For its first move the pawn may advance either one square or two, but after the opening move the pawn moves only one square at a time.

The knight's move is a point-to-point move and is thus unaffected by the presence of any intervening pieces. All of the other moves are restricted to the distance that the piece may move without encountering any other, whether the player's own or his opponent's.

All pieces except the pawn capture by moving in the normal manner to the square occupied by the piece being captured. The captured piece is removed from the board. The pawn captures diagonally forward.

(Capturing *en passant* and castling are the two additional moves, but they will not be needed in the exercises.)

For the programming exercises we have a two-dimensional integer array named BOARD, in which the rows and columns are numbered as in Figure 5.19. Each element of BOARD contains a number to identify what is on the square, according to the following coding of the pieces:

1   pawn
2   rook
3   knight
4   bishop
5   queen
6   king

If a given square is not occupied, the corresponding element of BOARD is zero. Positive values for the piece codings indicate white pieces and negative black. The integer variable *I*1 and *J*1 in all exercises give the row and column, respectively, of a piece under consideration. *I*2 and *J*2 give the location of some other square, when appropriate. We assume throughout that the game has been in progress for some time, so that the pieces are considerably removed from their starting positions.

*(a) Write a routine to print the row and column numbers of all unoccupied squares adjacent to *I*1, *J*1. The possibility that the subject square will be on

the edge of the board must be taken into account.

(b) Write a routine to print the row and column numbers of all unoccupied squares that can be reached in a single move by a knight at $I1, J1$.

*(c) A rook is on square $I1, J1$. If the path from there to square $I2, J2$ is unobstructed, set MOVE to .TRUE., and to .FALSE. otherwise. (The square $I2, J2$ *itself* may or may not be occupied.) Do this only if $I1 = I2$ or $J1 = J2$; if neither of these is true, set LEGAL to .FALSE..

(d) A bishop is on square $I1, J1$. If the path from there to $I2, J2$ is unobstructed, set MOVE to .TRUE., and to .FALSE. otherwise. Make these moves only if the path is on a diagonal; if not, set LEGAL to .FALSE..

*(e) The following scale, among others, is used to evaluate the relative value of the pieces:

pawn	1
knight	3
bishop	3
castle	5
queen	10

No weight is given to the king, since capture of the king ends the game.

Write a program to compute the value of all pieces, including pawns, for white, and place this integer in WPIECE.

(f) The black king is at $I1, J1$. White claims to have the black king in check (under attack) by an unspecified piece on an unspecified square. Write a routine to determine whether the black king actually is in check. (This is much harder than the preceding exercises!)

6 INPUT AND OUTPUT

6.1 INTRODUCTION

The beginning programmer necessarily concentrates at first on the basic ideas of data processing: what constitutes a good algorithm, how to translate a flow-charted procedure into a correct program, how to make effective use of the features of the programming language being used, and so on. Once these things are under at least partial control, however, most people discover that the work of the programmer revolves to a large extent around questions of input and output.

These questions range from matters of convenience and accuracy in card preparation, to the effective presentation of results in an easily understood and pleasing arrangement, and the best way to utilize an operating system to provide flexibility in program execution, to name some.

In this chapter we shall primarily be extending the reader's command of input and output techniques beyond the somewhat elementary methods presented when we were concentrating on other topics. However, in order to make the chapter more useful as a reference, we shall mention again some matters that have been covered before.

6.2 BASICS

Reading input data or writing results requires the programmer to provide four categories of information.

1. The selection of an input or output device, which is handled by a combination of the statement verb and the unit designation. We write READ or WRITE to indicate input or output, and then the first number in parentheses after the verb to designate which of the various input or output (I/0) devices available on the system is to be used. Until now we have almost always assumed that input was from cards and that output was to a printer. We here explore the full range of I/0 devices, and learn that there is considerably more to the story. The use of disk devices for storage of data after it has been read from cards is of special importance.

2. The variables to receive new input values or to have their values sent to an output device, specified by the list of variables in the I/0 statement.

3. The order in which the values are to be transmitted, which is governed by the order in which the variables are named in the list.

4. The format in which the data appears, for input, or is to be written, for output, which is specified by a FORMAT statement that must be referenced by the input or output statement in all but a few special cases.

Each of these four areas has been discussed in preceding chapters, and there have been many examples of their application. Each of them is now the subject of further elaboration in the interest either of simplicity of programming, or, more commonly, of more powerful techniques directed toward greater usefulness of the total computing system.

After considering these matters from the standpoint of what we do in writing the Fortran source program, we shall need to learn enough about operating system concepts to be able to discuss the ways in which some of the things that are done in the source program can be done instead with job control language (JCL) statements. We shall also consider how programs can be written to take advantage of the great flexibility provided by the ability to postpone many decisions about I/0 devices until the object program is run.

6.3 THE LIST OF AN INPUT OR OUTPUT STATEMENT

The simplest type of list is one in which all the variables are named explicitly and in the order in which they are to be transmitted. There are more complicated (and more powerful) types of lists, as we shall see shortly. In all cases, however, the fundamental idea of "scanning" carries through: the first data field is associated with the first variable name and with the first field descriptor and so on.

The first additional list feature is a useful one that does not complicate the scanning process: it is permissible to use integer variables in a list as subscripts elsewhere in the list. This is subject to one restriction: when it is done with input, any variable used as a subscript must appear in the list as an input variable *before* it appears as a subscript. "Before" means in the sense of the scanning process, but it also means, in fact, "to the left." For an example, we might arrange for a data card to contain an element number and a data value. Then we could write

```
      READ (5, 160) K, POWER(K)
160   FORMAT (I2, F10.0)
```

The value of K read from the card would immediately be used to determine where in the POWER array to place the data value.

Although completely legal, this technique does carry dangers, and cannot be recommended for indiscriminate use. If anything goes wrong in the preparation of the data cards, so that the element number is not valid, the program may be completely disabled. Not only will the one data item be stored incorrectly, but the entire program operation may be disrupted. For this reason we ordinarily read both the element number and the data value into temporary stor-

age locations, not utilizing subscripting, then make validity checks before storing the value in the array if everything is in order. We have employed such a scheme, for instance, in Case Study 10, where this point was discussed on page 112.

When entire arrays or parts of arrays are to be transmitted, it is often not necessary to name each element explicitly. To transmit an entire array, it is necessary only to name the array in a list without any subscripts. The name of the array must, of course, appear elsewhere in the program in a DIMENSION statement or in a COMMON statement that gives dimensioning information, but in the list it need not carry any subscripting information. Ordinarily, all the elements have the same field descriptors; this one field descriptor may be given by itself in the FORMAT statement. For instance, we can write

```
      WRITE (6, 320) A
320   FORMAT (1PE20.8)
```

where A is an array of any size.

Whenever an entire array is moved this way, the elements are transmitted in a sequence in which the first subscript varies the most rapidly and the last subscript the least rapidly, as discussed on page 80.

When only some of the array elements are to be transferred, or when the "natural order" just mentioned is not wanted, it is often still possible to avoid naming each element explicitly. The elements can be specified instead in the list in a way that parallels a DO loop. For instance, the statements

```
      READ (5, 200) (A(1, J), J = 1, 10)
200   FORMAT (10F7.0)
```

would call for 10 numbers to be read from a card and stored as the first 10 elements of the first row of an array named A. The same 10 numbers would be stored as the first 10 elements of the first *column* of A by

```
READ (5, 200) (A(I, 1), I = 1, 10)
```

We see that the indexed variable (or variables), along with the indexing information, must be enclosed in parentheses.

Just as it is possible to have nests of DO's, it is possible to have nests of *implied DO's,* as they are called. Suppose, for example, that we want to print 60 numbers, taking the first 12 from the first row of R, the next 12 from the *third* row of R, the next 12 from the *fifth* row of R, and so on. This can be done with

```
      WRITE(6,90)((R(I,J),J=1,12),I=1,9,2)
90    FORMAT (4E20.7)
```

In a certain sense this list may be thought of as equivalent to the schematic nest:

```
      DO 462 I = 1, 9, 2
      DO 462 J = 1, 12
462   R(I, J)
```

We see that the idea of inner and outer DO's carries over to inner and outer list indexing. A comma is always required between the last variable name in an implied DO and the indexing information.

The implied DO is a powerful feature of the input and output capability of Fortran. The serious student will take the trouble to learn it thoroughly. In fact, some people urge the use of implied DO's even where it might be possible to write the name of an array without subscripts. The implied DO is simple and precise, whereas experience shows that the use of array names without subscripting can cause complications. On the other hand, writing the array name without subscripts and without using implied DO's usually results in much faster execution of the object program. If this is an important consideration, the reader will do well to look carefully into Excursion IV, where the matter is treated in more detail.

The scanning of a list can be considerably more complex than it is in a simple list that names each variable explicitly. Still, the sequence of transmission of values is completely specified in all cases. It should also be realized that the scanning of the list and the scanning of the FORMAT statement entries keep in step: each time another variable is obtained from the list the next field descriptor is obtained from the FORMAT statement. If the closing parenthesis of the FORMAT is reached while more variables still remain in the list, a new card or a new line is called for and FORMAT scanning returns to the start of the FORMAT statement. Thus, if A is a one-dimensional array with 20 elements, the statements

```
      WRITE (6, 582) A
582   FORMAT (1PE16.6)
```

would print 20 separate lines with one value each. On the other hand, these statements

```
      WRITE (6, 583) A
583   FORMAT (1P5E16.6)
```

would print five numbers on each of four lines. And we could also write

```
      WRITE (6, 584) A
584   FORMAT (F10.1,F10.2,F10.3,F10.4)
```

which would put four numbers on each of five lines. *In each line* the first number would have one decimal place, the second two, and so on.

This "repeat scanning," as we might call it, is an important feature of FORMAT statement usage. We shall discuss it further in Section 6.5, in which we shall also see how it can be modified by parentheses within the FORMAT.

6.4 THE FORMAT STATEMENT

The FORMAT statement describes how information is arranged on input or is to be arranged on output. To each value transmitted there must correspond a field descriptor that lists the kind of information the field contains (in terms of its internal representation) and what it "looks like" externally.

The subject may conveniently be described under two headings: (1) what each of the types of field descriptors does and (2) how the field descriptors may be arranged in the FORMAT statement, in keeping with the scanning process. Item (1) is the subject of this section and item (2), of the next.

We shall discuss nine types of field descriptors. In each case a complete field descriptor consists of the following:

1. A letter (I, F, E, D, G, L, A, H, or X) to designate the kind of information and how it is to be handled.
2. A number to designate how many card columns or printing positions are in use.

The D, E, F, and G field descriptors require a second number to prescribe decimal-point handling.

To save repetition, we may note a few items that apply to D, E, F, G, and I field descriptors.

On *input,* a sign, if any, must be the first nonblank character of the field. The use of a plus sign is always optional; if no sign appears, the number is considered positive. Blanks are taken to be zeros. A field that is entirely blank is taken to be zero.

On *output,* the number will appear at the right of the output field if more character positions are specified for the field than there are characters in the number. If too few character positions are specified, asterisks are substituted for the value, in most systems. Plus signs are neither punched nor printed in most Fortran systems.

In all types except H and X it is permissible to specify that the same field descriptor applies to several successive fields by writing a *repeat count* in front of the field descriptor.

Whenever a scale factor is written with a D, E, F, or G field descriptor, it automatically applies to all succeeding D, E, F, and G field descriptors in the same FORMAT statement, until some other scale factor is encountered. If a given scale factor is to apply to one field descriptor only, the next field descriptor must have an 0P scale factor.

Field Descriptor I (Integer)

The form of this descriptor is Iw. *I* specifies conversion between an internal integer and an external decimal integer. The total number of characters in the field, including sign and any blanks, is w. Decimal points are not permitted.

Field Descriptor F (External Fixed Point)

The form of this descriptor is Fw.d. The *F* indicates conversion between an internal real value and an external number written without an exponent. The total number of characters in the field, including sign, decimal point, and any blanks, is w. The number of decimal places after the decimal point is d.

On *input,* the use of a decimal point is optional; if one is supplied in the card, it overrides d. (The use of an explicit decimal point is recommended practice.)

On *output,* there will be d places to the right of the decimal point, which is always supplied, and which counts in w.

A scale factor may be used with the F field descriptor by writing the descriptor in the general form

$$sPrFw.d$$

where s is the scale factor and r the repeat count. The effect is

$$\text{external number} = \text{internal number} \cdot 10^s$$

where "external number" is the number being read or printed, and "internal number" is the corresponding value in the computer. The scale factor may be positive or negative. The formula applies both to input and output, although use with input is rare. There are many possible reasons for using a scale factor. One would be to change units for printing. An internal number giving current in amperes could be printed as milliamperes by use of scale factor 3. This was illustrated in Case Study 9.

Field Descriptor E (Floating Point)

The form of this descriptor is Ew.d. *E* specifies conversion between an internal real value and an external number written with an exponent. The total number of characters in the external medium is w, including sign, decimal point, exponent, and any blanks. The number of decimal places after the decimal point (not counting the exponent) is d.

On *input,* the use of an actual decimal point is optional; if it is supplied in the card, it overrides d. The exponent part of the field takes the general form $E \pm ee$, as in a floating point constant in a statement. However, several shortcuts are permitted to simplify card punching. A positive exponent may appear with the + omitted or replaced with a blank, that is, E ee or Eee. If the first digit of the exponent is zero, it may be omitted. If the exponent is written with a sign, the E may be omitted. Thus all of the following are permissible and equivalent forms for the exponent *plus 2:* E+02, E 02, E02, E+2, E2, +2.

The exponent, if present, must be punched at the extreme right of the card field to convey the correct meaning, since blanks are taken to be zeros.

For example, all of the following data fields convert to the same internal number (1234.5678) if read in under control of E14.7, remembering that an actual decimal point overrides d in the field descriptor:

```
+12345678E03
 12345678.E-4
  1234.5678E0
+0.12345678+4
```

On *output,* the number will normally appear in the form $\pm 0.nn \ldots E\pm ee$ (except that plus signs are replaced with blanks), in which the number of places after the decimal point is specified by *d*.

A scale factor has no effect on input with an E field descriptor, assuming there is an actual exponent part in the input field. On output the effect is to multiply the "fractional" part by 10^s and to reduce the exponent by *s*. The scale factor may be positive or negative.

Field Descriptor D (Double Precision)
In the Dw.d descriptor the internal value must be double-precision. The exponent is written with *D* instead of *E*, but in all other respects this is analogous to the E field specification.

Field Descriptor G (Generalized)
This is a convenient field descriptor for situations where the programmer wants to write a FORMAT statement with a minimum of effort, and is not greatly concerned about the details of appearance of output; it has obvious usefulness for beginners who wish to concentrate on other matters at the outset.

The form is Gw.d. For input of real data, the effect is exactly equivalent to Ew.d. That is, the use of an exponent is optional, an actual decimal point overrides the effect of the *d*, and so on. For output of real data, the form in which the data is printed depends on the size of the number. If it is possible to print the number without an exponent and not lose any significant digits, that is done; otherwise an exponent is used. The precise effect of the descriptor can be defined, but it is just about as useful simply to give an example. Suppose that the descriptor was 1PG14.5; then a series of numbers of varying sizes as shown could be printed:

```
1.23457E 06
1.23457E 05
 12346.
 1234.6
 123.46
 12.346
 1.2346
 0.12346
1.23457E-02
1.23457E-03
1.23457E-04
1.23457E-05
```

On Fortran for the IBM 360, the generalization is carried even further: the variable associated with a G field descriptor may be of any type, including integer and logical. In the latter two cases the *d* portion of the descriptor is ignored, and the effect is as though we had written Iw or Lw. This makes it possible to write some suitably chosen field descriptor, such as 1P8G15.6, and use a FORMAT statement containing that descriptor indiscriminately for all output. The system will consider the type of the variable in determining how to interpret the contents of the G field descriptor.

Field Descriptor L (Logical)
In the Lw form the *L* specifies conversion between an internal logical value (.TRUE. or .FALSE.) and one of the letters *T* or *F* externally. The total number of character positions is *w*.

On *input,* the first nonblank character in the field must be *T* or *F*, which will cause storage of a value of .TRUE. or .FALSE., respectively. Any other letters following the *T* or *F* are ignored, making it possible, for instance, to specify L5 and then to punch the word TRUE or FALSE in the card.

On *output,* the letter *T* or *F* is placed at the extreme right of the allotted space, preceded by *w*-1 blanks.

Field Descriptor A (Alphanumeric)
In the Aw form of field descriptor the associated variable may be of any kind. The field descriptor causes *w* characters to be read into, or written from, the associated list element. The alphanumeric characters may be any symbols representable in the particular computer: letters, digits, punctuation, and the "character" *blank*. The precise action depends on the number of characters held in one storage location in the particular machine, which, as a general indication, ranges from four to eight. Call this number *g*.

On *input,* if *w* is greater than or equal to *g*, the rightmost *g* characters will be taken from the external input field; these *g* characters fill the storage location. If *w* is less than *g*, the *w* characters will appear "left justified" (at the extreme left) in storage, followed by trailing blanks.

On *output,* if *w* is greater than *g*, the external result will consist of *w*-*g* blanks followed by the *g* characters. If *w* is less than or equal to *g*, the external result will be the leftmost *w* characters from storage.

For instance, in Case Study 11 we shall see field descriptors of A1 used for input and output. On input, this places one character in the leftmost character position of a storage location. When this location is later printed under control of A1, that one leftmost character is the one printed.

Field Descriptor H (Hollerith)
This descriptor takes the form wH. The w characters immediately following the letter H are printed or punched in the position indicated by the position of the Hollerith field descriptor in the FORMAT statement. The Hollerith field descriptor is different from the others so far discussed in that it does not call for the transmission of any values from the list. Instead, it calls for the input or output of the text *itself*. Any character available in the computer may be used, as it can with the A field descriptor. This, incidentally, is the only case in which a blank in a statement is not ignored by the Fortran compiler.

No indication of the presence of the Hollerith text is required in the list of the input or output statement that refers to the FORMAT statement containing the text. Whenever a Hollerith field descriptor is encountered in the scanning of the FORMAT statement, the text is transmitted without any variable from the list having been transmitted.

On *input*, the w characters from the input record are inserted into the FORMAT statement. This makes it possible to change Hollerith information within a FORMAT. The variation of FORMAT statements, however, is more commonly accomplished with FORMAT descriptors in arrays, as will be discussed in Section 6.6.

On *output*, the w characters following the letter H are written out.

Hollerith field descriptors are commonly used to provide headings and other identification on printed reports, as we have seen.

Another very frequent application controls the spacing of lines in printing. The first character of the line printed with a WRITE statement is ordinarily not actually printed, but is used instead to control spacing, according to the table at the top of the next column.

Common practice, and strongly recommended, is to start every FORMAT statement for output with a Hollerith field giving the desired vertical spacing. If, by accident, the first data

Control Character	Action
Blank	Normal single spacing
0	Double space
1	Skip to top of next page before printing
+	Suppress spacing

field places a nonblank character into the carriage control position, *strange* spacing can result and the character will not be printed.

As we have seen, many Fortran systems provide what we have called the quoted literal as an alternative to the Hollerith field descriptor. When both are available, the programmer must balance positive and negative factors of the following sort.

In favor of the quoted literal is ease of use: it is not necessary to count the number of characters in the Hollerith text. Errors in this counting are easy to make, and often result in making the following field descriptor appear to be in error. Arguing against the quoted literal is the fact that it is not available on all systems, which causes a loss of transferability of your program from one Fortran system to another. Furthermore, if through any kind of error a quote mark is not matched by a closing quote, naturally everything after the opening quote is taken to be part of the literal, up to the end of the statement. This can create interesting diagnostic messages, too. On balance, the quoted literal seems to have a slight edge.

Field descriptor X (blank). This descriptor has the form wX.

On *input*, the effect is to skip over w columns. The reason might be that the columns are blank and that the purpose is to avoid having to make the succeeding field descriptor longer than it really is to take the blanks into account. On the other hand, the columns skipped might have punches that simply are not needed in the computer, such as card identification used only by the programmer and the computer operator.

On *output*, the effect is to insert w blanks into the output record. This is commonly done to space heading information or to spread out results across the line.

Two additional field descriptors are available on some Fortran implementations, although they are not included in the ANSI standard. The first of these applies only to machines in which hexadecimal representation of groups of four binary digits is used, but that includes a number of important systems.

Field Descriptor Z (Hexadecimal)

The form of this field descriptor is Zw. It calls for conversion between an external representation of hexadecimal digits (formed of the 16 characters 0, 1, 2, . . . , 9, A, B, C, D, E, and F) and groups of four bits in internal storage. On input, blanks in the data are taken to be zeros. Furthermore, since one storage location contains two hexadecimal digits, in the major machines where this descriptor is used, if the input consists of an odd number of digits the field is *padded* with a hexadecimal zero. On output, if the number of characters in the internal number is less than *w*, the leftmost print positions are filled with blanks. If the number of characters is greater than *w*, leftmost digits are dropped.

Field Descriptor T

This field descriptor does not itself call for the transmission of data, just as the X descriptor does not. Instead, it specifies the location within a group of characters being transmitted where the following field descriptor is to apply. For example, on output we could write

```
       WRITE (6, 100) X, Y
100    FORMAT('0',T40,F12.4,T81, F12.3)
```

This would mean that the 12 spaces allotted to X are to begin in position 40 and the 12 for Y in position 81. One handy use for this field descriptor is in specifying where the printing of literal data for headings and other identification is to begin.

6.5 ADDITIONAL FORMAT STATEMENT FEATURES

Just as it is possible to repeat a field descriptor by writing a repeat count in front of it, it is also possible to repeat a *group* of field descriptors. The group is enclosed in parentheses and the desired number of repetitions is written before it. For instance, suppose that eight fields on a card are alternately described by I2 and F10.0. We can write

```
4(I2, F10.0)
```

to get the desired action. This is *not* the same as

```
4I2, 4F10.0
```

which describes a card with four I2 fields, then four F10.0 fields, rather than the desired alternation.

Two levels of parentheses, in addition to those required by the FORMAT statement, are permitted. The second level facilitates the transmission of complex quantities, which require two field descriptors for each list variable. Some systems place no limit on the number of levels of parentheses.

When the list of an input or output statement is used to transmit more than one *record* (card or line) and the different records have different formats, a slash(/) is used to separate the format descriptors for the different lines. For example, suppose that two cards are to be read with a single READ statement; the first card has only a four-digit integer and the second has six real numbers. We could write

```
FORMAT (I4/6E14.0)
```

The slash terminates the reading of the first card (skipping over any other punching that it might contain) and, if list variables remain, it initiates the reading of another card, using the field descriptors after the slash.

It is possible to specify a special format for the first (one or more) records and a different format for all subsequent records. This is done by enclosing the last record descriptors in parentheses. For instance, if the first card of a deck has an integer and a real number and all following cards contain two integers and a real number, we could write

```
FORMAT (I4,E14.0/(2I4,E14.0))
```

The principle here is that when all field descriptors in a FORMAT statement have been used and more list variables remain, control reverts to the group-repeat descriptor terminated by the last preceding right parenthesis, if there is one, or the beginning of the statement. For instance, suppose we have

```
  FORMAT (2E10.3, 2(I2, I3),
1   (I4,2(F12.4,F12.6)), D26.16)
```

If more list variables remain after the D26.16 descriptor has been used, control reverts to the group-repeat descriptor (I4, 2(F12.4, F12.6)), which is the one terminated by the last preceding right parenthesis.

It is possible to call for the skipping of entire records by writing successive slashes, which are often useful when line spacing is desired and it is not convenient to use a carriage control character in the FORMAT statement for the next line. When $n + 1$ consecutive slashes appear at the end of a FORMAT descriptor, they are treated as follows: for input, $n + 1$ records are skipped; for output, n blank records are written, unless after doing so control reverts for the transmission of additional values, in which case $n + 1$ blank records are written. When $n + 1$ consecutive slashes appear in the middle of the FORMAT statement, n records are skipped or written. Different Fortrans, however, are not consistent on the handling of slashes at the end of a FORMAT.

If a FORMAT statement contains nothing but Hollerith and blank field descriptors, there must be no variables listed in the associated input or output statement. This is most commonly done with the WRITE statement to produce page and column headings or to cause line and page spacing. A common FORMAT statement is

```
FORMAT (1H1)
```

Referenced by a WRITE statement with no list, this causes the printer paper to space to the top of the next page.

6.6 OBJECT-TIME FORMAT STATEMENTS

The ability to read a FORMAT statement at the time of execution of the object program adds great flexibility to Fortran. To do this we must establish an array that will hold the format specifications in the form of alphanumeric data. The formats are read into this array at object time. To use these variable formats we reference the array *by name* in the READ or WRITE statement. Let us study an example.

Suppose that we wish to print the values of four variables named *I*, *J*, *X*, and *Y*, the first two being integers and the last two real. The formats for printing them are to be read in at object time. Let us assume further that our computer

has storage locations that hold four characters each. Consider the following program segment:

```
      DIMENSION FMT(7)
      READ (5, 209) FMT
  209 FORMAT (7A4)
      .
      .
      WRITE (6, FMT) I, J, X, Y
```

The DIMENSION statement establishes FMT as a one-dimensional array with seven elements, which will be considered as alphanumerical variables and can therefore hold 28 characters (seven words of four characters each). The READ statement references a FORMAT statement that says to expect seven groups of four characters each, and these characters are to go into the seven storage locations of the array named FMT. Notice that we have written the name of the array without subscripting, calling for all elements to be filled in succession from the card.

The card, starting in column 1, might contain something like this:

```
(I10, I16, 1PE20.8, 0PE16.2)
```

Counting the parentheses and the blanks, we have 28 characters up through the closing parenthesis. These fill out the FMT array. This is how the object-time format information must be entered: with the enclosing parentheses, but without the word FORMAT. The specifications just written would be entered into the FMT array exactly as they were punched on the card.

Later in the program we can use the formatting information that has been read into storage, as in the WRITE statement, by writing the name of the format array in place of the statement number of a FORMAT statement. The field descriptors will be taken from storage as they have been read. It is now possible to enter the formatting information right along with the data every time the program is read. When the format of the data changes, we simply revise the card that contains the formatting information. No changes in the program are required.

Reading in a complete set of format descriptors is by no means the only thing that can be done with object-time formats. Suppose we have an array named RESULT, which contains ten real numbers. These are to be printed across one line, using F8.2 descriptors for nonzero values and replacing zeros with blanks. This will avoid printing the 0.0 that most Fortran systems put out for zero values and that some users might not consider attractive. The lines are to be double spaced.

Figure 6.1 shows one way in which this requirement can be met. We establish the arrays for the format information and for the results. It is impossible to write a program of this sort without knowing how many characters there are in each computer word, so we do not apologize for using a machine-dependent REAL*8 statement to make the aphanumeric variables large enough to hold the longest item that any of them will contain. The READ statement should receive a card as described at the top of the next column, where small *b*'s stand for blanks. In FORM(1) we place LEFT, the opening left parenthesis. This is followed in storage by seven blanks, but blanks in a FORMAT are ignored except in a literal field (that is, a Hollerith field or a quoted literal). To get the desired double spacing we place a slash before the closing right

Columns	Contents	Program Name
1–8	(bbbbbbb	LEFT
9–16	/)bbbbbb	RIGHT
17–24	A8,bbbbb	ASPEC
25–32	F8.2,bbb	FSPEC
33–40	bbbbbbbb	BLANKS

parenthesis that appears in RIGHT, in FORM(12). (In many systems two slashes would be needed here.)

Now we have ten storage locations, FORM(2) to FORM(11), into which to place field descriptors corresponding to the ten values in the array RESULT. For each element in RESULT that is nonzero we shall place in the corresponding position of FORM the field descriptor "F8.2," including the comma. Each element of RESULT that is zero will be replaced in RESULT by an alphanumeric "value" consisting of blanks, and in the corresponding element of FORM we will place the field descriptor "A8," also including the comma.

```
        DIMENSION RESULT(10), FORM(12)
        REAL*8 FORM, LEFT, RIGHT, ASPEC, FSPEC, BLANKS
C
C READ A CARD CONTAINING THE FIELD DESCRIPTORS
        READ (5, 100) LEFT, RIGHT, ASPEC, FSPEC, BLANKS
 100    FORMAT (5A8)
C
C SET UP OPENING AND CLOSING PARENTHESES
        FORM(1) = LEFT
        FORM(12) = RIGHT
C
C LOOP TO READ SAMPLE DATA
        DO 20 I1 = 1, 5
        READ (5, 200) RESULT
 200    FORMAT (10F3.0)
C
C LOOP TO PROCESS ALL TEN ITEMS IN 'RESULT'
        DO 10 I = 1, 10
C
C PUT 'F8.2,' INTO STORED FORMAT, THEN REPLACE WITH 'A8,' IF
C NUMBER IS ZERO
        FORM(I+1) = FSPEC
        IF ( RESULT(I) .EQ. 0.0 ) FORM(I+1) = ASPEC
C
C IF ZERO, ALSO PUT BLANKS INTO DATA LOCATION
 10     IF ( RESULT(I) .EQ. 0.0 ) RESULT(I) = BLANKS
C
C WRITE THE ARRAY UNDER CONTROL OF THE COMPUTED FORMAT
 20     WRITE (6, FORM) RESULT
        STOP
        END
```

FIGURE 6.1. A program segment using object-time formatting to blank out zero values.

A simple DO loop runs through the 10 elements of RESULT, processing each appropriately, after which the array is printed under control of the format that we have assembled in FORM. FORM(2) corresponds to RESULT(1), etc.

Figure 6.2, in the first five lines, shows sample data printed by another program with F8.2 field descriptors throughout. The second five lines are the output of the program of Figure 6.1 for the same data values.

Very complex and flexible formatting can be built up by using techniques like these. The result can be a program that has more statements for input and output than for other data processing, which is more or less typical of the work of professional programming.

6.7 THE NAMELIST FEATURE

In everything we have done so far it has been necessary to state explicitly the name of every variable involved in an input or output operation. Now we pause to see how it is possible, in some systems that go beyond the ANSI standard, to relax this requirement.

The NAMELIST feature is usable on output, as we shall see, but the primary motivation for using it occurs in connection with input. The idea is that we shall designate, using the NAME-

LIST statement, certain variables that may potentially be involved in a somewhat different type of input operation—one where we do *not* name any variables in the READ statement. Instead, we provide a READ statement that refers to the NAMELIST statement, and that says, in effect, "Some or all of the variables named in the NAMELIST *may* appear in the input record. Any that do appear will have their names with them." Any variable names (and associated values) that do appear on the card will have new values assigned by the READ-NAMELIST combination; any variables named in the NAMELIST that do *not* occur in the READ are simply left unchanged.

For example, suppose that in a program we write

```
NAMELIST /INPUT/ TIN, TOUT,
1   LENGTH, MAXIT, EPS, OMEGA
```

This establishes INPUT as the name of a NAMELIST that includes the variables shown. Now we may write something like

```
READ (5, INPUT)
```

Observe that no variables are named. The specification of which variables are to receive new values will appear on the cards read by the READ. Those cards are required to conform to a fairly specific format, as follows.

The first character must be blank. The second

1.00	2.00	3.00	4.00	5.00	6.00	7.00	8.00	9.00	10.00
1.10	0.0	2.20	0.0	3.30	4.40	0.0	0.0	0.0	5.50
0.0	0.0	10.00	20.00	0.0	0.0	30.00	40.00	0.0	0.0
0.10	0.0	0.0	0.0	0.0	0.0	0.0	0.0	0.20	0.0
0.01	0.02	0.03	0.0	0.0	0.0	0.0	0.0	0.04	0.05

1.00	2.00	3.00	4.00	5.00	6.00	7.00	8.00	9.00	10.00
1.10		2.20		3.30	4.40				5.50
		10.00	20.00			30.00	40.00		
0.10								0.20	
0.01	0.02	0.03						0.04	0.05

FIGURE 6.2. Sample data values, printed with F8.2 field descriptors (first five lines), and the output of the program segment of Figure 6.1 for the same data values (second five lines).

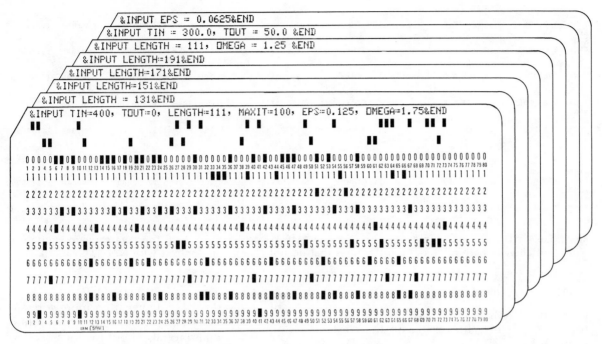

FIGURE 6.3. A set of data cards for reading with the NAMELIST feature.

character must be an ampersand (&); in the first record read by the READ, this ampersand must be followed immediately by the NAMELIST name and a space. The end of the data associated with a NAMELIST READ is signaled by &END. Between the NAMELIST name and the &END, for each value that is to be read, there should appear the combination

variable name = constant

with each combination followed by a comma if there are more than one. If values are being read into an array, the array name should be written without subscripts, then an equal sign, then values for all of the array elements written, separated by commas.

Some systems use a dollar sign instead of the ampersand on the data cards.

This may sound more complicated than it is. Figure 6.3 shows a set of eight data cards that could be read by the READ statement given above, with its associated NAMELIST statement. We see that on the first card values have been given to all the variables named in the NAME-LIST, but in the next four only LENGTH has been given a new value. This is typical of the way the NAMELIST feature would be used: set up initial

values, then name only the ones that actually change. On the sixth card LENGTH and OMEGA would both change, on the seventh only TIN and TOUT, and on the eighth only EPS. The notion is that we wish to be able to write the source program without having to know which variables will change in given runs.

The same concept does not really apply on output: when we write a WRITE statement there is no simple corresponding way to leave the selection of which variables to print to be decided at execution time. However, it is sometimes convenient to be able to produce cards that can later be read using the NAMELIST feature, so it is permitted for a WRITE statement (in systems that have the NAMELIST feature, of course) to refer to a NAMELIST instead of to a FORMAT. When this is done, all the variables named in the NAMELIST are written out in a form that makes it possible to read the cards by a NAMELIST READ. This would have primary usefulness when cards are punched, but it is permissible to do the same thing with printed output if desired. This does provide an explicit identification of each value, which is sometimes a useful feature in itself. Figure 6.4 shows a few lines printed by the statement

```
&INPUT
TIN=   400.00000   ,TOUT= 0.0         ,LENGTH=        111,MAXIT=        100,EPS= 0.12500000   ,OMEGA=  1.7500000
&END
&INPUT
TIN=   400.00000   ,TOUT= 0.0         ,LENGTH=        131,MAXIT=        100,EPS= 0.12500000   ,OMEGA=  1.7500000
&END
&INPUT
TIN=   400.00000   ,TOUT= 0.0         ,LENGTH=        151,MAXIT=        100,EPS= 0.12500000   ,OMEGA=  1.7500000
&END
&INPUT
TIN=   400.00000   ,TOUT= 0.0         ,LENGTH=        171,MAXIT=        100,EPS= 0.12500000   ,OMEGA=  1.7500000
&END
&INPUT
TIN=   400.00000   ,TOUT= 0.0         ,LENGTH=        191,MAXIT=        100,EPS= 0.12500000   ,OMEGA=  1.7500000
&END
&INPUT
TIN=   400.00000   ,TOUT= 0.0         ,LENGTH=        111,MAXIT=        100,EPS= 0.12500000   ,OMEGA=  1.2500000
&END
&INPUT
TIN=   300.00000   ,TOUT= 50.000000   ,LENGTH=        111,MAXIT=        100,EPS= 0.12500000   ,OMEGA=  1.2500000
&END
&INPUT
TIN=   300.00000   ,TOUT= 50.000000   ,LENGTH=        111,MAXIT=        100,EPS= 0.62500000E-01,OMEGA=  1.2500000
&END
```

FIGURE 6.4. The printed output using the same NAMELIST as was used with the data cards in Figure 6.4. Note that all values are printed, even the ones that do not change, in contrast with NAMELIST input.

```
WRITE (6, INPUT)
```

where the NAMELIST was as shown above, for the same sets of values given on the cards of Figure 6.3.

We see that the &INPUT and the &END always appear on separate lines; this is permissible form for the input also. These lines were printed, obviously; if the WRITE statement had referred to a data set on punched cards (see below, Section 6.13), the values would have been limited to the 80 positions available on a card, and each NAMELIST output would have produced four cards corresponding to each three lines here.

It is not necessary, of course, that values read with the NAMELIST feature be printed correspondingly. Once the values are in the computer, they can be printed any way we wish, and most commonly they probably would not be printed under control of a NAMELIST.

One reason for providing a name for the NAMELIST is that there can be more than one in a program. It is therefore possible (and necessary) to identify the input explicitly to determine which NAMELIST is meant. A variable can be named in more than one NAMELIST.

6.8 TWO TYPES OF DATA ORGANIZATION

In the balance of this chapter we shall be taking up some additional topics that go beyond the rather limited concepts of input and output that we have so far taken for granted. In order to be able to discuss these new matters more conveniently it will be helpful to introduce the notion of a *data set,* and to talk about two of the common ways that data can be *organized.*

It turns out to be helpful to think of all information coming into a computer or going out of it as being organized into data sets. A data set, also often called a *file,* is nothing more or less than a collection of information having some common purpose, and which is arranged in some fashion that makes it possible to deal with individual parts of the complete data set in some convenient way. For example, a deck of cards being read as program data is a data set. A reel of magnetic tape can be a data set, or a tape might contain several data sets, or a reel of tape might be part of a larger data set consisting of many reels of tape. An object program being read into the machine by an operating system can be thought of, at the time it is being read, as a data set. So, also, a stream of lines going to a printer is a data set.

There is nothing very complicated about this idea; don't look for something "deep" that isn't there!

A data set is made up of individual items called *records.* One card in a deck is a record; one line of 132 characters plus a carriage control character can be one record; a group of a few dozen digits on a magnetic disk can be one record, if so defined to the system.

We need the concept of a record, among other reasons, to be able to talk about how records are *accessed*, or retrieved. In everything we have done up to this point, we have been dealing with *sequential* data sets, which means simply that the only way to get records from the data set was to start at the beginning and take them one after the other. There is no way to skip to the middle of a sequential data set and pick up a couple of records, without accessing the intervening records. Think, for instance, of a deck of cards in a card reader: they must be taken in the order in which they appear. Or consider a magnetic tape: just as with an audio tape, there is no way to move directly to a record in the middle or at the other end without actually moving the tape to the desired point. It is possible, sometimes, to pass over undesired records at high speed, as when a home music tape is rewound, and sometimes we can do roughly equivalent things in a computer; but basically a sequential data set is a one-after-the-other thing.

A *direct-access* data set, on the other hand, does permit us to move directly to a desired record or group of records without accessing intervening records. Think of a phonograph disk: if you want to play the song in band six, you move the pickup arm to band six and play it. It is not necessary (although still possible) to play bands one through five in sequence to get to band six, as is necessary with a sequential storage medium such as tape.

It is now possible to sharpen our terminology somewhat on a matter that we have oversimplified up to now. When we write something like

    WRITE (6, 100) X

the 6 is properly called the *data set reference number*. We have up to now called it the unit number or something of the sort, which suggests that the statement refers to a physical *device*; actually it refers to a collection of data. One of the functions of an operating system is to establish the relationship between data sets and physical devices, which need not actually be done until just before the object program is run. Using suitable job control language cards we can, as we shall see, associate data set 6 with a printer, a tape, a disk, or maybe a card punch. Data set reference numbers 5, 6, and 7 are often taken by default to mean a card reader, a printer, and a card punch, respectively, if we say nothing to the contrary—but that is simply a convenient convention, and is by no means required.

6.9 THE READ, PRINT, AND PUNCH STATEMENTS, WITHOUT UNIT DESIGNATION

In the earliest versions of Fortran the only input and output devices were a card reader, a card punch, a line printer, and several magnetic tapes. The concept of the data set reference number was not employed, and we wrote statements like

    READ 200, A, X, I
    PRINT 300, G, K
    PUNCH 400, ARRAY

The function of the FORMAT statement number was the same, but the information now contained in the data set reference number was provided by the I/0 verb (READ, PUNCH, or PRINT).

For compatibility with Fortran programs written for earlier systems, many modern Fortrans still accept these statements although they are not part of ANSI Fortran. Their meaning is precisely the same as the following statements, assuming (as is most common) an installation where data set reference numbers 5, 6, and 7 refer by default to a card reader, a printer, and a card punch:

    READ (5, 200) A, X, I
    WRITE (6, 300) G, K
    WRITE (7, 400) ARRAY

This feature, which is also present in WATFOR and WATFIV, may sometimes be of benefit to the beginning programmer in simplifying the form of input and output statements.

6.10 THE BACKSPACE, REWIND, AND END FILE STATEMENTS; THE END AND ERR PARAMETERS

Fortran deals basically with sequential data sets, such as card decks, printed output, magnetic tapes, and sequential data sets on magnetic disks. For use with such data sets there are three Fortran statements that find occasional usefulness. They are named BACKSPACE, REWIND, and END FILE, the first two betraying their origin in the early days when they applied only to data sets on magnetic tape.

The statement BACKSPACE *n*, where *n* is the data set reference number of a suitable sequential data set, "backs up" one record. What this means physically depends on what physical device is involved and on certain other matters of data organization that we do not need to get entangled in at this point. On a magnetic tape, it might mean literally moving the tape backward—but it might also mean only changing the value of a pointer that picks out the current record in main storage. A complete explanation of what the BACKSPACE "really" does would take us very far afield. Suffice it to say that if we write

```
READ (5, 100) X
BACKSPACE 5
READ (5, 100) X
```

we read the *same* record twice: the BACKSPACE has moved us back one record in the data set. (Some systems, however, prohibit the use of these operations on data sets 5, 6, and 7.)

If the BACKSPACE statement is executed for a data set where it makes no sense, such as a computer terminal, or if it is executed at a time when it makes no sense, such as before reading the first record of a data set, it is simply ignored in most systems.

The BACKSPACE statement will find limited usefulness in most Fortran programs. If it were not so extremely costly in terms of execution time, it might be handy for things like reading a record once to determine what kind of information is in it, then rereading it by whichever part of the program is appropriate to its contents. But the time penalty is usually too great to permit extensive use in this way. One possible application would be in processing records that are found to contain erroneous data. If a record is found to contain illegal characters, for instance, it would be possible to BACKSPACE and then reread the record using an alphabetic field descriptor so that the bad data could at least be printed for identification and correction.

The REWIND *n* statement, where meaningful, returns a data set to its beginning, ready for the first record to be accessed again. We shall see an example of the usefulness of this statement in Case Study 12, where we shall need to read the matrix of coefficients of a very large system of simultaneous equations repeatedly.

The END FILE *n* statement is used to place an indication in a sequential data set that no

more valid records follow. This is useful when information is being written out that is to be reread later, and we wish to have something in the data set to signal its end—without ourselves providing a sentinel record. The marker that is placed in the data set by the END FILE statement is recognized by the routines that handle reading. If we attempt to read a record that turns out to be the end-of-file mark and have not indicated that we expected this to happen, our program is taken out of execution. We have occasionally in this book written programs to operate in this manner intentionally: simply read data and process it in an endless loop, knowing that eventually the program will run out of data and be tossed off.

That is acceptable if there is nothing more for the program to do when the end of data is detected, but what if at that point there are some wrap-up chores to be done? This is the situation for which the END option is provided in a number of Fortran systems. We are permitted to write, for example,

```
READ (5, 100, END=85) X, Y, Z
```

This means that when the end-of-file mark is detected in attempting to read a record, statement 85 will be executed next.

This is a logical place to mention another optional parameter that can be used in the READ statement on a number of Fortran systems, the ERR parameter. This refers to the detection of errors in the recording or transmission of data. In many forms of data recording additional information is carried, to provide some measure of error detection and sometimes also limited error correction. The additional information is often referred to as *parity bits* because it is related to whether the other binary digits (bits) in a character or word contain an odd or even number of binary 1's. (One meaning of "parity" relates to oddness or evenness.) If the system detects an error in reading, it usually attempts to read the record again, on the possibility that the error was transient—possibly caused by dust on a tape, for instance. If the error does go away, it is usual not even to inform the object program that anything happened. If the error persists either some indication is passed to the object program, or, in the usual Fortran case, program execution is terminated with an error message. If the programmer wishes to provide his own error-handling routine in such a case, and if the particular Fortran system permits it, he can write, for instance,

```
READ (5, 100, ERR=3000) X, Y, Z
```

to indicate that if an uncorrectable error occurs the program should transfer to statement 3000, where he will have provided a program segment to take whatever appropriate action he desires.

The END and ERR parameters may both be used in the same READ:

```
READ (5, 100, END=85, ERR=3000) X, Y, Z
```

6.11 UNFORMATTED INPUT AND OUTPUT

Until now we have assumed that every READ or WRITE statement names a FORMAT statement that describes the external form of the information. However, if we wish to write out some information to temporary storage for later rereading, without ever printing or punching it, it is possible to transmit the information in essentially the same form as it is represented within the computer, and not name a FORMAT statement.

The form of the READ or WRITE is just as before, except that no statement number or FORMAT array name appears. We can write

```
WRITE (9) XARRAY
```

for example, where XARRAY might be a large array of data. The data set reference number used in such a statement must *not* name a data set that is to be printed; the latter must always be associated with formatting information. All that can legitimately be done with a record that was written without formatting is to read it back, also without formatting:

```
READ (9) XARRAY
```

The primary advantage of unformatted I/0 is speed. It turns out that the actions that have to be taken to format information according to the descriptions contained in a FORMAT statement require a lot of time. In a program in which large quantities of data are being manipulated many times, the difference can definitely be appreciable.

This question is considered more fully in Excursion IV.

6.12 THE DEFINE FILE STATEMENT

As we have noted, Fortran deals almost entirely with sequential files. ("File" and "data set" have to be used essentially interchangeably because of local variations in usage and also for historical reasons.) Files may exist on many media, including magnetic disks, but even if the file is recorded on a disk it will ordinarily still be a sequential file in Fortran. When the direct-access organization is provided, it is always in terms of a feature that is unique to the particular Fortran implementation. The ANSI standard, for instance, speaks only of sequential files. To give an example of direct access techniques in Fortran, therefore, we shall have to turn to some specific system. As we often have done before, we shall pick one that is widely distributed and therefore hopefully of benefit to the largest group of readers. In other words, we are once again going to describe a feature of Fortran G and H for the IBM 360 and 370.

For a direct access data set we shall be required to specify several items of information having to do with record size and organization, number of records, and accessing. The DEFINE FILE statement is used to provide this information; it is essentially a declaration, describing the file, before any actual transfer of data takes place. The general form is:

DEFINE FILE a(m, r, f, v)

(Actually, one DEFINE FILE can describe any number of data sets, with the descriptor groups separated by commas.) In the general form above, the letters have the following meanings.

a is the data set reference number; it can be any integer of one or two digits, although some installations may restrict the total number of separate data sets in a program.

m is an integer constant that specifies the number of records in the data set.

r represents the maximum size of each record in the data set. The units in which r is measured depends on the value of f, so we shall describe both together.

f specifies whether the data set is to be read and written with format control, according to the following scheme:

E indicates that the data set will always be read and written under format control, that is, with a FORMAT statement. In this case, *r* is measured in characters.

U indicates that the data set is always read and written without format control. In this case *r* is measured in *words,* where one word in the IBM 360 holds four characters.

L indicates that the data set may be read and written either with or without format control. The record size (*r*) in this case is measured in characters.

v is a nonsubscripted integer variable called the *associated variable,* the function of which is described below.

For an example of a DEFINE FILE statement, we might write:

```
DEFINE FILE 12(200, 30, U, IRECRD)
```

This means that data set 12 contains 200 records, is always read and written without format information, and has records that are a maximum of 30 words long. (One word in the 360 holds a single real number or a single integer number of length four. A DOUBLE PRECISION number takes up two words.) The associated variable is IRECRD. The statement

```
DEFINE FILE 4(1200, 80, E, KPOINT)
```

describes direct access data set number 4, which has 1200 records of at most 80 characters each, always read and written in conjunction with a FORMAT statement; the associated variable is KPOINT.

A READ or WRITE for a direct access data set is like that for a sequential data set, with one important difference. In addition to specifying the data set reference number, a FORMAT statement number or array name (if appropriate), the ERR parameter on READ if desired, and an I/O list if appropriate, we must also state which record within the file is to be processed. This is done by following the data set reference number with an apostrophe (single quote) and an integer expression that represents the relative position of a record within the data set. For example, if we write:

```
READ (4'1, 200) A
```

we call for the first record in data set 4, read under control of FORMAT statement number 200. If we write:

```
WRITE (12'IRECRD) XARRAY
```

we specify writing the contents of XARRAY onto data set 12, starting with the record identified by the current value of IRECRD, without format control. If we write:

```
READ (12'IRECRD+5) XARRAY
```

we are referring to the fifth record past the one identified by the current value of IRECRD.

We are now in a position of describing the function of the associated variable, and to see its usefulness. After every READ or WRITE of a direct access data set, the associated variable is given a value equal to the record number of the record *after* the one most recently processed. If we now want to process that next record, then the associated variable can be used to identify the record number.

For example, suppose we want to read the first ten records of the file described in the DEFINE FILE below, doing some processing on each:

```
DEFINE FILE 14(200, 20, U, KPOINT)
KPOINT = 1
DO 10 I = 1, 10
READ (14'KPOINT) ZARRAY
    .
    .
    .
10  CONTINUE
```

Before entering the loop we have given KPOINT the value 1, so that the first time the READ is executed we are specifying record number 1. After processing that record, KPOINT is given the value 2 (by the input routines), so that when we execute the READ again, we get the second record, and so on.

It might seem that we could have made KPOINT the index of the DO statement, but the automatic incrementing of the associated variable would then constitute an illegal redefinition of the index of a DO within its range.

The number of records processed by a direct access READ or WRITE depends on the interaction of the READ or WRITE, the DEFINE FILE, and the FORMAT, if any. For instance, if the DEFINE FILE specifies that a record contains a maximum of 20 words but the WRITE transmits 80 words and the FORMAT describes four records, four records will be written. This is not essentially different from what happens when we provide a FORMAT that calls for the writing of a number of lines on a printer through the use of slashes, since we should think of each line on the printer output as a record.

It may seem as though what we are calling a direct access data set is still rather sequential, since every record has a number, the numbers run consecutively, and if more than one record is called for by an I/O operation the subsequent records are taken in numerical order. The point is that, despite these characteristics, it is not necessary to start at the beginning nor to take records in sequence. If a file has 2000 records, we could process record number 1729 first, then record 6, then 1730, then 1500, then 2000, and end with 2. There may be minor time penalties associated with this jumping around, but they are strictly trivial compared with what would happen if we tried to do the same thing with a tape file.

In fact, a direct access data set on the IBM 360 would almost always reside physically on a magnetic disk. Without going into great detail on the hardware involved, we may note that magnetic disks are read and written by magnetic heads that are usually mounted on movable arms. When we execute a READ or WRITE of a record on disk, the time delay before data transmission begins consists of any time needed to move the arm (unless it was already positioned in the right track) plus the time required for the disk to turn so that the desired record is under the read/write head. The latter is a statistical matter over which we have no real control; that is, nothing we can do in the program will ordinarily diminish the rotational delay. The time to move the read/write head, however, can sometimes be overlapped with other operations, if it is possible to anticipate the need for a record. Thus, if we know that after some unrelated actions have been completed we shall need to read record number 97, it may speed up program execution if we notify the system in advance that we shall be wanting it. This is the function of a new statement, FIND. We write, for example,

```
FIND (14'97)
```

and then proceed with other processing not involving data set 14. When we later return to execute,

```
READ (14'97, 200) ZARRAY
```

any arm movement will already have been initiated, and, if we took long enough doing other things, the movement may have been completed. Instead of 97 we could, of course, have a variable name, which would often be even more valuable.

The times involved here are in the order of tens of milliseconds per record, which is obviously of no importance in small jobs. In programs that process many thousands of records repeatedly, however, which are not rare, savings of this sort may be quite important.

6.13 TIME-SHARING AND OPERATING SYSTEM CONSIDERATIONS

One of the desirable characteristics of a time-sharing system or an operating system is simplicity of input and output programming at the applications level. That is, the Fortran programmer, for instance, should be relieved of as much as possible of the great effort required to write an efficient and flexible I/O system. One important aspect of the desired simplicity is that it should be possible to write a Fortran program without knowing in advance much about how a data set will actually be stored. We would like to be able, for instance, to write a program so that when it is later run the intermediate storage that it uses may be provided either by tape or disk. Or we might like occasionally to run the program with the output going to disk storage instead of being printed, so that we can inspect a portion of the output for usefulness before deciding whether to print all of it.

For our purposes here, we can approach this large and complex subject—or as much of it as we shall explore—by posing the following question: How does the time-sharing system or the operating system find out what we meant by each data set reference number in our program? If we write, for instance,

```
WRITE (12, 150) A, B, C
```

how do we communicate that the 12 means a printer? Or how do we change that, when we run the program next week, so that the 12 means a high-density 9-track tape?

Answering these questions and others that we shall mention is the function of a time-sharing command with a name like FILEDEF or something of the sort, with which we provide the needed information about our file (data set). In an operating system we provide the information through what is called a data definition (DD), file allocation, file assign, or something similar.

Very commonly there are *default* values for most of the characteristics of data sets, that is, values that are assumed if we do not specify anything to the contrary. For instance, all the programs in this book use data set 5 as the system input, without our having had to specify anything about the data set at all. Even if we are dealing with some data set that does not have a *complete* set of default characteristics, there may be *some* defaults. For instance, in the system used to run the programs in this book, data sets 1 to 5 all have default record lengths of 80 characters, whereas data sets 8 and 12 have default record lengths of 133 characters (corresponding to the printers normally used). Generally speaking, when we provide information about a data set it is necessary to specify only those characteristics that are to be different from their default values.

The subject of file definitions can become quite involved, and there is a good deal of information to be mastered if one wishes to understand the subject thoroughly. Most beginning programmers find the whole subject mystifying, not to say terrifying. To give courage to the faint of heart before proceeding, let us emphasize that many common operations are quite simple and easy to carry out. For example, on the time-sharing system used to prepare this program in this book, that of National CSS, Inc., changing data set 5 to refer to a disk file named FCS10 instead of the time-sharing terminal requires merely executing the command

```
FILEDEF 5 DSK FCS10 DATA
```

Doing the same thing in Operating System 360 (OS/360) for the IBM System 360 might require a Data Definition as simple as

```
//GO.FT05F001 DD DSNAME=FCS10
```

The introduction of some of the basic concepts that follows is general, in the sense that it does not specifically refer to any particular time-sharing system or operating system. A certain degree of IBM bias in the terminology will not be denied, but the fundamental ideas are much the same for all systems, at least at the level of this elementary introduction.

Examples will be deferred to Case Study 12, where they can be placed in the context of a meaningful application.

One concept that is essential to a full understanding of input and output is that of the *blocking* of records, which involves the distinction between a *physical record* and a *logical record*. We can best get into this subject with an example. Suppose that we are writing 80-character records onto a magnetic tape that has a recording density of 1600 characters per inch. The 80 characters will accordingly occupy 0.05 inch of tape. If we write each group of 80 characters as a separate group on tape, we shall be using far more space for the gaps between records, which might be 0.6 inch, than for data. The time wasted will also be appreciable because it will take a great deal longer to get the tape started moving each time than to read the information.

Accordingly, we would ordinarily block the records. That is, we regard the basic group of 80 characters as a *logical record* and place perhaps 50 of these in a *physical record,* also called a *blocked record.* Such a physical record thus contains 4000 characters and occupies 2.5 inches of tape. We then say that the logical record length is 80, the block size is 4000, and the blocking factor is 50.

Suppose that we have prepared such a tape with a previous program and now want to read it. Within the program, we wish to obtain one *logical* record, but the tape unit can deal only with *physical* records; it is impossible to read only part of a physical record from the tape. Accordingly, the input routine (supplied as part of the time-sharing system or the operating system) must read a physical record into an area of main storage 4000 characters long, called a *buffer.* It must then give us access to the first logical record.

What happens the next time we ask for a logical record? Now, nothing whatever is read from tape because the second logical record is already in storage ready to be processed. The input routine accordingly need only make the second logical record available to us. (We cautiously say "make available" rather than "move" because many programming techniques are available to the writer of the input routines; perhaps all that "really" happens is that the value of a record pointer is changed.) This process continues until all 50 logical records have been processed. The next time after that when we ask for a logical record, the input routine actually does have to read a physical record from tape.

Unless, that is, two buffers have been provided. Since all modern computers can carry out I/O operations simultaneously with processing, why not be filling the second buffer while the data in the first one is being processed? Then when the data in the first has been exhausted, there need be no delay while the program waits for a physical record to be read from tape. Instead, the routine simply begins supplying logical records from the second buffer, while simultaneously reading another physical record into the first buffer so that it will be ready when we have used up the data in the second. The two buffers thus alternate between being read into and supplying logical records to the applications program.

Similar concepts apply to output.

As one small indication of the multitude of factors that have to be considered by the writer of the system I/O routines, consider that the last block in a file may not be full. Unless the number of logical records is an exact multiple of the blocking factor, the last block will have fewer logical records than all the others. It must still be written, of course, but with some kind of indication that it is not full. This is just one example of a great many things that the Fortran programmer never has to worry about. (As a matter of fact, many Fortran programmers are completely unaware that there is such a thing as record blocking.)

We have now introduced several of the items of information that must be provided about a data set, either explicitly or by default:

Block size
Logical record length (which will be the same if records are not blocked)
Number of buffers
Record format

Record format refers to several factors. One is whether the record is blocked. Another is whether, on an output data set, the first character is a printer control character. Another is something new: Are the records of fixed or variable length? For some purposes we would like to let the records be of variable size, in order to save the space that would be wasted if all records were made as long as the longest.

A small amount of additional information is ordinarily carried along with a variable length record, namely its length. If variable length records are blocked, the input routines have to have some way to figure out where each logical records begins and ends. This is provided by placing at the beginning of the block a number giving the total number of characters or words in the block, and at the beginning of each logical record its length. This additional space must be taken into account in specifying the block size and the logical record length.

For data sets that are to reside on magnetic disk, it is sometimes necessary to specify how much space the system should allocate.

Some data sets, especially those residing on magnetic tapes, contain *labels* at the beginning. These provide such information as the name of the file, its format, perhaps the date on which it was created, and the date after which it may be discarded. When a new file is being created, any information needed for the label must be provided. When a labelled file is read, the label can often provide much of the information about the file, making it unnecessary for us to put much into the data definition.

For any file, however, one item of information is essential: Where is it? That is, on what kind of medium is it recorded (cards, printer, disk, drum, tape, and so on), and if it is an existing data set that we are preparing to read, and if the data set resides on a removable device such as a disk pack or a reel of tape, exactly which disk or tape is it? In some systems, a particular disk pack, tape reel, or whatever, is called a *volume,* and we then speak of the identification of the particular item as the *volume serial number.*

Finally, for this quick introductory sketch, one last item of information must be provided: What is to be done with the data set after it has been processed? Some of the possibilities follow.

Delete it: we have no further need for the data.

Keep it: it is intended for later use.

Keep it and catalog it: it is intended for later use and we wish not to have to restate all the attributes.

Pass it along to a later step in the same job.

To summarize, we have to provide some or all of the following information about any data set we refer to in a program, although defaults may make it unnecessary to specify every item. In parentheses are shown the abbreviations for these items that are used in OS/360.

1. The name of the data set to be processed (DSNAME).

2. Record format: (RECFM) whether the records are fixed or variable length, whether they are blocked, and whether the first character is a carriage control character.

3. Blocksize (BLKSIZE).

4. Logical record length (LRECL), if different.

5. Disposition of the data set after processing (DISP).

6. Label information (LABEL).

7. Amount of space to be allocated (SPACE).

8. The type of device on which the data set resides (UNIT).

9. If applicable, the particular disk or tape involved (VOL).

6.14 CASE STUDY 11: GRAPHING

Sometimes in the early stages of a study, a person wants from a computer only a *general* idea of how a proposed system will work. Great accuracy may be of very little importance. In many cases a graphical presentation may be the best solution.

In others, the nature of the problem may be such that a graphical presentation will give the best intuitive understanding of the system, even though considerable accuracy may be required in the calculation.

In this case study we shall see an example of each of these points as indications of what can be done to make computer results more meaningful than they sometimes are when presented as a stack of numbers.

It should be realized that any reader who actually wants to do any serious graphing should borrow a routine designed for the purpose; it would be a waste of time and effort to repeat the programming effort when many graphing routines already exist. As in the case of Case Study 10 on simultaneous equations, we present this material to demonstrate programming techniques of importance and broad applicability, even though the wise programmer would not set out to write this particular kind of program for himself.

For the first example let us graph the results of the damped oscillation calculation we produced in Case Study 9. We shall produce a graph in which the *y* axis is a line of dots *across* the

page and the *x* axis is a row of dots *down* the page, printed one to each line. Each line printed (after the initial line of dots) will contain the letter *X* somewhere in the line; this is the plotted point. The page can be turned sideways for normal viewing. The reader may wish to glance ahead at Figures 6.6 and 6.7 to get a clear picture of what we shall be doing. Figure 6.6 is a page of output (one graph) in the orientation of the printer, somewhat reduced. Figure 6.7 shows three other graphs, turned on the page and very much reduced.

We have chosen to provide 61 printing positions in each line, a line, remember, being parallel to the *y* axis as we interpret the graph. The choice of 61 was arbitrary. There can be as many lines as there are points; in other words, the graph is of indefinite length in the *x* direction (down the page).

Figure 6.5 contains additions required to the program of Figure 5.9. We set up a one-dimensional variable LINE that will contain 61 alphanumeric elements, each containing one character. We get the symbols we shall be using by reading a card in which the first three columns contain a blank, a decimal point, and the letter *X*, in that order. In the program these symbols are named BLANK, DOT, and X. A simple DO loop fills all 61 elements of LINE with decimal points, which we then print. LINE is written without subscripts, since we want all 61 elements in the natural order. The associated FORMAT statement has a carriage-control character of 1 to space to the top of the next page. These decimal points are replaced with blanks, and a decimal point is put back in the middle of the line.

After each value of *I* (the current) has been found, we wish to use it to decide where in the line to place an *X*, to stand for the point. There are many ways to do this; the system here is indicative of what can be done. We know from the formulation of the problem that *IM* is the maximum absolute value of *I* that can ever arise. The formula

$$J = 30.0*(I/IM + 1.0) + 1.5$$

transforms I/IM, which lies between -1 and $+1$, into a number that falls between 1 and 61, the range of subscripts, as follows. The 1.0 inside the parentheses changes the range from $(-1, 1)$ to $(0, 2)$; the multiplier of 30 changes it to $(0, 60)$; and the added 1.5 changes it to $(1, 61)$; we

```
C CASE STUDY 11A
C DAMPED OSCILLATION WITH GRAPHING
C
C
      REAL I, IM, Q, R, C, L, F0, F1, C1, C2, T, DELTAT, TEMP, LINE
      INTEGER CYCLES, NPERCY, LIMIT
      DIMENSION LINE(61)
C
C READ PLOTTING SYMBOLS
      READ (5, 90) BLANK, DOT, X
  90  FORMAT (3A1)
C
C COMPUTE COMMONLY-USED FACTORS
      TWOPI = 2.0 * 3.141593
      REC2PI = 1.0 / TWOPI
C
C READ PARAMETERS
      READ (5, 100) Q, R, C, L, CYCLES, NPERCY
 100  FORMAT (4F10.0, 2I2)
C
C CHECK FOR INVALID DATA
      IF (        Q        .LE. 0.0
     1      .OR. CYCLES .LE. 0
     2      .OR. NPERCY .LE. 0
     3      .OR. R**2    .GE. 4.0*L/C ) STOP
C
C PRINT A LINE OF DOTS, WHICH WILL BE VERTICAL AXIS WHEN PAGE IS TURNED
      DO 6 J = 1, 61
  6   LINE(J) = DOT
C
C NOTE THAT INDEXING IS NOT REQUIRED, SINCE ENTIRE ARRAY IS PRINTED
      WRITE (6, 110) LINE
 110  FORMAT ('1', 61A1)
C
C BLANK THE LINE
      DO 8 J = 1, 61
  8   LINE(J) = BLANK
C
C PUT A DOT IN LINE(31), TO PRODUCE HORIZONTAL AXIS WHEN PAGE IS TURNED
      LINE(31) = DOT
C
C COMPUTE INTERMEDIATE VARIABLES
      F0 = REC2PI / SQRT(L * C)
      F1 = REC2PI * SQRT(1.0/(L*C) - R**2/(4.0*L**2))
      TEMP = NPERCY
      DELTAT = 1.0 / (TEMP * F0)
      IM = TWOPI * F0**2 * Q / F1
      C1 = R / (2.0 * L)
      C2 = TWOPI * F1
C
C START T AT ZERO BEFORE ENTERING LOOP
      T = 0.0
C
C COMPUTE THE NUMBER OF POINTS NEEDED
      LIMIT = CYCLES * NPERCY
C
C COMPUTING LOOP - DO USED FOR COUNTING THE NUMBER OF EXECUTIONS
      DO 10 J1 = 1, LIMIT
         I = IM * EXP(-C1 * T) * SIN(C2 * T)
C
C         ... COMPUTE DESIRED LOCATION OF PLOTTING SYMBOL
         J = 30.0 * (I/IM + 1.0) + 1.5
C
C         ... PUT X IN SELECTED POSITION, AND PRINT LINE
         LINE(J) = X
         WRITE (6, 120) LINE
 120     FORMAT (' ', 61A1)
C
C         ... PUT A BLANK IN SELECTED POSITION
         LINE(J) = BLANK
C
C         ... PUT A DOT IN AXIS LOCATION, IN CASE IT WAS JUST BLANKED
         LINE(31) = DOT
         T = T + DELTAT
  10  CONTINUE
      STOP
      END
```

FIGURE 6.5.   The program of Figure 5.9, modified to produce a graph rather than numeric data values. (Case Study 11a.)

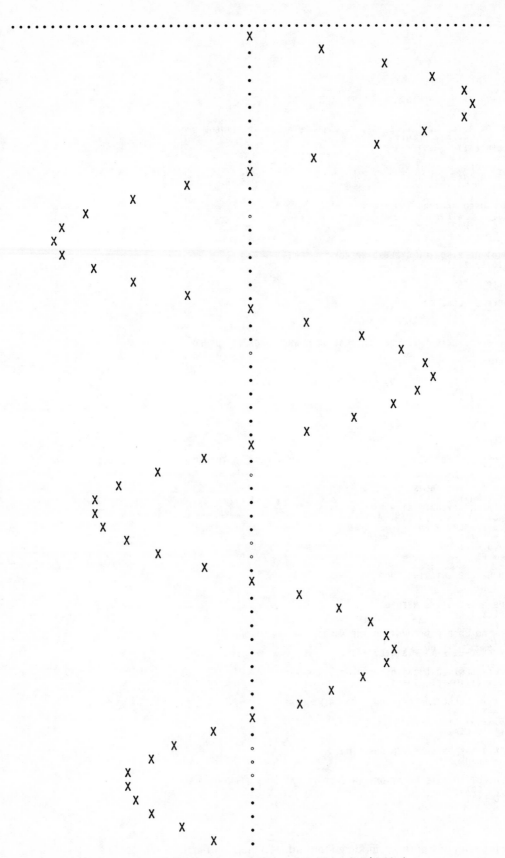

FIGURE 6.6.   The output of the program of Figure 6.5. (Case Study 11a.)

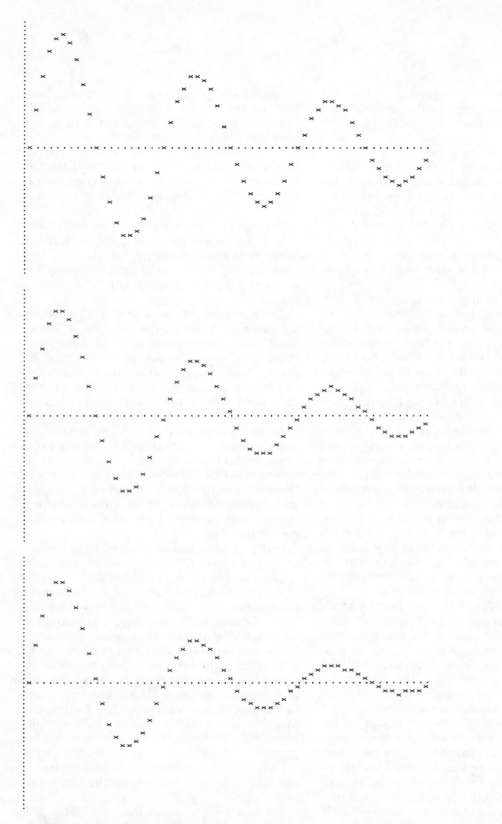

FIGURE 6.7. The output of the program of Figure 6.5, for other values of the resistance. The plots have been turned on the page for normal viewing. (Case Study 11a.)

remember that in the conversion of the real expression into an integer any fractional part will be truncated. The extra 0.5 in 1.5 is for rounding.

This subscript may now be used to place the X in one of the 61 elements of LINE, after which we print the line. The FORMAT statement for this WRITE must have a carriage-control character of blank to get single spacing. (The first version of this program was tried thoughtlessly, using FORMAT 110 for this purpose, which meant that the printer spaced to the top of a new page for every line. This is a bit wasteful of paper.)

After printing the line we replace the X with a blank and then put a decimal point in LINE(31) against the possibility that the X, which we would have erased, had been there. A test could be made to see whether the X had been in LINE(31), but it would be more trouble than the untested assignment statement.

The actions programmed at the bottom of the page in Figure 6.5 are carried out for every computed value of I, producing one line for each.

The usefulness of this kind of output is perhaps best seen in Figure 6.7, in which we have plots for different values of resistance. The damping caused by the increased resistance is clearly pictured in this way.

It would have been good practice, of course, to have printed some kind of identification on these plots. It was not done here partly because the identification would have been unreadable in Figure 6.7 after the reduction necessary to produce them in printable size.

This program illustrates only one of many approaches to the graphing of this kind of function. The method shown has the advantage that the plotting can be done as the points are produced, without requiring any storage of the values.

It is quite possible to print a complete graph on one page in normal orientation. It is most easily done if there is sufficient storage in the computer to be able to set up a two-dimensional array with as many rows as we need lines and as many columns as we need horizontal printing positions. This array could be as large as about 60×120, or 7200 storage locations, which in most computers is no problem at all.

With such an array, translation formulas, such as the foregoing, can translate x and y values into subscript values, which can then be used

to place a plotting point in the computed location. Unless a great deal is known about the function being plotted (e.g., that it decreases monotonically), it is impossible to print any of the graph until it is all ready, which, of course, is why we must have a two-dimensional array. It is entirely possible to print grid lines, indications of units on the axes, and axis identifications.

Problem 11 in the Suggestions for Term Problems at the back of the book outlines the specifications for one possible plotting program. This could be read for an idea of what such programs do, even if the reader has no interest in tackling the job.

The two examples presented in this section are intended to demonstrate the use of Fortran input and output operations, and accordingly show how to use a line printer to produce graphs. There are, of course, many other ways to produce graphs. Many types of plotters can be driven by the output of a computer program, either through a direct connection to the computer or through the intermediate medium of paper or magnetic tape. Figure 6.8 shows a plot produced on one of the smaller models of plotter marketed by California Computer Products. Everything in this figure, including the legend and the identifications of the curves, was produced under control of a Fortran program run on the IBM 1130.

This plot was graciously supplied to the author by Thomas J. Huston, whose work also appears on the cover of the book.

A second example of graphing involves a rather different sort of thing. In this problem we have a 61×61 array containing temperatures in the range of 0 to 200°. There are 529 elements in the middle of the array that contain no values, but not counting these elements, there are still 3192 temperatures to be presented, and the problem is to be solved for five different values of the temperature inside the pipe. Getting any meaning out of such a mass of data is virtually impossible, so we turn to a way of making it graphic.

Each temperature will be translated into a blank or a letter, according to the pattern of Table 6.1.

The basic idea here is that each letter will represent a band of temperatures about 11.7° wide. Between each of these bands will be a band of the same width for which a blank will

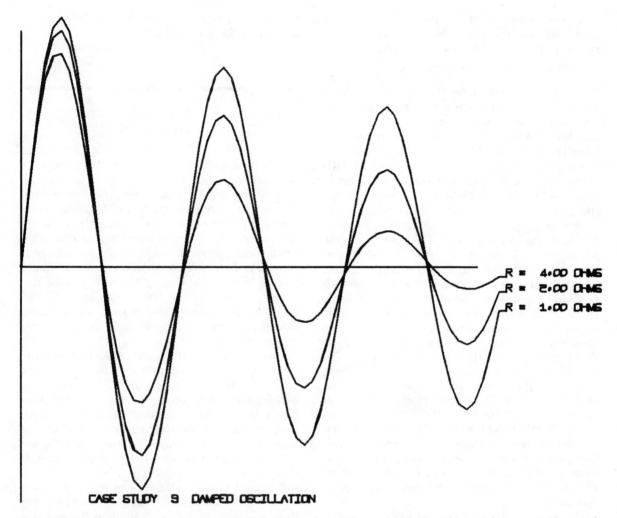

CASE STUDY 9 DAMPED OSCILLATION

R = 4.00 OHMS
R = 2.00 OHMS
R = 1.00 OHMS

FIGURE 6.8. The output of a program similar to that of Figure 6.5, modified to drive a plotter manufactured by California Computer Products, Inc. Courtesy Thomas J. Huston, Computra, Box 608, Upland, Indiana, and the Taylor University Computing Center. (Case Study 11a.)

TABLE 6.1

Temperature	Symbol
0–11.7	A
23.6–35.3	B
47.1–58.7	C
70.6–82.3	D
94.2–105.8	E
117.9–129.4	F
141.4–152.9	G
164.8–176.3	H
188.3–200.0	K

be printed. The temperatures in the 61×61 array are the solution to Laplace's equation for a certain square pipe, so that when the temperatures are plotted there will be bands of constant temperature, each band represented in our system by a letter. The letters to be used were selected to be of about the same size, visually, which will perhaps make the graph easier to interpret.

The program in Figure 6.9 includes the solution of Laplace's equation for those who may be interested. Our concern here, however, is with plotting, which is a rather small part of the total program, as it turns out.

At the beginning of the program we read a card that contains the following characters in columns 1 to 17, including the blanks:

A B C D E F G H K

The A is in column 1 on the data card. These 17 characters become the 17 elements of the one-dimensional array named SYMBOL. The variable BLANK receives the character in column 18, which is a blank.

From this point down through statement 1200 is the setup of the problem and its solution.

In the WRITE statement at 110 we reference the FORMAT at 1300 without an output list to cause page spacing. The subscripting scheme for working through the 61 lines and the 61 elements is of no interest to us in this case study. The long logical IF statement asks whether the element selected by the row-and-column subscripts is one of those in the middle because we wish to produce blanks in this area. If not, we come to a translation formula that converts a temperature into a symbol. Division of a temperature in the range (0, 200) by 11.765 provides a quotient in the range (0, 16.999); adding 1.0 produces a number in the range of (1, 17.999); when this is truncated to an integer value for the variable K, the range becomes (1, 17). SYMBOL(K) is then a blank or one of the letters contained in Table 6.1. The selected symbol goes into the appropriate place in an array named GRAPH, which has 61 elements. When a complete line of symbols has been assembled, it is printed.

The result is shown in Figure 6.10, somewhat reduced. The physical problem was this. We have a square pipe, with an inside dimension of 4 in. and an outside dimension of 10 in. The pipe is half submerged along its length in ice water at 0°; the temperature along the vertical sides increases linearly from 0° at the water level to 100° at the top, which is also the temperature along the top. The pipe is carrying a fluid at 200°. The output in Figure 6.10 shows the temperature at the interior points after solution of the differential equation. The picture is not square because there are 10 printing positions per inch horizontally but only 6 lines per inch vertically. This is no serious inconvenience.

One effective use of this program is in visualizing the effect of changing the internal fluid temperature on the temperature distribution through the pipe material. Figure 6.11 shows

plots, considerably reduced, for inside temperatures of 0, 50, 100, and 150°.

6.15 CASE STUDY 12: THE GAUSS-SEIDEL METHOD WITH LARGE SYSTEMS AND COEFFICIENTS ON TAPE OR DISK

In this case study we shall modify the program of Case Study 10 to make it apply to systems of as many as 400 equations. The coefficients for such a system number 160,000, which exceeds the central storage capacity for many computers. The coefficients are accordingly written onto tape or disk in a preliminary program and then read back from the intermediate storage repeatedly during the solution of the system. It is one of the advantages of the Gauss-Seidel method that it requires only one row of coefficients to be in main storage at any one time.

The emphasis in this case study will be twofold. First, we shall see how it is possible to work with intermediate storage on tape or disk. This part applies to any mode of operation, whether batch, time sharing, or stand-alone. Second, we shall consider how to convey to a batch or time-sharing system our intentions regarding the assignment of data sets to particular physical devices.

A reader whose system does not permit the latter, or who anticipates no immediate need for the capability, might wish to skim this section the first time through. It is no doubt the most difficult case study we have so far encountered, but it is really not impossible. The crucial issue, and the thing the reader should continually be asking himself, is: *Where is the data?* And: *How do we tell the system where the data is?*

As always in these matters, some of the details pertain strictly to the particular system used in running programs for this book. As usual, we can only urge that the general principles underlying the details are valid in any operating system, time sharing or batch.

Since the complete system of coefficients will have to be read repeatedly, as many times as there are iterations, it will be important to try to speed the reading of the data. This argues in favor of unformatted input statements, so the coefficients will have to be written out in that manner as well. The program shown in Figure 6.12 has this function, working specifically with the system of equations used to test the program of Case Study 10. (Seven equations is *not* a "large" system, of course, but for testing we prefer small samples.)

Since the data for Case Study 10 (as it happens) is still residing on disk from its earlier use, we shall pick it up from there, using a FILEDEF to establish data set 5 as being a disk rather than the time-sharing terminal. The unformatted output is written on data set 9, which we shall also define with a FILEDEF that will be displayed shortly.

The logic of this preliminary program is simply to read the data from disk into a two-dimensional array, then write it out one row at a time to data set 9. Reviewing the data as it was prepared for use in Case Study 10, we recall that the first record consisted of data about the system of equations: the number of equations, the maximum number of iterations to be permitted, and so forth. We shall need that information later, in actually solving the system, but for the purposes of this preliminary program, which only rearranges the coefficients and constant terms of the system, we wish to skip over that first record. The simplest way to do this is to execute a READ statement without a list—something that is not done very often. Then we go into a loop that reads the coefficients into the array named A, looking for a sentinel consisting of a 99 where the row number would normally be. We omit the normal data validation operations, to simplify and shorten the program.

We recall that the data prepared for the earlier case study consisted of only the nonzero elements of the system of coefficients. We accordingly begin the program by zeroing out the A array into which the coefficients will be read.

The writing of the rows to data set 9 could be carried out using implied DO indexing in a WRITE statement, but to emphasize the point that writing an array without subscripting is a good deal faster, we have written the program to transfer each row to a separate one-dimensional array before writing. Naturally, this transfer takes time, too, but ordinarily far less than the time saved in writing.

After all the rows have been written, we do an END FILE on the data set. This is not absolutely necessary if the program that later reads the data set is correct, but it does no harm and

could simplify checking out the other program. We then rewind the data set. This actually is not meaningful if the data set turns out to be on disk or drum, but it does no harm. Furthermore, if the program that later uses this data set begins by rewinding the tape, as it will, this rewind is not even needed. On the other hand, if the later program should for any reason fail to be executed and this program had not rewound the tape, it would cause the computer operator a minor inconvenience. What we have done here is conservative coding practice: an extra rewind where one would have been sufficient can do no harm, and in unexpected circumstances it might save somebody a bit of trouble.

We now move to the program to carry out the solution of the system of equations, shown in Figure 6.13. Observe the use of a "box" composed of asterisks to set off the new comments.

To emphasize the point that we have rather complete and flexible control over the assignment of data sets at the time of execution of the object program, we shall read the coefficients from data set 17 instead of 9. We shall show shortly the quite simple operations necessary to establish that data set 17 here is the same as the data set 9 that was produced by the program of Figure 6.12.

The array for the coefficients is now *one*-dimensional because we shall never have more than one row of coefficients in main storage at once. After clearing the X array we read the control parameters from data set 5, which is the same one from which the coefficients were taken by the program of Figure 6.12. Now we are ready to begin an iteration, at the beginning of which we immediately rewind data set 17. This may seem pointless the first time through, since the data set has not yet been read and should already be at its beginning. If the data set happens to reside on a magnetic tape, however, it is always necessary to issue an initial rewind to be absolutely certain that in the process of mounting the tape it did not get positioned past the beginning of the data.

In reading a row of coefficients into the array named A, it is necessary to use implied DO indexing because we wish to read only $N+1$ elements, not 401. This will slow the execution of the program somewhat, but it is unavoidable with the techniques so far available to us.

The program is not greatly different from that of Figure 5.12, except that the subscripting is a

```
C CASE STUDY 11B
C GRAPHING A PIPE TEMPERATURE MAP
C
C
      DIMENSION U(61, 61), GRAPH(61), SYMBOL(17)
C
C READ GRAPHING SYMBOLS AND A BLANK
      READ (5, 1000) (SYMBOL(K), K = 1, 17), BLANK
 1000 FORMAT (18A1)
C
C FROM HERE THROUGH STATEMENT 100 IS THE TEMPERATURE COMPUTATION
    5 READ (5, 1100, END=150) OMEGA, EPS, TEMP, MAXIT
 1100 FORMAT (3F10.0, I3)
C
C SET UP BOUNDARIES AND INITIAL APPROXIMATIONS (ZEROS)
      DO 20 I = 1, 61
          DO 10 J = 1, 61
              U(I, J) = 0.0
   10     CONTINUE
   20 CONTINUE
      DO 30 J = 32, 61
          FJ = J
          BOUND = 100.0 * (FJ - 31.0) / 30.0
          U(1, J) = BOUND
          U(61, J) = BOUND
   30 CONTINUE
      DO 40 I = 2, 60
          U(I, 61) = 100.0
   40 CONTINUE
      DO 50 I = 19, 43
          U(I, 43) = TEMP
          U(I, 19) = TEMP
   50 CONTINUE
      DO 60 J = 19, 43
          U(43, J) = TEMP
          U(19, J) = TEMP
   60 CONTINUE
C
C SET UP COMMON FACTORS
      A = OMEGA / 4.0
      B = 1.0 - OMEGA
C
C START DO TO COUNT ITERATIONS AND CHECK AGAINST MAXIMUM
      DO 100 ITN = 1, MAXIT
C
C START BIGGEST RESIDUAL AT ZERO
   70     BIGRES = 0.0
C
C COMPUTE NEW APPROXIMATION AT EACH POINT IN PIPE
          DO 90 J = 2, 60
              DO 80 I = 2, 60
                  IF (       (I .GE. 19)
     1              .AND. (I .LE. 43)
     2              .AND. (J .GE. 19)
     3              .AND. (J .LE. 43) ) GO TO 80
                  UNEW = A*(U(I+1,J) + U(I-1,J) + U(I,J+1) + U(I,J-1))
     1              + B*U(I,J)
                  RESID = ABS(UNEW - U(I,J))
                  IF ( RESID .GT. BIGRES ) BIGRES = RESID
                  U(I, J) = UNEW
   80         CONTINUE
   90     CONTINUE
C
```

FIGURE 6.9.   A program for solving LaPlace's equation for a certain square pipe, and plotting the solution. (Case Study 11b.)

```
C CHECK FOR CONVERGENCE
         IF ( BIGRES .LT. EPS ) GO TO 110
 100   CONTINUE
C
C IF THIS DO IS EVER SATISFIED MORE THAN 'MAXIT' ITERATIONS WOULD BE
C    NEEDED FOR CONVERGENCE -- WRITE COMMENT AND PRINT GRAPH ANYWAY
       WRITE (6, 1200) MAXIT, BIGRES
 1200 FORMAT (1H1, 'DIDN''T CONVERGE IN ', I3, '    ITERATIONS.'/
      1 'BIGGEST RESIDUAL WAS ', F12.4, ';    PRINTING GRAPH ANYWAY.')
C
C COMPUTATION COMPLETE -- MOVE TO TOP OF NEW PAGE TO START GRAPH
 110   WRITE (6, 1300)
 1300 FORMAT (1H1)
C
C SET ROW INDEX, J, TO 61 FOR TOP ROW
      J = 61
C
C RUN THROUGH COMPLETE ROW
 120   DO 140 I = 1, 61
C
C CHECK IF POINT IS IN CENTER OF PIPE
         IF (         (I .GE. 20)
      1        .AND. (I .LE. 42)
      2        .AND. (J .GE. 20)
      3        .AND. (J .LE. 42) ) GO TO 130
C
C NOT IN CENTER -- SELECT LETTER OR BLANK TO REPRESENT TEMPERATURE
         K = U(I,J) / 11.765 + 1.0
C
C PLACE SELECTED SYMBOL IN APPROPRIATE POSITION IN LINE
         GRAPH(I) = SYMBOL(K)
         GO TO 140
C
C INSERT BLANK FOR CENTER OF PIPE
 130     GRAPH(I) = BLANK
 140   CONTINUE
C
C WRITE ENTIRE LINE -- INDEXING NOT REQUIRED
       WRITE (6, 1400) GRAPH
 1400 FORMAT (1H , 61A1)
C
C MOVE TO NEXT ROW OF MAP
      J = J - 1
C
C CHECK FOR COMPLETION
      IF ( J .NE. 0 ) GO TO 120
C
C GRAPH COMPLETE -- GO BACK FOR MORE DATA IF ANY
      GO TO 5
C
C STOP AT END OF FILE ON INPUT DATA SET
 150   STOP
       END
```

FIGURE 6.9.   (Cont.)

```
EEEEEEEEEEEEEEEEEEEEEEEEEEEEEEEEEEEEEEEEEEEEEEEEEEEEEEEEEEEEEEEEEEEEEEEEE
EEEEEEEEEEEEEEEEEEEEEEEEEEEEEEEEEEEEEEEEEEEEEEEEEEEEEEEEEEEEEEEEEEEEEEEE
  EEEEEEEEEEEEEEEEE                              EEEEEEEEEEEEEEEEE
    EEEEEEEEE                                      EEEEEEEEE
      EEEEEEEE            FFFFFFFFFFFFF              EEEEEEEE
        EEEEE          FFFFFFFFFFFFFFFFFFFFFFF         EEEEE
D        EEEEE        FFFFFFFFFFFFFFFFFFFFFFFFFFFF      EEEEE        D
DD       EEEE       FFFFFFF              FFFFFFF        EEEE        DD
DDD       EEE      FFFFF                    FFFFF       EEE       DDD
DDD       EEE     FFF        GGGGGGGGGGGGGGGG      FFF      EEE       DDD
DDD       EEE     FFF     GGGGGGGGGGGGGGGGGGGGGG   FFF      EEE       DDD
 DDD      EEE    FFF    GGGGGG              GGGGGG  FFF     EEE      DDD
  DD      EEE    FF    GGGG                    GGGG  FF     EEE      DD
C  DD     EEE    FF   GGG       HHHHHHHHHHHHH    GGG  FF    EEE     DD  C
C  DD     EE    FF    GG     HHHHHHHHHHHHHHHHHHHHH GG  FF    EE    DD  C
CC  DD    E     FF    G    HHHH                 HHHH G FF    E    DD  CC
C  DD     E    FF  GG HH                         HH GG FF    E    DD  C
CC DD     E    F    G HH   KKKKKKKKKKKKKKKKKKKKK  HH G  F    E    DD CC
CC  D     E    F    G H  KKKKKKKKKKKKKKKKKKKKKKKKKKK  H G    F    E    D  CC
  C  D    E    F  GG H K                           K H GG    F    E    D   C
B CC  D   E    F  G   H K                         K H   G    F    E   D CC B
B  C DD   E    F  G H  K                           K  H G    F    E DD  C  B
B  C DD   E    F  G H KK                         KK H G    F    E DD  C  B
  B  C    D E    F  G H KK                       KK H  G    F    E D   C B
  B CC    D E    F  G H KK                       KK H  G    F    E D CC  B
  B  C D  EE F    G H KK                         KK H G    FF EE  D  C  B
BB  C D   EE F    G H KK                         KK H G    FF EE  D C BB
A  B C D    E    F  G H KK                       KK H  GFE    D   C B A
A  B C DD   E    F  G H KK                       KK H  G FE DD  C B A
A  B C    D E    F  G H KK                       KK H  GFED    C B A
A B CC    D E    F  G H KK                       KK H  G F ED CC B A
A BB  C   D E    F  G H KK                       KK H  G F ED  C BB A
AA  B C   D E    F  GG H KK                       KK H  G F ED  C B AA
AA  B C   D E    F  GG H K                         K H GG F    ED  C B AA
AA  B C   D E     F  GH K                          K H G  F    ED C B AA
AA  B C   D EE    F  G H K                          K H G  F EE D C B AA
AA  B C   DD E    F  G H K                          K H G  F EDD C B AA
AA  B C    D E    F  G H K                          K H G  FED    C B AA
AA  B CC  D E    F  G H K                           K H G  FE DCC B AA
AA  B     C D E   F  G H K                          K H G  FED C   B AA
AA  B     C  D E   F  GH K                          K HG F  D   C  B AA
AA BB  C  DD E    F  G   K                         K  G FE DD  C BB AA
AA BB  C   D E    F  G  HKKKKKKKKKKKKKKKKKKKKKKKKKKKH G FE D   C BB AA
AA BB CC  D   E    F  G H                          H G FE  D CC BB AA
AA  B   C   D EE  F  G   HHHHHHHHHHHHHHHHHHHHHHHH   G F EE D   C B   AA
AA  B  CC DD E   F  GGG                          GGG F E DD CC B   AA
AA  BB CC   D  E   FF   GGGGGGGGGGGGGGGGGGGGGG  FF  E D   CC BB   AA
AA  BB  CC DD  EE  FFF                          FFF  EE  DD CC  BB   AA
AAA   BB  C   DD   EE    FFFFFFFFFFFFFFFFFFFFFF   EE  DD   CC  BB   AAA
AAA   BB  CC   DDD  EEE                          EEE DDD   CC  BB   AAA
AAA   BBB  CC    DDD    EEEEEEEEEEEEEEEEEEEEEE   DDD    CC  BBB   AAA
AAA   BBB  CCC    DDDD                          DDDD   CCC   BB    AAA
AAAA   BBB   CCC    DDDDDDDDD   DDDDDDDDD   CCC   BB   AAAA
AAAA   BBBB    CCCCC       DDDDDDDDD       CCCCC   BBBB   AAAA
AAAAA    BBBB     CCCCCCCC            CCCCCCCC     BBBB    AAAAA
AAAAA     BBBBB        CCCCCCCCCCCCCCCC         BBBBB     AAAAA
AAAAAAA       BBBBBBBB                       BBBBBBBB       AAAAAAA
AAAAAAAA         BBBBBBBBBBBBBBBBBBBBBBBBBBBBB         AAAAAAAA
AAAAAAAAAAAA                                      AAAAAAAAAAAA
AAAAAAAAAAAAAAAAAAAAAAAAAAAAAAAAAAAAAAAAAAAAAAAAAAAAAAAAAAAAAA
AAAAAAAAAAAAAAAAAAAAAAAAAAAAAAAAAAAAAAAAAAAAAAAAAAAAAAAAAAAAAA
```

FIGURE 6.10. The output of the program of Figure 6.9. This is a graphical presentation of the solution of LaPlace's equation in a pipe carrying a hot liquid and partially immersed in ice water. (Case Study 11b.)

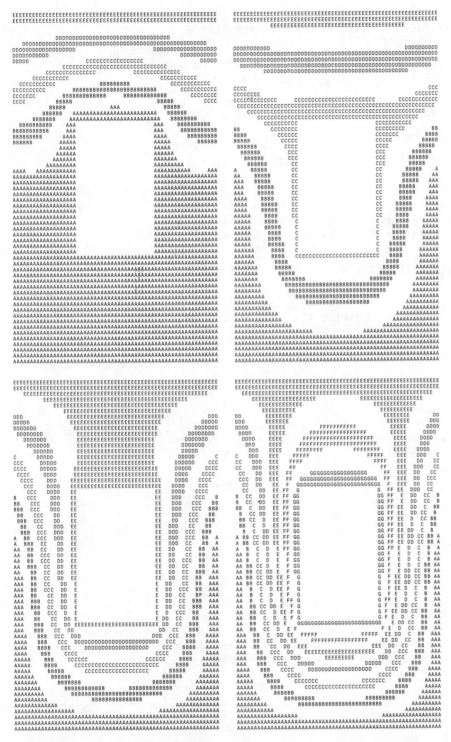

FIGURE 6.11.   The output of the program of Figure 6.9, considerably reduced,
for four other temperatures of the liquid inside the pipe. (Case Study 11b.)

```
C CASE STUDY 12
C A PROGRAM TO PREPARE THE UNFORMATTED DATA FOR VERY LARGE
C SYSTEMS OF SIMULTANEOUS EQUATIONS
C
C (THIS EXAMPLE, HOWEVER, IS BASED ON THE SYSTEM OF SEVEN
C   EQUATIONS USED IN CASE STUDY 10.)
C
C THE DATA IS TAKEN FROM DATA SET 5, WHERE IT APPEARS IN FORMATTED
C FORM, AND PLACED ON DATA SET 9 IN UNFORMATTED FORM.
C
      DIMENSION A(7, 8), ROW(8)
C
C ZERO OUT THE ARRAY SO ONLY NON-ZERO ELEMENTS NEED BE READ
      DO 10 I = 1, 7
      DO 10 J = 1, 8
  10  A(I, J) = 0.0
C
C REWIND THE DATA SET TO BE SURE IT IS AT ITS BEGINNING --
C THIS HAS NO EFFECT IF THE DATA SET WAS ALREADY AT ITS BEGINNING
      REWIND 9
C
C THIS READ ESSENTIALLY SKIPS OVER AN UNWANTED FIRST RECORD
      READ (5, 100)
 100  FORMAT (1X)
C
C NOW WE READ THE DATA RECORDS, LOOKING FOR AN I = 99 SENTINEL
  20  READ (5, 110) I, J, TEMP
 110  FORMAT (2I2, F10.0)
      IF ( I .EQ. 99 ) GO TO 30
C
C (ANY DATA VALIDATION WOULD BE DONE HERE)
      A(I, J) = TEMP
      GO TO 20
C
C WRITE OUT THE ROWS, ONE FULL ROW AT A TIME
C EACH ROW IS MOVED TO A ONE-DIMENSIONAL ARRAY BEFORE WRITING,
C TO SPEED THE OUTPUT OPERATION.
  30  DO 50 I = 1, 7
          DO 40 J = 1, 8
              ROW(J) = A(I, J)
  40      CONTINUE
          WRITE (9) ROW
  50  CONTINUE
C
C WRITE END OF FILE ON DATA SET 9
      END FILE 9
C
C REWIND DATA SET 9
      REWIND 9
      STOP
      END
```

FIGURE 6.12.   A program to prepare the unformatted data for a very large system of simultaneous equations. The file definition for data set 9 is given separately, using an operating system command. (Case Study 12.)

bit different because the array that holds the coefficients is now one-dimensional.

We are now ready to run the programs. Let us review the data sets used by each:

The program of Figure 6.12 reads data set 5, which is a disk file named (as it happens) FCS10; it writes data set 9, which we wish to make a disk file named FCS12DAT. (These names were selected to be meaningful to the author.)

The program of Figure 6.13 reads data set 5, which is the same as before; it also reads data set 17, which we wish to establish as being the same as the earlier data set 9; it writes data set 6, which we wish to be the time-sharing console.

We compile the program of Figure 6.12 in the ordinary way, but before executing it we carry out the following operations in the time-sharing system being used, which, to repeat, is that of

National CSS, Inc., Stamford, Conn., and Sunny-vale, Calif.

```
FILEDEF 5 DSK FCS10 DATA
FILEDEF 9 DSK FCS12DAT DATA RECFM V
```

The FILEDEF command stands for "file define." In the first of these, we identify data set 5 as residing on disk (DSK), as having the name FCS10 (which was established when the data set was written in connection with Case Study 10), and the file type of DATA, which distinguishes it from another file named FCS10 with the file type of FORTRAN that contains the source program. The second FILEDEF defines data set 9 as residing on a disk, having the name FCS12DAT and the file type DATA, and it also states that the record format (RECFM) is *variable* (V). This is necessary because we want the program to work for whatever size of system may

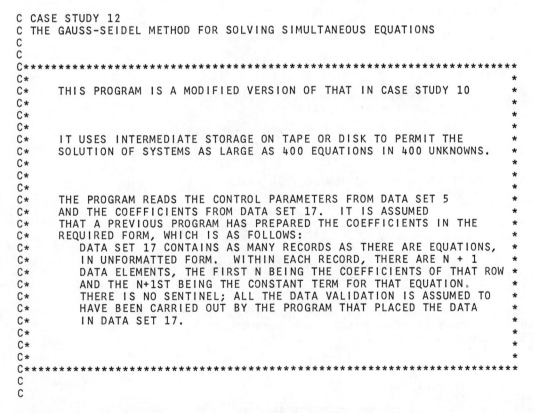

```
C CASE STUDY 12
C THE GAUSS-SEIDEL METHOD FOR SOLVING SIMULTANEOUS EQUATIONS
C
C
C*******************************************************************
C*                                                                 *
C*      THIS PROGRAM IS A MODIFIED VERSION OF THAT IN CASE STUDY 10 *
C*                                                                 *
C*                                                                 *
C*                                                                 *
C*      IT USES INTERMEDIATE STORAGE ON TAPE OR DISK TO PERMIT THE  *
C*      SOLUTION OF SYSTEMS AS LARGE AS 400 EQUATIONS IN 400 UNKNOWNS. *
C*                                                                 *
C*                                                                 *
C*                                                                 *
C*      THE PROGRAM READS THE CONTROL PARAMETERS FROM DATA SET 5    *
C*      AND THE COEFFICIENTS FROM DATA SET 17.  IT IS ASSUMED       *
C*      THAT A PREVIOUS PROGRAM HAS PREPARED THE COEFFICIENTS IN THE *
C*      REQUIRED FORM, WHICH IS AS FOLLOWS:                         *
C*          DATA SET 17 CONTAINS AS MANY RECORDS AS THERE ARE EQUATIONS, *
C*          IN UNFORMATTED FORM.  WITHIN EACH RECORD, THERE ARE N + 1 *
C*          DATA ELEMENTS, THE FIRST N BEING THE COEFFICIENTS OF THAT ROW *
C*          AND THE N+1ST BEING THE CONSTANT TERM FOR THAT EQUATION. *
C*          THERE IS NO SENTINEL; ALL THE DATA VALIDATION IS ASSUMED TO *
C*          HAVE BEEN CARRIED OUT BY THE PROGRAM THAT PLACED THE DATA *
C*          IN DATA SET 17.                                         *
C*                                                                 *
C*                                                                 *
C*                                                                 *
C*******************************************************************
C
C
```

FIGURE 6.13. A program for solving a system as large as 400 equations in 400 unknowns, using the Gauss-Seidel method, with the coefficients and constant terms stored on tape or disk. Compare with the program of Figure 5.12. (Case Study 12.)

```
        DIMENSION A(401), X(400)
C
C CLEAR THE X ARRAY
        DO 10 I = 1, 400
            X(I) = 0.0
   10   CONTINUE
C
C READ PARAMETERS DESCRIBED IN INTRODUCTORY COMMENTS IN CASE STUDY 10
        READ (5, 100) N, MAXIT, EPSLON
        NPLUS1 = N + 1
C
C       BEGIN ITERATION SCHEME -- DO LOOP COUNTS THE NUMBER OF ITERATIONS
        DO 70 ITER = 1, MAXIT
C
C           ... NEXT 2 STATEMENTS ARE EXECUTED ONCE PER SWEEP OF THE SYSTEM
            RESID = 0.0
C
C           ... REWIND THE DATA SET TO ITS BEGINNING
            REWIND 17
C
C           ... INDEX I SELECTS A ROW
            DO 60 I = 1, N
C
C               ... NEXT 2 STATEMENTS ARE EXECUTED ONCE PER ROW
                SUM = 0.0
C
C               GET I-TH ROW OF COEFFICIENTS
                READ (17) (A(L), L = 1, NPLUS1)
C
C               ...GET SUM OF TERMS IN I-TH ROW, NOT INCLUDING DIAGONAL TERM
                DO 50 J = 1, N
                    IF ( J .NE. I ) SUM = SUM + A(J)*X(J)
   50           CONTINUE
C
C               ... COMPUTE THE NEW APPROXIMATION TO VARIABLE X(I)
                TEMP = (A(NPLUS1) - SUM) / A(I)
C
C               ... AT THE END OF A SWEEP OF ALL EQUATIONS, THE FOLLOWING
C               ... STATEMENT WILL HAVE PUT LARGEST RESIDUAL IN RESID
                IF ( ABS(TEMP - X(I)) .GT. RESID ) RESID = ABS(TEMP - X(I))
C
C               ... STORE NEW APPROXIMATION TO I-TH VARIABLE
                X(I) = TEMP
   60       CONTINUE
C
C           ... ONE SWEEP HAS NOW BEEN COMPLETED --  PRINT VARIABLES
            WRITE (6, 140) (X(K), K = 1, N)
C
C           ... IF LARGEST RESIDUAL LESS THAN EPSLON, PROCESS HAS CONVERGED
            IF ( RESID .LT. EPSLON ) STOP
   70   CONTINUE
C
C IF THIS OUTER DO IS EVER SATISFIED, MORE THAN MAXIT ITERATIONS WOULD
C    BE NEEDED FOR CONVERGENCE -- WRITE ERROR COMMENT AND GIVE UP
        WRITE (6, 150) MAXIT
        STOP
C
C
  100   FORMAT (2I2, 3F10.0)
  140   FORMAT ('0', 8F12.5)
  150   FORMAT ('0', 'PROCESS DID NOT CONVERGE IN', I4, ' ITERATIONS')
        END
```

FIGURE 6.13.   (Cont.)

turn up in running the job, which precludes fixed-length records. We have not supplied a block size, although we could have; we shall accept the system default value.

After issuing these FILEDEFs we command the time-sharing system to execute the program of Figure 6.12. Since the only output goes to disk, nothing is printed at the console and after a few seconds the system reports that it has completed running the program.

Now we are ready to run the program of Figure 6.13. The FILEDEF for data set 5 is still correct, but now we need to instruct the system that data set 17 is the same one that we just called data set 9. This is done with the command:

```
FILEDEF 17 DSK FCS12DAT DATA RECFM V
```

Data set 6 automatically defaults to the time-sharing console in the CSS system, so nothing has to be done about that.

Now we call for the execution of the object program corresponding to the source program of Figure 6.13. The control parameters come from data set 5 on disk, the coefficients from data set 17 on disk, and the output goes to the time-sharing terminal. The output is identical to that shown in Figure 5.14, indicating that everything worked as desired.

Now let us run the same programs using magnetic tape for intermediate storage instead of magnetic disk. Everything is done just as before, except that the file definitions for data sets 9 and 17 this time are

```
FILEDEF 9 TAP RECFM V
FILEDEF 17 TAP RECFM V
```

Notice that there are no file names or file types here, since a tape reel can hold only one file.* The machine being used here, a very large IBM 360 Model 67, has many tape units; by not speci-

---

*Strictly speaking, this statement is an oversimplification, but the precise details are of no importance to us.

fying which one, we accept the default. So long as it is the same tape unit for both writing and reading, we really have no interest in what its unit designation might be. (It is necessary, however, to instruct the input/output operator to mount a tape for our use. Since for the purposes of this example we have no interest in keeping the tape—and therefore paying rental on it—we instruct the operator to use a *scratch tape*, that is, one that will not be saved.)

With these FILEDEFs for 9 and 17, and with the same FILEDEF for 5 as before, the two programs can be run once again, without any change whatsoever in the programs. The printed results are once again identical with those in Figure 5.14.

This kind of flexibility is also available with batch operating systems, and indeed was one of the primary motivations for the development of operating systems.

The batch operating system commands that would be required to specify the actions we have called for with the FILEDEFs above would differ for various operating systems. In OS/360 for the IBM System 360 and 370 the term is Data Definition (DD); in EXEC 8 for the Univac 1108 the term is Assign Control Statement (ASG); in the Master Control Program for the Burroughs B6000 equipment we speak of a label table; the Control Data Corporation SCOPE program for the 6000 Computer Systems refers to a File Environment Table (FET). All such commands have to specify about the same kinds of information, along the lines of the concepts introduced in Section 6.8 and 6.13 and illustrated in the current case study. The formats of the commands do vary markedly from one system to another, however, and we doubt whether very many readers would benefit greatly by examples for any one system, beyond the illustrations already presented above.

We therefore leave the reader to the mercies of the manuals for his particular operating system, and wish him good luck.

EXERCISES

1. Show how the given data values would be printed under control of the field descriptors stated.

   (a) I5: 0, 1, 10, −587, 90062, 123456
   (b) F7.2: 0.0, 1.0, 16.77, −586.21, 0.04, 12.34
   (c) F5.0: 0.0, 1.0, 16.87, −12.32
   (d) E10.3: 0.0, 0.00072, 601000., −473., −0.0123
   (e) 1PE10.3: 0.0, 10.0, 0.000076, 6780000., −627., −0.000456

2. Given that the values of three variables are as follows

$$M = 12$$
$$X = 407.8$$
$$Y = -32.9$$

   Show exactly what would be printed by

   WRITE (6, 107) M, X, Y

   with each of the following FORMAT statements.

   *a. 107   FORMAT (1H , 3HM= , I3, 3HX= ,
       1   F6.1, 3HY= , F6.1)

   b. 107   FORMAT (1H1, 17HREADING NUMBER = ,
       1   I3/1H0, 11HPRESSURE = , F6.1,
       2   7HTEMP = , F6.1)

   c. 107   FORMAT (1H1, 17HREADING NUMBER = ,
       1   I3/1H0, 8HPRESSURE, 6X,
       2   11HTEMPERATURE/1H0, F7.1, 9X,
       3   F6.1)

   *3. Four numbers are punched on a card; they are new values of real variables named BOS, EWR, PHX, and DCA. Each number is punched in eight columns, the first beginning in column 1. Each number contains a decimal point. Write READ and FORMAT statements to read the card.

   4. Same as Exercise 3, except that there is no decimal point. The numbers are to be treated as if they had two decimal places, that is, two places to the right of an assumed decimal point.

   5. Same as Exercise 3, except that each num-

ber occupies 14 columns and is punched with a decimal point and an exponent.

*6. A card is punched in the following format.

Columns	Sample Format	Variable Name
1–3	±xx	LAX
4–6	xxx	JFK
7–20	±x.xxxxxxxE ± ee	PDX
21–34	±x.xxxxxxxE ± ee	SFO

LAX and JFK are integer variables; PDX and SFO are real. The small letters stand for any digits. Write statements to read such a card.

*7. Given a WRITE statement,

WRITE (6, 92) I, J, R, S

I and J are integer variables and R and S are real. For each of the following, write a FORMAT statement that could produce such a line or lines with the given WRITE statement. [Write only one FORMAT statement for (f).] The letters in (e) and (f) are in column 1.

a.   -16   92017   16.82   437.89

b.   -16   92017   17.   438.

c.   -16   92017   0.16824E 02   0.43789E 03

d.   -16   92017   1.6824E 01   4.3789E 02

e. I=   -16   J= 92017   R= 16.8   S= 437.9

f. I=   -16
   J= 92017
   R= 16.8
   S= 437.9

8. Same as Exercise 7, but given the WRITE statement

WRITE (6, 93) M, P, Q, R

M is an integer variable and the others are real. [Write only one FORMAT statement each for (d) and (e).]

a. 9 -33. 1.6E-04 1.439024E 06

b. 9 -32.62 0.00016   0.1439024E 07

c. 9 -32.62 0.16E-03 1439024.

d. M   RHO   GAIN   OUTPUT
    9 -32.62 1.6E-04   1.439024E 06

e. M= 9   RHO= -32.62   GAIN= 1.6E-04
   OUTPUT= 1.439024E 06

A GUIDE TO FORTRAN IV PROGRAMMING

*9. DATA is a one-dimensional array of 10 elements. A card is punched with a value of N in columns 1 and 2 and with 1 to 10 elements of DATA in succeeding columns. The number of values is given by the value of N. Each number is punched with a decimal point but no exponent, in seven columns. Write statements to read such a card and place the values in the first N elements of DATA.

10. Same as Exercise 9 except that the numbers are the *odd-numbered* elements of DATA; there are therefore at most five of them. N is the *element number* of the last one, not the total number of elements.

*11. Describe in words what card format and deck make-up would be required for each of the following groups of statements to be meaningful:

a.
```
   DIMENSION X(10)
   READ (5, 69) (X(I), I = 1, 7)
69 FORMAT (10F4.0)
```

b.
```
   DIMENSION X(10)
   READ (5, 70) N, (X(I), I = 1, N)
70 FORMAT (I2, 10F4.0)
```

c.
```
   DIMENSION X(10)
   READ (5, 71) N, (X(I), I = 1, N)
71 FORMAT (I2/10F4.0)
```

d.
```
   DIMENSION X(10)
   READ (5, 72) N, (X(I), I = 1, N)
72 FORMAT (I2/(F9.0))
```

12. Same as Exercise 11.

a.
```
   DIMENSION Y(10, 10)
   READ (5, 79) K, (Y(K, I),I=1,10)
79 FORMAT (I2, 10F5.0)
```

b.
```
   DIMENSION Y(10, 10)
   READ (5,80) K, M, (Y(K,I),I=1,M)
80 FORMAT (2I2, 10F5.0)
```

c.
```
   DIMENSION Y(10, 10)
   READ(5,81)M,N,((Y(I,J),J=1,N),I=1,M)
81 FORMAT (2I2/(10F8.0))
```

d.
```
   DIMENSION Y(10, 10)
83 READ (5, 82) I, J, Y(I,J), L
82 FORMAT (2I2, F10.0, I1)
   IF ( L .EQ. 0 ) GO TO 83
```

*13. The values of the real variables A, B, X, and Z are to be printed on one line. A and B are to be printed without exponents, X and Z with exponents. Twelve spaces should be allowed for A and B, and they should have

four decimal places. Twenty spaces should be allowed for X and Z, and they should be printed with eight decimal places and no scale factor. Write appropriate statements.

14. Same as Exercise 13 except that a positive integer named K is to be printed in six spaces between A and B and the decimal point is to be moved one place to the right in X and Z.

*15. A two-dimensional array named PHL consists of 10 rows and 4 columns. Write a program to print a page as follows: at the top of the page is the heading MATRIX PHL. After two blank lines the elements are printed in the normal row-and-column arrangement for a two-dimensional array, using 1PE20.7 field descriptors. (*Hint.* Be sure that exactly four numbers are printed on each line.)

16. A one-dimensional array named CVG contains a maximum of 40 elements. The input deck to be read has one element per card; each card contains the element number in columns 1 and 2 and the element itself in columns 3 to 12, punched with a decimal point but without an exponent. The cards cannot be assumed to be in sequence on the element numbers. It is not known how many cards there are, but the last card of the deck is blank, which will look like an element number of zero. Write a program segment to read the deck and place each value in the correct location in the array.

*17. A two-dimensional array named STL is named in the statement

```
DIMENSION STL(10, 13)
```

The actual number of rows and columns is given by the values of the variables M and N, respectively. Write a program to punch on cards as many elements as there actually are in the array, in row order. Each element should be punched on a separate card along with its row and column numbers. Use I2 for the integers and 1PE20.7 for the real numbers.

*18. Given an integer variable I, assuming $1 \leq I \leq 12$, set up a program that will print in three printing positions one of the abbreviations JAN, FEB, MAR, APR, etc., depending on the value of I. Assume a computer in which one alphanumeric variable can hold four characters.

19. Given an integer variable J, with $1 \leq J \leq 7$. Set up a program to print one of the words MONDAY, TUESDAY, etc., depending on the value of J. Assume a computer in which one alphanumeric variable can hold four characters, which, of course, is not enough to hold the words.

*20. Given the following program segment

```
      DIMENSION FMT(18), X(10)
101   READ (5, 102) (FMT(I),I=1,18)
102   FORMAT (18A4)
         .
         .
         .
      WRITE (6, FMT) (X(I), I=1,10)
```

Show exactly what should be punched on the card read by the foregoing READ statement in order to print the 10 numbers in each of the following ways.

(a) All 10 on one line, using F10.2 for each.
(b) Five on each of two lines, using 1PE20.6 for each number.
(c) X(1) on first line, using F10.2; second line blank; X(2), X(3), and X(4) on third line, 1PE20.6 for each; X(5), X(6), and X(7), on fourth line, 1PE20.6 for each; X(8), X(9), and X(10) on fifth line, 1PE20.6 for each.

21. Given the following program segment.

```
      DIMENSION FMT(18), A(80, 80)
201   READ (5, 202) (FMT(I),I=1,18)
202   FORMAT (18A4)
203   READ (5, FMT) I, J, T
      IF ( I .EQ. 0 ) GO TO 204
      A(I, J) =T
      GO TO 203
204
```

State what should be on the card read by the READ at 201 to permit cards of the following types to be read by the READ at 203.

(a) Columns 1-2: I
    Columns 3-4: J
    Columns 5-14: T, in form suitable for use with F10.0
(b) Columns 1-2: I
    Columns 3-4: J
    Columns 5-14: T, in form suitable for use with F10.4
(c) Columns 1-2: I

Columns 3-4: J
Columns 5-18: T, in form suitable for use with E14.7
(d) Columns 1-2: I
    Columns 3-4: J
    Columns 5-16: T, for use with F12.0

There are five such groups per card; the second starts in column 17, and so on.

(e) Columns 1-2: I
    Columns 3-4: J
    Columns 5-10: T, for use with F6.3

There are eight such groups per card; the second starts in column 11, and so on.

(f) Columns 21-22: I
    Columns 31-32: J
    Columns 47-61: T, for use with E15.6

Ignore the contents of all other columns on the card.

22. Modify the program of Figure 6.1 so that a zero value is replaced with the word ZERO instead of blank.

23. Modify the program of Figure 6.5 so that the vertical scale is variable. ("Vertical" means as the final graph is normally viewed, that is, after turning the page from the way it was printed.) Make a suitable change in the DIMENSION statement and in the conversion formula so that there may be between 20 and 100 points vertically.

*24. Following the scheme suggested on p. 148, write a routine to plot a unit circle on a graph. Use 48 lines vertically and 80 horizontally; assuming a printer with 6 lines per inch vertically and 10 printing positions per inch horizontally, such a graph will be square. Print rows of dots for the axes. Given the x-y coordinates of a point, it will be necessary to use two different conversion formulas to find the element in which to store the character for plotting. Let 1 in. = 1 unit on both axes.
    Generate and plot 40 points equally spaced around a circle of radius 1 with center at the origin.

25. Modify the program of Exercise 24 so that it reads two numbers from a data card, one of which gives the number of vertical lines that are to represent one unit and the other the number of horizontal printing posi-

tions. These numbers become parameters in the formulas that locate the element in which to store the plotting character.

26. Modify the program of Exercise 25 so that points in the first quadrant are plotted with the character "1," points in the second quadrant are plotted with the character "2," and so on.

27. Produce a plot of the unit circle with each point plotted as its quadrant number. Consider the graph to be the complex plane. For each point x + iy plot also the point CEXP(x + iy). If x + iy is in quadrant j, plot both the point itself and CEXP(x + iy) with the character j. In this case all of the function points will be in the first or fourth quadrants.

28. Write a routine that, given the array named BOARD described in Exercise 31 of Chapter 5, produces a picture of a chessboard along the lines of that shown in Figure 6.14. (The position shown is from the chess quiz in the New York Times, March 26, 1972. White to move and force a win, in three moves if Black accepts the inevitable.)

29. Given an array called LOTTRY containing 365 integers, write the statements necessary to produce Figure 5.18. You may generate another array containing the integers from 1 to 365 in sequence, but do not develop each line in an array before printing it. In other words, use implied DO indexing to pick up the correct arrangements of the areas for each line. Devise whatever "cheating" you wish to take care of the final line that contains only five values.

30. Refer to Problem 15 in Chapter 5. Given the value of N and the one-dimensional array, produce a print-out of the original system of equations in the triangular form in which the system is shown in the exercise. For simplicity, you may assume that N is sufficiently small that the last equation will fit on one line.

31. You are given a deck of cards that was mispunched in the following way. It was intended that all 80 columns of each card contain information, mostly alphabetic, and that the end of the variable-length information on each card terminate with an apostrophe (single quote). The person who prepared the deck, however, uninten-

tionally used an output routine that replaced the contents of columns 73 to 80 with a sequence number.

You are to write a routine that performs two actions. First, punch a new deck in which each card contains the contents of columns 1 to 72 of the input, and with 73 to 80 blank. Second, print out a line for every card on which information was destroyed by the insertion of the sequence number. This will be true for any card on which the rightmost nonblank character before column 73 is *not* an apostrophe. (The idea is that only a small percentage of the cards were harmed in this way, and that they can be corrected manually.) On the printed records, include the sequence number, for ease of identification.

You may assume that the data cards contain no embedded blanks.

32. Write a routine that determines whether a ten digit number read from an input device is properly *self-checking* according to the following scheme.

The number is to be thought of as a nine-digit account number for a department store followed by a rightmost check digit. This digit (which was computed when the account number was assigned to the customer) consists of the last digit of the sum found by adding together the second, fourth, sixth, and eighth digits, together with three times the sum of the first, third, fifth, seventh, and ninth digits. For instance, if a nine-digit account number is 123456789, the check digit is the last digit of the sum

$$(2 + 4 + 6 + 8)$$
$$+ 3(1 + 3 + 5 + 7 + 9) = 95$$

The last digit is five, so the complete account number would be 1234567895.

There is a certain protection against fraud here; unless the person attempting the fraud knows the system, there is only one chance in ten that an invented account number will be a valid one.

More important, perhaps, there is considerable protection against clerical error. If any one digit is miscopied, the erroneous account number will not pass the check. Furthermore, most transpositions of two adjacent digits will cause the check to fail.

```
--------- --------- --------- --------- --------- --------- --------- ---------
|         |////////|          |////////|          |////////|          |////////|
|         |/      /|          |/      /|          |/      /|          |/      /|
|   BR    |/      /|    BB    |/      /|    BR    |/      /|    BK    |/      /|
|         |/      /|          |/      /|          |/      /|          |/      /|
|         |////////|          |////////|          |////////|          |////////|
--------- --------- --------- --------- --------- --------- --------- ---------
|////////|          |////////|          |////////|          |////////|         |
|/      /|          |/      /|          |/      /|          |/      /|         |
|/      /|    BP    |/  BQ  /|    BN    |/      /|    BP    |/      /|    BP   |
|/      /|          |/      /|          |/      /|          |/      /|         |
|////////|          |////////|          |////////|          |////////|         |
--------- --------- --------- --------- --------- --------- --------- ---------
|         |////////|          |////////|          |////////|          |////////|
|         |/      /|          |/      /|          |/      /|          |/      /|
|   BP    |/      /|          |/  BP  /|          |/      /|    BP    |/  WQ  /|
|         |/      /|          |/      /|          |/      /|          |/      /|
|         |////////|          |////////|          |////////|          |////////|
--------- --------- --------- --------- --------- --------- --------- ---------
|////////|          |////////|          |////////|          |////////|         |
|/      /|          |/      /|          |/      /|          |/      /|         |
|/      /|          |/  BP  /|    WP    |/      /|          |/      /|         |
|/      /|          |/      /|          |/      /|          |/      /|         |
|////////|          |////////|          |////////|          |////////|         |
--------- --------- --------- --------- --------- --------- --------- ---------
|         |////////|          |////////|          |////////|          |////////|
|         |/      /|          |/      /|          |/      /|          |/      /|
|   WP    |/      /|    WP    |/      /|          |/      /|          |/      /|
|         |/      /|          |/      /|          |/      /|          |/      /|
|         |////////|          |////////|          |////////|          |////////|
--------- --------- --------- --------- --------- --------- --------- ---------
|////////|          |////////|          |////////|          |////////|         |
|/      /|          |/      /|          |/      /|          |/      /|         |
|/      /|          |/  WN  /|          |/      /|          |/  WN  /|    WP   |
|/      /|          |/      /|          |/      /|          |/      /|         |
|////////|          |////////|          |////////|          |////////|         |
--------- --------- --------- --------- --------- --------- --------- ---------
|         |////////|          |////////|          |////////|          |////////|
|         |/      /|          |/      /|          |/      /|          |/      /|
|         |/  WP  /|    BN    |/      /|    WB    |/  WP  /|    WP    |/      /|
|         |/      /|          |/      /|          |/      /|          |/      /|
|         |////////|          |////////|          |////////|          |////////|
--------- --------- --------- --------- --------- --------- --------- ---------
|////////|          |////////|          |////////|          |////////|         |
|/      /|          |/      /|          |/      /|          |/      /|         |
|/      /|          |/      /|          |/  WR  /|    WR    |/  WK  /|         |
|/      /|          |/      /|          |/      /|          |/      /|         |
|////////|          |////////|          |////////|          |////////|         |
--------- --------- --------- --------- --------- --------- --------- ---------
```

FIGURE 6.14. A graphical representation of a chess position. See Exercise 28.

For instance, the check digit for 132456789 would be

$$(3 + 4 + 6 + 8) + 3(1 + 2 + 5 + 7 + 9) = 93$$

The computed check digit of 3 is obviously not the same as the one in the number, so the account number is rejected as invalid.

Your program should print the number together with the word "YES" or "NO" to show whether it passed this test for a self-checking number.

33. Write a program that handles the input/output portion of the following problem.

The input of the problem consists of a loan amount in dollars and cents, an annual interest rate, a number of payments to be made, the number of the month in which the debt was contracted, and the year in which the debt was contracted.

The program should produce output similar to that shown in Figure 6.15.

Omit the payment calculation and use some dummy numbers for testing your FORMATs.

Based on Case Study 3 in Thomas J. Schriber, *Fortran Case Studies for Business Applications,* New York, Wiley, 1969.

34. Write a routine to print a dollars and cents amount with a *floating dollar sign* as a protection against alteration of the amount of a check. This means that a dollar sign must appear immediately to the left of the most significant digit of the amount. Here are some examples of the form in which amounts of various sizes should be printed.

```
$12345.67
 $1234.56
  $123.45
   $12.34
    $1.23
    $0.12
    $0.01
```

The number you are to print is a Fortran

REAL number expressed in units of dollars. That is, the cents portion actually is a fraction of a dollar inside the machine. If you are working with a nondecimal computer (which is almost everybody) you will need to consider that the cents portion of the amount may not be represented exactly correctly inside the machine. If the amount you are printing, for instance, should be $12.34 but what is inside the machine is approximately $12.339999 and your output routine does not round, then you are going to print $12.33—which is not acceptable.

35. Same as Exercise 34 except that you are to insert commas for amounts over $999.99. In other words, you are to produce output that follows these examples.

```
$12,345.67
 $1,234.56
   $123.45
    $12.34
     $1.23
     $0.12
     $0.01
```

THE FOLLOWING AMORTIZATION SCHEDULE HAS
BEEN DEVELOPED FOR THIS DEBT SITUATION:

```
         INITIAL SIZE OF DEBT:    20000.00
         NUMBER OF PAYMENTS USED TO LIQUIDATE DEBT:   240
         EFFECTIVE ANNUAL INTEREST RATE:  6.00 %
         REQUIRED SIZE OF MONTHLY PAYMENT: 141.46
```

NO. OF PAYMENT	DATE OF PAYMENT	YEAR	SIZE OF PAYMENT	INTEREST DUE	AMOUNT OF DEBT REDUCTION	UPDATED SIZE OF DEBT
0	AUGUST 1	1969	(DEBT INCURRED ON THIS DATE)			20000.00
1	SEPTEMBER 1	1969	141.46	97.35	44.11	19955.89
2	OCTOBER 1	1969	141.46	97.14	44.32	19911.57
3	NOVEMBER 1	1969	141.46	96.92	44.54	19867.03
4	DECEMBER 1	1969	141.46	96.70	44.76	19822.27
5	JANUARY 1	1970	141.46	96.49	44.97	19777.30
6	FEBRUARY 1	1970	141.46	96.27	45.19	19732.11
7	MARCH 1	1970	141.46	96.05	45.41	19686.70

THE INTERMEDIATE PORTION OF THE AMORTIZATION SCHEDULE IS NOT SHOWN

235	MARCH 1	1989	141.46	4.06	137.40	696.52
236	APRIL 1	1989	141.46	3.39	138.07	558.45
237	MAY 1	1989	141.46	2.72	138.74	419.71
238	JUNE 1	1989	141.46	2.04	139.42	280.29
239	JULY 1	1989	141.46	1.36	140.10	140.19
240	AUGUST 1	1989	140.87	0.68	140.19	0.0

TOTALS: 13949.81   20000.00

FIGURE 6.15.   Output of the type to be produced by the program written for Exercise 33.

36. Look up the function of the COBOL PIC-TURE clause. (See, for example, Daniel D. McCracken and Umberto Garbassi, *A Guide to COBOL Programming*, 2nd ed., New York, Wiley, 1970, pp. 89–95.) Define a subset of the PICTURE clause elements to make the job manageable and write a routine that accepts a PICTURE from the first card of a deck and then a succession of numbers to be edited according to that PICTURE. For each input number, print a line showing the edited and unedited forms.

(It should be understood that this is a finger-work exercise and that in programming actual commercial data processing applications no programmer would *ever* have to write routines like this himself. Such editing functions are always provided as part of any language that would be used for such applications.)

37. Write a program to encode and decode messages according to a substitution cipher, as follows.

On the first card of the deck are punched all of the characters that will ever appear in a message. (Remember to include blank as one of the characters!) You might choose to make this character set simply all the characters that can be punched on your input device, or you might limit it to letters only, or letters and punctuation, or whatever you please. The second card contains in each column the character that is to be substituted for the character in the corresponding column of the first card. The second card ought to contain the same number of characters as the first, counting blank as one of the characters on the first. The second card should not contain any character more than once (at least not if you hope to be able to decode the encoded message!). The program must read these first two cards, count the characters on the first card to determine how large the character set is and set up the substitution tables. It should then read subsequent cards in the deck, making the appropriate substitution for every character, and write out the encoded message.

The simplest way to see whether the program works is to produce the output as a deck of punched cards except that the output deck should have cards 1 and 2 reversed from the order in which they appear in the input. Rerunning the program with this output deck as the input ought to produce a copy of the original deck.

This program can be written with a great deal less effort in various other programming languages, such as APL or SNOBOL, that have features facilitating the processing of character strings. It might be interesting to ask someone who knows one of these languages to write a program to carry out this exercise, as a demonstration that Fortran is not the ideal language for all tasks.

38. Write a program to compute and print bowling scores. The input for each game

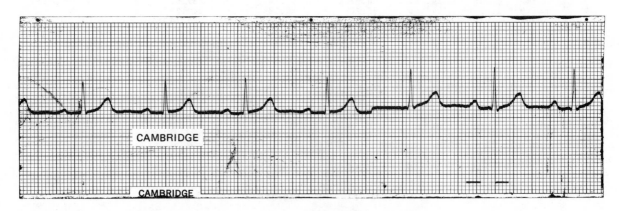

FIGURE 6.16. A portion of the author's electrocardiograph. See Exercise 39.

will consist of a card giving the number of pins knocked down with each ball. The number of values is, of course, variable; it could consist of twelve tens for a 300 game or 20 zeros for 20 gutter balls. For a description of how to approach this problem, see Problem H6, "The Game of Bowling," in Fred Gruenberger and George Jaffray, *Problems For Computer Solution,* New York, Wiley, 1965, pp. 266–269.

39. Figure 6.16 shows a few cycles from the author's most recent electrocardiograph. Assume you are given a magnetic tape on which this curve appears in digitized form. This consists of a succession of 100-word records representing the potential in millivolts, at two millisecond intervals.

    Write a routine that reads several of these records, computes the time intervals between ten successive peak voltages, and then prints the average heart beat rate in beats per minute, rounded to the nearest integer.

    If you are in medical school or have friends who are, there are obviously a great many more interesting things you can find to do with a digital computer on this problem. See, for example, Ralph W. Stacey and Bruce D. Waxman, *Computers in Biomedical Research,* New York, Academic Press, 1968.

40. (The following two exercises involve writing Job Control Language commands to carry out some typical operations under an operating system. They therefore depend heavily on the details of physical equipment and of operating system characteristics and languages. It may be necessary to modify them to fit your situation.)

    Consider the data presented in Figure 5.18 in connection with Exercise 28 of Chapter 5. Punch the data on cards and then read onto disk for use by other students doing the exercise. Print the table and check it thoroughly before releasing it for other peoples' use. Prepare a brief statement of what READ and FORMAT statements others should use to read the data set, together with any necessary Job Control Language statements.

    If you are entering the data from a time-sharing console, you should set up a little program to supply you with each day of the year, to which you respond with the lottery number for that day. This will require some kind of sentinel, however, so that if you mispunch something or otherwise get out of step with the input routine you can get restarted other than by beginning all over again.

41. Rerun the programs in Case Study 12 on your system, providing whatever information is required to specify the locations of the various data sets. Investigate the ways you might be able to speed up the execution of the program of Figure 6.13 by altering the blocking factor defaults supplied by your operating system. As an adjunct to the last suggestion, you might like to run some experiments to see what the differences in execution times actually are for various blocking factors and for formatted versus unformatted I/O. You will need to find out how to write program statements to read your computer's digital clock, which may involve a subroutine call as discussed in the next chapter, but that is not very difficult. Bear in mind that to get meaningful timing figures you will probably have to set up a somewhat larger system than used in the text because otherwise the program execution time may be lost in the system overhead. Finally, you will have to be sure what the clock measures: on some systems it is CPU time only, with time spent waiting for I/O not included.

42. As an exercise in using direct-access files, as discussed in the IBM context in Section 6.12, write a demonstration information retrieval system.

    For something specific, suppose you are working with a time-sharing system, and that it is desired to let the user ask questions about the states in the United States, in random order, naturally. You might designate the states by the Postal Service's two-letter codes (AL for Alabama, AK for Alaska, AZ for Arizona, etc.) or by some other abbreviation. (Don't be so lazy as to require the user to look up the state's number in a table, however; that's what computers are for.) Then, using some coding of your devising, the user should be able to ask for such items as population, capital city, size in square miles, possibly bordering states, and so on.

You must prepare the *data base,* that is, the information on a disk file, and the program that accepts the user's queries and provides the answers from the data base.

This exercise can be big or little, de-pending on how much you try to do. If you provide only a little information, all of fixed length, and make no provision for handling input errors, it is not much of a job. But a more ambitious effort could easily turn into a term problem.

7 FUNCTIONS AND SPECIFICATION STATEMENTS

7.1 INTRODUCTION: WHY USE FUNCTIONS?

A *function*, as the word is used in discussions of computer programming, is a program segment that has—in some sense—an independent existence, and that can be called into operation by other program segments. We have already made extensive use of one type of function available in Fortran, the supplied function. When we write SQRT, for instance, we call into play a program segment written by someone associated with the development of the Fortran compiler. The square root routine is made a part of our program, in effect, with no more expenditure of effort on our part than that required to write down the name.

There are three primary motivations for the use of functions, all illustrated—more or less well—by the square root example.

1. If someone else has already written a program segment that we can utilize without modification, we obviously save time and effort. This applies not only to the basic task of writing the function but the work of checking it out and the time almost certain to be wasted in ferreting out errors caused by our programming mistakes.

This can be a major factor. There exist large collections of programs already written and checked out, in many fields, such as statistics, specialized branches of engineering, or computer input and output operations. Sometimes these packages are available for the cost of a reel of tape onto which they are written for you by a librarian of a user's organization. In other cases they are proprietary products available for sale or rental. Several organizations make a business of providing up-to-date lists of what is available. International Computer Programs, Inc., of Indianapolis, for example, publishes a quarterly summary of programs available for sale or rental. The current issue runs over 400 pages, with typically half a dozen entries per page.

2. If a certain programming operation needs to be carried out at several points in a program, and the operation requires a sizable amount of programming, it is wasteful of storage space to provide duplicate copies of the program segment. Using functions, we are able to write one copy of the program segment, then call that one copy into action from many other places in other programs.

This advantage, when it applies, is of equal force whether the function in question was written by ourselves or was from another source.

3. Often a program that makes effective use of functions is easier to understand and to prove for accuracy of intended operation than one that is written without the use of functions. This advantage, when it applies, may be quite independent of the other two. For instance, we might make a function of something that is used only once in the program, and that we write ourselves.

We turn now to a study of the various types of functions available in Fortran. In this discussion and in the case studies we shall see examples of how the three major advantages cited above work out in practice.

We also introduce in this chapter two additional statements, COMMON and EQUIVALENCE, that are in part related to effective use of two types of functions, although, as we shall see, they have other values as well. Finally, we consider a means of entering program data with the program, using the DATA statement.

7.2 SUPPLIED FUNCTIONS

Most Fortran systems provide several dozen functions to compute such things as trigonometric functions, logarithms, and absolute values. The exact list depends not only on the computer and the version of Fortran used, but on the particular installation. Most installations provide special-purpose functions to meet their individual needs. An installation doing orbit calculations, for instance, might have a special function to compute air density as a function of altitude. Each programmer must have an up-to-date list of the functions available at his installation, as well as a precise write-up containing such information as accuracy, speed, the form of the data (whether angles are in degrees or radians, for instance), and so on.

The functions listed in Appendix 2, it is expected, will be found in virtually all Fortran systems.

In order to use these functions, it is necessary only to write their names where they are needed, entering the desired expression(s) for the argument(s). (Many permit several arguments, such as the function that finds the smallest of the values of the arguments listed.)

The names of these functions are established in advance, and the programmer must write them exactly as specified. Although he has no control over their naming, we may note that if the value produced by the supplied function is real or integer, the first letter of the function name must comply with the IJKLMN naming convention.

The functions available as part of the system are actually of two different kinds, depending on the mechanics of their insertion into the object program. The *open* or *in-line* functions require only a few machine instructions, which are inserted into the object program every time the function is used. The *closed* functions, in general, are considerably longer; they are inserted into the object program in one place only, and the object program transfers to that one place whenever it is needed. The closed functions are more common.

7.3 STATEMENT FUNCTIONS

Often a programmer will find some relatively simple computation recurring through his program, making it desirable to be able to set up a function to carry out the computation. This function would be needed in only the one program, so that there would be no point in setting up a new supplied function for the purpose—which is a bit of work. Instead, a function can be defined for the purpose of the one program and then used whenever desired in that program. It has no effect on any other program.

A statement function is *defined,* by writing a single statement of the form $a = b$, where a is the name of the function and b is an expression. The name, which is invented by the programmer, is formed according to the same rules that apply to a variable name: one to six letters or digits, the first of which must be a letter. If the name of the statement function is mentioned in a prior type statement, there is no restriction on the initial letter; if the name is not mentioned in a type statement, the initial letter distinguishes between real and integer in the usual way.

The name of the function is followed by parentheses enclosing the argument(s), which must be separated by commas if there is more than one. The arguments *in the definition* must not be subscripted.

The right-hand side of the definition statement may be any expression not involving subscripted variables. It may use variables not specified as arguments and it may use other functions (except itself). All function definitions must appear before the first executable statement of the program. If the right-hand side of a statement function uses another statement function, the other function definition must have appeared *earlier* in the program.

As an illustration, suppose that in a certain program it is frequently necessary to compute one root of the quadratic equation,

$ax^2 + bx + c = 0$, given values of a, b, and c. A function can be defined to carry out this computation by writing

```
ROOT(A, B, C) =
1   (-B+SQRT(B**2 - 4.0*A*C))/(2.0*A)
```

(The definition is written on two lines here only because of size limitations in this book.) The compiler will produce a sequence of instructions in the object program to compute the value of the function, given three values to use in the computation.

This is only the *definition* of the function; it does not cause computation to take place. The variable names used as arguments are only dummies; they may be the same as variable names appearing elsewhere in the program. The argument names are unimportant, except as they may distinguish between integer and real.

A statement function is *used* by writing its name wherever the function value is desired and substituting appropriate expressions for the arguments. "Appropriate" here means, in particular, that if a variable in the definition is real the expression substituted for that variable must also be real and similarly for the other types of variables. The values of these expressions will be substituted into the program segment established by the definition and the value of the function computed. The actual arguments may be subscripted if desired.

Suppose, now, that we wish to use this function with 16.9 for a, R − S for b, and T + 6.9 for c; the value of the function (root) is to be added to the cosine of x and the sum stored as the new value of ANS. All this can be done with the statement

```
ANS = ROOT(16.9,R-S,T+6.9) + COS(X)
```

Suppose that later in the program it is necessary to compute the function with DATA(I) for a, DATA(I + 1) for b, and 0.087 for c; the function value is to be cubed and stored as the value of TEMP:

```
TEMP=ROOT(DATA(I),DATA(I+1),0.087)**3
```

It must be emphasized that the variables A, B, and C in the function definition have no relation to any variables of the same names that may appear elsewhere in the program. To illustrate, suppose that the value of the root is needed for the equation

$$22.97x^2 + ax + b = 0$$

where a and b are variables in the program. The root may be found by writing

```
VAL = ROOT(22.97, A, B)
```

The A and B that appear here in the *use* of the function are completely unrelated to the A and B in the *definition* of the function. In summary, the definition variables are dummies that establish how the expression values in the use should be substituted into the object program set up from the definition.

For another example of the usefulness of statement functions, suppose that in a certain program it is frequently necessary to evaluate the function

$$E = \frac{1}{x^5(e^{1.432/Tx} - 1)}$$

The argument this time is to be just x. This is easily set up as a function:

```
E(X)=1.0/(X**5*(EXP(1.432/(T*X))-1.0))
```

The X here, as always in a function definition, is only a dummy variable that defines a computational procedure; when an expression is later written in using the function, the same actions are carried out on the actual value of the argument as are shown being done with X in the definition.

There is no prohibition against using X as an actual variable. The function just defined could be used in statements like these:

```
SUM4 = SUM4 + E(X)
SUM2 = SUM2 + E(X+H)
EFFIC=64.77*H/3.0*(4.0*SUM4+2.0*SUM2
1   + E(A) + 4.0*E(B-H) + E(B))/T**4
```

We see in this function an example of something that was mentioned earlier: the use of a variable in the function definition that is not an argument. The only argument here is X; this is a dummy. T, however, since it is not an argument, is *not* a dummy: it is the same T that presumably appears elsewhere in the program. This use of variables that are not arguments is perfectly legal; as we see, it saves the effort of making arguments out of variables for which we shall never want to substitute anything but their own values. (It is *logically* possible to think of a statement function with *no* arguments: all the variables would simply take on their current values in the program, as T did in the last example. This is not permitted with statement functions. We shall see that it *can* be done with a SUBROUTINE subprogram.)

It is permissible for the name of a programmer-written statement function to be the same as that of a supplied function, if explicitly so desired. The effect is to override the supplied function with the statement function. For instance, we might write

```
SQRT(X) = DSQRT(X)
```

to replace all references to the single-length square root function with the double-precision square root function. This sort of application should be used with care, however, and in some Fortrans may require type statements to provide the information that the function SQRT—which is now a statement function, not a supplied function—is of the type DOUBLE PRECISION.

7.4 FUNCTION AND SUBROUTINE SUBPROGRAMS

Although a statement function is often useful, it does have two rather serious restrictions: the definition is limited to one statement and it can compute only one value. The FUNCTION and SUBROUTINE subprograms remove these restrictions.

This is only half the story, however. The outstanding feature of these two is that they are *subprograms;* they can be compiled independently of any main program in which they are used. Their variable names are completely independent of the variable names in the main program and in other subprograms. They may have their own DIMENSION statements (and the other specification statements described below). In short, FUNCTION and SUBROUTINE subprograms can be completely independent of any main program—yet it is quite easy to set up "communication" between a main program and subprogram(s). This means that a large program can be divided into parts that can be compiled independently, making possible two important kinds of flexibility in writing programs.

The ability to compile a subprogram independently of the main program of which it is a part means that one subprogram can be used with different main programs. For instance, many different programmers in an installation may need a subprogram to solve a system of simultaneous equations. Since arrays are involved and since many statements are required, statement functions are out of the question. However, a SUBROUTINE subprogram can be written to do the job. It can be compiled by itself, and the compiled object program can be combined with *any* main program. All that is necessary is for the main program to have been written with the conventions of the subprogram in mind.

The other flexibility provided by separate compilation is the freedom to compile and run segments of one program independently of each other. This means that parts of a program can be checked out as they are written, which can be an important advantage. For example, if there are many subprograms, all called by one main program, individual subprograms can be checked out and tested before all of the others are finished.

As with the arithmetic statement functions, we must distinguish carefully between the definition and the use. The computation desired in a FUNCTION subprogram is *defined* by writing the necessary statements in a segment, writing the word FUNCTION and the name of the function before the segment, and writing the word END after it. The name is formed as for variables and statement functions: one to six letters or digits, the first of which must be a letter. The letter must be chosen according to the naming convention in the absence of a type declaration. If the naming convention is to be overridden, or if the type is other than real or integer, the word FUNCTION is preceded by one of the five types (REAL, INTEGER, DOUBLE PRECISION, COMPLEX, or LOGICAL).

The name of the subprogram is followed by parentheses enclosing the arguments, which are separated by commas if more than one.

The name of the function must appear at least once in the subprogram as a variable on the left-hand side of an assignment statement or in the list of an input statement. In other words, the name of a FUNCTION subprogram is associated with a value; a value must therefore be given to it in the subprogram.

As before, the arguments in the subprogram definition are only dummy variables. The arguments in the function definition must be distinct nonsubscripted variables or array names. Within the subprogram itself, however, subscripted variables may be used freely. The subprogram must contain at least one RETURN statement, for reasons that we shall see shortly.

To *use* a FUNCTION subprogram it is necessary only to write the name of the function where its value is desired, with suitable expressions for arguments. The mechanics of the operation of the object program are as follows: the FUNCTION subprogram is compiled as a set of machine instructions in one place in storage, and wherever the name of the subprogram appears in the source program a transfer to the subprogram is set up in the object program. When the computations of the subprogram have been completed, a transfer is made back to the section of the program that brought the subprogram into action. The RETURN statement(s) in the subprogram results in object program instructions to transfer back to the place in the main program from which the subprogram was called. (This is actually quite similar to the way a statement function is set up, except that in that case there can be only one statement in the definition and there is no question when the function's operations are complete.)

As a simple example of the use of a FUNCTION subprogram, suppose that in a certain program there is frequent need for the function shown on page 30. The function can be defined with the statements shown below in which the name Y has been given to the function.

```
FUNCTION Y(X)
IF ( X .LE. 2.1 ) Y = 0.5*X + 0.95
IF ( X .GT. 2.1 ) Y = 0.7*X + 0.53
RETURN
END
```

If we now want to compute the value of this function for an argument equal to GRS − 6.8 and divide the result by 12.99 to get the value of EWR, we can write

```
EWR = Y(GRS - 6.8) / 12.99
```

To get the value of this function of the square root of one plus RHO, with SFO set equal to the square root of the result, we can write

```
SFO = SQRT(Y(SQRT(1.0+RHO)))
```

A FUNCTION subprogram can be set up to have many arguments, including arrays. For example, suppose that it is necessary to find the product of the main diagonal elements (those having the same row and column number) of square arrays. The arrays from which this prod-

uct is computed must have been mentioned in a DIMENSION statement in the "calling" program, as always, and all the arrays must have the same dimensions. (We shall see shortly how to remove the same-dimension restriction.) The array names in the FUNCTION argument list and subprogram will be dummies, but the dummy array names must still be mentioned in a DIMENSION statement in the subprogram. Suppose that the arrays in question are all 10×10, but that only some of the element positions are filled with data; the value of an integer variable gives the number of rows and columns that contain useful data. The subprogram could be as follows:

```
      FUNCTION DIAGPR(A, N)
      DIMENSION A(10, 10)
      DIAGPR = A(1, 1)
      DO 10 I= 2, N
   10 DIAGPR =DIAGPR * A(I, I)
      RETURN
      END
```

Now, if we want the product of the main diagonal elements of a 10×10 array named X, in which the actual size is 8×8, with the extra elements containing nothing, we can write

```
DET = DIAGPR(X, 8)
```

To find the square of the product of the main diagonal elements of an array named SAM, in which the number of rows and columns containing meaningful data is given by the value of an integer variable named JACK, we could write

```
EIG = DIAGPR(SAM, JACK) ** 2
```

A FUNCTION subprogram is seen to be quite similar to a statement function, except that it can use many statements instead of just one and it can use any of the Fortran statements instead of just an assignment statement. A subprogram can call on other subprograms as long as it does not call itself and as long as two subprograms do not call each other.*

---

*A subprogram that calls itself is said to be *recursive*. This *is* permitted in the ALGOL language and others, in which it finds greatest utility in nonnumerical applications, such as compiler programs, processing natural languages (such as English), and in operations on the *symbols* of mathematics as distinguished from their values. Recursiveness can be accomplished in some cases in Fortran by "stacking" arguments in arrays. We shall see a rudimentary example of some of these ideas in Case Study 14, on the translation from ordinary algebraic notation to Polish notation.

A FUNCTION subprogram has been described as computing just one value, the one associated with the name of the FUNCTION. Actually, there can be any number of output values: any of the arguments may refer to output. For an example of how this can be useful, consider the following extension of the requirements of the preceding illustration. Suppose that if the product of the main diagonal elements is less than or equal to 100 we wish to go to statement 12; if it is between 100 and 1000, we wish to go to statement 13; if it is greater than or equal to 1000, we wish to go to statement 14. All of these statement numbers refer to statements in the *main* program. This could, of course, be done with IF statements in the main program, but if it has to be done frequently we prefer a simpler way.

To accomplish the simplification, let us first add a type specification to make the value associated with the name of the integer type. This is done by writing the word INTEGER in front of the word FUNCTION in the subprogram definition. We then write the modified subprogram so that the value of DIAGPR is negative, zero, or positive, depending on whether the product is less or equal to 100, between 100 and 1000, or greater or equal to 1000. We also add PROD as an argument and within the subprogram give it the value of the product of the main diagonal elements. The modified program is as follows.

```
      INTEGER FUNCTION DIAGPR(A, N, PROD)
      DIMENSION A(10, 10)
      PROD = A(1, 1)
      DO 10 I = 2, N
   10 PROD = PROD * A(I, I)
      IF (    PROD .LE. 100.0 )DIAGPR = -1
      IF (    PROD .GT. 100.0
     1 .AND. PROD .LT. 1000.0 )DIAGPR = 0
      IF (    PROD .GE. 1000.0 )DIAGPR = 1
      RETURN
      END
```

Now suppose that we want the product of the main diagonal elements of a 10×10 array named BETA in which seven rows and seven columns are used; the product is to be called GAMMA. We are to transfer to one of the three statements numbered 12, 13, or 14, as already described.

```
      IF ( DIAGPR(BETA,7,GAMMA) ) 12, 13, 14
```

The appearance of the name of the function, written with appropriate arguments, causes the function to be called into operation, in the course of which a value is given to its name and also to the other output parameter, which is GAMMA in this case. Control returns from the subprogram to the arithmetic IF statement in the main program, where the proper transfer is made. At any of these locations the newly computed value of GAMMA may be used.

The basics of a SUBROUTINE subprogram, although quite similar to those of a FUNCTION subprogram, show three differences.

1. A SUBROUTINE has no value associated with its name. All outputs are defined in terms of arguments; there may be any number of outputs.

2. A SUBROUTINE is not called into action simply by writing its name, since no value is associated with the name. Instead, we write a CALL statement to bring it into operation; this specifies the arguments and results in storing all the output values.

3. Since the output of a SUBROUTINE may be any combination of the various types of values, there is no type associated with the name and likewise no convention attached to the first letter of the name. The naming of a SUBROUTINE is otherwise the same as the naming of a FUNCTION.

In all other respects the two subprograms are entirely analogous.

The essential features of the SUBROUTINE subprogram are illustrated in the following example. Suppose that in a certain program it is frequently necessary to find the largest element (in absolute value) in a specified row of a 50×50 array. The input to the SUBROUTINE is therefore the array name and the row number. The output will be the absolute value of the largest element in that row and its column number. The SUBROUTINE could be as follows.

```
      SUBROUTINE LARGE(ARRAY, I, BIG, J)
      DIMENSION ARRAY(50, 50)
      BIG = ABS(ARRAY(I, 1))
      J = 1
      DO 9 K = 2, 50
      IF (ABS(ARRAY(I,K)).LT.BIG) GO TO 9
      BIG = ABS(ARRAY(I,K))
      J = K
    9 CONTINUE
      RETURN
      END
```

Now suppose that the largest element in the third row of a 50 × 50 array named ZETA is needed. The absolute value of the element is to be called DIVIS and the column number is to be called NCOL. We write the statement

```
CALL LARGE (ZETA, 3, DIVIS, NCOL)
```

This brings the subprogram into operation, stores the values of DIVIS and NCOL found by the subprogram, and returns control to the statement following the CALL. If, later, it is necessary to find the largest element in row M + 2 of an array named DETAIL, storing its absolute value in SIZE and the column number in KW, we can write

```
CALL LARGE (DETAIL, M+2, SIZE, KW)
```

To emphasize the independence of the variable names between the main program and any subprograms we note that it would be possible and legal to write the statement

```
CALL LARGE (ARRAY, I, BIG, J)
```

If this is done, all the input variables to the subprogram must be defined and given values in the calling program and all output variables from the subprogram must be defined in the subprogram. The name I in the calling program and the name I in the subprogram are unrelated. And this must logically be so: the name I in the subprogram tells *what to do with* a value from the calling program, whereas the name I in the calling program must *specify a value,* one that has already been computed by the calling program. In the case of output variables, J, for instance, the variable J in the subprogram identifies a value that the subprogram computes, whereas J in the calling program identifies a result transmitted from the subprogram.

7.5 ADJUSTABLE DIMENSIONS

It is possible for a subprogram to be defined in terms of arrays that are of adjustable size. We do this by writing in the subprogram a DIMENSION statement in which we write integer variable names instead of integer constants. The integer variables must appear in the argument list and be given values by the calling program.

This is much easier to understand in an example. Consider the following program.

```
SUBROUTINE LARGE(ARRAY,N,I,BIG,J)
DIMENSION ARRAY(N, N)
BIG = ABS(ARRAY(I, 1))
J = 1
DO 9 K = 2, N
IF (ABS(ARRAY(I,K)) .LT. BIG)GO TO 9
BIG = ABS(ARRAY(I, K))
J = K
9 CONTINUE
RETURN
END
```

It will be noted that another variable, N, has been added to the argument list, which gives the number of rows and columns in the array to be searched. The DIMENSION statement says that the array is N × N, and the DO statement says to inspect rows 2 through N.

With this revision, the subroutine can be used to find the largest element in a specified row of *any* square array. We might write, for instance,

```
CALL LARGE (ALPHA, 49, 6, BIGGST, M)
```

This will find the largest element in row 6 of a 49 × 49 array named ALPHA, placing the largest element in BIGGST and its row number in M. Or we might write

```
CALL LARGE (GAMMA, L, M, DELTA, K98)
```

The array this time is L × L, where L would have to have been given a value before the call.

The adjustable dimension facility has a number of advantages. One, of course, is that a very general sort of subprogram can be adapted to the needs of a particular main program, without the awkwardness and potentially wasted storage of specifying a maximum size and then using only some of the elements. A given subprogram can be called many times from one main program, each time if necessary with arrays of different sizes. Looking at another aspect of the usefulness of subprograms, a pre-written subprogram can serve the rather different requirements of many programmers.

We have noted that it is permissible for one subprogram to call another. When this is done, adjustable dimension information may be "passed through" subprograms. For instance, a main program might call a subprogram with array dimension information given by the value of a variable in the argument list. The subprogram called might in turn call another subprogram, "passing" the dimensioning information to the subprogram *it* called.

The restrictions on the usage of adjustable dimensions are reasonable. The subprogram must not use a subscript value greater than specified in the call; the subprogram must not redefine the value of an adjustable dimension; the calling program must not leave the value of a dimensioning variable undefined. We may also note at this point that an array mentioned in a COMMON statement (see Section 7.7) must not have adjustable dimensions.

7.6 SUMMARY OF THE FOUR TYPES OF FUNCTIONS

Fortran provides for four types of functions: those supplied with the system, statement functions, FUNCTION subprograms, and SUBROUTINE subprograms. The salient features of the four types are summarized in Table 7.1.

7.7 THE EQUIVALENCE AND COMMON STATEMENTS

These two nonexecutable statements make possible certain conveniences in the naming of variables and the assignment of storage locations to them.

The EQUIVALENCE statement causes two or more variables to be assigned to the same storage location, which is useful in two rather different ways.

In one usage the EQUIVALENCE statement allows the programmer to define two or more variable names as meaning the same thing. It might be that after writing a long program the programmer will realize that he has inadvertently changed variable names and that X, X1, and RST7 all mean the same thing. Rather than going back and changing the variables names in the program, a time-consuming and error-prone process, he can write

```
EQUIVALENCE (X, X1, RST7)
```

and the mistake is corrected.

The other application, and the more important, is in making use of the same storage loca-

tion to contain two or more variables that are different but are never needed at the same time. Suppose that in a certain program the variable I27 appears in the initial READ statement and in a few subsequent statements but is never used after that. Later in the program a value is given to the variable NPL, which is then used as a DO parameter. Later the variable JJM2 is applied to a similar purpose. At the end of the program the variable NEXT1 is given a value and then used in the final WRITE statement. As things now stand, four storage locations will be allocated to these variables, which is pointless, since their usage never overlaps. If the programmer is short of storage space, he can assign all four variables to one location by writing

```
EQUIVALENCE (I27, NPL, JJM2, NEXT1)
```

The same thing could, of course, be accomplished by changing the variable names, but using an EQUIVALENCE is obviously simpler. Furthermore, a programmer often does not know he is going to be short of storage when he first writes the program, perhaps discovering that fact only after getting into the checkout process.

These two applications of EQUIVALENCE differ only in viewpoint; the statement and its treatment by the compiler are the same in either case.

One EQUIVALENCE statement can establish equivalences between any number of sets of variables. For instance, if A and B are to be made equivalent, as are X, Y, and Z, we can write

```
EQUIVALENCE (A, B), (X, Y, Z)
```

Seldom is storage so "tight" that the EQUIVALENCE statement is *really* needed for nonsubscripted variables. The value comes in establishing equivalences between arrays.

In many versions of Fortran array names must be mentioned with a single constant subscript, regardless of the actual dimensionality of the array. We might, for instance, have statements like

```
DIMENSION A(50), B(5, 10), C(2, 5, 5)
EQUIVALENCE (A(1), B(1), C(1))
```

This EQUIVALENCE statement causes storage to be assigned so that the elements of the three arrays occupy the same 50 storage locations. It is not required, however, that the arrays made equivalent have the same number of elements.

TABLE 7.1

	Supplied	**Statement**	**Function**	**Subroutine**
Naming	1–6 characters, first of which is a letter	1–6 characters, first of which is a letter	1–6 characters, first of which is a letter	1–6 characters, first of which is a letter
Type	Implied by first letter; can be over-ridden in some Fortrans by REAL, INTEGER, COMPLEX, LOGICAL, or DOUBLE PRECISION	Implied by first letter unless over-ridden by REAL, INTEGER, COMPLEX, LOGICAL, or DOUBLE PRECISION	Implied by first letter unless over-ridden by REAL, INTEGER, COMPLEX, LOGICAL, or DOUBLE PRECISION	None—no value associated with name
Definition	Provided with the compiler	One arithmetic statement before first usage of function	Any number of statements after word FUNCTION	Any number of statements after word SUBROUTINE
How called	Writing name where function value is desired	Writing name where function value is desired	Writing name where function value is desired	CALL statement
Number of arguments	One or more, as defined	One or more, as defined	One or more, as defined	Any number, including *none*, as defined
Number of outputs	One	One	One is associated with function name; others may be specified as arguments	Any number

If they do not, and if the arrays in the EQUIVALENCE statements all have element number 1, as above, then the extra elements at the end of the longer array will simply not be shared locations.

It is also permissible to specify that equivalence be established between element locations other than the first. If, for instance, X is a one-dimensional array with ten elements, and D, E, and F are all nonsubscripted variables, we might write

```
EQUIVALENCE(X(1),D),(X(2),E),(X(10),F)
```

The single variable D would be assigned to the same location as the first element of X, E would be assigned to the same location as the second element of X, and F would be assigned to the same location as the tenth element of X.

Arrays can be overlapped by the same techniques. We might write

```
EQUIVALENCE (A(1), B(20))
```

The general idea is that the storage assignments are made in such a manner that the specified equivalence is established, and both arrays are stored in consecutive locations just as arrays always are. The question we need to be able to answer, often, is, "In a two- or three-dimensional array, which element *is* the twentieth or the Nth?"

The answer is given by the *element successor* rule, which tells where a given element is stored in the linear sequence of storage locations. Table 7.2 gives the needed information. A, B, and C in this table are dimensions, as given by a DIMENSION, COMMON, or type statement;

TABLE 7.2

Dimensionality	Subscript Declarator	Subscript	Subscript Value
1	(A)	(a)	a
2	(A,B)	(a,b)	$a + A \cdot (b - 1)$
3	(A,B,C)	(a,b,c)	$a + A \cdot (b - 1) + A \cdot B \cdot (c - 1)$

a, b, and c are the values of subscript expressions. By "subscript declarator" we mean the dimensioning information given in the DIMENSION, or COMMON, or type statement. For instance, in

    DIMENSION X(3, 12)

the subscript declarator is (3,12).

Consider an example. In the statement just given, in terms of the notation of Table 7.2, $A = 3$, $B = 12$. Now where, for instance, is the element in row 2, column 9, that is, X(2,9)? Table 7.2 says that the "value" of this subscript is $2 + 3 \cdot (9 - 1) = 26$. In other words, we are to think of the 36 elements of the array arranged in a linear sequence in storage. Then, if element (1,1) is in position 1 in this string, element (2,9) is in position 26.

Study will show that Table 7.2 is a formal expression of the rule given earlier: arrays are stored in such a way that the first subscript varies most rapidly and the last varies least rapidly. This was the convention described in connection with using array names in input or output statements without subscripts.

All of the preceding has assumed that the variables in question were real, integer, or logical and furthermore that each takes up one storage location. (There are local exceptions to the latter.) In the case of complex and double precision variables two storage locations usually are required for each element, and when a single element is made equivalent to a double element it is the first part of the double element that is involved.

The reader is cautioned that the various versions of Fortran vary considerably on the matter of storage assignments for arrays, in the effect of complicated EQUIVALENCE and COMMON statements, in the presence or absence of special rules governing complex and double precision arrays, etc., etc. Different Fortrans vary as much in this area as anywhere. The description given here conforms to ANSI Fortran, but every programmer must get the details for his system.

The COMMON Statement

It has been stated that each subprogram has its own variable names: the name X in the main program is not necessarily taken to be the same as the name X in a subprogram. However, if the programmer *wishes* them to mean the same thing, he can write

    COMMON X

in *both* the main program and the subprogram. The compiler will then assign the two variables (and they still are distinct, in principle) to the same storage location, which, as a practical matter, makes them the same.

But the statement is not limited to this kind of use. Suppose we write

    COMMON X, Y, I   in a main program
    COMMON A, B, J   in a subprogram

Then X and A are assigned to the same storage location, as are Y and B, and as are I and J. Therefore, if we change the value of the variable named X in the main program, we have also changed the value of the variable named A in the subprogram; since both names refer to the same storage location, the two are effectively the same variable under two different names.

EQUIVALENCE and COMMON have a somewhat similar function. What is the difference between them?

EQUIVALENCE assigns two variables *within the same main program or within the same subprogram* to the same storage location; COMMON assigns two variables *in different subprograms or in a main program and a subprogram* to the same location.

When an array is named in an EQUIVALENCE statement *and* in a COMMON statement, the equivalence is established in the same general way as described earlier. This may increase the size of the COMMON block of storage and thus change the correspondences between the COMMON block described and some other COMMON block in another program.

For instance, consider a program containing the following three statements

```
DIMENSION A(4), B(4)
COMMON A, C
EQUIVALENCE (A(3), B(1))
```

Without the EQUIVALENCE statement, the COMMON block would contain five storage locations in the sequence

```
A(1), A(2), A(3), A(4), C
```

With the EQUIVALENCE statement, the B array is brought into COMMON, so to speak, and requires the following sequence of storage locations

```
A(1), A(2), A(3), A(4), C
         B(1), B(2), B(3), B(4)
```

COMMON is now six storage locations long.

COMMON may be lengthened in this way, but it may *not* be lengthened by any attempt to push the start of a COMMON block forward. For instance, with the same DIMENSION and COMMON statement just considered, the following EQUIVALENCE would be illegal.

```
EQUIVALENCE (A(1), B(2))
```

The storage assignment in COMMON would need to be

```
         A(1), A(2), A(3), A(4), C
B(1), B(2), B(3), B(4)
```

Since B is not mentioned in the COMMON statement, but is brought into COMMON by the EQUIVALENCE, the first element of B now precedes the start of the block of COMMON. This is not permitted.

As we have mentioned several times in passing, a variable named in a COMMON or type statement may have subscripting information. We might write

```
COMMON A(23), J(2, 8), LOGIC(3, 3, 7)
REAL X(10)
DOUBLE PRECISION VARNCE(5, 20)
```

A variable that is written with subscripting information in a COMMON or type statement must *not* be mentioned in a DIMENSION statement. On the other hand, it is still permissible

to name a variable in a DIMENSION statement and also to name it, without subscripting information, in a COMMON or type statement.

Two variables in COMMON must not both be named in an EQUIVALENCE statement. The reason for this is instructive. EQUIVALENCE says that two or more variables in *one program* (main program or subprogram) are to be assigned to the same storage location. COMMON says that variables in *different programs* are to be assigned to the same location. The way COMMON works is that all the variables named in a COMMON statement are assigned to storage in the sequence in which the names appear in the COMMON statement. This is true even when there is only one COMMON statement, in which case COMMON does not cause multiple assignments at all. But then if there are two or more COMMON statements, correspondences are established simply because the COMMON statement is treated the same way wherever it appears.

For example, if in a main program we write

```
COMMON A, B, C, D
```

the four variables named are assigned to storage locations in the order named, in a special section of storage called "COMMON storage." Thus A is a specific storage location, followed by B, and so on. Now suppose that in some subprogram we have

```
COMMON W, X, Y, Z
```

This means that W is assigned to the first storage location in COMMON, X is assigned to the next one, and so on, and the "COMMON block" used by the subprogram is the same as that used in the main program. Ergo, A and W have been assigned to the same location—without the compiler ever knowing about more than one COMMON statement at a time. Indeed, the two programs may very well have been compiled entirely separately.

Now suppose that we had the combination

```
COMMON A, B, C, D
EQUIVALENCE (A, B)
```

The net effect is a contradiction: the COMMON says to put the four variables named into a special area of storage, in the order named and *in separate locations,* whereas the EQUIVALENCE says that A and B are to be assigned to the *same* location.

In the description just given we have said that there is only one COMMON block in storage. This is actually too limited: we can establish as many distinct blocks of COMMON storage as we please by *labeling* COMMON. What we have been discussing so far is in fact called *blank* COMMON to signify that it has no label.

Each COMMON block—blank COMMON and as many labeled COMMON blocks as there may be—is set up as described above. That is, variables and arrays are assigned storage locations in the order in which they are listed. Any rearrangements made necessary by EQUIVALENCE statements are made.

Labeled COMMON may be used, if there is some need to do so, simply to guarantee a particular arrangement of storage locations. This is probably rare in normal usage, being limited to what might be called "extralegal" programming. (For instance, in a particular compiler and computer it may be possible to refer to the data adjacent to an array by using subscripts larger than the maximum given in dimensioning information.)

In "normal" or "legal" usage, the value of labeled COMMON is to have two COMMON blocks with the same name in two programs that are executed together. When this is done, the two blocks must be the same length. Assuming this to be the case, the variables in the two blocks are assigned to the same storage locations, just as with blank COMMON.

Labels are written between slashes in front of the variable names. We might write, for instance

```
COMMON /X/A, B, C
```

If a single COMMON statement includes labeled COMMON and blank COMMON, the blank COMMON portion may either be written first without a name, as we have done heretofore, or the name may be omitted between slashes.

For a final example, suppose we were to write the following two statements in a main program and in a subprogram.

```
COMMON A,B,C/B1/D,E/B2/F(20),G(2,5)
COMMON R,S,T/B1/U,V/B2/X(10),Y(10,2)
```

Blank COMMON would contain A, B, and C, in that order, in the program containing the first COMMON, and R, S, and T in the program containing the second. A and R would thus be assigned to the same storage location, as would

B and S, and C and T. The COMMON block labeled B1 would establish D and U in the same location and E and V in the same. We assume that all of the foregoing variables were not mentioned elsewhere in a DIMENSION statement. B2 in the first program contains the 20 elements of F and the 10 elements of G. The same 30 locations would also contain the 10 elements of X and the 20 elements of Y. The overlap between the four arrays involved would cause the compiler no difficulty—indeed the compiler would never really consider the situation. Such a pair of statements would put F(11) and Y(1,1) in the same location, for instance. If that is the intended action, then everything will work nicely. If not, naturally there will be some surprises in store for the programmer. As a matter of fact, the intricacies of things like labeled COMMON and the interrelationships between COMMON and EQUIVALENCE account for a disproportionate percentage of the questions programmers have to ask about Fortran, and the problems of program conversion from one machine to another.

COMMON and EQUIVALENCE offer considerable power to the programmer who understands them and uses them wisely. One of the most frequent applications of the COMMON statement is in setting up communication between a main program and one or more subprograms. By placing identical COMMON statements in all the programs and subprograms involved, it becomes unnecessary to list the variables so designated in the FUNCTION reference or SUBROUTINE call. We shall see an example of this important application in Case Study 13.

7.8 THE DATA STATEMENT

More frequently than one might imagine it happens to be convenient to compile data into the object program from source program statements. We saw an example in the case studies involving plotting, where in Figure 6.9, for instance, we needed to enter 18 alphanumeric values. There is no such thing in Fortran as an alphanumeric constant, so we had to read a data card to get the characters entered. This works, but it is slightly annoying, since the card has to be read every time the program is executed even though it never changes. Other examples could be cited.

The DATA statement provides the capability we need. It takes the form

DATA list/$d_1, d_2, \ldots, d_n$/,
    list/$d_1, d_2, k*d_3, \ldots d_m$/ . . .

In this symbolic description a "list" contains the names of the variables to receive values, the d's are the values, and k, if it is used, is an integer constant. Consider some examples.

```
DATA A, B, C/14.7, 62.1, 1.5E-20/
```

This statement would assign the value 14.7 to A, 62.1 to B, and 1.5×10^{-20} to C. *This is done prior to the time of execution of the object program. The DATA statement is not executable.* The values assigned by the DATA statement are placed in storage when the object program is loaded and that is the end of the actions instituted by the DATA statement. It is legal to redefine the values of these variables, but having done so it is NOT possible to "re-execute" the DATA statement to put the variables back to their initial values.

The following two statements have the same effect; the choice is a matter of personal preference.

```
DATA A/67.87/, B/54.72/, C/5.0/
DATA A, B, C/67.87, 54.72, 5.0/
```

The following statement assigns the value 21.7 to all six variables.

```
DATA R, S, T, U, V, W/6*21.7/
```

A DATA statement may contain Hollerith text written either with the H field descriptor or with quoted literals if available.

```
DATA DOT, X, BLANK/1H., 1HX, 1H /
DATA DOT, X, BLANK/'.', 'X', ' '/
```

If the number of characters of text is not the same as the number of characters in a storage location, the treatment is the same as that for reading alphanumeric data from cards. In the foregoing example, the period would be left-adjusted in DOT and the rest of DOT filled with blanks, and similarly with X. BLANK would be filled entirely with blanks, as intended in this case.

A DATA statement may use an implied DO to specify the elements of an array, as we see in the following statement, which handles the example cited at the beginning of this section.

```
DATA (SYMBOL(L), L = 1, 17)/'A',
1   ' ', 'B', ' ', 'C', ' ', 'D', ' ',
2   'E', ' ', 'F', ' ', 'G', ' ', 'H',
3   ' ', 'K'/, BLANK/' '/
```

This feature, however, is an extension of the ANSI standard, and is not found in all compilers.

Data may never be entered into blank COMMON with a DATA statement. In order to enter data into labeled COMMON it is necessary to write a BLOCK DATA subprogram. This is a subprogram that begins with the words BLOCK DATA and that contains only the DATA, COMMON, DIMENSION, EQUIVALENCE, and type statements associated with the data being defined. It must not contain executable statements.

The segment below illustrates a BLOCK DATA subprogram. We see two labeled COMMON blocks, BLK1 and BLK2. All the variables in each block must be listed, even though not all variables receive values from the DATA statement (T does not appear there). We see examples of all three ways of writing the dimensioning information for a subscripted variable: in a DIMENSION statement, in the COMMON statement, and in a type statement.

```
BLOCK DATA
COMMON /BLK1/R, S, T/BLK2/X, Y(2)
DIMENSION R(6)
COMPLEX S
INTEGER T(2)
LOGICAL X
DATA (R(I), I = 1, 6)/1.0,2.0,4*7.5/,
1   S/(1.0, 2.0)/, X/.TRUE./,
2   Y(1), Y(2)/7.5, 8.0/
END
```

7.9 FUNCTIONS AS ARGUMENTS: THE EXTERNAL STATEMENT

Fortran permits the use of a function name as an argument in a subprogram call. When this is done, it is necessary to list the function name in an EXTERNAL statement in the calling program to distinguish the function name from a variable name.

As an example of what can be done, Figure 7.1 contains a main (calling) program that calls a SUBROUTINE subprogram. The subprogram contains exactly one executable statement:

```
Y = F(X)
```

```
C PROGRAM USING EXTERNAL STATEMENT
C
        EXTERNAL SIN, COS, SQRT
C
C CALL SUBR WITH SINE AS ARGUMENT
        CALL SUBR (2.0, SIN, RESULT)
        WRITE (6, 100) RESULT
 100    FORMAT ('0SIN(2.0) = ', F10.6)
C
C CALL SUBR WITH COSINE AS ARGUMENT
        CALL SUBR (2.0, COS, RESULT)
        WRITE (6, 200) RESULT
 200    FORMAT ('0COS(2.0) = ', F10.6)
C
C CALL SUBR WITH SQRT AS ARGUMENT
        CALL SUBR (2.0, SQRT, RESULT)
        WRITE (6, 300) RESULT
 300    FORMAT ('0SQRT(2.0) = ', F10.6)
        STOP
        END
```

FIGURE 7.1. A main program that calls a subprogram with function names as arguments, and therefore uses the EXTERNAL statement.

The arguments listed are X, F, and Y, making the function F a matter of choice in the subprogram call.

The main program calls this subprogram three times. Each time the value of X is 2.0 and the actual variable corresponding to Y is RESULT. The arguments corresponding to F are successively SIN, COS, and SQRT; these three supplied function names are listed in an EXTERNAL statement. Figure 7.2 shows the three lines printed, indicating that the subprogram really was executed with three different functions for F.

In place of the standard mathematical functions, we could also have specified FUNCTION subprograms that we might have written.

7.10 CASE STUDY 13: QUADRATIC EQUATION SOLUTION WITH SUBPROGRAMS

This case study illustrates some of the ideas about subprograms and the COMMON statement that we have been discussing. The numer-

```
SIN(2.0) =    0.909297

COS(2.0) =   -0.416147

SQRT(2.0) =   1.414213
```

FIGURE 7.2. The output of the program of Figure 7.1.

ical aspects of the example are quite simple; the solution of quadratic equations by the familiar formula presents no new concepts. The emphasis instead is on program organization and input-output formats.

A program is to be set up to solve the quadratic equation $Ax^2 + Bx + C = 0$. The program must be able to read from cards the coefficients of many such equations—possibly hundreds—and to produce an easily readable report showing for each equation the coefficients and the roots. A data card contains the coefficients of two equations, six values in all. However, each equation is to be written on a line by itself. The roots can be real or complex, although we shall do all arithmetic using Fortran real variables. A heading is to be printed at the top of each page, the pages are to be numbered, and the lines are to be counted as they are printed, so that each page will contain only 20 lines of output, double-spaced.

The program will be written to use two SUBROUTINE subprograms. Each subprogram will be called twice for each data card, avoiding duplications and perhaps making the complete program easier to correct and modify. The main routine will handle reading of data cards, printing of page headings, page numbering, line counting, and detecting the end of the deck, which will be done using a zero value at A as a sentinel.

The first subprogram will get the solutions, taking into account that if the discriminant $B^2 - 4AC$ is negative the roots are complex. The input to this subprogram, named SOLVE, consists of the names of the three coefficients; they are named as arguments of the subprogram. The output consists of the real and imaginary parts of the two roots, which are named X1REAL, X1IMAG, X2REAL, and X2IMAG. These four variables are needed in the main program and in both subprograms. They are named in COMMON statements in all three places, making it unnecessary to write them as arguments of the subprograms.

The second subprogram, named OUTPUT, writes the coefficients and the roots. It is desired to print the results in such a way that the reader can tell at a glance if the roots are pure real or pure imaginary. If the roots are real, the space for the imaginary parts is to be left blank, and if they are pure imaginary the space for the real parts is to be left blank. We recall that complex roots always occur as complex conjugates; it can never happen that only one root is complex or that two complex roots have different real parts.

Figure 7.3 is a flowchart of the main program, which has been drawn on the assumption that DO statements will be used to implement the line- and page-counting operations. See page 108 for a description of the flowcharting symbol used in this book to denote the operation of a DO statement. The first DO controls a page-numbering variable that is also used to set a maximum limit on the amount of output; it is assumed that 100 pages would be far more than normal, and that exceeding this limit would indicate incorrect data. The second DO controls the number of lines printed, using LINE as the index, but since the coefficients for two equations appear on each card, we have to read only 10 cards to get 20 lines. What is being done might have been more obvious if we had used somethings like KARDS as the index instead of LINE. The rest of the flowchart is straightforward.

Figure 7.4 is a flowchart of the subprogram for finding the roots. The procedure shown steers a middle course between the bare minimum required to distinguish between real and complex roots and the more complicated tests that could be made to take advantage of every special situation. The bare minimum would be to go to the complex section if the discriminant is negative and to the real section if it is zero or positive. Since the arithmetic IF statement automatically gives a three-way branch, it seems reasonable to take special action if the discriminant is zero to avoid computing the square root of zero. We could, however, go further with this testing for special conditions. If C is zero, both roots are real, one being zero and the other $-B/A$. If B is zero, the formulas simplify slightly. If B and C are both zero, then, of course, both roots are zero—but it is hard to see why such a case would ever be entered.

In any such case it is necessary to draw the line somewhere. Time can indeed be saved in the execution of the object program by taking advantage of special situations, unless testing for them wastes all the saving. Even where there is a net saving, though, a thorough series of tests may simply not be worth the trouble and the program complexity.

The flowchart of the output subprogram, Figure 7.5, is also fairly simple. Notice that it is not necessary to test both imaginary components for zero values, since both will always be zero

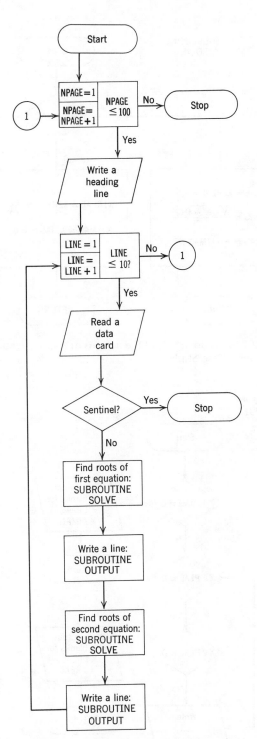

FIGURE 7.3. A flowchart of the actions of a main program for finding the roots of quadratic equations. (Case Study 13.)

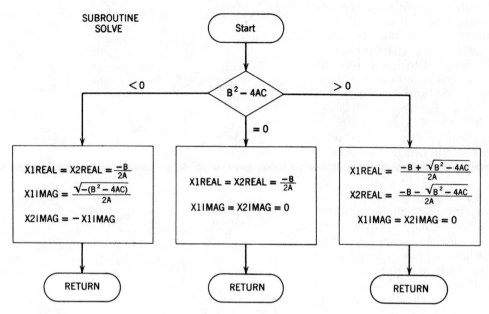

SUBROUTINE
SOLVE

Start

< 0

$B^2 - 4AC$

> 0

$= 0$

X1REAL = X2REAL = $\frac{-B}{2A}$

X1IMAG = $\frac{\sqrt{-(B^2 - 4AC)}}{2A}$

X2IMAG = $-$X1IMAG

X1REAL = X2REAL = $\frac{-B}{2A}$

X1IMAG = X2IMAG = 0

X1REAL = $\frac{-B + \sqrt{B^2 - 4AC}}{2A}$

X2REAL = $\frac{-B - \sqrt{B^2 - 4AC}}{2A}$

X1IMAG = X2IMAG = 0

RETURN

RETURN

RETURN

FIGURE 7.4.   A flowchart of the actions of a subprogram for finding the roots of quadratic equations. (Case Study 13.)

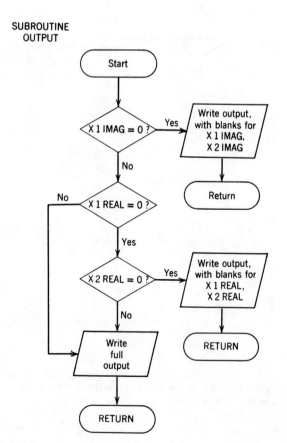

SUBROUTINE
OUTPUT

Start

X 1 IMAG = 0 ?   Yes → Write output, with blanks for X 1 IMAG, X 2 IMAG → Return

No

X 1 REAL = 0 ?   No →

Yes

X 2 REAL = 0 ?   Yes → Write output, with blanks for X 1 REAL, X 2 REAL → RETURN

No

Write full output

RETURN

or both nonzero. This is not true of the real parts, since they could be two different real roots.

The main program is shown in Figure 7.6. We begin with a COMMON statement naming the real and imaginary parts of the two roots. The same statement appears in both subprograms, so that these four variables are assigned to the same storage locations by all three programs, even though the three will be compiled separately. They would not be so assigned, of course, without the COMMON statements.

Next we have the DO statement that counts the pages and sets the limit of 100 pages of output. At the top of each page we write a heading line that contains column identifications and the page number. Then another DO counts the number of cards read, as noted in discussing the flowchart. For each data card we first ask whether the first number on the card is zero. This is the coefficient of x^2 for the first equation; if this is zero the equation is not a

FIGURE 7.5.   A flowchart of the actions of a subprogram for printing the roots of quadratic equations. (Case Study 13.)

```
C CASE STUDY 13
C QUADRATIC EQUATION SOLUTION WITH SUBROUTINES
C
C THIS IS THE MAIN PROGRAM
C
C
      COMMON X1REAL, X1IMAG, X2REAL, X2IMAG
C
C     ... USE DO TO COUNT PAGES AND SET LIMIT ON OUTPUT
      DO 40 NPAGE = 1, 100
C
C         ... WRITE HEADING LINE AT TOP OF NEW PAGE
          WRITE (6, 10) NPAGE
   10     FORMAT ('1', 9X, 'A', 14X, 'B', 14X, 'C', 11X, 'X1 REAL', 8X,
      1        'X1 IMAG', 8X, 'X2 REAL', 8X, 'X2 IMAG        PAGE', I4//)
C
C         ... USE ANOTHER DO, TO COUNT LINES;
C         ... THERE WILL BE TWO LINES PRINTED PER DATA CARD READ.
          DO 30 LINE = 1, 10
C
C             ... READ A DATA CARD
              READ (5, 20) A1, B1, C1, A2, B2, C2
   20         FORMAT (6F10.0)
C
C             ... CHECK FOR SENTINEL
              IF ( A1 .EQ. 0.0 ) STOP
C
C             ... SOLVE BOTH EQUATIONS AND PRINT RESULTS
              CALL SOLVE (A1, B1, C1)
              CALL OUTPUT (A1, B1, C1)
              CALL SOLVE (A2, B2, C2)
              CALL OUTPUT (A2, B2, C2)
   30     CONTINUE
   40 CONTINUE
      STOP
      END
```

FIGURE 7.6. The main program for finding roots of quadratic equations. (Case Study 13.)

quadratic, so there is little likelihood that anyone would want to use zero as a legitimate
value.

Now we are ready to find the roots for the
first set of coefficients, and we call into operation the subprogram that solves the equation.
The arguments are the first set of coefficients.
When control returns from SOLVE, values will
have been given to X1REAL, X1IMAG, X2REAL,
and X2IMAG. Now we call the subprogram for
writing the output, naming only the three coefficients; the four parts of the roots are com-
municated via COMMON. Another call of each
of the subprograms computes and writes the
roots for the second set of coefficients from the
data card.

The coding of the two subprograms, Figures
7.7 and 7.8, should not be hard to follow. Two
new variables, DISC and S, are set up in the
SOLVE subprogram to avoid computing certain
expressions twice. Advantage is taken of the fact
that complex roots occur only as complex conjugates, once again to avoid computing an expression twice.

The OUTPUT subprogram is not complicated,
but the FORMAT statements should be studied
carefully. The blank spaces for the two special
cases of pure real and pure imaginary roots are
introduced by 15X field descriptors. Notice also
the carriage control characters to get double
spacing.

The main program of Figure 7.6 and the subprograms of Figures 7.7 and 7.8 were compiled
one at a time, each leading to a separate object
program. Since they were run on a time-sharing
system, the physical form of the object programs was simply magnetic disk storage. In
some situations they might have been produced
as actual decks of cards. At a later time the
system was asked to load all three object pro-

```
C CASE STUDY 13
C QUADRATIC EQUATION SOLUTION WITH SUBROUTINES
C
C THIS IS THE SUBROUTINE FOR FINDING THE ROOTS
C
C
      SUBROUTINE SOLVE (A, B, C)
      COMMON X1REAL, X1IMAG, X2REAL, X2IMAG
C
C MAKE INTERMEDIATE VARIABLE OF THE DISCRIMINANT
      DISC = B**2 - 4.0*A*C
C
C TEST DISCRIMINANT, USING ARITHMETIC IF STATEMENT
      IF ( DISC ) 10, 20, 30
C
C HERE IF DISCRIMINANT IS NEGATIVE -- ROOTS ARE COMPLEX
   10 X1REAL = -B / (2.0 * A)
      X2REAL = X1REAL
      X1IMAG = SQRT(-DISC) / (2.0 * A)
      X2IMAG = -X1IMAG
      RETURN
C
C HERE IF DISCRIMINANT IS ZERO -- ROOTS ARE REAL AND EQUAL
   20 X1REAL = -B / (2.0 * A)
      X2REAL = X1REAL
      X1IMAG = 0.0
      X2IMAG = 0.0
      RETURN
C
C HERE IF DISCRIMINANT IS POSITIVE -- ROOTS ARE REAL AND UNEQUAL
   30 S = SQRT(DISC)
      X1REAL = (-B + S) / (2.0 * A)
      X2REAL = (-B - S) / (2.0 * A)
      X1IMAG = 0.0
      X2IMAG = 0.0
      RETURN
      END
```

FIGURE 7.7. The subprogram for finding the roots of quadratic equations. (Case Study 13.)

grams, an operation that is much more involved than it might sound, because of the necessity of setting up the communications between the three independent programs and incorporating all the input/output routines and other supplied functions that they call into action. Once all three were loaded, the system was instructed to begin executing the main program, which it did, producing the output of Figure 7.9.

7.11 CASE STUDY 14: TRANSLATING ALGEBRAIC EXPRESSIONS TO POLISH NOTATION

In this case study we shall consider an application that, although highly practical, is quite different from others in this book. The appli-

cation is that of translating an expression written in ordinary algebraic notation, with parentheses and operators written between the forms they operate on, into what is called *Polish notation,** in which there are never any parentheses and in which operators are written *after* the forms on which they operate.

Let us start by seeing what an expression written in Polish notation means. Consider the expression

AB+C*

The plus sign applies to the two operands to the left of it; the plus sign is the first operator that appears in a left-to-right "scan" of the ex-

*So called because it was developed by the Polish logician J. Lukasiewicz.

```
C CASE STUDY 13
C QUADRATIC EQUATION SOLUTION WITH SUBROUTINES
C
C THIS IS THE SUBROUTINE FOR PRINTING THE RESULTS
C
C
      SUBROUTINE OUTPUT (A, B, C)
      COMMON X1REAL, X1IMAG, X2REAL, X2IMAG
C
C CHECK IF ROOTS ARE PURE REAL
      IF ( X1IMAG .EQ. 0.0 ) WRITE (6, 10) A, B, C, X1REAL, X2REAL
   10 FORMAT ('0', 1P4E15.4, 15X, 1PE15.4)
      IF ( X1IMAG .EQ. 0.0 ) RETURN
C
C CHECK IF ROOTS ARE PURE IMAGINARY
      IF ( (X1REAL .EQ. 0.0) .AND. (X2REAL .EQ. 0.0 ) )
     1    WRITE (6, 20) A, B, C, X1IMAG, X2IMAG
   20 FORMAT ('0', 1P3E15.4, 15X, 1PE15.4, 15X, 1PE15.4)
      IF ( (X1REAL .EQ. 0.0) .AND. (X2REAL .EQ. 0.0) ) RETURN
C
C IF WE GET HERE, ROOTS ARE NEITHER PURE REAL NOR PURE IMAGINARY
      WRITE (6, 30) A, B, C, X1REAL, X1IMAG, X2REAL, X2IMAG
   30 FORMAT ('0', 1P7E15.4)
      RETURN
      END
```

FIGURE 7.8. The subprogram for printing the results of the computations of the programs of Figures 7.6 and 7.7. (Case Study 13.)

pression, and it is carried out first. After doing the addition, we keep scanning the expression, looking for another operator. When we find it, it is applied to the two quantities preceding it, which now are A + B and C. The Polish expression is thus equivalent to the ordinary algebraic expression (A + B)*C.

Consider the Polish expression

ABC+*

We scan across the expression looking for an operator; when we find the plus sign, we apply it to the last two operands preceding it, to get B + C. Finding the asterisk, we apply it to the last two things in the list, which are now A and B + C. The expression is thus equivalent to A*(B + C).

Here are a few more Polish expressions and their ordinary equivalents.

Polish	Algebraic
AB+C+D+	A+B+C+D
ABC*+D+	A+B*C+D
AB+CD+*	(A+B)*(C+D)
ABCDEF+*+++	A+B*(C+D*(E+F))

Figure 7.13, the output of the program we shall write, contains some more pairs of this sort.

The work of this case study will be to translate an expression written in the ordinary manner into Polish notation. We shall work entirely with the expression, never evaluating it or even asking what the values of the variables might be. The example thus illustrates one type of *nonnumeric* data processing. The application is entirely practical: things of this general sort are an essential part of many compilers, for instance, along with many other important areas of computer application.

The program we shall consider will read an expression from a card. We shall restrict ourselves to expressions involving variables only (no constants), with variable names that are always just one letter. We shall further restrict ourselves to the four arithmetic operations of addition, subtraction, multiplication, and division. Exponentiation is excluded, as is the unary subtraction operator. (In the expression $-(A - B)$, for instance, the first minus is a unary operator, since it operates on only one operand.) These and many other forms could be included, of course, but we prefer to restrict the complexity in order to gain a full understanding of the basic ideas. We shall assume, finally, that there are no errors of any sort in the input expression.

PAGE   1

A	B	C	X1 REAL	X1 IMAG	X2 REAL	X2 IMAG
1.0000E 00	-2.0000E 00	1.0000E 00	1.0000E 00		1.0000E 00	
1.0000E 00	-1.0000E 01	2.5000E 01	5.0000E 00		5.0000E 00	
1.0000E 00	-3.0000E 00	2.0000E 00	2.0000E 00		1.0000E 00	
2.0000E 00	-6.0000E 00	4.0000E 00	2.0000E 00		1.0000E 00	
1.0000E 00	1.0000E 00	-2.5500E 03	5.0000E 01		-5.1000E 01	
1.0000E 01	-2.0000E 01	1.0000E 01	1.0000E 00		1.0000E 00	
1.0000E 03	-2.0000E 03	1.0000E 03	1.0000E 00		1.0000E 00	
2.0000E-02	-4.0000E-02	2.0000E-02	1.0004E 00		9.9962E-01	
1.4320E 00	9.8760E 00	-4.5670E 00	4.3500E-01		-7.3316E 00	
8.8130E 00	-1.3100E 00	0.0	1.4864E-01		0.0	
2.3003E 00	1.9917E 00	0.0	0.0		-8.6584E-01	
1.0000E 00	0.0	-1.0000E 00	1.0000E 00		-1.0000E 00	
1.0000E 00	0.0	1.0000E 00		1.0000E 00		-1.0000E 00
9.0000E 00	0.0	3.6000E 01		2.0000E 00		-2.0000E 00
1.0000E 00	2.0000E 00	5.0000E 00	-1.0000E 00	2.0000E 00	-1.0000E 00	-2.0000E 00
5.3500E 02	2.2000E 01	1.5830E 03	-2.0561E-02	1.7200E 00	-2.0561E-02	-1.7200E 00
-9.0000E 00	2.3000E 01	3.7000E 01	-1.1189E 00		3.6744E 00	
6.1000E 01	2.0000E 00	8.7000E 01	-1.6393E-02	1.1941E 00	-1.6393E-02	-1.1941E 00
6.1000E 01	1.5900E 02	8.7000E 01	-7.8145E-01		-1.8251E 00	
1.0000E 02	9.9000E 01	9.8000E 01	-4.9500E-01	8.5731E-01	-4.9500E-01	-8.5731E-01

FIGURE 7.9. The output produced when the object programs from the programs of Figures 7.6, 7.7, and 7.8 were combined and run with suitable data. (Case Study 13.)

The first action in the program, after reading the expression from a card, is to identify the various characters as operators or operands. The operators are

- + * / ( )

The operands are the letter variables. Then for each operator we must assign a number that gives its "rank" or "strength." This will determine when the operator enters the final Polish expression. This is the way we implement the convention that multiplications and divisions are executed before additions and subtractions, in the absence of parentheses, and it is the way we take parentheses into account. The hierarchy numbers are

(	1
)	2
+, -	3
*, /	4

A hierarchy number of zero will identify an operand.

These rankings become the entries in another array, this one having 80 integer elements. The input string is called SOURCE and the associated hierarchy array SHIER (for Source HIERarchy).

The basic scheme of the translation is as follows.* Operands are always transferred to the output string (POLISH) as soon as they are encountered. Operators other than a right parenthesis are always transferred to another stack (OPSTCK, for OPerator STaCK) to await transfer to the output string. As operators are transferred to the operator stack OPSTCK, their hierarchies go to the corresponding elements of an array called OHIER (for Operator HIERarchy).

After the transfer of an operand to the output string a check is made to see if the last entry in the operator stack has a higher hierarchy than the next operator in the input, or the same hierarchy; in either case, the operator from operator stack is transferred to the output. Whenever a right parenthesis is found in the input, it is ig-

*This translation scheme is based on a publication of the Burroughs Corporation called a "Compilogram," a "game" that graphically illustrates concepts like those involved here.

nored, and the matching left parenthesis, which will always be the last entry in the operator stack at this point, is also ignored.

The reader will want to study the translation system in examples. This can best be done by following the definition given in the flowcharts of Figures 7.10 and 7.11. Figure 7.10 diagrams a straightforward examination of each character of the input string, on the basis of which a hierarchy number is placed in the corresponding element of SHIER. The variable M is the count of characters in the SOURCE string up to the first blank column on the card, since we assume no embedded blanks in the input expression. M will be used later to stop the translation process. The program is to be applied to a series of cards, one expression per card; a blank card will signal the end of the deck.

In Figure 7.11 we have what amounts to a definition of the translation algorithm as it was outlined above. The reader who wishes to understand the details of this case study will want to follow through the steps of Figure 7.11 with several examples.

The program of Figure 7.12 follows the logic of the flowcharts quite closely. The logic would be virtually impossible to decode given only the program, but with the flowchart for comparison the program has little that is new. The only feature not already illustrated in earlier case studies is the DATA statement, with which we enter the alphanumeric values BLANK, LPAREN, RPAREN PLUS, MINUS, ASTRSK, and SLASH.

All the data variables were included in INTEGER statements to avoid diagnostics that say, in effect, "you can't compare SOURCE(L) and LPAREN—they are not of the same type." We know that they are both alphanumeric, but there is no separate alphanumeric type. We can put alphanumeric values into *any* type variable as long as *we* know what we are doing. The logical IF statement will compare two alphanumeric values just as though they contained ordinary numerical values; if they are equal, they are equal—and it matters not that symbols are involved rather than numbers.

Figure 7.13 displays several pairs of input expressions and translated Polish equivalents.

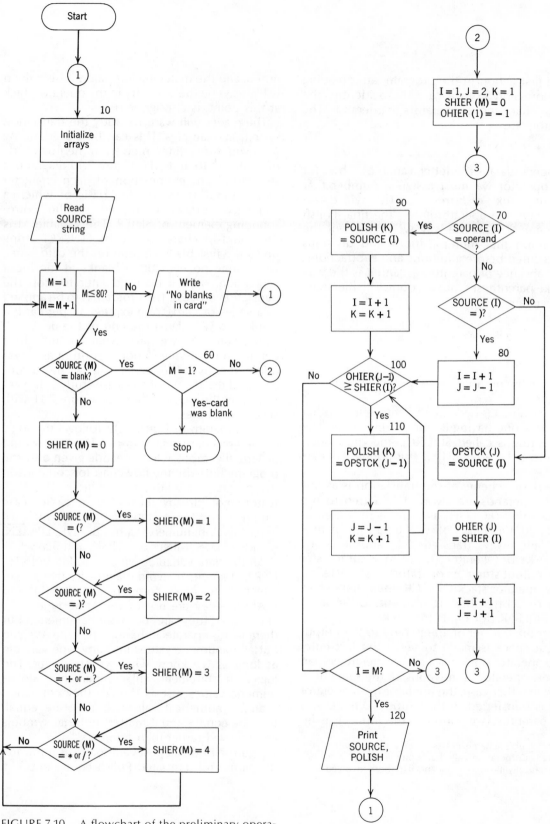

FIGURE 7.10. A flowchart of the preliminary operations in converting an expression from ordinary algebraic notation to Polish notation. See page 108 for an explanation of the flowchart symbol used to denote the operations of the DO statement. (Case Study 14.)

FIGURE 7.11. A flowchart of the procedure for converting an expression from ordinary algebraic notation to Polish notation, once the preliminary operations shown in Figure 7.10 are complete. (Case Study 14.)

```
C CASE STUDY 14
C TRANSLATING ALGEBRAIC EXPRESSIONS TO POLISH NOTATION
C
C THE VARIABLE NAMES AND THEIR MEANINGS ARE AS FOLLOWS:
C     SOURCE      THE INPUT STRING, IN NORMAL ALGEBRAIC FORM
C     SHIER       ARRAY CONTAINING THE HIERARCHY NUMBERS OF THE INPUT
C     OPSTCK      'OPERATOR STACK': THE OPERATORS FROM THE INPUT
C     OHIER       ARRAY CONTAINING THE HIERARCHY NUMBERS OF THE OPERATORS
C     POLISH      THE OUTPUT STRING, IN POLISH NOTATION
C
C     L           DO INDEX USED IN INITIALIZING
C     M           DO INDEX USED IN SETTING UP SHIER ARRAY
C     I           POINTER TO INPUT STRING (SOURCE AND SHIER)
C     J           POINTER TO OPERATOR STACK (OPSTCK AND OHIER)
C     K           POINTER TO OUTPUT STRING (POLISH)
C
C     THE OTHER VARIABLES ARE ACTUALLY CONSTANTS, AND ARE
C     DEFINED IN THE DATA STATEMENT.
C
C
      INTEGER*2 SOURCE(80), SHIER(80), OPSTCK(80), OHIER(80), POLISH(80)
      INTEGER*2 BLANK, LPAREN, RPAREN, PLUS, MINUS, ASTRSK, SLASH
      DATA BLANK/' '/, LPAREN/'('/, RPAREN/')'/, PLUS/'+'/,
     1    MINUS/'-'/, ASTRSK/'*'/, SLASH/'/'/
C
C INITIALIZE ARRAYS TO ZERO OR BLANK, AS APPROPRIATE
   10 DO 20 L = 1, 80
          SHIER(L) = 0
          OHIER(L) = 0
          OPSTCK(L) = BLANK
          POLISH(L) = BLANK
   20 CONTINUE
C
C READ A 'DATA' CARD
      READ (5, 30) SOURCE
   30 FORMAT (80A1)
C
C IN THE FOLLOWING DO-LOOP, M POINTS TO CARD COLUMNS, FROM LEFT TO RIGHT
C FIRST BLANK SIGNALS END OF STRING (EMBEDDED BLANKS ARE NOT ALLOWED)
C IT IS ASSUMED THAT IF A CHARACTER IS NOT AN OPERATOR OR A
C    PARENTHESIS, IT IS A VARIABLE
      DO 40 M = 1, 80
          IF ( SOURCE(M) .EQ. BLANK ) GO TO 60
C
C SET SHIER(M) TO ZERO, THEN CHANGE IT IF THE CHARACTER IS AN OPERATOR
          SHIER(M) = 0
          IF (       SOURCE(M) .EQ. LPAREN ) SHIER(M) = 1
          IF (       SOURCE(M) .EQ. RPAREN ) SHIER(M) = 2
          IF (       SOURCE(M) .EQ. PLUS
     1        .OR. SOURCE(M) .EQ. MINUS  ) SHIER(M) = 3
          IF (       SOURCE(M) .EQ. ASTRSK
     1        .OR. SOURCE(M) .EQ. SLASH  ) SHIER(M) = 4
   40 CONTINUE
C
C IF NORMAL EXIT IS TAKEN, THE CARD DID NOT CONTAIN A BLANK
      WRITE (6, 50)
   50 FORMAT (1X, 'DATA CARD IN ERROR - NO BLANKS')
      GO TO 10
C
C IF SOURCE-STRING POINTER = 1 ON EXIT FROM DO, CARD WAS ALL BLANK
   60 IF ( M .EQ. 1 ) STOP
```

FIGURE 7.12.   A program for converting expressions from algebraic to Polish notation. (Case Study 14.)

```
C
C OTHERWISE PROCEED TO TRANSLATION
C INITIALIZE HIERARCHY NUMBERS TO GET STARTED PROPERLY
      SHIER(M) = 0
      OHIER(1) = -1
C
C INITIALIZE POINTERS
      I = 1
      J = 2
      K = 1
C
C CHECK FOR OPERAND
  70  IF ( SHIER(I) .EQ. 0 ) GO TO 90
C
C CHECK FOR RIGHT PARENTHESIS
      IF ( SHIER(I) .EQ. 2 ) GO TO 80
C
C SOME OTHER OPERATOR IF HERE -- MOVE TO OPERATOR STACK
      OPSTCK(J) = SOURCE(I)
      OHIER(J) = SHIER(I)
C
C ADVANCE POINTERS
      I = I + 1
      J = J + 1
      GO TO 70
C
C DELETE CORRESPONDING LEFT PARENTHESIS
  80  I = I + 1
      J = J - 1
      GO TO 100
C
C MOVE OPERAND TO POLISH STRING
  90  POLISH(K) = SOURCE(I)
      I = I + 1
      K = K + 1
C
C CHECK HIERARCHY RANKINGS
 100  IF ( OHIER(J-1) .GE. SHIER(I) ) GO TO 110
C
C CHECK FOR END OF SOURCE STRING
      IF ( I .EQ. M ) GO TO 120
      GO TO 70
C
C MOVE OPERATOR TO POLISH STRING
 110  POLISH(K) = OPSTCK(J-1)
      K = K + 1
      J = J - 1
      GO TO 100
C
C WRITE SOURCE AND POLISH STRINGS
 120  WRITE (6, 130) SOURCE, POLISH
 130  FORMAT (1H0, 80A1/1H , 80A1)
      GO TO 10
      END
```

FIGURE 7.12.   (Cont.)

```
A*(B+C)
ABC+*

(A+B)*C
AB+C*

A+B*C+D
ABC*+D+

(A+B)*(C+D)
AB+CD+*

A-B/C
ABC/-

(A-B)/C
AB-C/

A/B+C
AB/C+

A/(B+C+D)
ABC+D+/

A/B/C
AB/C/

(A/B)/C
AB/C/

A*B-C+D
AB*C-D+

A*B-(C+D)
AB*CD+-

A
A

(((((A)))))
A

((A)+((B)))
AB+

A+B+C+D
AB+C+D+

(A+B)+(C+D)
AB+CD++

(E+V)*(D*(A*N))
EV+DAN***

(C-(H-A/S))*(J-(U-D/E))
CHAS/--JUDE/--*

C*(I*(N*(D+Y)))+(G/(I/(N/(N/(I-E)))))
CINDY+***GINNIE-////+

(R+(A+C*H))/(L+(I+Z*A))/(T+O*M)
RACH*++LIZA*++/TOM*+/
```

FIGURE 7.13.   The output of the program of Figure
7.12. (Case Study 14.)

EXERCISES

Note: Now that the full resources of the Fortran language are available to the reader, any of the problems in the Suggestions for Term Problems (Appendix 3) may be considered. Many of them can best be approached in terms of a group of subprograms.

*1. Define a statement function to compute

$$DENOM(X) = X^2 + \sqrt{1 + 2X + 3X^2}$$

Then use the function to compute

$$ALPHA = \frac{6.9 + Y}{Y^2 + \sqrt{1 + 2Y + 3Y^2}}$$

$$BETA = \frac{2.1Z + Z^4}{Z^2 + \sqrt{1 + 2Z + 3Z^2}}$$

$$GAMMA = \frac{\sin Y}{Y^4 + \sqrt{1 + 2Y^2 + 3Y^4}}$$

$$DELTA = \frac{1}{\sin^2 Y + \sqrt{1 + 2\sin Y + 3\sin^2 Y}}$$

2. Define a statement function to compute

$$SLG(A) = 2.549 \log\left(A + A^2 + \frac{1}{A}\right)$$

Then use the function to compute

$$R = X + \log X + 2.549 \log\left(A + A^2 + \frac{1}{A}\right)$$

$$S = \cos X + 2.549 \log$$
$$\left(1 + X + (1 + X)^2 + \frac{1}{1 + X}\right)$$

$$T = 2.549 \log$$
$$\left[(A - B)^3 + (A - B)^6 + \frac{1}{(A - B)^3}\right]$$

$$U = [B(I) + 6]^2$$
$$+ 2.549 \log\left[\frac{1}{B(I)} + \frac{1}{B(I)^2} + B(I)\right]$$

*3. Define a logical statement function to compute the "exclusive or" of two logical variables. The exclusive or is true when exactly one of the inputs is true; it is false when both inputs are false and when both inputs are true. Then write the statements that would be needed to test whether the exclusive or is associative, that is, whether

$$(A \circ B) \circ C = A \circ (B \circ C)$$

in which a circle has been used to indicate the exclusive or.

4. Given three logical variables, A, B, and C, a full binary adder accepts three inputs and provides two outputs, the sum and the carry. The sum is true if any one of the three inputs is true and the others are false, or if all three inputs are true. The carry is true if any two or more of the inputs is true. Write logical statement functions to compute these two functions.

*5. Given two one-dimensional arrays of N logical elements each, named A and B, that are to be viewed as the digits of two binary numbers. The two numbers are to be added in binary to produce the N + 1 elements of an array named C. Use the functions developed in Exercise 4 in a loop.

*6. Write a FUNCTION subprogram to compute

$$Y(X) = \begin{cases} 1 + \sqrt{1 + X^2} & \text{if } X < 0 \\ 0 & \text{if } X = 0 \\ 1 - \sqrt{1 + X^2} & \text{if } X > 0 \end{cases}$$

Then write statements to evaluate the following expressions.

$$F = 2 + Y(A + Z)$$

$$G = \frac{Y[X(K)] + Y[X(K + 1)]}{2}$$

$$H = Y[\cos(2\pi X)] + \sqrt{1 + Y(2\pi X)}$$

7. Write a FUNCTION subprogram to compute

$$RHO(A, B, N) = \frac{A}{2\pi} \sum_{i=1}^{N} B_i$$

in which B is a one-dimensional array of 50 elements ($N \leq 50$).

Then use it to compute $\frac{1}{2}\pi$ times the sum of the first 18 elements of an array named A; call this SOME.

8. Rewrite the program for Exercise 7 so that N represents the number of elements in the array, which may then have adjustable dimensions.

9. A is any 20 x 20 array. Write a FUNCTION subprogram to compute

$$PD(A, I, J)$$
$$= \frac{A(I-1, J) + A(I+1, J) + A(I, J-1) + A(I, J+1)}{4}$$

Then use it to compute

$$B_{ij} = (1 - \alpha)B_{ij}$$
$$+ \alpha \frac{B_{i-1,j} + B_{i+1,j} + B_{i,j-1} + B_{i,j+1}}{4}$$

(Could a statement function be used here? Why not?)

*10. Write a FUNCTION subprogram for which the argument list contains A, M, and N, where A is an array name, and M and N are the numbers of rows and columns. The function value is to be the sum of the absolute values of all the elements. The dimensions are to be adjustable.

11. Devise a FUNCTION subprogram that could be called in either of the forms

```
AVER(ROW, L, ARRAY, M, N)
AVER(COLUMN, L, ARRAY, M, N)
```

The intent is to be able to ask for the algebraic sum of the elements in *row or column* L of an M × N adjustable array. Bear in mind that what is transmitted to the subprogram as a result of writing an argument is, in effect, the *value* of the argument: the characters 'ROW' or 'COLUMN' are not *themselves* transmitted. Not, that is, unless you put them in quotes as just done and arrange for the subprogram to accept the characters as alphanumeric input, if that is permissible in your system. Failing this, you will have to have given appropriate value to the variable named ROW or COLUMN so that the subprogram can make its decision as to what you wanted on the basis of the *value* of the first argument. In that case, using the variable names ROW and COLUMN is purely a documentation device, of possibly arguable worth.

This is indeed confusing, and the example is not very important in itself—but the distinctions involved are fundamental.

*12. A is a one-dimensional array with 50 elements. Write a SUBROUTINE subprogram to compute the average of the first N elements and a count of the number of these elements that are zero. Call the subprogram AVERNZ(A, N, AVER, NZ).

Then use the subprogram to get the average of the first 20 elements of an array named ZETA and place the average in ZMEAN and the count of zero elements in NZCNT.

13. Write a SUBROUTINE subprogram that uses the FUNCTION of Exercise 11 and find the row of an M × N array that has the largest sum; the outputs are the row number and the sum.

Then use the subprogram to operate on an array named OMEGA which has 15 rows and 29 columns; place the largest sum in OMEGAL and the row number in NROW.

This combination of subprograms involves passing adjustable dimensions through a subprogram.

14. Given single variables A, B, X, and L, write a SUBROUTINE subprogram to compute R, S, and T from

$$R = \sqrt{A + BX + X^L}$$
$$S = \cos(2\pi X + A) \cdot e^{BX}$$

$$T = \left(\frac{A + BX}{2}\right)^{L+1} - \left(\frac{A + BX}{2}\right)^{L-1}$$

15. Identify any errors in the following:

a. `COMMON A, B(2, 19), R(40)`

b. `COMMON //R, S, T/LABEL,/U, V, W`

c. `COMMON G, H, P, Q, Y, Z`
   `EQUIVALENCE (A, P, R), (B, H, S, Z)`

d. `COMMON A(12), B, C(14)`
   `DIMENSION D(9)`
   `EQUIVALENCE (A(2), D(8), G)`

e. `EQUIVALENCE (A(3),B(2),C(4)),`
   `1   (A(4),B(6),D(9))`

16. Sketch the storage layout that would result from the following:

*a. `DIMENSION A(3), B(4)`
    `EQUIVALENCE (A(2), B(1))`

*b. `DIMENSION C(2,3), D(3,2)`
    `EQUIVALENCE (C(1), D(3))`

c. `DIMENSION E(2,2,2), F(4)`
   `EQUIVALENCE (E(5), F(2))`

17. Assume a computer in which an integer number and a real number take the same amount of storage space and in which a complex number and a double precision number each take twice as much storage space as a real or integer number. Further, when a complex or double precision number or array element is referenced in an EQUIVALENCE statement, it is always the

first of the two storage locations that is meant. Sketch the storage layout that would result from the following:

*a.
```
DIMENSION I(2), R(4), C(3)
INTEGER I
REAL R
COMPLEX C
EQUIVALENCE (I(1),C(1)), (R(1),C(2))
```

*b.
```
DIMENSION D(4), I(5)
DOUBLE PRECISION D
REAL R1, R2
INTEGER I
EQUIVALENCE (D(1),R1), (D(2),R2),
1    (D(3),I(2))
```

c.
```
DIMENSION C(5), D(3), S(1), T(1)
COMPLEX C
DOUBLE PRECISION D
EQUIVALENCE (C(1),S(1)), (C(2),T(2)),
1    (C(2),D(1))
```

d.
```
DIMENSION C(3,3), D(2,2,2), R(20)
COMPLEX C
DOUBLE PRECISION D
REAL R
EQUIVALENCE (C(4),D(7),R(12))
```

18. Consider the following plan. We wish to make the diagonal elements of a 4×4 array A the same as the four elements of a one-dimensional array DIAG. It is proposed to do this with the statement

```
EQUIVALENCE (A(1),DIAG(1)),
1          (A(6),DIAG(2)),
2          (A(11),DIAG(3)),
3          (A(16),DIAG(4))
```

This is quite impossible. Formulate a rule of which this would be a violation and explain why the rule is necessary.

19. Write DATA statements to do the following.

*(a) Initialize A to contain 21.9; initialize the complex variable C to contain $1 + 2i$; initialize all 23 elements of STRING to contain 2.0.

*(b) Put the words ONE, TWO, THREE, and FOUR in the four elements of NUMBER.

(c) Replace the example near the end of Section 7.8 with a statement in which the Hollerith *blank* field appears only once.

(d) Place in each location of an integer array named K the element number of the element. The array has 10 elements.

20. Extend the program of Figure 7.12 to include an exponentiation operator, represented by some single character of your choosing, having higher precedence than multiplication or division. Also, remove the requirement that there be no imbedded blanks and no errors in the input statement. Finally, modify the program to accept variable names of more than one character. This will require an initial pass through the input for *lexical* analysis, as distinguished from the *syntactic* analysis performed by the program as it stands.

The reader who finds this type of thing interesting may wish to know more about how compilers work. A good tutorial introduction to the subject is David Gries, *Compiler Construction for Digital Computers,* New York, Wiley, 1971.

21. Make the program of Figure 5.12, not including the input and output, into a subroutine. Use adjustable dimensions, so that the argument list can include the size of the system.

Write a small main program to read some data, call this subroutine, then print the results.

22. Given the array BOARD described in Exercise 31 of Chapter 5, write a subroutine to produce a chessboard picture along the lines of that shown in Figure 6.14.

EXCURSIONS I–IV
APPENDICES I–IV
ANSWERS TO EXERCISES

EXCURSION I: A DIARY OF A TIME-SHARING SESSION

By Daniel D. McCracken*

By far the most convenient way to prepare programs is with the aid of a good time-sharing system. At the present time (1972) it is somewhat more expensive than using a card punch and a batch compiler, but when allowance is made for the increased efficiency of the programmer, the cost differential is not too great. Furthermore, the costs are rapidly decreasing, so that the use of time sharing is growing rapidly.

We accordingly present here a sketch of how a representative time-sharing system can be used for programming in Fortran. This really will be only a sketch, since time sharing can be used for many languages other than Fortran; it can be used in ways that do not involve conventional programming at all; and it can be used in ways far more elaborate and powerful than we shall attempt to present here. Nevertheless, the sample session will give an adequate flavor of the subject.

The first part of the session concerns writing a simple example program, to demonstrate some of the concepts. The second part displays the program that will be used a little later in the book production process to prepare the index for the book, and shows it in operation.

It seems that the only sensible way to describe something of this sort is in the first person. What follows is therefore in the form of a diary of a terminal session, with the paragraphs of the text keyed to the numbers shown in circles on the printout on the facing page. It should be understood that terminal paper is ordinarily supplied as a continuous form; we have cut it apart so that the terminal printout and the description of it can always be seen without turning pages.

1. I dial the CSS number in White Plains, New York, a few miles from my office. The computer is in Stamford, Conn., and until CSS installed a multiplexor in White Plains, which accepts five or ten local calls and forwards them to Stamford over a higher-speed telephone line, I used to have to call Stamford. After the right lights on my terminal come on, I press the carrier return, from which the computer figures out what kind of terminal I have, and sends me the "CSS Online" message. I *log in;* MCRACKEN is my user identification (limited to eight characters, so I dropped one "C" when the identification was assigned). The system recognizes my identification as valid, and asks for my password. To protect me if I worked in an office where some one might try to poach on my account, the system types the blackout characters to make it impossible to tell what my current password is. (If you think you can read it, be assured that it has been changed!) It then asks for accounting information. This is for my benefit: when I get my bill, the charges are broken down by account, using the accounting information I supply. This would be more useful in an office where a number of people use the same user identification, but I do use it to keep track of what I spend on different projects.

"CSS" originally stood for "Conversational Software System." Now it is simply part of the company name, National CSS, Inc.

2. The system says it is ready to go, and states which version is running: it's version 201, which went up on 2/10/72. New versions, containing improvements and corrections, are currently installed every couple of months at CSS. It is no reflection on the company to observe that sometimes new versions have errors in them, so that the user might wish to know—when something doesn't work—whether it is the fault of the system. It rarely is, of course, but this identification is available just in case.

By and large, things that are typed in lower case are things that I typed; the system generally answers in UPPER CASE. As we shall see later, there are times when I want to control that matter, and I can.

Not all time-sharing terminals have both upper and lower case, however, and many have a somewhat shorter line length than the 130 characters on my terminal, which is the NOVAR Model 5-41. This terminal is manufactured by NOVAR using a Selectric® typewriter mechanism purchased from IBM, as are the terminals made by a number of other manufacturers. I therefore have available the full capability of changing the typing element to get different type styles.

*With grateful acknowledgement of the assistance of the staff of National CSS, Inc., Stamford, Conn., especially Mrs. Ursula Connor and Douglas B. Kuhn.

① CSS Online   XRR Qsyosu

login mcracken
PASSWORD:
▨▨▨XXXXX
A/C INFO:
fiv
② READY AT 15.44.25 ON 03/30/72
CSS.201 02/10/72

3. When the system is ready for me to issue an instruction to it, it types the time of day. Shortly after 3:44 PM on March 30, 1972, accordingly, I said to the system *"edit triangle fortran."* The *"edit"* is a command to CSS; *"triangle"* is the name of the file I intend to create, and *"fortran"* is the *type* of the file. The type distinguishes this file named *triangle* from other files named *triangle* that will be created later in the session, and it also implies some actions to the editor. For instance, with a file type of *fortran,* all lower case letters that I type will be automatically converted to upper case.

The system checks to see whether this file already exists, and, since it doesn't, the system immediately prepares to accept input.

4. I type in my Fortran program, taking advantage of the lower-case-to-upper-case conversion most of the time. (If I type upper case letters, they just stay that way.) I make a typing error in the second line, which I notice before striking CR (carrier return, or carriage return) to enter the line, but I decide to leave it there and fix it later.

5. In typing the READ statement I hit a 6 where I meant 5; I caught this as soon as I did it, so I immediately typed the character @, which wipes out the immediately preceding character. (If I needed to be able to enter the character @, I could issue an instruction changing or cancelling this effect.) I use this facility in the IF statement as well, and at many other times in the session.

6. In typing the second FORMAT statement, I get so fouled up in my typing that I decide to kill the whole line and start over. If the last character on a line is ¢, the line is simply not entered. There is an error in the continuation of the FORMAT, but I didn't see it at the time.

7. When I get to the GO TO I realize that I have not put a statement number on the READ. I make up a number, and make a mental note to fix up the READ later.

8. The blank line, called a *null line,* signals the editor that I want to get out of input mode. The editor comes back with the word EDIT. In any time-sharing system it is essential to know at all times which *environment* you are in, and everyone forgets from time to time, issuing a command in one environment that makes sense only in some other environment. A good time-sharing system, therefore, provides a lot of clues as to where you are, and answers any null line

with an indication of what environment you are in.

9. The *"top"* is an edit command, saying that the editor should position itself at the top of the file. We shall find it useful to think in terms of a *line pointer* concept; at all times during editing, there is some line that is under consideration. We may want to look at it, change it, delete it, add something after it, or do any of a lot of other things; all these actions are referenced in terms of the line currently being "pointed at."

Most time-sharing systems associate a *line number* with each line; in many systems the line number is usually printed along with the line. Using the line number it is possible to say "go to line 43," or something to that effect, to move the line pointer to the given line. This capability is available in the CSS system, but I generally find it more convenient to refer to lines in other ways, as will be demonstrated later.

10. I move the pointer to the top of the file to ask for the entire file to be printed. If I wanted to count the number of lines in the file, I could have been precise and said *"print 14,"* but since I want the whole thing, I just give a large number; the editor can't print more than there is. The entire file is accordingly printed. Observe the upper case letters, the corrections called for by the @ and ¢, and the fact that my typing errors are still there! The EOF means "end of file": I said to print 90 lines, but the editor naturally could not find that many, and told me that it had come to the end.

11. After moving the pointer back to the top, I say *"next,"* to move the pointer to the first line of the file. The *"top"* needs to refer to something *above* the first line, in case I should wish to insert some new lines before the first. When I say "next" the editor not only moves the pointer but also prints the line. If I were pretty sure what the line was and didn't want to see it, I could have typed a period after the *"next,"* to kill printing. If I want to kill all such printing, I can issue a command to that effect.

There are abbreviations for almost all commands in this time-sharing system. If this were not a demonstration, I would have typed just *"n"* instead of *"next."* Since the reader is presumably reading this diary more for the flavor than for the specifics, I have generally avoided the abbreviations.

<circle>3</circle> 15.44.38 edit triangle fortran
NEW FILE.
INPUT:
c a program to demonstrate some of the features of
<circle>4</circle> c time&hsaring. given the two sides of a right triangle,
c it computes and prints the hypotenuse and area
c
<circle>5</circle>   read (6@5, 100) a, b
  100   format (2f10.0)
        o@if (a .eq. 0.0) stop
        hyp = sqrt(a**2 + b**2)
        area = A*B/2.0
        write (6, 200) a, b, hyp, area
<circle>6</circle> 200   format (1x, 'a = ',f8.2'b = ,'¢
   200   format (1x, 'a = ', f8.2, ' b = ', f8.2,
      1   ' hyp = ', f8.2, ' area = ', f8.3
<circle>7</circle>   go to 10
        end
<circle>8</circle>
EDIT:
<circle>9</circle> top
<circle>10</circle> print 90
C A PROGRAM TO DEMONSTRATE SOME OF THE FEATURES OF
C TIME&HSARING. GIVEN THE TWO SIDES OF A RIGHT TRIANGLE,
C IT COMPUTES AND PRINTS THE HYPOTENUSE AND AREA
C
        READ (5, 100) A, B
  100   FORMAT (2F10.0)
        IF (A .EQ. 0.0) STOP
        HYP = SQRT(A**2 + B**2)
        AREA = A*B/2.0
        WRITE (6, 200) A, B, HYP, AREA
  200   FORMAT (1X, 'A = ', F8.2, ' B = ', F8.2,
      1   ' HYP = ', F8.2, ' AREA = ', F8.3
        GO TO 10
        END
EOF:
top
<circle>11</circle> next
C A PROGRAM TO DEMONSTRATE SOME OF THE FEATURES OF

12. What I wanted, actually, was the second line, so I say *"next"* again, and reach the line that needs correction.

13. I say *"change"* and then give the old and new character-strings, delimited by slashes. If the string being changed contains a slash, naturally I cannot use a slash for a delimiter, but this is no problem: the editor takes the first character that appears after the *"change"* (or *"c"* if abbreviated) as the delimiter.

14. I decide to add a period at the end of the sentence.

15. I say *"find"* and specify the word *"read"* in columns 7 to 10. (The exact positioning of the *"read"* would get us into the action of the tab key in time sharing, which is a hopelessly confusing subject that I propose to ignore.) The editor starts searching for the characters READ in the positions specified, starting with the line at which the pointer is presently pointing. It finds and prints it.

16. I say to *"overlay"* the current line with the characters 10, again with some magic about the positioning. In this case, column 1 is considered to begin after one blank space beyond the *edit* command. Anyway, the 10 is inserted into the line; if there had already been something in the two character positions involved, they would have been destroyed ("overlaid"). The net effect is to give me the statement number I forgot when I first typed the line.

17. I figure I have a workable program, so I tell the editor to *"file"* it. This means to put it in the disk storage space assigned to me. Since I didn't say otherwise, it is filed under the name *triangle*, with the file type *fortran*, as stated in the original *"edit."* If I had wanted to change my mind and give the file some other name, I could have done so. This can be useful in developing a modified version of an existing file: edit it under one name, modify it, then file the new version under a new name. The new and old versions will both then be on disk.

18. The time-of-day message (15.50.57, so I spent about five minutes typing in the program and making the corrections) tells me I am back in the CSS environment. The commands that make sense in this environment are naturally different from those that make sense in the editing environment; if I were to say *"top"* or

"change" now, the system would come back with INVALID CSS COMMAND. In the CSS environment, *"fortran"* is a command to compile the file named, which had better have the file type of *fortran* for the command to make sense, so I don't have to give the file type.

The compiler finds the error in the FORMAT statement and gives me a diagnostic. Actually, in the line below the erroneous statement there was a dollar sign at the far right, off the paper, as a pointer. This makes the diagnostic message SYNTAX a little more meaningful, since it does more or less indicate something missing at the end of the statement. The response !!E(00008)!! is an error-severity message from the compiler and means, as it happens, that moderately serious errors were found. I didn't ask for execution of the object program, but if I had the system would have attempted to do so despite the error.

19. Obviously, I need to work on my program. I ask to *edit* the file named *triangle* with the file type of *fortran,* just as I did at the beginning of the session; this time, it is not a new file, and the response is simply to inform me that I am in the edit environment. I ask the editor to *"locate"* the line containing the string /hyp =/. It turns out that such a string occurs earlier in the program than the line I am looking for, which I forgot, so I simply ask to have the same edit command repeated, by saying *"again."* This time I get the offending line, and proceed to change it. The major problem was a missing right parenthesis, of course, but while I'm making that correction I notice that I did not use consistent field descriptors, so I make that change at the same time. I am not aware of any other errors in the program, so I file it after making this one change.

20. Now I ask for the program to be compiled. There are no diagnostic messages, and after a few seconds I get the time-of-day message indicating that the compilation is complete. That is 13 seconds of *elapsed* time, and, of course, includes the typing of the command. There are dozens of other people using the computer along with me, and I don't get the full resources of the system. The actual CPU (central processing unit) time used for such a small problem would have been under a second, probably.

```
⑫  next
    C TIME&HSARING.  GIVEN THE TWO SIDES OF A RIGHT TRIANGLE,
⑬  change /&hs/-sh/
    C TIME-SHARING.  GIVEN THE TWO SIDES OF A RIGHT TRIANGLE,
    next
    C IT COMPUTES AND PRINTS THE HYPOTENUSE AND AREA
⑭  change /area/area./
    C IT COMPUTES AND PRINTS THE HYPOTENUSE AND AREA.
⑮  find   read
          READ (5, 100) A, B
⑯  overlay   10
       10  READ (5, 100) A, B
⑰  file

⑱  15.50.57 fortran triangle
              1   '  HYP = ',  F8.2, '  AREA = ', F8.3

    01)  IEY0131 SYNTAX
     !!E(00008)!!

⑲  15.51.09 edit triangle fortran
    EDIT:
    locate /hyp =/
          HYP = SQRT(A**2 + B**2)
    again
          1   '  HYP = ', F8.2, '  AREA = ', F8.3
    c /f8.3/f8.2)/
          1   '  HYP = ', F8.2, '  AREA = ', F8.2)
    file

⑳  15.52.01 fortran triangle
```

21. Now I execute another CSS command, *"listf"* (for *list file*). I specify the file name, but by placing an asterisk in the file-type position I ask for a listing of all files having that name. It turns out that there are two: the Fortran source program I wrote using the editor, and a file with the file-type of *text* which is, in effect, the object program. (We shall ignore the *file mode* for the purposes of this Excursion. It will be P1 on all files used here, and the matter is not very interesting for our purposes.)

22. Now I say *"run triangle"* to indicate that the object program should be loaded into my section of main storage and executed. When the program has been loaded, CSS types out EXE-CUTION and, since the program asks for data from data set 5—which defaults to the console—the keyboard unlocks and waits for me to enter data. I type in two numbers, using commas between them so that I can ignore the field descriptors in the FORMAT statement, and press CR. The program executes, in the course of which it prints the output line shown, and transfers back to ask for more data. I try three more triangles, then enter a zero sentinel to get out of execution.

Many other time-sharing systems type a question mark to indicate readiness to accept input.

23. I decide I would like to change the output field descriptor, to get three decimal places instead of two. I accordingly ask to edit the *triangle fortran* file, then call for a *"change"* of a little different sort. Without bothering to locate a line, I say to change every occurrence of the string f8.2 to f9.3. The two asterisks say, in effect, to make this change every time the string occurs in any line. The editor searches through the file for all occurrences of the string f8.2, and whenever it finds the string makes the change and prints the changed line. That is all I wanted to do this time, so I file the modified version, thus automatically replacing the earlier version.

24. I now need to recompile the program and execute it. The combination of compile and execute is something I do so often that I have

set up my own CSS command for it, using something called the Executive Language. To show the reader what is involved here, I have printed the file named *frun* having the file type of *exec*, using the CSS command *printf* (*"print file"*). My *frun* is a very simple command. It first turns off typing, so that the subsequent commands will not be typed at my terminal. It then says FORTRAN &1, which means to execute the CSS command *fortran* for whatever file I name when I use the EXEC. In a moment, for example, I will say *"frun triangle"*; the name *"triangle"* will be substituted for the &1 when the EXEC is executed. Likewise with the *"run."* In other words, I have made up a new CSS command that combines the functions of the actual CSS commands *fortran* and *run*. The command *frun* will apply only to my work; this has no effect on other people using the system.

25. I now ask to compile and execute the modified program. We see that the FORMAT was changed as desired.

26. I would now like to put the program data into a file, so that I don't have to type it in as the program executes. I accordingly ask to *edit* (which means *"create"* in this case) a file named *triangle* having the file-type of *data*. I enter some data values and file them.

27. Now when I ask for a listing of all the files named *triangle*, of whatever file type, we find three.

28. The default for data set 5 is the console. If I want to read from somewhere else, I need to tell CSS about it. I therefore do a *filedef* (*"file define"*) that says data set 5 is a disk file having the name *triangle* and the file type *data*. It is *not* necessary that the file name be the same as that of the program that will use the data; it just happens to be convenient in terms of an EXEC I have previously set up.

29. Now when I ask to *run triangle*, the data values are read from disk, and accordingly do not appear on the listing as they did at paragraphs 22 and 25.

```
㉑  15.52.14 listf triangle *
    FILENAME FILETYPE MODE   ITEMS
    TRIANGLE FORTRAN  P1     014
    TRIANGLE TEXT     P1     022

㉒  15.52.23 run triangle
    EXECUTION:
    3.0,4.0,
    A =     3.00  B =      4.00  HYP =      5.00  AREA =      6.00
    5.0,12.0,
    A =     5.00  B =     12.00  HYP =     13.00  AREA =     30.00
    2.,2.,
    A =     2.00  B =      2.00  HYP =      2.83  AREA =      2.00
    67.91,23.88,
    A =    67.91  B =     23.88  HYP =     71.99  AREA =    810.84
    0.0

㉓  15.53.51 edit triangle fortran
    EDIT:
    change /f8.2/f9.3/ * *
     200  FORMAT (1X, 'A = ', F9.3, ' B = ', F9.3,
        1    ' HYP = ', F9.3, ' AREA = ', F9.3)
    EOF:
    file

㉔  15.55.04 printf frun exec

    &TYPE OFF
    FORTRAN &1
    RUN &1


㉕  15.55.15 frun triangle
    EXECUTION:
    3.0,4.0,
    A =     3.000  B =      4.000  HYP =      5.000  AREA =      6.000
    9.999,2.002
    A =     9.999  B =      2.002  HYP =     10.197  AREA =     10.009

㉖  15.56.18 edit triangle data
    NEW FILE.
    INPUT:
    1.0,2.0,
    3.0,4.0,
    56.,67.,
    0.0,0.0

    EDIT:
    file

㉗  15.56.53 listf triangle *
    FILENAME FILETYPE MODE   ITEMS
    TRIANGLE FORTRAN  P1     014
    TRIANGLE TEXT     P1     022
    TRIANGLE DATA     P1     004

㉘  15.57.03 filedef 5 dsk triangle data

㉙  15.57.23 run triangle
    EXECUTION:
    A =     1.000  B =      2.000  HYP =      2.236  AREA =      1.000
    A =     3.000  B =      4.000  HYP =      5.000  AREA =      6.000
    A =    56.000  B =     67.000  HYP =     87.321  AREA =   1876.000
```

30. I decide it might be nice to show off a couple of other features of the editor. (A good text editor is perhaps the most valuable feature of a time-sharing system.) I *edit triangle data,* and begin with a *"putd"* (*"put and delete"*) command, specifying two lines. This places the current line and the one after it in a special buffer, awaiting whatever I may decide to do with them. I move the pointer to the top and print the entire file, to prove to the reader that the first two lines really have been deleted. The printing puts me at the end of the file, so I move up two lines, then use the "insert" command to put in an entirely new line. Now I say *"get"* to pick up the two records previously placed in the buffer, move to the top again, and print the entire file.

The convenience of a good editor is hard to convey to someone who has never had the privilege of using one. Take a look at Figure 6.14 and imagine how long it would have taken a poor typist like me to prepare without the CSS editor to do most of the work!

31. It might be nice to show the output going somewhere else other than the console, so I do a *filedef* on data set 6 to send it to a disk file. The name again was *triangle* (also not required) but with a file type of *listing;* there are defaults associated with this file-type that are useful to me here.

32. Now I ask to run triangle, and get no output printed. But that's right! I ask to see the file named *triangle* having the file-type of *listing,* and there are my results.

33. At this point I wanted to show all the files named *triangle,* but I evidently hit two keys at once or something, and got thrown back into VP (for *"virtual processor"*), which is another environment of the system. There are several things I might have done at this point, in truth, but what I chose to do was an *ipl* (*"initial program load"*) to get back into CSS. (The distinction between the VP and CSS environments is important sometimes, but not to us here.)

34. I list my files named *triangle,* and sure enough, there are four of them. The number of *items* in each case means, very roughly, the number of lines. The details of this have to do with variable versus fixed-length records, record blocking, and all that. See Section 6.13. This

matters some to me when I am trying to figure out how to minimize my use of disk storage and thus reduce my monthly bill from National CSS, but is not essential to us here.

35. I'm curious how much money I've spent, so to speak, so I ask for a summary of what I've done in this session. It turns out that I have used 4.652 CPU seconds, have been connected to the machine for about 20 minutes, and have used 768 input/output operations. The precise definition of the latter would take 17 pages to explain, presumably—I've never understood it myself. Anyway, by the National CSS rate structure as of March, 1972, I have so far spent $5.94 of anticipated royalties (plus telephone). I will not break down the rate structure further, since it will inevitably change during the life of the book, and thus it would be unfair to National CSS to quote it.

36. I am also curious about how much disk space I have left, so I ask for *"stat"* (*"statistics"*). The results are shown, a cylinder being IBM terminology used with the particular storage device in question; as organized for customer use by National CSS, a cylinder holds about 120,000 characters.

37. The triangle demonstration being over, I erase all files having the name *triangle,* of whatever file type. When I now ask for statistics, I see that I have thus released seven records, a record being 800 characters.

38. We now move to the second section of the demonstration, that having to do with the preparation of the index for the book. I cannot remember whether I have saved the object program, so I ask for a listing of all the files having the name *index.* The *text* version is indeed there, together with *two* versions of the source program. The one having the file type of *fortranp* (*"fortran packed"*) was produced using an editor option that removes blanks from files, along the lines of Exercise 21 in Chapter 5. The unpacked version takes 160 items of 80 characters each (the length of the items can be determined using an option of the *listf* command), versus 9 items of 800 characters each, thus saving nearly half the storage space. Why I did not erase the unpacked version after packing it is a good question; that would ordinarily have been the idea.

```
30  15.57.44 edit triangle data
    EDIT:
    putd 2
    top
    print 90
    56.,67.,
    0.0,0.0
    EOF:
    up
    0.0,0.0
    up
    56.,67.,
    insert 5.0,12.0,
    get
    3.0,4.0,
    top
    print 90
    56.,67.,
    5.0,12.0,
    1.0,2.0,
    3.0,4.0,
    0.0,0.0
    EOF:
    file

31  15.59.22 filedef 6 dsk triangle listing

32  15.59.34 run triangle
    EXECUTION:

    15.59.55 printf triangle listing

    A =     56.000  B =     67.000  HYP =     87.321  AREA =  1876.000
    A =      5.000  B =     12.000  HYP =     13.000  AREA =    30.000
    A =      1.000  B =      2.000  HYP =      2.236  AREA =     1.000
    A =      3.000  B =      4.000  HYP =      5.000  AREA =     6.000


33  16.00.24 listf triangle *

    VP


    ipl css
    CSS.201 02/10/72

34  16.01.11 listf triangle *
    FILENAME FILETYPE MODE    ITEMS
    TRIANGLE DATA     P1       005
    TRIANGLE FORTRAN  P1       014
    TRIANGLE TEXT     P1       022
    TRIANGLE LISTING  P1       004

35  16.01.17 query time
    4.652 CPU SECS, .34 CONNECT HRS, 768 I/O

36  16.03.19 stat
    P-DSK(WT): 00608 USED. 00136 LEFT (OF 00744), 82% (OF 005 CYL)

37  16.03.32 erase triangle *

    16.03.45 stat
    P-DSK(WT): 00601 USED. 00143 LEFT (OF 00744), 81% (OF 005 CYL)

38  16.03.48 listf index *
    FILENAME FILETYPE MODE    ITEMS
    INDEX    FORTRANP P1       009
    INDEX    MEMO     P1       013
    INDEX    TEXT     P1       060
    INDEX    FORTRAN  P1       160
```

39. Now I want to remind myself what I put into the *index memo* file to use for sample data, so I ask to have the file printed. Unfortunately, however, I made a typing error in the command—namely, spacing and then backspacing in the middle of the file name. It turns out that the CSS command analyzer cannot handle this (it's OK in data) and rejected the command.

40. This time everything works fine, and we get a listing of the file, which consists of a few entries from the index for the first edition of this book.

41. I need a little more data than this to test the program properly, so I edit the file, using the *next* command in the abbreviated form of *n,* and using an *insert* to get in a new line. The *bottom* command puts me at the end of the file, and at that point I do a *save.* This puts the file

(as it now stands) out on disk, so that if the telephone connection is broken, for instance, or if National CSS has a machine outage (which happens once in a while in the best of families), the editing work I have done up to this point will not have been lost. The response to a *save* is to return to the input mode, which is fine with me: I do want to enter some more data.

The edit commands *file* and *save* both store the file on disk. The difference is that *file* returns to CSS environment whereas *save* returns to the edit input environment.

Observe that I am using upper and lower case here. For the purposes of this file, I definitely do want to maintain the distinction. This is one of the defaults associated with a file of the type *memo:* there is no automatic conversion from lower to upper case.

㊴ 16.04.00 printf index memo
INCORRECT 'PRINTF' PARAMETER-LIST
!!E(00001)!!

㊵ 16.04.33 printf index memo
A field specification, 85, 94$
Absolute value function: complex, 45, 65, 136$
>double precision, 42, 137$
>integer, 137$
>real, 9, 32, 137$
Ac circuit (Case Study 2), 25$
Addition, 5, 6, 40, 44, 135$
Adjustable dimension, 112, 132$
Advanced Scientific Instruments, 131$
Aircraft position exercise, 38$
ALGOL, 110$
Algorithm, 127$
Alphameric variable, 85, 110, 127$

㊶ 16.05.17 edit index memo
EDIT:
n
A field specification, 85, 94$
insert Absolute value of a complex number, 45, 47, 65$
bottom
Alphameric variable, 85, 110, 127$
save
INPUT:
American Standards Association, 131$
Amplitude ofcomplex number, 45, 47$
/@AND operator, 23, 49, 50$
Approximation methods, 31, 37, 74, 120$
Arctangent function: double precision, 136$
>real, 9 48, 49, 136$
Area of triangle (Case Study 1), 15@6$
Argument of function, 9 106, 110, 113,$
Arithmetic: assignment statement, 4, 9, 107$
>expression, 5$
>IF statement, 20, 21, 69$
operation¢
>operation, 3, 5$
Array, .¢
Array, 57, 79, 87, 111@0, 114, 132$
Array name without subscripts, 60, 83$
Assembly, 33, 34$
Assignement sa@tatmeent¢
Assignment statement: arithmetic, 4, 9, 70, 107$
>logical, 49, 53, 107$
$
BACKSPACE statement, 90$
BCD, 89, 90$
$
$
$

42. When I want out of the input mode, I issue a null line, as always, and again *save*. This time I do not want to do any more input; the *save* this time really was just for protection. So I enter another null line and ask to *locate* (abbreviated "l") the string /ofcomplex/, which I notice I have mistyped. The editor starts looking at whatever line it is currently pointing to and goes to the end of the file without finding such a string; it therefore types EOF and quits. I realize that the string in question was *above* the current line, so I ask for the command to be executed again, causing the editor to go to the top of the file and try the whole operation again. This time it finds the offending line, which I change by inserting a blank as needed.

43. I ask for the next line—for what reason I cannot recall as I write this a day later. Then I ask the editor to find the string /,$/, which includes an unintended comma. After making a few more corrections I file.

Now I begin to try to print out the *index fortran* file, but run into a discouraging series of *transmission errors*. These are exhibited as a pause in the typing, an error light on my terminal, and then some kind of garbled line. Whether the cause is the telephone company, the computer, or my terminal, I have no way of knowing. I sign off and recall the computer, going directly to the Stamford number, and get the same problem, so I have to guess it is not the telephone company. About this time my other phone rings and a coauthor wants to talk about something else altogether, so I put my terminal out of its misery and forget about the whole thing until the next morning. I skip over quite a few pages of useless garbled printing.

44. The next morning, undaunted, I try the White Plains number again. Behold, the transmission error problem has evaporated. Before printing out the index program, however, I decide it would be handy to have an EXEC to handle the printing on the size paper I want to use. I write an EXEC having the name *p* that accepts two line numbers and prints from the file named *index* having the file-type *fortran*, between those line numbers. This is mildly interesting in another way: until I defined my own EXEC named *p*, an acceptable abbreviation for the CSS command *printf* was *p*—but not now. My list of EXECs is examined first when I type a CSS command, and therefore my newly defined EXEC takes precedence over what is supplied with the system.

45. I try it out, asking for just the first two lines of the file. It works. Using this EXEC, I print out the program, which is shown in Figure E1.1. Comments have been used very heavily, and I shall take it that any reader who wants to understand the program will be able to figure it out for himself.

The program demonstrates an attempt to apply the suggestions in Excursion III for writing readable Fortran programs, and it uses a SUBROUTINE primarily to assist in understandability. In terms of the application, it shows that Fortran can be used for text processing, even if it is sometimes awkward. The same program, rewritten in APL or SNOBOL, would be a small fraction of this length—although it would take more CPU time to run.

46. Everything seems to be in order. The program was rather thoroughly tested in the course of using it to prepare the index for another book, as noted in the comments, so I do not expect any trouble with the program itself. On the other hand, it has been several months since I used it, so I may have forgotten some of the details.

Indeed I have. Specifically, I have forgotten that the text comes from data set 4, and that I have not done a *filedef* for that data set. I get a set of lines chiding me for my oversights, and trying to help me straighten it out. As soon as the first line prints I know what the problem is, but I let it print. The error severity message !!E(00016)!! means that the program was unexecutable.

(42) EDIT:
      save
      INPUT:

      EDIT:
      l /ofcomplex/
      EOF:
      again
      Amplitude ofcomplex number, 45, 47$
      c /of/of /
      Amplitude of complex number, 45, 47$
(43) n
      AND operator, 23, 49, 50$
      l /,$/
      Argument of function, 9 106, 110, 113,$
      c /,$/$/
      Argument of function, 9 106, 110, 113$
      c /9/9,/
      Argument of function, 9, 106, 110, 113$
      file

      CSS Online   XRR Qsyosu

      login mcracken
      PASSWORD:
      ▩▨▩▨▨▨▨▨
      A/C INFO:
      fiv
      READY AT 09.58.56 ON 03/31/72
      CSS.201 02/10/72

(44) 09.59.02 e p exec
      NEW FILE.
      INPUT:
      &type off
      printf index forr@tran &1 &2

      EDIT:
      file

(45) 09.59.49 p 1 2

      C CASE STUDY 18
      C PRINTING A PROPERLY SPACED INDEX FROM A MEMO FILE

(46) 10.15.48 run index
      EXECUTION:

      FT04F001 NOT OPENED...09

      IHC900I EXECUTION TERMINATING DUE TO ERROR COUNT FOR ERROR NUMBER 219

      IHC219I FIOCS - MISSING DD CARD FOR FT04F001

      TRACEBACK   ROUTINE   CALLED FROM ISN   REG. 14   REG. 15   REG. 0   REG.

                  IBCOM   000121E8   00012680   00000000   0000D908

                  INDEX   0000DDA0   00012000   0000011A   0000

      ENTRY POINT= 00012000
       !!E(00016)!!

47. Before fixing up this problem, I alter the name of the data file to prove that there is no necessity for a program and its data to have the same name. When I now ask for a listing of all my files named *index* the one with the file type of *memo* is no longer to be seen.

48. Now I do a *filedef* for data set 4.

49. At this point I am not absolutely certain that the object program (*text* file) named *index* really is the latest version of the program, so I recompile using my *frun* EXEC. After compil- ation, the program executes, starting with the prompt for the maximum number of characters per line and the maximum number of lines per page. I specify 25 characters per line and 10 lines per "page," for testing.

50. I'm tired of looking at this, so I press the *attention* key on my console. In the National CSS system this throws me back into VP (never mind!), and I do an *ipl* (*initial program load*) to get back to the CSS environment.

㊼ 10.19.40 alter index memo * xyz memo *

10.19.53 listf index *
FILENAME FILETYPE MODE   ITEMS
INDEX   FORTRANP P1   009
INDEX   TEXT   P1   060
INDEX   FORTRAN P1   160

㊽ 10.19.59 filedef 4 dsk xyz e@memo

㊾ 10.20.27 frun index
EXECUTION:
ENTER MAX CHARS AND MAX LINES, PER SAMPLE: 25,55,
25,10,
A field specification,
     85, 94
Absolute value of a
     complex number, 45,
     47, 65
Absolute value function:
     complex, 45, 65, 136
   double precision, 42,
     137
   integer, 137

   real, 9, 32, 137
Ac circuit (Case Study
     2), 25
Addition, 5, 6, 40, 44,
     135
Adjustable dimension,
     112, 132
Advanced Scientific
     Instruments, 131
Aircraft position

     exercise, 38
ALGOL, 110
Algorithm, 127
㊿ Alphameric variable, 8 #
VP

ipl css
CSS.201 02/10/72

51. The *ipl* operation wipes out all nonstandard *filedefs,* so I redefine data set 4 and run the program again, except that I use different parameters this time to demonstrate the operation of the program. Everything seems to be in order.

52. I carelessly omitted the END= option in writing the program, so when it comes to the end of the data set it starts to give me a long-winded message about my error. I am not terribly interested, so I press the *attention* key to stop the message.

```
(51) 10.27.07 filedef 4 xyz memo
DISK FILE ASSUMED

10.27.16 run index
EXECUTION:
ENTER MAX CHARS AND MAX LINES, PER SAMPLE: 25,55,
36,18,
A field specification, 85, 94
Absolute value of a complex number,
    45, 47, 65
Absolute value function: complex,
    45, 65, 136
  double precision, 42, 137
  integer, 137
  real, 9, 32, 137
Ac circuit (Case Study 2), 25
Addition, 5, 6, 40, 44, 135
Adjustable dimension, 112, 132
Advanced Scientific Instruments, 131
Aircraft position exercise, 38
ALGOL, 110
Algorithm, 127
Alphameric variable, 85, 110, 127
American Standards Association, 131
Amplitude of complex number, 45, 47



AND operator, 23, 49, 50
Approximation methods, 31, 37, 74,
    120
Arctangent function: double
    precision, 136
  real, 9 48, 49, 136
Area of triangle (Case Study 1), 16
Argument of function, 9, 106, 110,
    113
Arithmetic: assignment statement, 4,
    9, 107
  expression, 5
  IF statement, 20, 21, 69
  operation, 3, 5
Array, 57, 79, 87; 110, 114, 132
Array name without subscripts, 60,
    83
Assembly, 33, 34


Assignment statement: arithmetic, 4,
    9, 70, 107
  logical, 49, 53, 107

BACKSPACE statement, 90
BCD, 89, 90


(52) IHC217I FIOCS - END OF DATA SET ON UNIT     4

TRACEBACK  ROUTINE  CALL #
VP
```

53. At this point I stare out the window a while deciding what to do next. When I make up my mind, I forget what environment I am in and, not having done an *ipl,* get the response shown.

54. At this point I'm a little apprehensive about what EXECs I have created in the last few sessions, and decide to see if everything is still needed. The storage space is not too important, but I might have abbreviations for CSS commands (like *p*) that could get me in trouble next week.

55. For example! I cannot remember what the *st* EXEC is, so I ask to see it, using the CSS abbreviation *p* for *printf*. But *p* is at this moment my EXEC for something else entirely, so I get an error message. After erasing the *p* EXEC, I look at *st,* decide I no longer need it, and erase it. I similarly erase several other EXECs that I no longer need.

56. The *profile* EXEC is one that is automatically executed every time I *log in* or do an *ipl.* What it contains is up to me. I have chosen to inform the system of my mailing address, in case there is printed output to be mailed; I have defined certain standard tab settings; and I have asked that my machine configuration be saved for a few minutes if there is a telephone line break.

57. Out of general curiosity, I ask for my disk space statistics, in case I might need to request additional space for things I plan to do in coming days.

58. Again mostly out of curiosity, I ask for the current accounting figures. This CPU time is a little high, to my taste; this represents mostly the effort involved in the index text editing, at which Fortran is not ideal.

59. I log off the system, getting a summary of the session.

```
(53) listf * exec
     INVALID VP REQUEST

     ipl css
     CSS.201 02/10/72

(54) 10.30.06 listf * exec
     FILENAME FILETYPE MODE   ITEMS
     CONIN    EXEC     P1     002
     FRUN     EXEC     P1     003
     PRTALL   EXEC     P1     006
     FRUND    EXEC     P1     004
     RUNDD    EXEC     P1     003
     DSKIN    EXEC     P1     002
     PROFILE  EXEC     P1     004
     ST       EXEC     P1     002
     FD   EXEC         P1     003
     FD9  EXEC         P1     002
     BATCH    EXEC     P1     003
     TAB5     EXEC     P1     002
     PR       EXEC     P1     002
     P    EXEC         P1     002

(55) 10.30.31 p st exec
     FILE NOT FOUND.

     10.30.59 erase p exec

     10.31.13 p st exec

     &TYPE OFF
     START FCS12X


     10.31.17 erase st exec

     10.31.29 erase pr exec

     10.31.46 erase fd exec

     10.32.20 erase fd9 exec

     10.32.25 p profile exec

(56) &TYPE OFF
     SET TADDR ADDRESS MEMO
     TABSET 1 7 10 20 30 40 50 60 70 80 90 100
     SET SAVMACH ON


(57) 10.32.36 stat
     P-DSK(WT): 00601 USED. 00143 LEFT (OF 00744), 81% (OF 005 CYL)

(58) 10.32.54 query time
     8.074 CPU SECS, .59 CONNECT HRS, 963 I/O

(59) 10.33.03 logout
     8.087 CPU SECS, .59 CONNECT HRS, 963 I/O
     LOGGED OFF AT 10.33.11 ON 03/31/72
```

```
C PRINTING A PROPERLY SPACED INDEX FROM A MEMO FILE
C
C
C     THE PROGRAM ACCEPTS 80-CHARACTER RECORDS FROM A FILE ON DISK.
C THE FILE CONTAINS BOTH UPPER AND LOWER CASE CHARACTERS, HAVING
C BEEN ENTERED FROM A TIME-SHARING TERMINAL IN 'MEMO' MODE.
C THE PURPOSE OF THE PROGRAM IS TO PREPARE CAMERA-READY COPY FOR THE
C INDEX OF A BOOK; IT WAS USED TO PREPARE THE INDEX FOR
C 'NUMERICAL METHODS WITH FORTRAN IV CASE STUDIES,' BY
C WILLIAM S. DORN AND DANIEL D. MCCRACKEN, AND WILL BE USED TO
C PREPARE THE INDEX FOR THIS BOOK.
C     THE PROGRAM MUST BE ABLE TO ACCEPT NUMBERS DEFINING THE MAXIMUM
C LINE LENGTH AND THE MAXIMUM PAGE LENGTH, SO THAT THE DECISION ON
C THESE PARAMETERS CAN BE LEFT TO THE LAST MINUTE TO COORDINATE
C PROPERLY WITH PUBLISHING REQUIREMENTS.
C     THE MAJOR PROBLEM THAT THE PROGRAM MUST DEAL WITH IS THE CASE
C OF INPUT LINES THAT ARE LONGER THAN THE MAXIMUM LINE LENGTH; THESE
C HAVE TO BE BROKEN AT A POINT WHERE THERE IS A BLANK SPACE, WHICH
C THE PROGRAM MUST LOCATE, AND THEN 'TURN OVER' THE CONTINUATION,
C I. E., INDENT IT FOUR SPACES.  FURTHERMORE, SOME LINES OF INPUT
C ARE MARKED (IN THEIR FIRST CHARACTER) AS NEEDING TO BE INDENTED
C TWO SPACES, SINCE THEY REPRESENT SECOND-LEVEL ENTRIES.
C (A GLANCE AT THE INDEX WILL SHOW THE APPEARANCE THAT IS REQUIRED.)
C
C VARIABLE NAMES AND USAGES:
C
C     INDENT  LOGICAL; IF TRUE, LINE MUST BE INDENTED 2 SPACES
C     TRNOVR  LOGICAL; IF TRUE, LINE MUST BE INDENTED 4 SPACES
C     TEXT    ALPHABETIC; CONTAINS LINE OF TEXT FROM DISK
C     INDMRK  ALPHABETIC; '>' TO DESIGNATE LINE TO BE INDENTED
C     EOL     ALPHABETIC; '$' TO MARK END-OF-LINE IN INPUT RECORD
C     BLANK   ALPHABETIC; ' ' USED TO SEARCH FOR PLACE TO BREAK LINE
C     LCOUNT  INTEGER; LINE COUNTER
C     MAXLIN  INTEGER; READ AS CONSOLE DATA; MAX CHARACTERS PER LINE
C     MAXCNT  INTEGER; READ AS CONSOLE DATA; MAX LINES PER PAGE
C     INITL   INTEGER; POINTER TO FIRST CHARACTER OF LINE BEING
C             PRINTED FROM INPUT RECORD
C     LAST    INTEGER; POINTER TO LAST CHARACTER OF LINE BEING
C             PRINTED FROM INPUT RECORD
C     LINEL   INTEGER; LINE LENGTH--VARIES BECAUSE OF INDENTS AND
C             TURNOVERS
C
C
C     A SUBROUTINE IS USED TO HANDLE THE PRINTING OF A LINE.
C THIS WAS DONE BECAUSE THERE ARE THREE POINTS IN THE PROGRAM
C AT WHICH OUTPUT IS NEEDED, AND AT EACH OF THESE IT IS NECESSARY
C TO MAKE THE INDENTATION AND LINE COUNT DECISIONS.  A SUBROUTINE
C PERMITS ALL THIS TO BE DONE WITHOUT CONFUSING TRANSFERS.  THERE
C ARE NO PARAMETERS IN THE SUBROUTINE CALL; A COMMON STATEMENT HAS
C BEEN USED TO MAKE ALL THE NEEDED VARIABLES GLOBAL.
C     AN ENTRY STATEMENT IS USED TO GET INTO THE SUBROUTINE AT A
C SPECIAL POINT FOR SPACING LINES BETWEEN LETTER-GROUPS; THIS IS
C NOT A FEATURE OF ANSI FORTRAN.
C
C
```

FIGURE E1.1.   A program and a related subprogram for printing a properly spaced index from a file containing the index entries. The index of this book was produced by the program.

```
       LOGICAL INDENT, TRNOVR
       INTEGER*2 TEXT(80), INDMRK, EOL, BLANK
       DATA INDMRK/'>'/, EOL/'$'/, BLANK/' '/
       COMMON LCOUNT, MAXCNT, INITL, LAST, INDENT, TRNOVR, TEXT
C
C WRITE PROMPT FOR MAXIMUM CHARACTERS PER LINE AND LINES PER PAGE
       WRITE (6, 100)
 100   FORMAT (1X, 'ENTER MAX CHARS AND MAX LINES, PER SAMPLE: 25,55,')
       READ (5, 200) MAXLIN, MAXCNT
 200   FORMAT (2I3)
C
C INITIALIZE LINE COUNTER
       LCOUNT = 0
C
C READ A LINE OF TEXT
  10   READ (4, 300) TEXT
 300   FORMAT (80A1)
C
C CHECK FOR INITIAL END-OF-LINE (EOL) MARK, SIGNIFYING
C    THAT A BLANK LINE IS DESIRED
       IF ( TEXT(1) .EQ. EOL ) CALL BLKOUT
       IF ( TEXT(1) .EQ. EOL ) GO TO 10
C
C CHECK WHETHER LINE IS TO BE INDENTED
       LINEL = MAXLIN
       INDENT = .FALSE.
       INITL = 1
       IF ( TEXT(1) .EQ. INDMRK ) INDENT = .TRUE.
       IF ( INDENT ) INITL = 2
       IF ( INDENT ) LINEL = MAXLIN - 2
C
C SET TURNOVER SWITCH OFF
       TRNOVR = .FALSE.
C
C CHECK WHETHER LINE IS SHORT ENOUGH TO PRINT ON ONE LINE
C    PRINT IT AND GO BACK FOR ANOTHER LINE IF SO
  20   DO 30 I = 1, LINEL
          LAST = INITL + I
          IF ( TEXT(LAST) .EQ. EOL ) CALL OUT
          IF ( TEXT(LAST) .EQ. EOL ) GO TO 10
  30   CONTINUE
C
C IF HERE, LINE OF TEXT IS TOO LONG - MUST BREAK
  40   IF ( TEXT(LAST) .EQ. BLANK ) GO TO 50
C
C BACK UP ONE CHARACTER POSITION
       LAST = LAST - 1
       GO TO 40
C
C HAVE FOUND A PLACE TO BREAK - PRINT LINE
  50   CALL OUT
C
C SET UP TO TURN OVER SUCCEEDING LINES UNTIL FINDING EOL
       TRNOVR = .TRUE.
C
C ALLOW FOR TURNOVER IN CHECKING MAXIMUM LINE LENGTH
       LINEL = MAXLIN - 4
C
C MOVE POINTER TO NEXT CHARACTER AFTER LINE JUST PRINTED
       INITL = LAST + 1
C
C GO BACK TO CONTINUE PRINTING THE LINE THAT HAD TO BE BROKEN
       GO TO 20
       END
```

FIGURE E1.1   (Cont.)

```
C SUBROUTINE TO DO THE OUTPUT AND CHECK THE LINE COUNTER
C USES AN ENTRY STATEMENT TO GET IN FOR PRINTING BLANK LINE
C
C
      SUBROUTINE OUT
      COMMON LCOUNT, MAXCNT, INITL, LAST, INDENT, TRNOVR, TEXT
      INTEGER*2 TEXT(80)
      LOGICAL INDENT, TRNOVR
C
C PRINT A LINE, WITH OR WITHOUT INDENTATION
      M = LAST - 1
      IF (         .NOT. INDENT
     1      .AND. .NOT. TRNOVR ) WRITE (6, 400) (TEXT(J), J = INITL, M)
      IF (               INDENT
     1      .AND. .NOT. TRNOVR ) WRITE (6, 500) (TEXT(J), J = INITL, M)
      IF (               TRNOVR ) WRITE (6, 600) (TEXT(J), J = INITL, M)
C
C SKIP AROUND ENTRY POINT FOR BLANK OUTPUT
      GO TO 60
      ENTRY BLKOUT
      WRITE (6, 400)
C
C INCREMENT AND CHECK LINE COUNTER
  60  LCOUNT = LCOUNT + 1
      IF ( LCOUNT .LT. MAXCNT ) RETURN
C
C READ A NULL LINE, TO STOP PRINTING WHILE PAPER IS CHANGED
      READ (5, 400)
C
C RESET LINE COUNTER
      LCOUNT = 0
C
      RETURN
C
 400  FORMAT (1X, 50A1)
 500  FORMAT (3X, 50A1)
 600  FORMAT (5X, 50A1)
      END
```

FIGURE E1.1   (Cont.)

EXCURSION II PROGRAMMING FOR DATA ENTRY AND VALIDATION

By Daniel D. McCracken

One of the toughest problems facing the management of a data processing operation is the correct, timely, and economical entry of data into the computing system. The subject is far too broad for complete treatment in a book on Fortran programming, and in this excursion we shall deal only with one part—but a part that is under the control of the Fortran programmer when a program is being written in the first place.

The general approach is based on the following outlook. Sound data center management will undertake to prepare data correctly, whether this involves the punching of cards, key-to-disk methods, or whatever. It is impossible to attain 100% accuracy, however, and even if it were possible it would probably not be economically wise to do so. Furthermore, even if the data is prepared correctly, there are various other ways to get into trouble, such as reading the wrong data, putting cards in the reader upside down, and a lot of other funny things that do not happen very often but that cause misery when they do.

It is the responsibility of the programmer, therefore, to *validate* the data that his program is to process. (Sometimes programs are written that have no other function than to validate data and pass it along to processing programs if acceptable.) The attitude of the programmer writing a validation routine should be that Murphy's law holds universally: If anything can go wrong, it will. The programmer accordingly takes nothing for granted, checks everything he can think of to check and, generally speaking, looks for trouble.

The balance of this Excursion describes some approaches to this task that may be found useful. A certain part of the job depends on the application, and what follows cannot be followed blindly as a checklist, but it should serve as a good starting point.

Reading data into nonexistent array locations, caused by erroneous subscript values read from cards, is permitted by many compilers,* and causes no end of grief. The smart programmer accordingly takes it for granted that all subscript values found in data will be wrong, and makes absolutely no use of them until they have been explicitly checked and found to fall within the allowable range. A statement of the type

```
READ (5, 100) I, J, A(I, J)
```

will mess things up very thoroughly (in most systems) if I or J is negative, zero, or larger than the size specified in the DIMENSION statement for A.

All data values should be tested for validity in terms of the application. If a negative speed makes no sense in a particular job, test the speed data to make sure it is positive. If you are reading a United States Social Security number, make sure it is exactly nine characters long and all numeric. If one variable is always supposed to be larger than another, check them. If the data records are supposed to be in sequence on a certain quantity, make sure they are. If the cards are supposed to be serially numbered,

---

*Not including WATFOR and WATFIV, we might note. This is just one of the many ways WATFOR and WATFIV assist the programmer by providing run-time checking.

221

make sure every number from 1 to N really does occur.

This part of the job naturally requires knowledge of the application, and we can only give general indications, as above, of what should be done. There probably is a limit beyond which this kind of checking constitutes diminishing returns, but we would venture that in ordinary practice programmers almost never do too much data validation.

When a data record is found to be erroneous, for whatever reason, write out the entire record along with a diagnostic message. Nothing is so maddening as to get back a job with the cryptic note DATA ERRORS—JOB NOT RUN, with no indication of where or what the error was.

Sometimes this will require a bit of effort. One kind of data error is the presence of nonnumeric information where it is not expected—two decimal points in one field, for example, or letters where there should be only digits. In many systems, such a record will not be read into the program's data locations at all, since it cannot be interpreted according to the specifications contained in the program. On the IBM Fortran G and H compilers, and some others, it is possible to specify what should be done when such errors occur, rather than simply accepting the system default correction or being thrown off the machine. Ideally, what should be done in such a situation is to reread the record, using a long alphabetic field descriptor, so that it can at least be printed out for identification to the person who will later have to correct the data. The problem is, how do you reread a record that has already been read once? If a BACKSPACE is permissible for the data set in question, that offers one possibility. Another is a subprogram available in some systems called REREAD, which simply accepts again the record most recently read. The second time around we would be using a different FORMAT, presumably, but it is still the same record. Some other systems offer a separate pair of FORTRAN extensions, called CODE and DECODE, that can sometimes be used for the same purpose.

Most arrays are intentionally dimensioned larger than the typical case will require, so as to permit variation in the size of the data actually handled. It follows that most arrays are seldom filled with data. Then everywhere in the program that there is a reference to the size of the array, a variable giving today's size (or variables, for multidimensioned arrays) should be referenced. Furthermore, each and every subscript read with the data should be checked against the valid maximum for that run.

It is assumed, we should note, that all data being entered into arrays should be self-identifying, that is, should contain some explicit identification of which array element it represents. A procedure such as blindly reading the cards in sequence and placing them in an array in the order in which they appear in the deck cannot be discouraged too strongly as a general practice. (Just one missing or misplaced card, and everything goes wildly wrong.)

With this much background we can now suggest a scheme for reading data into arrays, which is one of the most common operations; with a few obvious modifications it will also apply to reading data other than into arrays.

1. Dimension the array larger than needed (but not grossly); make the actual dimensions variable. That is, set a variable to the actual size, either through an assignment statement at the beginning of the program or with a DATA statement. Then when the DIMENSION statement is changed, you need change only that variable because everywhere in the program you have referred to the maximum size of that array through that variable.

This also permits the convenience of setting the array sizes to small values for checkout, then changing them to realistic sizes for actual production runs.

2. Read a size card that gives the actual size of today's use of the array. Check it for validity against the variables set above and against the smallest meaningful size for the array.

3. Set an error count to zero.

4. Establish a convention for the end-of-data signal (such as a subscript of 99).

5. Zero out the array, to today's size (thus elements of value zero need not be read).

6. Read a data card into temporary storage. If it is the end sentinal, go to 7 below. If it is not the sentinal, check for the validity of the subscript(s). If possible, check for validity of the data value also, as sketched above. If an error is discovered, print the entire card contents along with a descriptive error message telling why it was rejected. Add one to the error count. If the data is OK, move it into the array. Continue reading. Predetermine a maximum error count and stop the program if it is reached. Make this maximum quite large, so if it is met it is probably because somebody loaded the card deck upside down or these are somebody else's data cards or something else is grossly wrong.

7. When the sentinal is reached, check the error count; if it is zero, begin the program's calculations on the data. If it is not zero, terminate this case, but go back around for the data of the next case. There is no point aborting a complete run just because one case has bad data.

A final word may be added about testing a validation program. Naturally, you will devise invalid data to establish that the program does properly reject it, but it is worth pondering whether this is enough. The real "enemy," after all, is the general perversity of nature; how can you anticipate all the ridiculous things that *might* happen in the next five years while this program is being used?

The difficulty is not so much the danger of rejecting valid data and thus requiring an unnecessary "correction"; that is annoying but seldom seriously damaging. The real problem is wrong data that slips through your tests. There is theoretically apparently no absolute answer to this question: there is no way to prove that a program will never accept bad data.

But you can at least make a serious effort to generate bad data and yet avoid the problem of being limited by what your imagination can do for you. The trick is to generate *random* data and see what your program does with it. Sit at a card punch for 20 minutes punching cards with miscellaneous punches, and then try running the program with that deck. Or run your program with a random collection of valid data from *other* programs. The shock of seeing your program accept as valid a card containing utter nonsense—which will almost certainly happen if you try long enough—will make you a believer in data validation.

EXCURSION III HOW TO WRITE A READABLE FORTRAN PROGRAM

By Daniel D. McCracken and Gerald M. Weinberg*

All programs have to be checked out to try to prove that they perform as intended, and virtually all programs have to be modified over a period of time as they are used. For both of these reasons it is imperative that programs be adequately *documented* so that someone studying them (including the original programmer six months after) can determine what they were intended to do.

A complete package of documentation ideally contains at least the following.

1. A precise statement of what the program is supposed to do. Depending on the application, this might consist of a verbal description, or a set of equations together with a statement of the numerical methods used, or conceivably a graphical presentation.

2. A complete set of flowcharts. Ordinarily, in a program of any size, there will need to be flowcharts at two or more levels of detail. The broadest level shows the general sequence of major operations, whereas the most detailed comes as close to the actual logic of the program as is necessary to provide full understanding.

3. The program itself, liberally sprinkled with comment cards and written so as to be understandable. This is the primary subject of this Excursion, and will be treated in detail below. *This must be the latest version.*

4. A complete set of sample input and output, including test cases that can be run to determine whether any modified version of the program still operates correctly on the parts that were not changed.

5. A set of operating instructions for the computer operator, if appropriate, describing tape mounting, special forms, and so on.

6. A set of instructions for the preparation of input, if appropriate.

7. A sketch of areas for possible program improvement.

8. A narrative history of past program changes.

9. The names and present places of employment of programmers who have worked on the program. A current list of telephone numbers is also helpful.

Item 9 is added in despair: if a program has been documented properly, it should not be necessary to call the original programmer to try to figure out how the program works. (He won't

*State University of New York at Binghamton.

It is a pleasure to acknowledge the contributions of the following people who participated in the development of the ideas presented here, by their comments and suggestions in correspondence about an earlier draft of the Excursion.

   Miss Christine Braun, The University of Toronto.
   William S. Dorn, The University of Denver.
   Robert R. Fenichel, The Massachusetts General Hospital.
   Mrs. Joyce Fodor, The University of Wisconsin.
   Charles J. Gibbons, The University of Nebraska, Omaha.
   C. C. Gotlieb, The University of Toronto.
   David Gries, Cornell University.
   Mrs. Susan E. Jaedecke, The University of Denver.
   Thomas A. Keenan, The National Science Foundation.
   Jerry L. Ray, The University of Nebraska, Omaha.
   John E. Skelton, The University of Denver.

remember anyway.) But programs are only rarely documented correctly, in part because it is generally regarded as a tedious and distasteful chore to be done at the end of the job. (Which is about like saying, "We'll build the building first and then put the architecture on.")

It is doubtful whether programmers as a class will ever come to regard documentation with joy. We offer the thoughts below on the principle that if an important part of the total documentation effort can be accomplished in the writing of the program in the first place, it becomes somewhat more likely that the job will be at least partially accomplished.

In this spirit, therefore, we approach the question of what the programmer can do in writing a program to make it as clear as possible what it is supposed to do. This will be to the benefit, we repeat, both of the original programmer in checkout and to anyone who subsequently has to modify or correct the program.

Much of what follows has been presented piecemeal elsewhere in the book, and most of it has been followed in writing the illustrative programs. Some of the items might be considered to be optional, depending on the length and complexity of the program and perhaps as well on the temperament of the programmer.

1. Comment cards must be used freely and wisely. Each program and subprogram should have an initial section of comments that completely describes the program, what it does, what it needs for input, what it produces for output, and generally how the processing is accomplished. If all other documentation should be omitted, there will be at least this much. A shrewd programming manager will rigidly enforce the rule that these initial comments *must be written before the first compilation of the program.*

Comments should be used freely within the program, especially at what might be called "logical paragraphs," that is, logical groupings of the actions of the program. It adds considerably to the readability if it is possible to specify that such paragraphs begin at the top of a new page. This requires, however, some facility for instructing the compiler as to the spacing of the program listing, such as the $EJECT command in WATFOR and WATFIV. (This is a command to control the spacing of the *program*

listing, not the output of program when it is later executed.)

In this book we have usually preceded each comment card in the body of a program by a "blank comment card," that is, one containing only a C in column 1. Some programmers prefer to precede *and follow* each comment with a blank; the decision not to do so in this book was governed mostly by considerations of space and the desire to keep as many programs as possible to one page or to two facing pages, for ease of study.

If the page ejection facility described in the previous paragraph is not available (as it currently is not in most Fortran systems), a passable substitute is to insert three or four blank comment cards. The extra space serves to set off the program sections to the eye, even if only semiconsciously.

Comments have to be written with a certain sense of style and with a feeling for what is going to help the reader understand the program. Writing a comment that says "ADD 1 TO N" before the statement N = N + 1 is no particular help. A program can consist of 70% comment cards and be poorly documented. The goal is to anticipate the questions that a later reader will have and answer them in advance, just as in good writing in any medium.

2. The GO TO statement should be used sparingly. Programs containing excessive GO TOs are inherently difficult to document and understand, since they are heavily interlocked and decidedly nonlocal. For documentation to work, it should be possible to understand the implications of a given program segment in a mostly *local context,* that is, without taking into account remote parts of the program. Moreover, interlocking nonlinear structures are simply more difficult for the human mind to follow.

E. A. Youngs has verified the general agreement about the undesirability of GO TOs in a series of experiments.* His results show that statements involving branching operations are *five times* more error-prone than the average statement not involving branching. If a statement is that much more difficult for the original programmer, imagine how impossible it will be for someone else! Other workers have appro-

*E. A. Youngs, *Error-Proneness in Programming* (University of North Carolina doctoral thesis). Ann Arbor, University Microfilms, 1970.

ached the problem from other directions, both empirical and theoretical.* All results point in the same direction, and the programmer who ignores the weight of this evidence will be a bother not only to others but to himself.

Situations that would seem to require heavy use of GO TOs, especially assigned or computed GO TOs, may sometimes actually be better programmed as subroutines. One of the best techniques for promoting clarity in any event is the intelligent use of subroutines to break a program up into pieces that can be understood and checked out *separately*, without the requirement of keeping simultaneously in mind the actions of large blocks of the program.

In other cases, the excessive use of GO TOs can be avoided by free use of the logical IF statement. If a few statements are to be executed only if some condition is met, it is a simple matter to set a logical variable to .TRUE. if the condition is true, then use a series of logical IFs containing just that logical variable as the logical expression. The loss of computer time involved in repeating the test of the logical variable is very small in most cases, and will be more than compensated for by increased clarity. (See the statements just before statement 30 in Figure 5.12 for an example of how the technique described in this paragraph looks in a program.)

These strictures against the GO TO apply equally to the unconditional, assigned, and computed GO TOs, and to the arithmetic IF statement.

Many other programming languages, such as ALGOL and PL/I and their derivatives, provide features that make GO TOs unnecessary. For example, the construction

    IF (condition) THEN S1 ELSE S2

where S1 and S2 are statements, obviates the need for GO TOs in many common situations. If the language further permits the grouping of

*Edsger W. Dijkstra, "Structured Programming," in John N. Buxton and Brian Randell, *Software Engineering Techniques*. Brussels, NATO Science Committee, 1970.
Donald E. Knuth and Robert W. Floyd, "Notes on Avoiding 'go to' Statements," Information Processing Letter, Vol. 1, No. 1, (Feb., 1971), pp. 23–31.
Ralph L. London, "Bibliography on Proving the Correctness of Computer Programs," *Machine Intelligence* 5, 1970, pp. 569–580.
Gerald M. Weinberg, *The Psychology of Computer Programming*. New York, Van Nostrand Reinhold, 1971.

statements between *statement brackets* such as BEGIN and END, so that S1 and S2 can be *groups* of statements rather than single statements, more GO TOs disappear and program clarity takes another leap forward. If, furthermore, the DO statement—or its equivalent under some other name—permits its controlled variable and indexing parameters to be of type REAL instead of only INTEGER, it is possible to write statements like

    DO 12 X = 1.2, G+9.1, B/2.0

calling for the range to be executed for X starting at 1.2, incremented by B/2.0, until reaching the value G + 9.1. Finally, the DO statement—or its equivalent, as always—may permit a construction of the form

    DO 12 WHILE (BIGRES > EPSLON)

When language features such as these are available, GO TO statements have virtually no legitimate use, and the readability of properly constructed programs is greatly enhanced.

3. Every DO statement should refer to a CONTINUE as the end of its range, and every DO should refer to a different CONTINUE. The statements contained in the range of the DO should be indented by some consistent amount—three spaces in this book. In the programs in this book the CONTINUE itself has not been indented. One of the authors of this Excursion (Weinberg) would prefer to see the CONTINUE also indented, to lessen the danger of forgetting that the CONTINUE is itself included in the range of the DO. Such also is the practice adopted by several other authors.

There may be occasions when following this suggestion would be less than helpful; the exercise of good judgment is in order. An example might be a DO that is used to control the number of iterations of some iterative process, where the range of the DO covers almost the entire program. With the possible exception of such special cases, however, an attempt to follow the rule should be made. If you find yourself saying frequently that it is no help, maybe you need to simplify your program structures anyway, such as by using more subprograms.

4. When an IF statement contains compound conditions, parenthesize the separate simple conditions to make the range and strength of the logical operators (.AND., .OR., and .NOT.)

crystal clear. If there are more than two simple conditions, use continuation cards to put each condition on a separate line and align the conditions vertically. In this book we have generally put the separate conditions on separate lines, but have not always parenthesized.

5. The free use of parentheses in general is to be strongly encouraged. There is no penalty, in modern compilers, for the use of "unnecessary" parentheses inserted for the sake of clarity. If you are not absolutely sure whether A/B*C means (A/B)*C or A/(B*C), regardless of whether your uncertainty refers to the ANSI Standard or to your compiler, write parentheses so that there can be no possible doubt as to what your program will do.

The writing of programs with an absolute minimum of parentheses is *not* a mark of a good programmer. It is the mark of a programmer who is wasting time on something utterly nonessential that will almost certainly periodically get him in trouble.

6. Assign statement numbers in some systematic fashion that will facilitate understanding. We say this rather vaguely because there are a great many things that one can think of to do, and trying to do them all would probably be more trouble than it is worth; good judgment is called for. Here are some possibilities, not all of which have been followed consistently in this book.

Assign statement number in ascending sequence, initially by 10's so that if new numbered statements have to be inserted it can be done without requiring renumbering. (This recommendation is made rather strongly; it generally should be followed.)

Assign statement numbers with the first and second digits indicating broad program segments. For instance, all statements in the 1000's would be in segment 1, all 2000's in segment 2, and so on.

Use the last digit to indicate the number of other statements that refer to this one. A statement ending in 1, then, would indicate that there is only one other statement anywhere in the program that refers to this one, whether some kind of GO TO, a DO, or a FORMAT. A statement ending in zero would then be one not referenced anywhere in the program—but why are you putting statement numbers on statements that are never referred to? An argument can be made that, other things being equal, the best program is the one that has the fewest statement numbers in it. (In other languages where statements are *labelled* rather than just numbered, alphabetic labels are often used for identification and clarity; these don't count in the above generalization.)

Put all FORMAT statements together in a section at the end of the program, with some unique identifying system. For example, FORMAT statement numbers might always have four digits and begin with a 9. On the other hand, many people prefer that if a FORMAT is referred to by only one I/O statement, the FORMAT should immediately follow the statement that uses it. In this case, the sequential ascending sequence rule should probably take precedence.

Applying all of these rules, or even some of them, gets to be a chore, and seems like the sort of thing a computer ought to be doing. In fact, commercial programs are available to reassign all statement numbers in a Fortran program in ascending sequence, changing all references to them as well. For that matter, it is no great problem for the compiler, as a minor extension of its work of the analysis of loops, to present a properly indented listing showing the scope of each DO. An optional feature along these lines is available in the IBM Fortran (H) compiler. Such a feature should not be used, however, as a crutch to evade good programming practice in writing the original program.

7. Assign variable names so as to be as meaningful as possible. The restriction to six characters is definitely a handicap, but there is still a great deal the programmer can do. XMEAN says more to the reader of a program in statistics than XM; EOQ should obviously be used for economic order quantity; and EPSLON is a better name for the Greek letter *epsilon* that occurs in many mathematics formulas than is E6.

This can definitely mean more work for the programmer, although not nearly as much as in other languages that do not have the limitation of six character variable names.

Never use the same variable in different contexts in the same program, just to save space. Doing so is confusing to the reader, makes checkout harder, and leads to massive confusion if you later change one of the meanings in such a way as to (unintentionally) alter something else. In modern computers storage space is virtually never that "tight," except sometimes for large arrays.

Applying these rules is unquestionably a matter of some effort. Almost every programmer will object that they are good in theory, and everybody else ought to do them, but in the particular job he is working on at the moment they would not be needed. The point we are trying to urge is that if writing programs along these general lines is taught as the only way to do the job correctly, then when a program is completed there already exists a minimum level of documentation.

One of the major advantages of time-sharing systems is that they almost always include a text editor, which is a great aid in carrying out the operations involved in following some of the suggestions above. In truth, if the programs in this book had had to be punched on a card punch instead of being developed with a good time-sharing system, it is highly doubtful whether the author of the book would have followed his own advice.

For instance, the program in Figure 4.3 was initially written with SX2 as the name for the variable that accumulates the sum of the squares of the X values. On reflection it became clear that this was not the most meaningful variable name that could be devised by someone who was planning to urge others to write meaningful names. Accordingly, the time-sharing text editor was instructed, using a one-line command, to change all occurrences of the name SX2 to SUMXSQ. This took roughly ten seconds of elapsed time and cost possibly four cents. Doing the same thing with a deck of cards at a card punch would, obviously, have been a tiresome, frustrating, and error-prone operation. (The new name is longer than the old, so everything else in a statement following the old variable name would have to be changed too. This is done automatically by the text editor.) Or a decision to revise the indentation scheme of a portion of a program can be carried out with a series of relatively simple commands to the editor. Many other operations leading to a consistent application of suggestions along the lines of those above are very much simpler with a good text editor than when done at a card punch.

Most readers of this book, at least at the time of publication (1972), probably are not using a time-sharing system to prepare their programs. Within the expected publishing life of the book, however, which would normally be about five years, it is quite possible that program preparation in the time-sharing mode will become the most common method. In the interest of readable programs without unreasonable programming effort, we may hope so.

EXCURSION IV THE EFFICIENT USE OF FORTRAN

By D. Chris Larson*

E4.1 INTRODUCTION

This text has stressed writing programs so that they are easy to understand. This is defensible for pedagogical reasons and has benefits in terms of getting a program running quickly and proving with some degree of assurance that it does what it was intended to do.

However, this approach may often lead to a program that, although carrying out the desired processing correctly, requires excessive time or storage space to do it. In such situations it is helpful to know what the programmer can do in writing or revising his source programs to lead to more efficient object programs.

Good judgment is clearly called for, however. If a program is to be run once or twice and does not involve too much computation anyway, great effort should be placed on getting it running quickly and correctly; everything in this Excursion probably should be ignored. Students early in their first computing course, who ought to be concentrating on understanding what an algorithm is and how to express one in the chosen language, should postpone any worry about most of the topics mentioned here. On the other hand, there are programs that, once checked out, run for several hours per week on

*Written while Mr. Larson was employed by Computer Synectics, Inc., Santa Clara, California. Adapted from an article in Datamation®, August 1, 1971, pp. 24-31. Reprinted with permission of Datamation®. Copyright, Technical Publishing Co., Barrington, Illinois 60010, 1971.

very large computers. In this kind of case, some one or two of the ideas suggested below might mean saving an hour a week on a machine that costs hundreds of dollars per hour.

In other words, the sophisticated programmer should definitely know about the kinds of things discussed here, but he will know when to make use of them and when it is not worth bothering.

E4.2 WHAT KINDS OF THINGS CAN THE SOURCE PROGRAMMER DO?

The Fortran user is concerned, basically, with four distinct factors, all of which influence turn-around time and job cost: compiler size, compiler speed, compiler-generated object program size, and compiler-generated object program speed.

The size and speed of the compiler are of interest to the Fortran user during the development and debugging stages of a program. If the compiler is relatively large, a Fortran job might often find itself at the bottom of the operating system scheduling queue competing for core space. On the other hand, the space requirement of any language translator is often (not always) an indicator of its speed—faster compilation speed in return for larger core requirements. For many compilers, the space requirement is also a function of the size and complexity of the source program being compiled.

231

Although both the size and the speed of the Fortran compiler are important factors during the development cycle of a program, the user typically has little or no control over them. Many installations have only one Fortran compiler available and, in developing a production program, the user would be ill-advised to code in such a way as to minimize compilation time or compile-time core space requirements. However, in installations where more than one compiler is available, it would be appropriate to compare their attributes and select a "development compiler" that would minimize program development costs. Many compilers provide the user with certain compile-time options, each of which has a direct effect on compiler performance and job cost. Again, it would be appropriate to study these options and set defaults (or prepare recommended option lists) that minimize compilation time for programs in the development stage. Perhaps the most glaring abuse of compilation options is the selection by many installations to print the compiler-generated object code by default.

When a Fortran program reaches the production stage, the user is concerned only with the performance of the compiler-produced object code. The set of compiler or compilation options selected to generate the production object code should be the one that most highly optimizes the object code for the target machine. Compilation time and compiler core space requirements for this process are no longer an issue because this is presumably the final compilation. If an optimizing compiler exists for a certain class of machines but its size or purchase price is prohibitive for a certain installation, it might prove economical to pay for a compilation of production programs at an installation where such a compiler is available, assuming the resulting object programs are not too large for the original installation.

Most language translators have no compile-time options that relate to object code optimization. This is not to say that such a compiler does not optimize object code, but rather that the compiler unconditionally applies a fixed set of optimizations to all programs. It is conceivable that such a compiler might produce more highly optimized object code than do compilers providing explicit optimization options.

The number and type of optimizations performed by compilers are many and varied. Basi-

cally, optimizations fall into two main categories:

1. Machine-independent optimizations.
2. Machine-dependent optimizations.

In each category there are optimizations for speed and for size of the object program. The optimizations for speed versus size are almost always in conflict.

In the absence of a definitive document describing precisely all optimizations performed by a given compiler, it is extremely difficult to determine the conditions under which optimizations are done.

Another significant point is that even the most sophisticated optimizing compiler has no way of knowing which sections of the program being compiled will be executed most frequently. If the compiler assigns equal weight to all sections, optimizations for infrequent paths often tend to interfere with optimizations for the more frequent paths.

It is important that the Fortran user become familiar with certain coding techniques that tend to result in fairly good object code regardless of the compiler. The remainder of this paper addresses itself to Fortran optimizations that the user can perform manually at the source code level to improve object code performance. Certain optimizations for speed will increase the size of the object program, and certain optimizations for size will increase execution time. It must be the user's decision as to whether any optimization will have any real payoff, based on the execution frequency of the code in question.

The use of these techniques clearly does not eliminate the need for an optimizing compiler because:

1. Many of the machine-dependent optimizations (such as central processor unit register assignment) cannot be anticipated and/or guided by the user's source program.
2. Even the most highly optimized source program can be enhanced by an optimizing compiler.

In fact, a few of the source code optimizations listed below may actually be detrimental in that they may obscure the intent to certain compilers, but this will be mentioned in each case.

The purpose of the following section is to describe how Fortran compilers deal with source code constructions written by the user. The intent is not to describe in detail how each compiler works or to provide lists of specific coding rules, because compilers are different, and each compiler would then require separate treatment. It is hoped that the following section will provide the user with a feel for those things in Fortran source coding that usually have a direct effect on the object code produced by most compilers.

Unless otherwise specified in the following sections, all examples will use standard Fortran naming conventions (that is, an INTEGER identifier begins with the letters I, J, K, L, M, or N, and everything else is REAL).

E4.3 INPUT/OUTPUT STATEMENTS

The most neglected area of optimization by Fortran compilers is in the handling of input/output statements. Typically, hundreds of non-I/O statements can be executed in the time it takes to execute one I/O statement, and this disparity can seldom be attributed to hardware I/O characteristics. Fortran programs that, from the source listing, appear to be I/O bound are, instead, usually CPU bound. That is, a program that, from the source program standpoint, looks as though the CPU would be waiting for I/O operations most of the time turns out to be the other way around. Compiler optimizations for I/O statements are difficult because of supervisory system constraints and the interpretive nature of I/O statement execution. Following are a few techniques for optimizing I/O statements at the source level.

1. All files that are created by Fortran programs and used only as temporary files or as input to other Fortran programs should be referenced via *unformatted* READ/WRITE statements. Unformatted I/O statements are executed more quickly than formatted ones because the unformatted mode requires no conversion or formatting of data from internal to external graphic representations or vice versa.
2. All I/O and file control statements are time

consuming because they result in calls to generalized Fortran subroutine library programs, which, in turn, make requests of the supervisory system. The user should attempt to minimize the number and frequency of such statements. (For example, two or more successive READ or WRITE statements referencing the same file might be combined into one statement.)
3. The time required to execute a READ/WRITE statement (formatted or unformatted) is a function of the number of data items in the I/O list. Most compilers produce one Fortran library call per data item in the I/O list. A scalar variable (that is, a nonsubscripted variable) is treated as one item, and an array name (with no subscripts) is treated as one item. A subscripted variable is equivalent to a scalar. However, an implied DO loop in an I/O list represents $n \times k$ items in most compilers, where n is the number of iterations of the loop and k is the number of variables under control of the DO. The user should therefore attempt to minimize the number of items in I/O lists. For example:

```
DIMENSION X(20), Y(10), Z(5, 30)
    .
    .
    .
35 WRITE(6,99) M,(X(I),I=1,20),Z(M,J)
```

The above WRITE statement, to most compilers, represents 22 data items. If it were changed to:

```
35 WRITE (6,99) M, X, Z(M,J)
```

it would represent only 3 data items. Changing the implied DO loop for X(I) to an array name without a subscript reduces the number of data items by 19.

Warnings

a. Because of hardware characteristics, a few compilers (but not many) store arrays backwards (with ascending subscripts corresponding to lower storage addresses). The above change would output X in the order $X(20), X(19) \ldots , X(1)$. However, if the file is a temporary file, the change could be made consistently for all references to the file with no adverse effects (that is, if an array is written out backwards, no harm is done if it is read in backwards later).
b. The elimination of implied DO loops for multidimensional arrays in I/O lists in favor

of array names is equivalent only if the implied DO loop is consistent with the implicit indexing used for array names (that is, which subscript varies most rapidly).

A few compilers do not permit an increment value in an implied DO loop in an I/O list, thereby fixing the increment at 1. Given this restriction, it is always possible for the compiler to effect the change in the above example, even if the range of indices in the implied DO spans only a portion of the array. For such compilers, the two WRITE statements above would produce identical object code. Some compilers, even with no such restriction, may effect the change automatically if the increment is 1.

A change like the above at the source code level produces equivalent code only when the increment value is 1 and the final value of the implied loop is equal to the dimension size of the variable involved.

Another, and perhaps the most optimum, way to reduce the number of items in an I/O list is to change the following:

```
DIMENSION X(20), A(10,4)
  .
  .
  .
WRITE (12) M, I, A, X, Z
```

to this

```
DIMENSION X(20), A(10,4), Q(63)
COMMON /BLOCK/ M, I, A, X, Z
EQUIVALENCE (M, Q(1))
  .
  .
  .
WRITE (12) Q
```

For I/O lists containing a large number of data items, the above change might result in a significant performance gain because a single data item replaces all items in the original list.

4. I/O statements that provide asynchronous input/output, if available in a given compiler, are almost always preferable to the READ/WRITE statements of Standard Fortran (for example, BUFFER IN/BUFFER OUT statements of CDC Fortran). The use of such statements places the burden of buffering and data conversion on the user, but a substantial increase in execution speed usually results.

5. If the facility exists, allocate large buffers for each Fortran file, which may minimize the number of supervisory I/O requests made by the Fortran subroutine library. For OS/360 Fortran, which imposes an upper limit of two buffers per file, programs with a large amount of printed output can be improved significantly by simply overriding the IBM-supplied GO step DD statement for the printer as follows:

```
//GO.FT06F001 DD SYSOUT=A,
//    DCB=(RECFM=FBA,LRECL=133,
//    BLKSIZE=7182)
```

6. As a last resort for production programs with heavy I/O usage, it might be worth the effort to replace all frequently executed I/O statements with CALLs to special user-written assembler language subroutines that perform the desired function.

E4.4 SUBSCRIPTS

Many Fortran compilers permit almost any valid arithmetic expression as a subscript. Most compilers, however, recognize certain "preferred" constructions of subscript expressions that permit optimizations to be made. Some Fortran compilers, in fact, restrict subscript expressions to this preferred set.

The preferred set of subscript expressions corresponds to the set of subscript expressions defined in ANSI Fortran:

1. V (scalar integer variable)

2. C (positive integer constant)

3. $V \pm C$ (scalar integer variable plus or minus a positive integer constant)

4. $C*V$ (positive integer constant times a scalar integer variable)

5. $C_1*V \pm C_2$ (positive integer constant times a scalar integer variable plus or minus a positive integer constant)

It is not sufficient that a subscript expression be *algebraically* equivalent to one of the preferred constructions—it must be *exactly* in the above form to be recognized. For example, $X(3+J)$ will usually result in a more lengthy object code expansion than will $X(J+3)$.

The above set of preferred constructions was not determined arbitrarily. Each one was chosen because it permits a partial evaluation at compile time so that, in the worst case (No. 5), at most one addition is required at execution time to isolate the array element for that dimension.

Consider the following sequence:

```
M = J - 5
X = A(M) + T
```

It is almost always more efficient to replace the above with

```
X = A(J-5) + T
```

because J-5 is computed at object time in the first case, whereas 5 is effectively subtracted from the base address of A at compile time in the second case. (The above change assumes that no path can be reached that contains a use of M prior to a definition of M.)

Subscript computations at object time are especially expensive for multidimensional arrays. It is always best to apply the rule "Never use a vector when scalars will do, and never use an N-dimensional array when an array of N-1 dimensions will do."

If arrays are necessary, it is best to use constant subscripts wherever possible. If a constant subscript is used with a vector, for example, X(7), the resulting object code will resemble a reference to a scalar. In general, a constant subscript in any dimension of an array reference will have the effect of reducing the rank of the array by one *at compile time*.

If multidimensional arrays are essential to an algorithm, the complexity of references may sometimes be reduced. Consider the following example:

```
DIMENSION X(10, 20, 8), Z(30, 30)
        .
        .
        .
        DO 5 I = 1, 10
        DO 5 J = 1, 20
        DO 5 K = 1, 8
    5   X(I, J, K) = 0.0
        .
        .
        .
        DO 75 I = 1, 30
   75   Z(I, I) = 1.0
        .
        .
        .
```

The above could be changed so that an improvement in both core space and execution time would be realized.

The following code is functionally equivalent to the above:

```
DIMENSION X(10, 20, 8), Z(30, 30)
DIMENSION XX(1600), ZZ(900)
EQUIVALENCE (XX(1), X(1, 1, 1))
EQUIVALENCE (ZZ(1), Z(1, 1))
        .
        .
        .
        DO 5 I = 1, 1600
    5   XX(I) = 0.0
        .
        .
        .
        DO 75 I = 1, 900, 31
   75   ZZ(I) = 1.0
        .
        .
        .
```

Changes such as these sometimes make the source coding harder to follow, forcing a choice between performance and ease of understanding—an unhappy decision to have to make. Sometimes it may be advisable to write the program initially in the easy-to-read fashion, then convert to the fast version but keep the original in the program by converting the original statements to comments.

E4.5 DATA TYPES AND CONVERSIONS

One of the most overlooked areas of source code optimization is minimizing the number of internal data conversions during execution. Strict ANSI Fortran compilers, in a way, force the user to think about conversions by not permitting mixed mode expressions. However, because mixed mode expressions are permitted by many compilers, it is easy to write programs that compile error-free and always produce correct output but that require many unnecessary data conversions during execution. In some compilers, such conversions result in calls to Fortran library subroutines; in others, in-line code performs the conversion.

Consider the following example:

```
X = I*Z - (I - 1)/T + I*6
```

Two conversions from INTEGER to REAL are required, and some compilers would produce three. The expression (I-1), because of the Fortran rules for expression evaluation, must be evaluated in integer mode and the result converted to REAL. The appearance of the variable I in two other places would cause either one or two additional conversions, depending on the compiler.

To reduce the number of conversions in the above example to one, use

```
V = I
X = V*(Z + 6.0) - (V - 1.0)/T
```

where I is converted to REAL by the assignment statement $V = I$. Collecting the first and last terms in the original example and factoring also saves execution time by reducing the number of multiplies, since addition is generally much faster than multiplication.

Following is another example illustrating that the most elegant algorithm may not be the most efficient:

```
    DO 4 J = 1, 1000
4 X(J) = J
```

This will result in 1000 conversions of J from INTEGER to REAL at execution time. The following code, although more lengthy in its source form, will execute faster and, for most compilers, take less core space because no conversions are required:

```
    Z = 0.0
    DO 4 J = 1, 1000
    Z = Z + 1.0
4 X(J) = Z
```

Conversions from INTEGER to REAL and vice versa are usually more costly than conversions from REAL to DOUBLE PRECISION. Conversions from DOUBLE PRECISION to REAL are usually free, as are conversions within the INTEGER category (that is, INTEGER*2 to INTEGER*4 and vice versa).

It would be wise for the user of a Fortran compiler to determine how the compiler handles constants with respect to data type. It would be easier for a compiler to ignore the context in which a constant is used and simply to preserve the type specified by the user rather than to perform a compile-time conversion of the constant to the type most optimum for execution. For example,

```
IF ( X .EQ. 17 ) K = 2.0
```

A "quick and dirty" compiler might emit object code that contains conversions of 17 from INTEGER to REAL and of 2.0 from REAL to INTEGER. If such is the case, the user should always attempt to match the constant type with the type of usage, which, for the above example, would become:

```
IF ( X .EQ. 17.0 ) K = 2
```

There is one type of mixed mode expression that is permitted by almost all FORTRAN compilers, which does not require data conversion and is recommended. This special case involves the raising of a real quantity to an integer power. In fact, this mixed mode expression is always preferable to its single mode (real) equivalent for reasons of execution time, accuracy, and compatibility. The expressions (X**27) or (X**N) would be rapidly evaluated by a series of multiplications, whereas (X**27.0) or (X**A) would involve the computation of logarithms and could introduce inaccuracies through round-off or truncation.

E4.6 EXTERNAL SUBPROGRAMS

It is always costly in terms of execution speed to invoke external subprograms. There are several different forms of external subprograms.

1. SUBROUTINE and FUNCTION subprograms supplied by and explicitly invoked by the user.

2. Intrinsic functions and subroutines provided by Fortran that are explicitly invoked by the user (for example, SIN, SQRT, FLOAT, CALL OVERFL).

3. Subroutines provided by Fortran that are invoked by I/O statements (for example, READ, WRITE, END FILE).

4. Subroutines provided by Fortran that are implicitly (and, in many cases, unknowingly) invoked by the user to accomplish such things as internal data conversion, exponentiation, and complex arithmetic. On a few machines, the Fortran compilers must use this mechanism to simulate DOUBLE PRECISION and possibly even REAL arithmetic.

Some compilers attempt to minimize external subprogram calls by expanding certain items in categories 2 and 4 as in-line coding. This often amounts to a considerable increase in execution speed at the expense of using more core space.

A few examples of functions in category 2 that may yield in-line coding, depending on the compiler and compilation options, are: MOD, IFIX, FLOAT, MIN, MAX, ABS, and so on.

Exponentiation (category 4) may produce in-line code only if the exponent is a positive integer constant *and* if the resulting in-line code (a sequence of multiply instructions) is shorter than the generalized out-of-line subroutine, which is usually determined by the compiler's inspection of the exponent value.

It is important to remember that many in-line copies of the same code sequence may appear when the compiler blindly produces in-line coding for many calls (either explicit or implicit) of the same function. Some compilers might determine the total number of calls of a particular function before choosing in-line expansions over a single copy of the out-of-line subroutine, but most compilers probably do not go to the trouble. And there is no compiler to my knowledge which, during the compilation of a single subprogram, emits both in-line and out-of-line code for the same function selectively, based on expected execution frequency. The only time when both in-line and out-of-line code for the same function is produced for a single subprogram is for MIN, MAX, exponentiation, etc., and the decision is based strictly on the number or size of function arguments and not on expected frequency of execution.

It is usually possible for the user to guarantee that only one copy of a function is present in the object code by declaring all such function names in an EXTERNAL statement. This is meaningful only for those functions in category 2 above.

To summarize, if core space is of no concern to the user, it is almost always best to permit in-line expansion of all functions that permit such expansion. The advantage to this approach is that no subroutine linkage is present in the resulting expansions and that such expansions are special-purpose subsets of the generalized out-of-line subroutine. On the other hand, if core space is to be conserved, it is best to declare such functions as EXTERNAL. Most Fortran compilers compile each subprogram independently of all others, so these functions should be declared as EXTERNAL *in each subprogram* to ensure that there is only one copy in the object code after all subprograms have been combined and link-edited for execution.

Fortran statement function definitions do not fall into any of the above categories because such functions are strictly local to the subprogram containing them. Such functions are always explicitly invoked by the user. Some compilers expand references to such functions with internal calls; others substitute in-line code for the definition at every reference, including expansions for nested inner references to other statement function definitions. However, the user never has a choice as to which method is to be used. If the user wants in-line expansions, he can always eliminate all statement function definitions and substitute the definition for every reference manually.

A previous section of this paper dealt with I/O statements, which always result in calls to Fortran library subroutines (category 3). Such subroutines are of necessity generalized and lengthy, so the user should attempt to minimize the number and frequency of I/O statements.

Like all other subprogram calls, a reference to an external user-supplied SUBROUTINE or FUNCTION (category 1) is expensive because of the linkage overhead, which is partly a function of the number of parameters and their usage. There is always a constant amount of linkage overhead, even if the subprogram has no explicit parameters. There is an additional burden placed on the object code of the calling program as a result of a SUBROUTINE CALL because the compiler must emit code which assumes that every variable in every COMMON block specified by the calling program must be available to, and may be changed by, the called subprogram. In some cases, the effect of this assumption on register load/store activity could produce more overhead in the calling program than in the linkage itself.

Many compilers, because of hardware architecture, produce more efficient object code for programs containing a minimum number of COMMON blocks. This is because the placement of COMMON blocks is not a function of the compiler but of the loader, and each COMMON block requires separate addressability which, for a program containing a large number of COMMON blocks, interferes with optimum register assignment. For machines with an elaborate indirect addressing capability, it would be possible for a compiler to emit code that is not hampered by this addressability problem. However, for most machines it is probably best from this standpoint for the user to combine all COMMON blocks into one.

As far as explicit subprogram parameters are concerned, it is generally best to minimize the number of parameters. Until recently, almost all Fortran compilers treated all parameters as *call-by-name,* which means that the called program requires the external address of the parameter at every reference. For a called program containing many references to external parameters, a considerable amount of overhead is introduced. For such programs, it is usually best to move all scalar parameters to local variables at the outset in the called program and then to use the local copy of the parameter at all subsequent references, which minimizes the number of explicit references to scalar parameters.

For example,

```
SUBROUTINE X(A, B, C, D, E, F, G)
DIMENSION C(10, 4), F(400), T(50)
Y = A
Z = B
W = D
S = G
  .
  .
  .
5 B = Z
E = V
RETURN
```

This assumes that A, D, and G are input-only parameters, that E is output-only, and that B is both input and output. The arrays C and F could be either or both. Regarding the scalars A, B, D, E, and G, notice that the minimum number of references is made to each, with the body of the subroutine using their local equivalents Y, Z, W, V, and S, respectively.

It is usually not worthwhile to move a scalar parameter to a local variable if the parameter is referenced only once or twice. It is never worthwhile to move array parameters to local arrays in the called program, especially for large arrays, because the overhead of moving them and the extra storage required probably far offset any performance gain that could be realized by so doing.

Some recent Fortran compilers have introduced a strain of the *call-by-value* concept whereby the user (in the SUBROUTINE or FUNCTION statement) declares which scalar parameters are to be moved to local variables within the subprogram. This capability elimi-

nates the need for the user to perform these moves explicitly in the subprogram.

To summarize, it is generally best to minimize the number of parameters of a subprogram and also to minimize the number of references in the called program to each parameter. If a program is called frequently, it might be well to investigate the effect of replacing the references with in-line source code, which, for multiple references, will increase the size of the program, but speed up the resulting object program. The decision to eliminate a subprogram in favor of in-line source code depends on the size of the subprogram and the number of references to it.

Also, there is no substitute for analyzing a problem before coding it. Consider the following statement, which contains a fairly commonplace construction used in numerical problems.

$$X = X*Y*((-1)**(I+J))$$

Most compilers would produce a call to the exponentiation subroutine and then convert the INTEGER result to REAL. The first improvement that comes to mind is changing (-1) to (-1.0), which produces a REAL result for the exponentiation. However, the exponentiation itself could be simplified and the conversion eliminated by using the following:

```
DIMENSION Z(3)
DATA Z/-1.0, 1.0, -1.0/
  .
  .
  .
K = MOD(I+J, 2)
X = X*Y*Z(K+2)
```

For compilers that emit in-line code for the MOD function, the generated code would contain no subprogram calls. This simplification in the source program is made with the assumption that the compiler has no equivalent "special case" optimization.

E4.7 EXPRESSION EVALUATION

The source programmer should always attempt to minimize the number of execution-time evaluations of an expression. Most compilers are able to do this automatically for the user for common subexpressions within a single statement only.

For example,

```
X(J*I) = ((A*B)/Y + T/(A*B)) + Z(J*I)
```

Most compilers would recognize that (A*B) and (J*I) are both used twice and would produce object code to evaluate each of these expressions only once.

Consider the following example.

```
Z=((A+(1.0/X))*(1.0/X))/(4-(A+(1.0/X)))
```

The expressions (1.0/X) and (A + (1.0/X)) would be evaluated only once. For compilers that recognize these common subexpressions within a single statement, two conditions are sometimes placed on the source code so that such subexpressions are detectable:

1. A subexpression is a candidate for detection as common only if it is parenthesized. Both examples above have parentheses surrounding the common subexpressions. If, in the first example, the first occurrence of the expression (A*B) had not been parenthesized A*B would not have been recognized as being common and would have been evaluated twice. Notice that subscript expressions are always candidates for this optimization because subscripts are always enclosed in parentheses (a comma separating subscripts for multidimensional arrays is an exception, but can be handled internally by the compiler with no problems).

2. Two parenthesized subexpressions are recognized as being common only if they are identical. It is not sufficient that they be algebraically equivalent—they must be identical. For example, (A*B) would not be recognized as being identical to (B*A), although they are equivalent expressions. The definition of "identical" depends on the compiler—some do a character-for-character comparison of the source code (which would mean that 1.0 is different from 1.00), and others perform the comparison after encoding the expression internally (where equivalent constants would be considered identical).

Within a single statement, multiple references with identical arguments to the same function will usually result in only one evaluation of the function, regardless of whether the references are parenthesized.

The recognition of common subexpressions within a single statement is fairly commonplace among Fortran compilers. However, only a few compilers are capable of detecting and eliminating redundant evaluations of expressions on a more global basis (that is, across many statements). But in the absence of information about any specific compiler, it is always possible for the user to write a source program so as to minimize the number of evaluations of an expression, regardless of the compiler being used.

Even though a certain expression may appear only once in the source program, the flow of the program may necessitate its evaluation many times. Consider the following example.

```
      DO 5 I = 1, 100
      Q(I) = 0.0
      DO 5 J = 1, 100
    5 Q(I) = Q(I) + A*B*X(J, I)
```

The subexpression A*B, although constant throughout both DO-loops, might be evaluated 10,000 times, depending on the compiler. Also, the effective address of Q(I) might be computed 10,100 times even though it is constant throughout the inner loop on J. To eliminate the possibility of these redundant evaluations, the above code could be changed to

```
      Z = A*B
      DO 5 I = 1, 100
      S = 0.0
      DO 4 J = 1, 100
    4 S = S + X(J, I)
    5 Q(I) = Z*S
```

Again, an optimizing compiler capable of recognizing common subexpressions on a global basis could have produced, for the first example, object code resembling the latter example, with two exceptions:

1. The multiplication by Z would appear in the inner loop if the compiler is incapable of algebraically factoring out the constant multiplier Z.

2. A new variable S would not be introduced, but the effective address of Q(I) would be computed only once (in the outer loop). In this regard, it might actually be detrimental to the object code to introduce the variable S in the source program.

Another source code optimization (which a sophisticated compiler can also perform) that may only save core space is shown in the following examples.

```
           .
           .
           .
     IF (    ) 6, 6, 3
   6 ......
           .
           .
     Z = A*B + T
           .
           .
           .
     GO TO 9
   3 ......
           .
           .
           .
     X = A*B*Q
           .
           .
           .
   9 ......
```

Because of the IF statement in the above example, the paths at labels 6 and 3 are mutually exclusive. At execution time, the expression A*B would be evaluated only once per execution of the IF statement, but the object code might contain the code for its evaluation in each path. This code could be eliminated by

```
     R = A*B
     IF (    ) 6, 6, 3
   6 ......
           .
           .
           .
     Z = R + T
           .
           .
           .
     GO TO 9
   3 ......
           .
           .
           .
     X = R*Q
           .
           .
           .
   9 ......
```

It is often desirable, for purposes of documentation, to include in the source program expressions containing only constants. For example,

```
M = (3159 - 2103) / 16
IF ( X .GT. 7.0/3.0 ) X = 5.0
Y = SQRT(ABS(SIN(2.174**1.638)))
```

Before using constant expressions in a source program, it is advisable for the user to determine how the target compiler treats such expressions. Some compilers would recognize that an expression contains only constants and would evaluate it at compile time; other compilers would emit object code for evaluating the expression at execution time. In the latter case, a constant expression within a loop could be costly in terms of execution time, especially so in the case of the last statement in the above example.

Some compilers attempt to optimize the evaluation of logical expressions, especially in logical IF statements. Consider the following logical expression:

$$(e_1).OR.(e_2), \ldots, .OR.(e_n)$$

Some compilers will attempt to minimize execution time for the above by terminating the evaluation on encountering the first .TRUE. e_i. If the operator were .AND. instead of .OR., evaluation would terminate on encountering the first .FALSE. e_i. In each case, the remaining e's would not require evaluation and would thereby save execution time. To take advantage of this optimization, the user should arrange the e_i subexpressions in a left-to-right order such that the leftmost would most frequently cause termination of the evaluation of the entire logical expression.

E4.8 MACHINE-DEPENDENT OPTIMIZATIONS

There are a few miscellaneous optimizations related to the evaluation of expressions that are machine dependent.

1. Since an add instruction is generally much faster than a multiply, it is usually best to replace a "multiply by 2" with an add:

$$(2.0*X) \text{ would become } (X + X)$$

a. This change should not be made for "preferred subscripts."
b. This change should not be made for a binary machine if the compiler is capable of replacing the multiply by a shift instruction.
2. Since a multiply instruction is usually faster than a divide, it is best to use multiplies wherever possible:

(X/4.0) would become (X*0.25)

3. For exponentiation using small constant integer exponents, it is usually best to replace the operation with a series of multiplies:

(X**4) would become (X*X*X*X)

A few compilers may be able to perform all the above optimizations automatically for the user. But, in the absence of information about specific compilers, the user should make these optimizations manually.

E4.9 MISCELLANEOUS OPTIMIZATIONS

1. Because of comparative execution speeds typical of most machines, the following general rules usually apply:
a. Never use a REAL variable when an INTEGER will suffice.
b. Never use a DOUBLE PRECISION variable when a REAL variable will suffice.
2. To save core space, use EQUIVALENCE statements to effect overlays of arrays when possible.
3. Whenever there is a choice, use compile-time FORMAT statements as opposed to variable object-time FORMAT statements. Some compilers encode compile-time FORMAT statements so that they may be more quickly interpreted at execution time.
4. For some compilers, it may be advantageous for the user to manually "unroll" loops to gain execution speed.
If

```
      DO 5 I = 1, 1000
    5 X(I) = 0.0
```

were changed to

```
      DO 5 I = 1, 1000, 2
      X(I) = 0.0
    5 X(I+1) = 0.0
```

a gain in execution speed might be realized. The loop-closing code produced by some compilers is fairly lengthy, and the above example reduces the frequency of such code by a factor of 2. The latter approach clearly takes more core space,

however. Also, there is a point of diminishing returns in applying the above approach to larger increment values in the DO statement. Taking this approach to its extreme, the loop would be completely eliminated in favor of in-line code (1000 source statements for the above example).
5. In regard to nested DO loops, consider the following example.

```
      DO 5 I = 1, 100      1 loop initialization
      DO 4 J = 1, 20       100 loop initializations
      DO 3 K = 1, 5        2000 loop initializations
       .
       .
       .
    3 CONTINUE             10,000 loop closings
    4 CONTINUE             2000 loop closings
    5 CONTINUE             100 loop closings
```

By simply reversing the order of nesting, observe that the execution frequency of certain statements is sharply reduced.

```
      DO 3 K = 1, 5        1 loop initialization
      DO 4 J = 1, 20       5 loop initializations
      DO 5 I = 1, 100      100 loop initializations
       .
       .
       .
    5 CONTINUE             10,000 loop closings
    4 CONTINUE             100 loop closings
    3 CONTINUE             5 loop closings
```

Notice that CONTINUEs have been added above for the sole purpose of exposition and that, in both cases, the execution frequencies of the loop closing code are not eliminated by terminating all three loops with one statement. This is an extreme illustration of a general rule to be followed with nested DO loops: nesting should occur from outer to inner with increasing iteration values.

On computers that use the technique called *paging* to achieve the effect (to the user) of a very large primary storage, additional considerations come to the fore. It can become very important, for example, to avoid skipping back and forth between widely separated object program segments, even though doing so in a non-paging machine would incur no cost whatever.

The reader concerned with these matters, which would tend to apply mostly to time-sharing systems, will find an excellent summary in "Programming in a Paging Environment," by R. L. Guertin, *Datamation*, February, 1972, pp. 48ff.

E4.10 CONCLUSION

Many of the recommendations set forth in the previous section seem to be defeating the purpose of a high-level language, which is to free the user from restrictions, details of machine characteristics, and so on. Although a language unencumbered by restrictions may be easier to use than a rigid one, it is usually more difficult for a compiler to optimize. Until compiler optimizations for a given language become extremely well-refined and universally applied, the user who is truly concerned about object code performance must be willing to share the optimization burden. Such a user could minimize the amount of his time required for optimization of source programs if compilers would optionally provide him with feedback data regarding the execution of his programs.

For Fortran, this could be accomplished if the compiler optionally inserted frequency collection code into the object program at every node and expanded all STOP statements into calls to a Fortran library subprogram that merged the original source program with the frequency data to form an *execution report*. Such a report can be obtained now by editing the source program prior to compilation, but it seems more appropriate and economical for compilers to provide this service as an option. Also, this report could conceivably be used as input to a subsequent compilation so that the compiler could place the optimization emphasis in the most frequently executed areas of the program.

APPENDIX I OPERATOR FORMATION RULES

Table A1.1 indicates the types of operands that may be combined by the four arithmetic operators other than exponentiation to form valid arithmetic expressions. If the operation is valid, the type of the result is given. An X indicates that the combination is illegal in all compilers. NR means Not Recommended: the combination is not permitted in the American National Standards Institute (ANSI) standard, and although it is legal in many compilers it should be used with caution. Table A1.2 gives the same information for exponentiation. Table A1.3 indicates how various types of operands may be combined by the six relational operands to form valid logical expressions.

TABLE A1.1

	+ − * /	Integer	Real	Double	Complex	Logical
TYPE OF LEFT OPERAND	Integer	Integer*	Real (NR)	Double (NR)	Complex (NR)	X
	Real	Real (NR)	Real	Double	Complex	X
	Double	Double (NR)	Double	Double	X	X
	Complex	Complex (NR)	Complex	X	Complex	X
	Logical	X	X	X	X	X

Column span header: TYPE OF RIGHT OPERAND

*Division of an integer by an integer gives a truncated integer quotient, discarding any remainder.

TABLE A1.2

TYPE OF LEFT OPERAND	**	Integer	Real	Double	Complex	Logical
		TYPE OF EXPONENT				
	Integer	Integer	Real (NR)	Double (NR)	X	X
	Real	Real	Real	Double	X	X
	Double	Double	Double	Double	X	X
	Complex	Complex	X	X	X	X
	Logical	X	X	X	X	X

TABLE A1.3

TYPE OF LEFT OPERAND	.EQ. .NE. .GT. .GE. .LT. .LE.	Integer	Real	Double	Complex	Logical
		TYPE OF RIGHT OPERAND				
	Integer	Logical	Logical (NR)	Logical (NR)	X	X
	Real	Logical (NR)	Logical*	Logical*	X	X
	Double	Logical (NR)	Logical*	Logical*	X	X
	Complex	X	X	X	X	X
	Logical	X	X	X	X	X

*In many compilers the comparison of anything but two integers may produce unexpected results. For example, two numbers written in the same form, one read from a card and the other written as a program constant, may compare as unequal because of differences in the input conversion routines.

APPENDIX II SUPPLIED FUNCTIONS

Table A2.1 lists the characteristics of the functions that may be expected to be supplied with most Fortran compilers. Those marked with a dagger (†) are not specified in the American National Standards Institute (ANSI) standard and are not found in some compilers.

(The standard distinguishes between external and intrinsic functions, a practice not followed here because many compilers do not follow the standard exactly and because the distinction is of little importance to the beginning programmer. In situations where it might matter, such as in renaming functions, specifying them as EXTERNAL, or in attempting to conserve storage space, the reader will need to have far more detailed information about his particular system than we could provide here in any case.)

TABLE A2.1 SUPPLIED FUNCTIONS

Function	Definition	Number of Arguments	Symbolic Name	Type of Argument	Type of Function
Exponential	e^a	1	EXP	Real	Real
		1	DEXP	Double	Double
		1	CEXP	Complex	Complex
Natural Logarithm	$\log_e (a)$	1	ALOG	Real	Real
		1	DLOG	Double	Double
		1	CLOG	Complex	Complex
Common Logarithm	$\log_{10} (a)$	1	ALOG10	Real	Real
			DLOG10	Double	Double
Trigonometric Sine (Argument in radians)	$\sin (a)$	1	SIN	Real	Real
		1	DSIN	Double	Double
		1	CSIN	Complex	Complex
Trigonometric Cosine (Argument in radians)	$\cos (a)$	1	COS	Real	Real
		1	DCOS	Double	Double
		1	CCOS	Complex	Complex
† Trigonometric Tangent (Argument in radians)	$\tan (a)$	1	TAN	Real	Real
		1	DTAN	Double	Double

TABLE A2.1 (*continued*)

Function	Definition	Number of Arguments	Symbolic Name	Type of Argument	Type of Function
† Hyperbolic Sine	sinh (a)	1	SINH	Real	Real
		1	DSINH	Double	Double
† Hyperbolic Cosine	cosh (a)	1	COSH	Real	Real
		1	DCOSH	Double	Double
Hyperbolic Tangent	tanh (a)	1	TANH	Real	Real
Square Root	$\sqrt{a}$	1	SQRT	Real	Real
		1	DSQRT	Double	Double
		1	CSQRT	Complex	Complex
† Arcsine	arcsin (a)	1	ARSIN	Real	Real
		1	DARSIN	Double	Double
† Arccosine	arccos (a)	1	ARCOS	Real	Real
		1	DARCOS	Double	Double
Arctangent	arctan (a)	1	ATAN	Real	Real
		1	DATAN	Double	Double
	arctan (a_1/a_2)	2	ATAN2	Real	Real
		2	DATAN2	Double	Double
Absolute Value	|a|	1	ABS	Real	Real
			IABS	Integer	Integer
			DABS	Double	Double
Modulus		1	CABS	Complex	Real
Truncation	Sign of a times largest integer ≤|a|	1	AINT	Real	Real
			INT	Real	Integer
			IDINT	Double	Integer
Remaindering*	a_1(mod a_2)	2	AMOD	Real	Real
			MOD	Integer	Integer
			DMOD	Double	Double
Choosing Largest Value	Max ($a_1, a_2, \ldots$)	≧ 2	AMAX0	Integer	Real
			AMAX1	Real	Real
			MAX0	Integer	Integer
			MAX1	Real	Integer
			DMAX1	Double	Double
Choosing Smallest Value	Min ($a_1, a_2, \ldots$)	≧2	AMIN0	Integer	Real
			AMIN1	Real	Real
			MIN0	Integer	Integer
			MIN1	Real	Integer
			DMIN1	Double	Double
Float	Conversion from integer to real	1	FLOAT	Integer	Real
Fix	Conversion from real to integer	1	IFIX	Real	Integer

Function	Definition	Number of Arguments	Symbolic Name	Type of Argument	Type of Function
Transfer of Sign	Sign of a_2 times $\lvert a_1 \rvert$	2	SIGN ISIGN DSIGN	Real Integer Double	Real Integer Double
Positive Difference	$a_1 - \text{Min}\ (a_1, a_2)$	2	DIM IDIM	Real Integer	Real Integer
Obtain Most Significant Part of Double Precision Argument		1	SNGL	Double	Real
Obtain Real Part of Complex Argument		1	REAL	Complex	Real
Obtain Imaginary Part of Complex Argument		1	AIMAG	Complex	Real
Express Single Precision Argument in Double Precision Form		1	DBLE	Real	Double
Express Two Real Arguments in Complex Form	$a_1 + a_2 \sqrt{-1}$	2	CMPLX	Real	Complex
Obtain Conjugate of a Complex Argument		1	CONJG	Complex	Complex

*The function MOD, AMOD, or DMOD (a_1, a_2) is defined as $a_1 - [a_1/a_2]a_2$, where $[x]$ is the integer whose magnitude does not exceed the magnitude of x and whose sign is the same as x.

APPENDIX III SUGGESTIONS FOR TERM PROBLEMS

The following list, it is hoped, will be suggestive of projects that a student who has spent several months studying Fortran might consider for a term problem. No attempt has been made to indicate the relative difficulty of the suggestions, largely because the difficulty depends mostly on how much of a complete job is attempted. Almost any of these could easily become far too large for a term problem in a one-semester course, and some of them are suitable for graduate thesis work. *It is essential that you write down a definition of the precise scope of the task you propose to attempt, and get your instructor's approval before proceeding.* It is sometimes remarkably difficult for the beginner to distinguish between a job that is too simple to be worth term problem status, and one that would be tough for a Ph. D. candidate.

Many of the exercises in the chapters, especially those at the end of the sets for Chapters 5 and 6, will suggest term problems if suitable scopes are established.

These suggestions are offered only on the thought that some readers may not have better ideas of their own. The goal of a term problem, after all, is to provide a transition from this course of study to the next one or to a realistic work situation. By far the best term problems are those that come from the reader's own field of interest: another course or his work. Even in these cases, however—or perhaps *especially* in these cases—it is essential to get guidance from an instructor or other experienced person before proceeding. Some rather simple-sounding jobs can turn out to be terribly difficult or complicated in ways that are not educational.

1. Desk calculator simulation.* Using typewriter terminal keys to simulate addition, subtraction, multiplication, and division, write a program that will cause a time-sharing system to act like a desk calculator. This problem may be done in terms of whatever "desk calculator" you wish; hand-held devices using LSI (large-scale integration) technology and costing about $100, are currently available to do considerably more than electromechanical devices costing ten times as much were able to do a few years ago.

2. Justified typing. Devise a program that will make Fortran simulate a justifying typewriter, so that after a line of English text has been entered the machine will adjust the spacing throughout so as to give flush left and flush right margins and spacing between the words that is as even as possible. (Do not try to hyphenate the words, unless you want to get into a *very* much larger problem.)

3. Language translation. Set up a dictionary of a few hundred words in some language you know (some *natural* language, that is, such as French or German) and their English equivalents. Write a routine to accept text in the source language and translate it into the target language.

4. Musical transposition. Write a program that will accept a tune, encoded in some suitable form, and transpose it into another key.

---

*The first six of these suggestions are adapted from "Problems for Students of Computers," by John W. Carr,III, in *Computers and Automation*, Vol. 4, No. 2 (Feb. 1955). Used by permission of Prof. Carr and *Computers and Automation*.

5. Track betting odds. Find out how the odds are calcuated on the win, place, and show pools at a race track, if you don't already know, and write a routine that will calculate the payoff on a given horse given the appropriate information. Recall that all payoffs are *truncated,* that is, any pennies above a multiple of 10¢ are dropped. (This is called the *breakage.* As an extension of the project, estimate what the total breakage amounts to for two months of racing at Aqueduct Racetrack.)

6. Bridge playing. Write a program that handles some aspects of the game of bridge. Possibilities: using a random number generator, deal out a hand; get the point-count of a hand; make a legal bid; make a bid according to some system; follow suit if possible, otherwise trump if possible, otherwise discard randomly.

7. Chess playing. Building on Exercise 31 in Chapter 5, write a rudimentary chess playing routine. To get any sort of decent play is a fairly big job and should not be attempted unless you have a lot of time to devote to it. For simple starters try writing a program that will determine whether a move made by the machine's opponent is legal; write a routine that will generate all legal moves open to the machine at a given point; write a routine that will determine whether any move that could now be made by the opponent would bring the machine's king into check; write a routine that will determine whether the machine has a checkmate available, that is, a check to which the opponent has no legal response; write a routine that will make some sort of weighted accounting of all pieces that both sides have in such a position as to influence control of the four center squares.

Warning: this kind of thing is addictive!

8. Graphic output. Write a routine that converts any string of eight or fewer characters to graphic symbols about 2 inches high. Such a routine is used at many computer installations to provide a title page that can be read at a distance by the computer operators.

9. Program grading. Write a grading routine that determines whether a student program is correct. As an example, for Case Study 1 the grader might specify that the student issue a SUBROUTINE CALL in which he names the input and output variables and his student number. The grader routine must determine whether the answer is correct and give the student an appropriate number of points in a class

register. If there are possibilities of partially correct answers, the grader should analyze the student's answers accordingly.

As an interesting extension, if you can get access to the necessary system data, try to analyze student programs for evidence of collusion. One clue is identical input, unless specified or permitted. Another clue is identical compilation, link editor, or loader error messages. None of these will be conclusive, probably, but they may be strongly indicative, and the existence of such checks might tend to inhibit cheating even if the checks are not very good.

10. A management information system. You are a systems analyst/programmer for the Fizzies Bottling Company. You have been asked to design and implement a small-scale management information system, along the following lines.

The company has four products: a cola, a root beer, a ginger ale, and a lime drink; each product can be packaged in 8-ounce bottles, 12-ounce cans, 12-ounce bottles, 16-ounce cans, and 32-ounce bottles, although not all of the 41 franchisers produce all products in all sizes. Sales history is kept in terms of each product, each size, and each franchiser, for each of the past 60 months, in terms of both cases and dollars.

You are to design a system that will permit any authorized company employee to be able to get rapid answers to questions of the following sort:

• What were the total sales for franchiser N in the last 12 months?
• What were the sales of root beer by all franchisers four months ago?
• How do franchisers M and N compare in sales of ginger ale on a month-by-month basis for the past two years?
• What were total company sales in the last month and in the month before that?
• What franchiser sold the most cola in month 16? What franchiser had the greatest sales of all products in the last year?

Assuming a fairly clean existing data base and experienced programmers, this job might take one to two man-years in a realistic situation, including designing the system, converting the data base to a form suitable for use, providing for weekly or monthly updates of the data, and so on. Cut the job down to something you can hope to finish in however much time you have. You will invent the data, of course, and you should cut the specifications down, by assuming only three or four franchisers, for instance. You should probably ignore the entire question of updating the data once the system is running.

You may assume that requests will be presented in a coded form, and part of your job will be to devise the codes. But it is crucial to observe the requirement that the questions be askable by "anyone." That doesn't really mean anyone in the whole world; a certain amount of intelligence, motivation, and a few hours of training may be assumed. But you may *not* assume any knowledge whatsoever of data processing in general or of programming.

If available to you, the project should of course be set up for interactive (time-sharing) operation, which is how it would be used in real life.

11. Write a series of subprograms to produce graphical output, along the following lines.*

It is important to note that printer characters are ordinarily spaced ten to the inch horizontally and six to the inch vertically. To produce square graphs, therefore, it is necessary that a character array similar to 83 wide by 50 high be used.

The programs are to produce a graph with scale markings, axes, horizontal and vertical axis identifications, and plotted points. The scales are to be variable under control of subprogram calls, although there are to be default values. A series of calls will set up the variable information, after which the points to be plotted will be entered into the array. When all points have been entered, a final call will cause printing of the entire array.

The package must include at least the following capabilities.

To clear the array, set defaults, and carry out any other necessary actions, there must be an initializing routine, that might be called by

CALL INIT

You might choose to make the name and size of the array parameters of this call.

The graph should be scaled from $v1$ to $v2$

*Adapted from a Harvard University Engineering Sciences assignment prepared by Robert R. Fenichel and Patrick C. Fischer.

along the left-hand edge, with calibrations every $(v2 - v1)/8$. The defaults should be $v1 = -10$, $v2 = 10$, unless overridden with

CALL SCALEV ($v1$, $v2$)

The graph should be scaled from $h1$ to $h2$ along the bottom edge, with calibrations every $(h2 - h1)/8$. The defaults should be $h1 = -10$, $h2 = 10$ unless overridden with

CALL SCALEH ($h1$, $h2$)

You may assume that $h1$, $h2$, $v1$, and $v2$ are all less than 10, and that $v2 \geq v1 + 1$.

A column at the left of the graph should be reserved for a vertical heading that may be requested with

CALL TITLEV (A, N)

where A is the name of an array that contains the characters of the title and N gives the number of words in the array. The default, if no title is requested, should be blanks. A similar horizontal title should be provided if called for by

CALL TITLEH (A, N)

The titles supplied by these calls should be approximately centered before printing.

Assuming that $v1 \leq y \leq v2$, the following call should cause a horizontal line of minus signs to cross the graph at the ordinate y:

CALL AXISH (y)

Likewise, for a vertical axis composed of upper case I's, and

CALL AXISV (x)

Assuming that $h1 \leq x \leq h2$ and $v1 \leq y \leq v2$, the following call should cause a point, given by the character variable CHAR, to be plotted at (x, y):

CALL POINT (x, y, CHAR)

The AXISH, AXISV, and POINT routines should ignore requests for plotting outside the range of the graph.

When the array has been completed in storage, it should be written in response to the call

CALL PLOT (N)

where N is the data set reference number that specifies where the output is to be written.

12. Write a program to produce the 157 decimal digits of the number 100! No Fortran system permits variables of that length, of course, so you will have to devise routines capable of handling such long integers as combinations of ordinary (shorter) integer variables.

This is a moderately difficult assignment, made somewhat simpler by the fact that you are dealing only with integers and therefore have no radix point problems to worry about, and by the fact that no divisions are involved.

13. Extend the routines indicated in Suggestion 12 to include decimal fractions and divisions, and use your routines to produce the first 500 digits of the decimal representation of e using the Taylor series:

$$e = 1 + \frac{1}{1!} + \frac{1}{2!} + \frac{1}{3!} + \cdots$$

Alternatively, produce 500 digits for the decimal representation of π using some series or combination of series that converges moderately rapidly. One possibility is:

$$\pi/4 = 4 \arctan 1/5 - \arctan 1/239$$

The value of π is now known to more than 500,000 decimal digits.

14. Let A be an R-digit number in base N. Form the largest and smallest numbers that can be obtained by permuting the digits of A, and subtract the smaller from the larger. Call the resulting difference the transformation T(A). This has been called the 6174 problem, since if A is a four-digit decimal number T(6174) = 6174, and applying T at most seven times to any four-digit decimal number produces 6174. For example, start with 1234. The largest number than can be formed is 4321 and the smallest is just 1234, so T(1234) = 4321 − 1234 = 3087 .T(3087) = 8730 − 0378 = 8352, and T(8352) = 8532 − 2358 = 6174.

For a starter, write a program in Fortran that will substantiate the claim that the 6174 transformation does work as described, for four-digit decimal numbers, with the exception of numbers of the form *nnnn*, since T(*nnnn*) = 0000. Then investigate how the transformation works on numbers of other than four digits and/or bases other than decimal. The author has tested enough cases to offer the conjecture that every three-digit number with an even base leads to some such phenomenon. For instance, all three-digit numbers of base 8 lead in at most five applications of the transformation to 374_8, of which the prime factors are 2, 2, 3, 3, and 7, and all three-digit numbers in base 42_{10} lead to $20_{10} \ 41_{10} \ 21_{10} = 37023_{10}$, of which the prime factors are 3, 7, 41, and 43.

The largest numbers tried were a four-digit numbers in base 160_{10}, which seemed in the cases tested always to lead to $96_{10} \ 31_{10} \ 127_{10} \ 64_{10} = 394029984_{10}$, of which the prime factors are 2, 2, 2, 2, 2, 3, 43, 53, and 1801.

See what patterns you can establish about this puzzle for other numbers and other number bases. If you know enough about number theory, try to explain the patterns in the factors.

This problem was related to the author by Professor Robert R. Fenichel, then of MIT, who reported that it was current there in 1970. Martin Gardner, whose feature "Mathematical Games" appears in *Scientific American,* has kindly supplied the following bibliography on this problem.

"An Interesting Property of the Number 6174," *Scripta Mathematica,* Vol. 21, 1955, p. 304.

"Self-Producing Sequences of Digits," *American Mathematical Monthly,* Vol. 71, Jan. 1964, p. 61.

"Kaprekar's Constant," *American Mathematical Monthly,* Vol. 78, Feb. 1971, p. 197.

APPENDIX IV WATFOR AND WATFIV

WATFOR is the name of a Fortran system developed by the Applied Analysis and Computer Science Department of the University of Waterloo, Ontario, Canada. The acronym stands for WATerloo FORtran. The first version ran on the IBM 7040 and was completed in 1965; a version for the IBM 360 was developed in 1967. When an improved version of the latter was prepared, it was named WATFIV ("the one after WATFOR," according to its developers), which also happens to stand for WATerloo Fortran IV.

It is no exaggeration to suggest that WATFOR revolutionized the use of computers in education. By greatly speeding up the compilation and execution of student programs, and by providing highly informative error diagnostic messages that made it possible to get programs running in fewer attempts, WATFOR made possible perhaps ten times as much educational benefit from the same hardware capability. WATFIV extends these capabilities.

This speed is obtained by a combination of factors. First, the assumption is made that speed of execution of the object program is of little importance, so virtually no effort was placed on code optimization in writing the compiler. A WATFOR or WATFIV program, therefore, will definitely run more slowly in most instances than one compiled using a more traditional compiler. Second, the entire system is *core-resident,* which means that the WATFOR or WATFIV system takes complete charge of the machine from the operating system, for as long as WATFOR or WATFIV programs are to be compiled and executed. Complete compilation and

execution of a student program accordingly take much less than one second on a large computer in most cases. Third, no permanent copy of the object program is produced; a WATFOR or WATFIV program must be recompiled every time it is used.

WATFOR and WATFIV provide a number of features that markedly facilitate the learning of Fortran programming by the beginner. As we have noted, the most important of these is the availability of input and output statements that do not require the use of FORMAT statements—a subject that is always confusing to the beginner and one that every instructor would like to be able to postpone. Another feature, indicative of the kinds of things that have been added, is the ability to write ordinary expressions in the list of an output statement rather than being restricted to the names of variables. Elementary examples of complete programs can therefore be constructed that consist in their entirety of a WRITE statement and an END statement.

When features such as these are used the WATFOR or WATFIV compiler generally flags them, to point out that although they are permitted in the WATFOR or WATFIV version of Fortran, they may not be accepted by other Fortrans. There are a fair number of other extensions, but most of them are of less far-reaching scope than the simplifications provided for input and output.

Beginning students are not the only ones who benefit by the availability of a very fast compiler that provides extremely thorough diagnostic error messages. A thoroughly experienced programmer writing a large production program also finds a WATFOR-type compiler useful in the following way. When the program has been written and desk-checked, it is first compiled using WATFOR or WATFIV, precisely to take advantage of the major features of these variations of Fortran: fast compilation and good diagnostics. A big program has essentially zero probability of running correctly the first few times it is compiled anyway, so the slowness of the object program is of no consequence whatever. The saving in the total number of compiler shots that is made possible by the better diagnostics, together with the improved assurance that the program actually does do what it is intended to do, is well worth the installation's trouble in maintaining the separate compiler. When the program has been determined to be correct, it is recompiled using a "normal" compiler, that is, one that does produce an object program so that it is not necessary to recompile every time the program is run, and one that does do at least some optimizing of the object code. Or, perhaps the final version is recompiled using an *optimizing compiler,* which is a relatively slow compiler that may also require extra main storage, but which produces object code that runs very rapidly.

Ideally, there would be at least two versions of the compilers for all major languages: one of the WATFOR variety for fast compiles and extensive diagnostics, and another to produce optimized code. This trend is in fact taking place, but at a somewhat slower pace than one might wish, presumably in part because of the high cost of producing and maintaining a major compiler. (This can easily run into the millions of dollars, counting program maintenance over a period of years.)

It is worth noting that the diagnostics provided by WATFOR and WATFIV apply both to compile-time and execution-time errors, and that they frequently catch errors that are in some sense "legal" in Fortran. For instance, they will catch the error of using the value of a variable to which no value has ever been assigned. There is nothing in the Fortran language that makes doing so illegal, and if the programmer has taken specific actions to clear storage to zero before execution it may not cause any

trouble. The practice is to be discouraged as strongly as possible, however, since it so often results from a programming error and leads to difficulties that are very difficult to track down.

The foregoing is an example of an error that can be caught at compile time. For an example of one that cannot, suppose we write the statement

```
DO 12 I = J, 100
```

and read the value of J from a card. There is no way the compiler can know what we are going to read, so it cannot be of any help in predicting a situation where J is zero or negative; this has to be done at execution time. Furthermore, although a value of zero here is clearly illegal according to the Fortran manual, very few compilers will even flag a statement like

```
DO 12 I = 0, 100
```

What such a statement will do is different on different systems. Even though such a statement would almost always represent a programming error and give erroneous results, it could be quite difficult to track down without diagnostic help from the system.

For a further discussion of the diagnostic capabilities of WATFOR and WATFIV, see Stan Siegel, "WATFOR . . . Speedy Fortran Debugger," *Datamation,* Vol. 17, No. 22 (Nov. 15, 1971), pp. 22–26.

The remainder of this appendix consists of the diagnostic error messages for WATFOR and WATFIV as they existed in early 1972. (Presumably they will change, over the years, in minor but not major ways.) These were graciously supplied by Sandra J. Ward and Professor J. Wesley Graham of the University of Waterloo. The author has made a few minor changes in the messages as they were supplied on cards, primarily such things as Americanizing the spelling of "programme" in the WATFOR messages.

For specific information on the precise nature of the WATFOR and WATFIV variations of the Fortran language, we recommend that the reader obtain the latest edition of a book written by three of the originators: Paul Cress, Paul Dirksen, and J. Wesley Graham, *FORTRAN IV with WATFOR and WATFIV,* Englewood Cliffs, New Jersey, Prentice-Hall, 1970.

'ASSIGN STATEMENTS AND VARIABLES'
AS-2   'ATTEMPT TO REDEFINE AN ASSIGNED VARIABLE IN AN ARITHMETIC STATEMENT'
AS-3   'ASSIGNED VARIABLE USED IN AN ARITHMETIC EXPRESSION'
AS-4   'ASSIGNED VARIABLE CANNOT BE HALF WORD INTEGER'
AS-5   'ATTEMPT TO REDEFINE AN ASSIGNED VARIABLE IN AN INPUT LIST'

'BLOCK DATA STATEMENTS'
BD-0   'EXECUTABLE STATEMENT IN BLOCK DATA SUBPROGRAM'
BD-1   'IMPROPER BLOCK DATA STATEMENT'

'CARD FORMAT AND CONTENTS'
CC-0   'COLUMNS 1-5 OF CONTINUATION CARD NOT BLANK'
                    PROBABLE CAUSE - STATEMENT PUNCHED TO LEFT OF COLUMN 7
CC-1   'TOO MANY CONTINUATION CARDS (MAXIMUM OF 5)'
CC-2   'INVALID CHARACTER IN FORTRAN STATEMENT '$' INSERTED IN SOURCE LISTING'
CC-3   'FIRST CARD OF A PROGRAM IS A CONTINUATION CARD'
                    PROBABLE CAUSE - STATEMENT PUNCHED TO LEFT OF COLUMN 7
CC-4   'STATEMENT TOO LONG TO COMPILE (SCAN-STACK OVERFLOW)'
CC-5   'BLANK CARD ENCOUNTERED'
CC-6   'KEYPUNCH USED DIFFERS FROM KEYPUNCH SPECIFIED ON JOB CARD'
CC-7   'FIRST CHARACTER OF STATEMENT NOT ALPHABETIC'
CC-8   'INVALID CHARACTER(S) CONCATENATED WITH FORTRAN KEYWORD'
CC-9   'INVALID CHARACTERS IN COL 1-5. STATEMENT NUMBER IGNORED'
                    PROBABLE CAUSE - STATEMENT PUNCHED TO LEFT OF COLUMN 7

'COMMON'
CM-0   'VARIABLE PREVIOUSLY PLACED IN COMMON'
CM-1   'NAME IN COMMON LIST PREVIOUSLY USED AS OTHER THAN VARIABLE'
CM-2   'SUBPROGRAM PARAMETER APPEARS IN COMMON STATEMENT'
CM-3   'INITIALIZING OF COMMON SHOULD BE DONE IN A BLOCK DATA SUBPROGRAM'
CM-4   'ILLEGAL USE OF BLOCK NAME'

'FORTRAN CONSTANTS'
CN-0   'MIXED REAL*4,REAL*8 IN COMPLEX CONSTANT'
CN-1   'INTEGER CONSTANT GREATER THAN 2,147,483,647 (2**31-1)'
CN-2   'EXPONENT OVERFLOW OR UNDERFLOW CONVERTING CONSTANT IN SOURCE STATEMENT'
CN-3   'EXPONENT ON REAL CONSTANT GREATER THAN 99'
CN-4   'REAL CONSTANT HAS MORE THAN 16 DIGITS, TRUNCATED TO 16'
CN-5   'INVALID HEXADECIMAL CONSTANT'
CN-6   'ILLEGAL USE OF DECIMAL POINT'
CN-8   'CONSTANT WITH E-TYPE EXPONENT HAS MORE THAN 7 DIGITS, ASSUME D-TYPE'
CN-9   'CONSTANT OR STATEMENT NUMBER GREATER THAN 99999'

'COMPILER ERRORS'
CP-0   'DETECTED IN PHASE RELOC'
CP-1   'DETECTED IN PHASE LINKR'
CP-2   'DUPLICATE PSEUDO STATEMENT NUMBERS'
CP-4   'DETECTED IN PHASE ARITH'
CP-5   'COMPILER INTERRUPT'

'DATA STATEMENT'
DA-0   'REPLICATION FACTOR GREATER THAN 32767; ASSUME 32767'
DA-1   'NON-CONSTANT IN DATA STATEMENT'
DA-2   'MORE VARIABLES THAN CONSTANTS IN DATA STATEMENT'
DA-3   'ATTEMPT TO INITIALIZE A SUBPROGRAM PARAMETER IN A DATA STATEMENT'
DA-4   'NON-CONSTANT SUBSCRIPTS IN A DATA STATEMENT INVALID IN /360 FORTRAN'
DA-5   '/360 FORTRAN DOES NOT HAVE IMPLIED DO IN DATA STATEMENT'
DA-6   'NON-AGREEMENT BETWEEN TYPE OF VARIABLE AND CONSTANT IN DATA STATEMENT'
DA-7   'MORE CONSTANTS THAN VARIABLES IN DATA STATEMENT'
DA-8   'VARIABLE PREVIOUSLY INITIALIZED. LATEST VALUE USED'
                    CHECK COMMON/EQUIVALENCED VARIABLES
DA-9   'INITIALIZING BLANK COMMON NOT ALLOWED IN /360 FORTRAN'
DA-A   'INVALID DELIMITER IN CONSTANT LIST PORTION OF DATA STATEMENT'
DA-B   'TRUNCATION OF LITERAL CONSTANT HAS OCCURRED'

'DIMENSION STATEMENTS'
DM-0   'NO DIMENSIONS SPECIFIED FOR A VARIABLE IN A DIMENSION STATEMENT'
DM-1   'OPTIONAL LENGTH SPECIFICATION IN DIMENSION STATEMENT IS ILLEGAL'
DM-2   'INITIALIZATION IN DIMENSION STATEMENT IS ILLEGAL'
DM-3   'ATTEMPT TO RE-DIMENSION A VARIABLE'
DM-4   'ATTEMPT TO DIMENSION AN INITIALIZED VARIABLE'

'DO LOOPS'
DO-0   'ILLEGAL STATEMENT USED AS OBJECT OF DO'
DO-1   'ILLEGAL TRANSFER INTO THE RANGE OF A DO-LOOP'
DO-2   'OBJECT OF A DO STATEMENT HAS ALREADY APPEARED'
DO-3   'IMPROPERLY NESTED DO-LOOPS'
DO-4   'ATTEMPT TO REDEFINE A DO-LOOP PARAMETER WITHIN RANGE OF LOOP'
DO-5   'INVALID DO-LOOP PARAMETER'
DO-6   'TOO MANY NESTED DO'S (MAXIMUM OF 20)'
DO-7   'DO-PARAMETER IS UNDEFINED OR OUTSIDE RANGE'
DO-8   'THIS DO LOOP WILL TERMINATE AFTER FIRST TIME THROUGH'
DO-9   'ATTEMPT TO REDEFINE A DO-LOOP PARAMETER IN AN INPUT LIST'

'EQUIVALENCE AND/OR COMMON'
EC-0   'TWO EQUIVALENCED VARIABLES APPEAR IN COMMON'
EC-1   'COMMON BLOCK HAS DIFFERENT LENGTH THAN IN A PREVIOUS SUBPROGRAM'
EC-2   'COMMON AND/OR EQUIVALENCE CAUSES INVALID ALIGNMENT. EXECUTION SLOWED'
          REMEDY - ORDER VARIABLES IN DESCENDING ORDER BY LENGTH
EC-3   'EQUIVALENCE EXTENDS COMMON DOWNWARDS'
EC-7   'COMMON/EQUIVALENCE STATEMENT DOES NOT PRECEDE PREVIOUS USE OF VARIABLE'
EC-8   'VARIABLE USED WITH NON-CONSTANT SUBSCRIPT IN COMMON/EQUIVALENCE LIST'
EC-9   'A NAME SUBSCRIPTED IN AN EQUIVALENCE STATEMENT WAS NOT DIMENSIONED'

'END STATEMENTS'
EN-0   'NO END STATEMENT IN PROGRAM -- END STATEMENT GENERATED'
EN-1   'END STATEMENT USED AS STOP STATEMENT AT EXECUTION'
EN-2   'IMPROPER END STATEMENT'
EN-3   'FIRST STATEMENT OF SUBPROGRAM IS END STATEMENT'

'EQUAL SIGNS'
EQ-6   'ILLEGAL QUANTITY ON LEFT OF EQUALS SIGN'
EQ-8   'ILLEGAL USE OF EQUAL SIGN'
EQ-A   'MULTIPLE ASSIGNMENT STATEMENTS NOT IN /360 FORTRAN'

'EQUIVALENCE STATEMENTS'
EV-0   'ATTEMPT TO EQUIVALENCE A VARIABLE TO ITSELF'
EV-1   'ATTEMPT TO EQUIVALENCE A SUBPROGRAM PARAMETER'
EV-2   'LESS THAN 2 MEMBERS IN AN EQUIVALENCE LIST'
EV-3   'TOO MANY EQUIVALENCE LISTS (MAX = 255)'
EV-4   'PREVIOUSLY EQUIVALENCED VARIABLE RE-EQUIVALENCED INCORRECTLY'

'POWERS AND EXPONENTIATION'
EX-0   'ILLEGAL COMPLEX EXPONENTIATION'
EX-2   'I**J WHERE I=J=0'
EX-3   'I**J WHERE I=0, J.LT.0'
EX-6   '0.0**Y WHERE Y.LE.0.0'
EX-7   '0.0**J WHERE J=0'
EX-8   '0.0**J WHERE J.LT.0'
EX-9   'X**Y WHERE X.LT.0.0, Y.NE.0.0'

'ENTRY STATEMENT'
EY-0   'SUBPROGRAM NAME IN ENTRY STATEMENT PREVIOUSLY DEFINED'
EY-1   'PREVIOUS DEFINITION OF FUNCTION NAME IN AN ENTRY IS INCORRECT'
EY-2   'USE OF SUBPROGRAM PARAMETER INCONSISTENT WITH PREVIOUS ENTRY'
EY-3   'ARGUMENT NAME HAS APPEARED IN AN EXECUTABLE STATEMENT,
              BUT WAS NOT A SUBPROGRAM PARAMETER'
EY-4   'ENTRY STATEMENT NOT PERMITTED IN MAIN PROGRAM'
EY-5   'ENTRY POINT INVALID INSIDE A DO-LOOP'
EY-6   'VARIABLE WAS NOT PREVIOUSLY USED AS A PARAMETER - PARAMETER ASSUMED'

```
'FORMAT'
   SOME FORMAT ERROR MESSAGES GIVE CHARACTERS IN WHICH ERROR WAS DETECTED
FM-0    'INVALID CHARACTER IN INPUT DATA'
FM-2    'NO STATEMENT NUMBER ON A FORMAT STATEMENT'
FM-5    'FORMAT SPECIFICATION AND DATA TYPE DO NOT MATCH'
FM-6    'INCORRECT SEQUENCE OF CHARACTERS IN INPUT DATA'
FM-7    'NON-TERMINATING FORMAT'

FT-0    'FIRST CHARACTER OF VARIABLE FORMAT NOT A LEFT PARENTHESIS'
FT-1    'INVALID CHARACTER ENCOUNTERED IN FORMAT'
FT-2    'INVALID FORM FOLLOWING A SPECIFICATION'
FT-3    'INVALID FIELD OR GROUP COUNT'
FT-4    'A FIELD OR GROUP COUNT GREATER THAN 255'
FT-5    'NO CLOSING PARENTHESIS ON VARIABLE FORMAT'
FT-6    'NO CLOSING QUOTE IN A HOLLERITH FIELD'
FT-7    'INVALID USE OF COMMA'
FT-8    'INSUFFICIENT SPACE TO COMPILE A FORMAT STATEMENT (SCAN-STACK OVERFLOW)'
FT-9    'INVALID USE OF P SPECIFICATION'
FT-A    'CHARACTER FOLLOWS CLOSING RIGHT PARENTHESIS'
FT-B    'INVALID USE OF PERIOD(.)'
FT-C    'MORE THAN THREE LEVELS OF PARENTHESES'
FT-D    'INVALID CHARACTER BEFORE A RIGHT PARENTHESIS'
FT-E    'MISSING OR ZERO LENGTH HOLLERITH ENCOUNTERED'
FT-F    'NO CLOSING RIGHT PARENTHESIS'

'FUNCTIONS AND SUBROUTINES'
FN-0    'NO ARGUMENTS IN A FUNCTION STATEMENT'
FN-3    'REPEATED ARGUMENT IN SUBPROGRAM OR STATEMENT FUNCTION DEFINITION'
FN-4    'SUBSCRIPTS ON RIGHT HAND SIDE OF STATEMENT FUNCTION'
                PROBABLE CAUSE - VARIABLE TO LEFT OF = NOT DIMENSIONED
FN-5    'MULTIPLE RETURNS ARE INVALID IN FUNCTION SUBPROGRAMS'
FN-6    'ILLEGAL LENGTH MODIFIER IN TYPE FUNCTION STATEMENT'
FN-7    'INVALID ARGUMENT IN ARITHMETIC OR LOGICAL STATEMENT FUNCTION'
FN-8    'ARGUMENT OF SUBPROGRAM IS SAME AS SUBPROGRAM NAME'

'GO TO STATEMENTS'
GO-0    'STATEMENT TRANSFERS TO ITSELF OR A NON-EXECUTABLE STATEMENT'
GO-1    'INVALID TRANSFER TO THIS STATEMENT'
GO-2    'INDEX OF COMPUTED 'GO TO' IS NEGATIVE, ZERO OR UNDEFINED'
GO-3    'ERROR IN VARIABLE OF 'GO TO' STATEMENT'
GO-4    'INDEX OF ASSIGNED 'GO TO' IS UNDEFINED OR NOT IN RANGE'

'HOLLERITH CONSTANTS'
HO-0    'ZERO LENGTH SPECIFIED FOR H-TYPE HOLLERITH'
HO-1    'ZERO LENGTH QUOTE-TYPE HOLLERITH'
HO-2    'NO CLOSING QUOTE OR NEXT CARD NOT CONTINUATION CARD'
HO-3    'HOLLERITH CONSTANT SHOULD APPEAR ONLY IN CALL STATEMENT'
HO-4    'UNEXPECTED HOLLERITH OR STATEMENT NUMBER CONSTANT'

'IF STATEMENTS (ARITHMETIC AND LOGICAL)'
IF-0    'STATEMENT INVALID AFTER A LOGICAL IF'
IF-3    'ARITHMETIC OR INVALID EXPRESSION IN LOGICAL IF'
IFF-4   'LOGICAL, COMPLEX, OR INVALID EXPRESSION IN ARITHMETIC IF'

'IMPLICIT STATEMENT'
IM-0    'INVALID MODE SPECIFIED IN AN IMPLICIT STATEMENT'
IM-1    'INVALID LENGTH SPECIFIED IN AN IMPLICIT OR TYPE STATEMENT'
IM-2    'ILLEGAL APPEARANCE OF $ IN A CHARACTER RANGE'
IM-3    'IMPROPER ALPHABETIC SEQUENCE IN CHARACTER RANGE'
IM-4    'SPECIFICATION MUST BE SINGLE ALPHABETIC CHARACTER, 1ST CHARACTER USED'
IM-5    'IMPLICIT STATEMENT DOES NOT PRECEDE OTHER SPECIFICATION STATEMENTS'
IM-6    'ATTEMPT TO ESTABLISH THE TYPE OF A CHARACTER MORE THAN ONCE'
IM-7    '/360 FORTRAN ALLOWS ONE IMPLICIT STATEMENT PER PROGRAM'
IM-8    'INVALID ELEMENT IN IMPLICIT STATEMENT'
IM-9    'INVALID DELIMITER IN IMPLICIT STATEMENT'
```

APPENDIX IV
257

'INPUT/OUTPUT'
IO-0   'MISSING COMMA IN I/O LIST OF I/O OR DATA STATEMENT'
IO-2   'STATEMENT NUMBER IN I/O STATEMENT NOT A FORMAT STATEMENT NUMBER'
IO-3   'FORMATTED LINE TOO LONG FOR I/O DEVICE (RECORD LENGTH EXCEEDED)'
IO-6   'VARIABLE FORMAT NOT AN ARRAY NAME'
IO-8   'INVALID ELEMENT IN INPUT LIST OR DATA LIST'
IO-9   'TYPE OF VARIABLE UNIT NOT INTEGER IN I/O STATEMENTS'
IO-A   'HALF-WORD INTEGER VARIABLE USED AS UNIT IN I/O STATEMENTS'
IO-B   'ASSIGNED INTEGER VARIABLE USED AS UNIT IN I/O STATEMENTS'
IO-C   'INVALID ELEMENT IN AN OUTPUT LIST'
IO-D   'MISSING OR INVALID UNIT IN I/O STATEMENT'
IO-E   'MISSING OR INVALID FORMAT IN READ/WRITE STATEMENT'
IO-F   'INVALID DELIMITER IN SPECIFICATION PART OF I/O STATEMENT'
IO-G   'MISSING STATEMENT NUMBER AFTER END= OR ERR='
IO-H   '/360 FORTRAN DOESN'T ALLOW END/ERR RETURNS IN WRITE STATEMENTS'
IO-J   'INVALID DELIMITER IN I/O LIST'
IO-K   'INVALID DELIMITER IN STOP, PAUSE, DATA, OR TAPE CONTROL STATEMENT'

'JOB CONTROL CARDS'
JB-1   'JOB CARD ENCOUNTERED DURING COMPILATION'
JB-2   'INVALID OPTION(S) SPECIFIED ON JOB CARD'
JB-3   'UNEXPECTED CONTROL CARD ENCOUNTERED DURING COMPILATION'

'JOB TERMINATION'
KO-0   'JOB TERMINATED IN EXECUTION BECAUSE OF COMPILE TIME ERROR'
KO-1   'FIXED-POINT DIVISION BY ZERO'
KO-2   'FLOATING-POINT DIVISION BY ZERO'
KO-3   'TOO MANY EXPONENT OVERFLOWS'
KO-4   'TOO MANY EXPONENT UNDERFLOWS'
KO-5   'TOO MANY FIXED-POINT OVERFLOWS'
KO-6   'JOB TIME EXCEEDED'
KO-7   'COMPILER ERROR - INTERRUPTION AT EXECUTION TIME,RETURN TO SYSTEM'
KO-8   'INTEGER IN INPUT DATA IS TOO LARGE (MAXIMUM IS 2147483647)'

'LOGICAL OPERATIONS'
LG-2   '.NOT. USED AS A BINARY OPERATOR'

'LIBRARY ROUTINES'
LI-0   'ARGUMENT OUT OF RANGE DGAMMA OR GAMMA. (1.382E-76 .LT. X .LT. 57.57)'
LI-1   'ABSOLUTE VALUE OF ARGUMENT .GT. 174.673, SINH,COSH,DSINH,DCOSH'
LI-2   'SENSE LIGHT OTHER THAN 0,1,2,3,4 FOR SLITE OR 1,2,3,4 FOR SLITET'
LI-3   'REAL PORTION OF ARGUMENT .GT. 174.673, CEXP OR CDEXP'
LI-4   'ABS(AIMAG(Z)) .GT. 174.673 FOR CSIN, CCOS, CDSIN OR CDCOS OF Z'
LI-5   'ABS(REAL(Z)) .GE. 3.537E15 FOR CSIN, CCOS, CDSIN OR CDCOS OF Z'
LI-6   'ABS(AIMAG(Z)) .GE. 3.537E15 FOR CEXP OR CDEXP OF Z'
LI-7   'ARGUMENT .GT. 174.673, EXP OR DEXP'
LI-8   'ARGUMENT IS ZERO, CLOG, CLOG10, CDLOG OR CDLG10'
LI-9   'ARGUMENT IS NEGATIVE OR ZERO, ALOG, ALOG10, DLOG OR DLOG10'
LI-A   'ABS(X) .GE. 3.537E15 FOR SIN, COS, DSIN OR DCOS OF X'
LI-B   'ABSOLUTE VALUE OF ARGUMENT .GT. 1, FOR ARSIN, ARCOS, DARSIN OR DARCOS'
LI-C   'ARGUMENT IS NEGATIVE, SQRT OR DSQRT'
LI-D   'BOTH ARGUMENTS OF DATAN2 OR ATAN2 ARE ZERO'
LI-E   'ARGUMENT TOO CLOSE TO A SINGULARITY, TAN, COTAN, DTAN OR DCOTAN'
LI-F   'ARGUMENT OUT OF RANGE DLGAMA OR ALGAMA. (0.0 .LT. X .LT. 4.29E73)'
LI-G   'ABSOLUTE VALUE OF ARGUMENT .GE. 3.537E15, TAN, COTAN, DTAN, DCOTAN'
LI-H   'FEWER THAN TWO ARGUMENTS FOR ONE OF MINO, MIN1, AMINO, ETC.'

'MIXED MODE'
MD-2   'RELATIONAL OPERATOR HAS A LOGICAL OPERAND'
MD-3   'RELATIONAL OPERATOR HAS A COMPLEX OPERAND'
MD-4   'MIXED MODE - LOGICAL WITH ARITHMETIC'
MD-6   'WARNING - SUBSCRIPT IS COMPLEX. REAL PART USED'

'MEMORY OVERFLOW'
MO-0   'SYMBOL TABLE OVERFLOWS OBJECT CODE. SOURCE ERROR CHECKING CONTINUES.
MO-1   'INSUFFICIENT MEMORY TO ASSIGN ARRAY STORAGE. JOB ABANDONED'
MO-2   'SYMBOL TABLE OVERFLOWS COMPILER, JOB ABANDONED'
MO-3   'DATA AREA OF SUBPROGRAM TOO LARGE -- SEGMENT SUBPROGRAM'
MO-4   'GETMAIN CANNOT PROVIDE BUFFER FOR WATLIB'

'PARENTHESES'
PC-0   'UNMATCHED PARENTHESES'
PC-1   'INVALID PARENTHESIS COUNT'

'PAUSE, STOP STATEMENTS'
PS-0   'STOP WITH OPERATOR MESSAGE NOT ALLOWED. SIMPLE STOP ASSUMED'
PS-1   'PAUSE WITH OPERATOR MESSAGE NOT ALLOWED. TREATED AS CONTINUE'

'RETURN STATEMENT'
RE-0   'FIRST CARD OF SUBPROGRAM IS A RETURN STATEMENT'
RE-1   'RETURN I, WHERE I IS ZERO,NEGATIVE OR TOO LARGE'
RE-2   'MULTIPLE RETURN NOT VALID IN FUNCTION SUBPROGRAM'
RE-3   'VARIABLE IN MULTIPLE RETURN IS NOT A SIMPLE INTEGER VARIABLE'
RE-4   'MULTIPLE RETURN NOT VALID IN MAIN PROGRAM'

'ARITHMETIC AND LOGICAL STATEMENT FUNCTIONS'
    PROBABLE CAUSE OF SF ERRORS - VARIABLE ON LEFT OF = WAS NOT DIMENSIONED
SF-1   'PREVIOUSLY REFERENCED STATEMENT NUMBER ON STATEMENT FUNCTION'
SF-2   'STATEMENT FUNCTION IS THE OBJECT OF A LOGICAL IF STATEMENT'
SF-3   'RECURSIVE STATEMENT FUNCTION, NAME APPEARS ON BOTH SIDES OF ='
SF-5   'ILLEGAL USE OF A STATEMENT FUNCTION'

'SUBPROGRAMS'
SR-0   'MISSING SUBPROGRAM'
SR-2   'SUBPROGRAM ASSIGNED DIFFERENT MODES IN DIFFERENT PROGRAM SEGMENTS'
SR-4   'INVALID TYPE OF ARGUMENT IN SUBPROGRAM REFERENCE'
SR-5   'SUBPROGRAM ATTEMPTS TO REDEFINE A CONSTANT,TEMPORARY OR DO PARAMETER'
SR-6   'ATTEMPT TO USE SUBPROGRAM RECURSIVELY'
SR-7   'WRONG NUMBER OF ARGUMENTS IN SUBPROGRAM REFERENCE'
SR-8   'SUBPROGRAM NAME PREVIOUSLY DEFINED -- FIRST REFERENCE USED'
SR-9   'NO MAIN PROGRAM'
SR-A   'ILLEGAL OR BLANK SUBPROGRAM NAME'

'SUBSCRIPTS'
SS-0   'ZERO SUBSCRIPT OR DIMENSION NOT ALLOWED'
SS-1   'SUBSCRIPT OUT OF RANGE'
SS-2   'INVALID VARIABLE OR NAME USED FOR DIMENSION'

'STATEMENTS AND STATEMENT NUMBERS'
ST-0   'MISSING STATEMENT NUMBER'
ST-1   'STATEMENT NUMBER GREATER THAN 99999'
ST-3   'MULTIPLY-DEFINED STATEMENT NUMBER'
ST-4   'NO STATEMENT NUMBER ON STATEMENT FOLLOWING TRANSFER STATEMENT'
ST-5   'UNDECODABLE STATEMENT'
ST-7   'STATEMENT NUMBER SPECIFIED IN A TRANSFER IS A NON-EXECUTABLE STATEMENT'
ST-8   'STATEMENT NUMBER CONSTANT MUST BE IN A CALL STATEMENT'
ST-9   'STATEMENT SPECIFIED IN A TRANSFER STATEMENT IS A FORMAT STATEMENT'
ST-A   'MISSING FORMAT STATEMENT'

'SUBSCRIPTED VARIABLES'
SV-0   'WRONG NUMBER OF SUBSCRIPTS'
SV-1   'ARRAY NAME OR SUBPROGRAM NAME USED INCORRECTLY WITHOUT LIST'
SV-2   'MORE THAN 7 DIMENSIONS NOT ALLOWED'
SV-3   'DIMENSION TOO LARGE'
SV-4   'VARIABLE WITH VARIABLE DIMENSIONS IS NOT A SUBPROGRAM PARAMETER'
SV-5   'VARIABLE DIMENSION NEITHER SIMPLE INTEGER VARIABLE NOR S/P PARAMETER'

'SYNTAX ERRORS'
SX-0   'MISSING OPERATOR'
SX-1   'SYNTAX ERROR-SEARCHING FOR SYMBOL,NONE FOUND'
SX-2   'SYNTAX ERROR-SEARCHING FOR CONSTANT; NONE FOUND'
SX-3   'SYNTAX ERROR-SEARCHING FOR SYMBOL OR CONSTANT; NONE FOUND'
SX-4   'SYNTAX ERROR-SEARCHING FOR STATEMENT NUMBER,NONE FOUND'
SX-5   'SYNTAX ERROR-SEARCHING FOR SIMPLE INTEGER VARIABLE,NONE FOUND'
SX-C   'ILLEGAL SEQUENCE OF OPERATORS IN EXPRESSION'
SX-D   'MISSING OPERAND OR OPERATOR'

'I/O OPERATIONS'
UN-0   'CONTROL CARD ENCOUNTERED ON UNIT 5 DURING EXECUTION'
               PROBABLE CAUSE - MISSING DATA OR IMPROPER FORMAT STATEMENTS
UN-1   'END OF FILE ENCOUNTERED'
UN-2   'I/O ERROR'
UN-3   'DATA SET REFERENCED FOR WHICH NO DD CARD SUPPLIED'
UN-4   'REWIND, ENDFILE, BACKSPACE REFERENCES UNIT 5, 6, 7'
UN-5   'ATTEMPT TO READ ON UNIT 5 AFTER IT HAS HAD END-OF-FILE'
UN-6   'UNIT NUMBER IS NEGATIVE, ZERO, GREATER THAN 7 OR UNDEFINED'
UN-7   'TOO MANY PAGES'
UN-8   'ATTEMPT TO DO SEQUENTIAL I/O ON A DIRECT ACCESS FILE'
UN-9   'WRITE REFERENCES 5, OR READ REFERENCES 6 OR 7'
UN-A   'ATTEMPT TO READ MORE DATA THAN CONTAINED IN LOGICAL RECORD'
UN-B   'TOO MANY PHYSICAL RECORDS IN A LOGICAL RECORD.INCREASE RECORD LENGTH.'
UN-C   'I/O ERROR ON WATLIB'
UN-D   'RECFM OTHER THAN V IS SPECIFIED FOR I/O WITHOUT FORMAT CONTROL'

'UNDEFINED VARIABLES'
UV-0   'UNDEFINED VARIABLE - SIMPLE VARIABLE'
UV-1   'UNDEFINED VARIABLE - EQUIVALENCED, COMMONED, OR DUMMY PARAMETER'
UV-2   'UNDEFINED VARIABLE - ARRAY MEMBER'
UV-3   'UNDEFINED VARIABLE - ARRAY NAME WHICH WAS USED AS A DUMMY PARAMETER'
UV-4   'UNDEFINED VARIABLE - SUBPROGRAM NAME USED AS DUMMY PARAMETER'
UV-5   'UNDEFINED VARIABLE - ARGUMENT OF THE LIBRARY SUBPROGRAM NAMED'
UV-6   'VARIABLE FORMAT CONTAINS UNDEFINED CHARACTER(S)'

'VARIABLE NAMES'
VA-0   'ATTEMPT TO REDEFINE TYPE OF A VARIABLE NAME'
VA-1   'SUBROUTINE NAME OR COMMON BLOCK NAME USED INCORRECTLY'
VA-2   'NAME LONGER THAN SIX CHARACTERS; TRUNCATED TO SIX'
VA-3   'ATTEMPT TO REDEFINE THE MODE OF A VARIABLE NAME'
VA-4   'ATTEMPT TO REDEFINE THE TYPE OF A VARIABLE NAME'
VA-6   'ILLEGAL USE OF A SUBROUTINE NAME'
VA-8   'ATTEMPT TO USE A PREVIOUSLY DEFINED NAME AS FUNCTION OR ARRAY'
VA-9   'ATTEMPT TO USE A PREVIOUSLY DEFINED NAME AS A STATEMENT FUNCTION'
VA-A   'ATTEMPT TO USE A PREVIOUSLY DEFINED NAME AS A SUBPROGRAM NAME'
VA-B   'NAME USED AS A COMMON BLOCK PREVIOUSLY USED AS A SUBPROGRAM NAME'
VA-C   'NAME USED AS SUBPROGRAM PREVIOUSLY USED AS A COMMON BLOCK NAME'
VA-D   'ILLEGAL DO-PARAMETER,ASSIGNED OR INITIALIZED VARIABLE IN SPECIFICATION'
VA-E   'ATTEMPT TO DIMENSION A CALL-BY-NAME PARAMETER'

'EXTERNAL STATEMENT'
XT-0   'INVALID ELEMENT IN EXTERNAL LIST'
XT-1   'INVALID DELIMITER IN EXTERNAL STATEMENT'
XT-2   'SUBPROGRAM PREVIOUSLY EXTERNALLED'

'ASSEMBLER LANGUAGE SUBPROGRAMS'
AL-0   'MISSING END CARD ON ASSEMBLY LANGUAGE OBJECT DECK'
AL-1   'ENTRY-POINT OR CSECT NAME IN AN OBJECT DECK WAS PREVIOUSLY
         DEFINED.FIRST DEFINITION USED'

'BLOCK DATA STATEMENTS'
BD-0   'EXECUTABLE STATEMENTS ARE ILLEGAL IN BLOCK DATA SUBPROGRAMS'
BD-1   'IMPROPER BLOCK DATA STATEMENT'

'CARD FORMAT AND CONTENTS'
CC-0   'COLUMNS 1-5 OF CONTINUATION CARD ARE NOT BLANK.
         PROBABLE CAUSE:STATEMENT PUNCHED TO LEFT OF COLUMN 7'
CC-1   'LIMIT OF 5 CONTINUATION CARDS EXCEEDED'
CC-2   'INVALID CHARACTER IN FORTRAN STATEMENT.
         A '$' WAS INSERTED IN THE SOURCE LISTING'
CC-3   'FIRST CARD OF A PROGRAM IS A CONTINUATION CARD.
         PROBABLE CAUSE:STATEMENT PUNCHED TO LEFT OF COLUMN 7'
CC-4   'STATEMENT TOO LONG TO COMPILE (SCAN-STACK OVERFLOW)'
CC-5   'A BLANK CARD WAS ENCOUNTERED'
CC-6   'KEYPUNCH USED DIFFERS FROM KEYPUNCH SPECIFIED ON JOB CARD'
CC-7   'THE FIRST CHARACTER OF THE STATEMENT WAS NOT ALPHABETIC'
CC-8   'INVALID CHARACTER(S) ARE CONCATENATED WITH THE FORTRAN KEYWORD'
CC-9   'INVALID CHARACTERS IN COLUMNS 1-5.STATEMENT NUMBER IGNORED.
         PROBABLE CAUSE:STATEMENT PUNCHED TO LEFT OF COLUMN 7'

'COMMON'
CM-0   'THE VARIABLE IS ALREADY IN COMMON'
CM-1   'OTHER COMPILERS MAY NOT ALLOW COMMONED VARIABLES TO BE INITIALIZED IN
         OTHER THAN A BLOCK DATA SUBPROGRAM'
CM-2   'ILLEGAL USE OF A COMMON BLOCK OR NAMELIST NAME'

'FORTRAN TYPE CONSTANTS'
CN-0   'MIXED REAL*4,REAL*8 IN COMPLEX CONSTANT;REAL*8 ASSUMED FOR BOTH'
CN-1   'AN INTEGER CONSTANT MAY NOT BE GREATER THAN 2,147,483,647 (2**31-1)'
CN-2   'EXPONENT ON A REAL CONSTANT IS GREATER THAN 2 DIGITS'
CN-3   'A REAL CONSTANT HAS MORE THAN 16 DIGITS.IT WAS TRUNCATED TO 16'
CN-4   'INVALID HEXADECIMAL CONSTANT'
CN-5   'ILLEGAL USE OF A DECIMAL POINT'
CN-6   'CONSTANT WITH MORE THAN 7 DIGITS BUT E-TYPE EXPONENT,ASSUMED TO
         REAL*4'
CN-7   'CONSTANT OR STATEMENT NUMBER GREATER THAN 99999'
CN-8   'AN EXPONENT OVERFLOW OR UNDERFLOW OCCURRED WHILE CONVERTING A CONSTANT
         IN A SOURCE STATEMENT'

'COMPILER ERRORS'
CP-0   'COMPILER ERROR - LANDR/ARITH'
CP-1   'COMPILER ERROR.LIKELY CAUSE:MORE THAN 255 DO STATEMENTS'
CP-4   'COMPILER ERROR - INTERRUPT AT COMPILE TIME,RETURN TO SYSTEM'

'CHARACTER VARIABLE'
CV-0   'A CHARACTER VARIABLE IS USED WITH A RELATIONAL OPERATOR'
CV-1   'LENGTH OF A CHARACTER VALUE ON RIGHT OF EQUAL SIGN EXCEEDS THAT ON
         LEFT. TRUNCATION WILL OCCUR'
CV-2   'UNFORMATTED CORE-TO-CORE I/O NOT IMPLEMENTED'

'DATA STATEMENT'
DA-0   'REPLICATION FACTOR IS ZERO OR GREATER THAN 32767.
         IT IS ASSUMED TO BE 32767'
DA-1   'MORE VARIABLES THAN CONSTANTS'
DA-2   'ATTEMPT TO INITIALIZE A SUBPROGRAM PARAMETER IN A DATA STATEMENT'
DA-3   'OTHER COMPILERS MAY NOT ALLOW NON-CONSTANT SUBSCRIPTS IN DATA
         STATEMENTS'

DA-4   'TYPE OF VARIABLE AND CONSTANT DO NOT AGREE. (MESSAGE ISSUED ONCE FOR
        AN ARRAY)'
DA-5   'MORE CONSTANTS THAN VARIABLES'
DA-6   'A VARIABLE WAS PREVIOUSLY INITIALIZED.THE LATEST VALUE IS USED.
        CHECK COMMONED AND EQUIVALENCED VARIABLES'
DA-7   'OTHER COMPILERS MAY NOT ALLOW INITIALIZATION OF BLANK COMMON'
DA-8   'A LITERAL CONSTANT HAS BEEN TRUNCATED'
DA-9   'OTHER COMPILERS MAY NOT ALLOW IMPLIED DO-LOOPS IN DATA STATEMENTS'

'DEFINE FILE STATEMENTS'
DF-0   'THE UNIT NUMBER IS MISSING'
DF-1   'INVALID FORMAT TYPE'
DF-2   'THE ASSOCIATED VARIABLE IS NOT A SIMPLE INTEGER VARIABLE'
DF-3   'NUMBER OF RECORDS OR RECORD SIZE IS ZERO OR GREATER THAN 32767'

'DIMENSION STATEMENTS'
DM-0   'NO DIMENSIONS ARE SPECIFIED FOR A VARIABLE IN A DIMENSION STATEMENT'
DM-1   'THE VARIABLE HAS ALREADY BEEN DIMENSIONED'
DM-2   'CALL-BY-LOCATION PARAMETERS MAY NOT BE DIMENSIONED'
DM-3   'THE DECLARED SIZE OF ARRAY EXCEEDS SPACE PROVIDED BY CALLING ARGUMENT'

'DO LOOPS'
DO-0   'THIS STATEMENT CANNOT BE THE OBJECT OF A DO-LOOP'
DO-1   'ILLEGAL TRANSFER INTO THE RANGE OF A DO-LOOP'
DO-2   'THE OBJECT OF THIS DO-LOOP HAS ALREADY APPEARED'
DO-3   'IMPROPERLY NESTED DO-LOOPS'
DO-4   'ATTEMPT TO REDEFINE A DO-LOOP PARAMETER WITHIN THE RANGE OF THE LOOP'
DO-5   'INVALID DO-LOOP PARAMETER'
DO-6   'ILLEGAL TRANSFER TO A STATEMENT WHICH IS INSIDE THE RANGE OF A DO-LOOP'
DO-7   'A DO-LOOP PARAMETER IS UNDEFINED OR OUT OF RANGE'
DO-8   'BECAUSE OF ONE OF THE PARAMETERS,THIS DO-LOOP WILL TERMINATE AFTER THE
        FIRST TIME THROUGH'
DO-9   'A DO-LOOP PARAMETER MAY NOT BE REDEFINED IN AN INPUT LIST'
DO-A   'OTHER COMPILERS MAY NOT ALLOW THIS STATEMENT TO END A DO-LOOP'

'EQUIVALENCE AND/OR COMMON'
EC-0   'EQUIVALENCED VARIABLE APPEARS IN A COMMON STATEMENT'
EC-1   'A COMMON BLOCK HAS A DIFFERENT LENGTH THAN IN A PREVIOUS
        SUBPROGRAM:GREATER LENGTH USED'
EC-2   'COMMON AND/OR EQUIVALENCE CAUSES INVALID ALIGNMENT.
        EXECUTION SLOWED.REMEDY:ORDER VARIABLES BY DECREASING LENGTH'
EC-3   'EQUIVALENCE EXTENDS COMMON DOWNWARDS'
EC-4   'A SUBPROGRAM PARAMETER APPEARS IN A COMMON OR EQUIVALENCE STATEMENT'
EC-5   'A VARIABLE WAS USED WITH SUBSCRIPTS IN AN EQUIVALENCE STATEMENT BUT HAS
        NOT BEEN PROPERLY DIMENSIONED'

'END STATEMENTS'
EN-0   'MISSING END STATEMENT:END STATEMENT GENERATED'
EN-1   'AN END STATEMENT WAS USED TO TERMINATE EXECUTION'
EN-2   'AN END STATEMENT CANNOT HAVE A STATEMENT NUMBER. STATEMENT NUMBER
        IGNORED'
EN-3   'END STATEMENT NOT PRECEDED BY A TRANSFER'

'EQUAL SIGNS'
EQ-0   'ILLEGAL QUANTITY ON LEFT OF EQUALS SIGN'
EQ-1   'ILLEGAL USE OF EQUAL SIGN'
EQ-2   'OTHER COMPILERS MAY NOT ALLOW MULTIPLE ASSIGNMENT STATEMENTS'
EQ-3   'MULTIPLE ASSIGNMENT IS NOT IMPLEMENTED FOR CHARACTER VARIABLES'

'EQUIVALENCE STATEMENTS'
EV-0   'ATTEMPT TO EQUIVALENCE A VARIABLE TO ITSELF'
EV-2   'A MULTI-SUBSCRIPTED EQUIVALENCED VARIABLE HAS BEEN INCORRECTLY
        RE-EQUIVALENCED.REMEDY:DIMENSION THE VARIABLE FIRST'

```
'POWERS AND EXPONENTIATION'
EX-0    'ILLEGAL COMPLEX EXPONENTIATION'
EX-1    'I**J WHERE I=J=0'
EX-2    'I**J WHERE I=0, J.LT.0'
EX-3    '0.0**Y WHERE Y.LE.0.0'
EX-4    '0.0**J WHERE J=0'
EX-5    '0.0**J WHERE J.LT.0'
EX-6    'X**Y WHERE X.LT.0.0, Y.NE.0.0'

'ENTRY STATEMENT'
EY-0    'ENTRY-POINT NAME WAS PREVIOUSLY DEFINED'
EY-1    'PREVIOUS DEFINITION OF FUNCTION NAME IN AN ENTRY IS INCORRECT'
EY-2    'THE USAGE OF A SUBPROGRAM PARAMETER IS INCONSISTENT WITH A PREVIOUS
         ENTRY-POINT'
EY-3    'A PARAMETER HAS APPEARED IN A EXECUTABLE STATEMENT BUT IS NOT A
         SUBPROGRAM PARAMETER'
EY-4    'ENTRY STATEMENTS ARE INVALID IN THE MAIN PROGRAM'
EY-5    'ENTRY STATEMENT INVALID INSIDE A DO-LOOP'

'FORMAT'
   SOME FORMAT ERROR MESSAGES GIVE CHARACTERS IN WHICH ERROR WAS DETECTED
FM-0    'IMPROPER CHARACTER SEQUENCE OR INVALID CHARACTER IN INPUT DATA'
FM-1    'NO STATEMENT NUMBER ON A FORMAT STATEMENT'
FM-2    'FORMAT CODE AND DATA TYPE DO NOT MATCH'
FM-4    'FORMAT PROVIDES NO CONVERSION SPECIFICATION FOR A VALUE IN I/O LIST'
FM-5    'AN INTEGER IN THE INPUT DATA IS TOO LARGE.
         (MAXIMUM=2,147,483,647=2**31-1)'
FM-6    'A REAL NUMBER IN THE INPUT DATA IS OUT OF MACHINE RANGE (1.E-78,1.E+75)'
FM-7    'UNREFERENCED FORMAT STATEMENT'
FT-0    'FIRST CHARACTER OF VARIABLE FORMAT IS NOT A LEFT PARENTHESIS'
FT-1    'INVALID CHARACTER ENCOUNTERED IN FORMAT'
FT-2    'INVALID FORM FOLLOWING A FORMAT CODE'
FT-3    'INVALID FIELD OR GROUP COUNT'
FT-4    'A FIELD OR GROUP COUNT GREATER THAN 255'
FT-5    'NO CLOSING PARENTHESIS ON VARIABLE FORMAT'
FT-6    'NO CLOSING QUOTE IN A HOLLERITH FIELD'
FT-7    'INVALID USE OF COMMA'
FT-8    'FORMAT STATEMENT TOO LONG TO COMPILE (SCAN-STACK OVERFLOW)'
FT-9    'INVALID USE OF P FORMAT CODE'
FT-A    'INVALID USE OF PERIOD(.)'
FT-B    'MORE THAN THREE LEVELS OF PARENTHESES'
FT-C    'INVALID CHARACTER BEFORE A RIGHT PARENTHESIS'
FT-D    'MISSING OR ZERO LENGTH HOLLERITH ENCOUNTERED'
FT-E    'NO CLOSING RIGHT PARENTHESIS'
FT-F    'CHARACTERS FOLLOW CLOSING RIGHT PARENTHESIS'
FT-G    'WRONG QUOTE USED FOR KEY-PUNCH SPECIFIED'
FT-H    'LENGTH OF HOLLERITH FIELD EXCEEDS 255'

'FUNCTIONS AND SUBROUTINES'
FN-1    'A PARAMETER APPEARS MORE THAN ONCE IN A SUBPROGRAM OR STATEMENT
         FUNCTION DEFINITION'
FN-2    'SUBSCRIPTS ON RIGHT-HAND SIDE OF STATEMENT FUNCTION.
         PROBABLE CAUSE:VARIABLE TO LEFT OF EQUAL SIGN NOT DIMENSIONED'
FN-3    'MULTIPLE RETURNS ARE INVALID IN FUNCTION SUBPROGRAMS'
FN-4    'ILLEGAL LENGTH MODIFIER'
FN-5    'INVALID PARAMETER'
FN-6    'A PARAMETER HAS THE SAME NAME AS THE SUBPROGRAM'

'GO TO STATEMENTS'
GO-0    'THIS STATEMENT COULD TRANSFER TO ITSELF'
GO-1    'THIS STATEMENT TRANSFERS TO A NON-EXECUTABLE STATEMENT'
GO-2    'ATTEMPT TO DEFINE ASSIGNED GOTO INDEX IN AN ARITHMETIC STATEMENT'
```

```
GO-3     'ASSIGNED GOTO INDEX MAY BE USED ONLY IN ASSIGNED GOTO AND ASSIGN
          STATEMENTS'
GO-4     'THE INDEX OF AN ASSIGNED GOTO IS UNDEFINED OR OUT OF RANGE,OR INDEX OF
          COMPUTED GOTO IS UNDEFINED'
GO-5     'ASSIGNED GOTO INDEX MAY NOT BE AN INTEGER*2 VARIABLE'

'HOLLERITH CONSTANTS'
HO-0     'ZERO LENGTH SPECIFIED FOR H-TYPE HOLLERITH'
HO-1     'ZERO LENGTH QUOTE-TYPE HOLLERITH'
HO-2     'NO CLOSING QUOTE OR NEXT CARD NOT A CONTINUATION CARD'
HO-3     'UNEXPECTED HOLLERITH OR STATEMENT NUMBER CONSTANT'

'IF STATEMENTS (ARITHMETIC AND LOGICAL)'
IF-0     'AN INVALID STATEMENT FOLLOWS THE LOGICAL IF'
IF-1     'ARITHMETIC OR INVALID EXPRESSION IN LOGICAL IF'
IF-2     'LOGICAL, COMPLEX OR INVALID EXPRESSION IN ARITHMETIC IF'

'IMPLICIT STATEMENT'
IM-0     'INVALID DATA TYPE'
IM-1     'INVALID OPTIONAL LENGTH'
IM-3     'IMPROPER ALPHABETIC SEQUENCE IN CHARACTER RANGE'
IM-4     'A SPECIFICATION IS NOT A SINGLE CHARACTER.THE FIRST CHARACTER IS USED'
IM-5     'IMPLICIT STATEMENT DOES NOT PRECEDE OTHER SPECIFICATION STATEMENTS'
IM-6     'ATTEMPT TO DECLARE THE TYPE OF A CHARACTER MORE THAN ONCE'
IM-7     'ONLY ONE IMPLICIT STATEMENT PER PROGRAM SEGMENT ALLOWED. THIS ONE
          IGNORED'

'INPUT/OUTPUT'
IO-0     'I/O STATEMENT REFERENCES A STATEMENT WHICH IS NOT A FORMAT STATEMENT'
IO-1     'A VARIABLE FORMAT MUST BE AN ARRAY NAME'
IO-2     'INVALID ELEMENT IN INPUT LIST OR DATA LIST'
IO-3     'OTHER COMPILERS MAY NOT ALLOW EXPRESSIONS IN OUTPUT LISTS'
IO-4     'ILLEGAL USE OF END= OR ERR= PARAMETERS'
IO-5     'INVALID UNIT NUMBER'
IO-6     'INVALID FORMAT'
IO-7     'ONLY CONSTANTS,SIMPLE INTEGER*4 VARIABLES,AND CHARACTER VARIABLES ARE
          ALLOWED AS UNIT'
IO-8     'ATTEMPT TO PERFORM I/O IN A FUNCTION WHICH IS CALLED IN AN OUTPUT
          STATEMENT'
IO-9     'UNFORMATTED WRITE STATEMENT MUST HAVE A LIST'

'JOB CONTROL CARDS'
JB-0     'CONTROL CARD ENCOUNTERED DURING COMPILATION;
          PROBABLE CAUSE:MISSING $ENTRY CARD'
JB-1     'MIS-PUNCHED JOB OPTION'

'JOB TERMINATION'
KO-0     'SOURCE ERROR ENCOUNTERED WHILE EXECUTING WITH RUN=FREE'
KO-1     'LIMIT EXCEEDED FOR FIXED-POINT DIVISION BY ZERO'
KO-2     'LIMIT EXCEEDED FOR FLOATING-POINT DIVISION BY ZERO'
KO-3     'EXPONENT OVERFLOW LIMIT EXCEEDED'
KO-4     'EXPONENT UNDERFLOW LIMIT EXCEEDED'
KO-5     'FIXED-POINT OVERFLOW LIMIT EXCEEDED'
KO-6     'JOB-TIME EXCEEDED'
KO-7     'COMPILER ERROR - EXECUTION TIME:RETURN TO SYSTEM'
KO-8     'TRACEBACK ERROR. TRACEBACK TERMINATED'
KO-9     'CANNOT OPEN WATFIV ERRTEXTS. RUN TERMINATED'
KO-A     'I/O ERROR ON TEXT FILE'

'LOGICAL OPERATIONS'
LG-0     '.NOT. WAS USED AS A BINARY OPERATOR'
```

'LIBRARY ROUTINES'
LI-0   'ARGUMENT OUT OF RANGE DGAMMA OR GAMMA. (1.382E-76 .LT. X .LT. 57.57)'
LI-1   'ABSOLUTE VALUE OF ARGUMENT .GT. 174.673, SINH,COSH,DSINH,DCOSH'
LI-2   'SENSE LIGHT OTHER THAN 0,1,2,3,4 FOR SLITE OR 1,2,3,4 FOR SLITET'
LI-3   'REAL PORTION OF ARGUMENT .GT. 174.673, CEXP OR CDEXP'
LI-4   'ABS(AIMAG(Z)) .GT. 174.673 FOR CSIN, CCOS, CDSIN OR CDCOS OF Z'
LI-5   'ABS(REAL(Z)) .GE. 3.537E15 FOR CSIN, CCOS, CDSIN OR CDCOS OF Z'
LI-6   'ABS(AIMAG(Z)) .GE. 3.537E15 FOR CEXP OR CDEXP OF Z'
LI-7   'ARGUMENT .GT. 174.673, EXP OR DEXP'
LI-8   'ARGUMENT IS ZERO, CLOG, CLOG10, CDLOG OR CDLG10'
LI-9   'ARGUMENT IS NEGATIVE OR ZERO, ALOG, ALOG10, DLOG OR DLOG10'
LI-A   'ABS(X) .GE. 3.537E15 FOR SIN, COS, DSIN OR DCOS OF X'
LI-B   'ABSOLUTE VALUE OF ARGUMENT .GT. 1, FOR ARSIN, ARCOS, DARSIN OR DARCOS'
LI-C   'ARGUMENT IS NEGATIVE, SQRT OR DSQRT'
LI-D   'BOTH ARGUMENTS OF DATAN2 OR ATAN2 ARE ZERO'
LI-E   'ARGUMENT TOO CLOSE TO A SINGULARITY, TAN, COTAN, DTAN OR DCOTAN'
LI-F   'ARGUMENT OUT OF RANGE DLGAMA OR ALGAMA. (0.0 .LT. X .LT. 4.29E73)'
LI-G   'ABSOLUTE VALUE OF ARGUMENT .GE. 3.537E15, TAN, COTAN, DTAN, DCOTAN'
LI-H   'LESS THAN TWO ARGUMENTS FOR ONE OF MIN0,MIN1,AMIN0,ETC.'

'MIXED MODE'
MD-0   'RELATIONAL OPERATOR HAS LOGICAL OPERAND'
MD-1   'RELATIONAL OPERATOR HAS COMPLEX OPERAND'
MD-2   'MIXED MODE - LOGICAL OR CHARACTER WITH ARITHMETIC'
MD-3   'OTHER COMPILERS MAY NOT ALLOW SUBSCRIPTS OF TYPE COMPLEX,LOGICAL OR
        CHARACTER'

'MEMORY OVERFLOW'
MO-0   'INSUFFICIENT MEMORY TO COMPILE THIS PROGRAM.REMAINDER WILL BE ERROR
        CHECKED ONLY'
MO-1   'INSUFFICIENT MEMORY TO ASSIGN ARRAY STORAGE. JOB ABANDONED'
MO-2   'SYMBOL TABLE EXCEEDS AVAILABLE SPACE,JOB ABANDONED'
MO-3   'DATA AREA OF SUBPROGRAM EXCEEDS 24K -- SEGMENT SUBPROGRAM'
MO-4   'INSUFFICIENT MEMORY TO ALLOCATE COMPILER WORK AREA OR WATLIB BUFFER'

'NAMELIST STATEMENTS'
NL-0   'NAMELIST ENTRY MUST BE A VARIABLE,NOT A SUBPROGRAM PARAMETER'
NL-1   'NAMELIST NAME PREVIOUSLY DEFINED'
NL-2   'VARIABLE NAME TOO LONG'
NL-3   'VARIABLE NAME NOT FOUND IN NAMELIST'
NL-4   'INVALID SYNTAX IN NAMELIST INPUT'
NL-6   'VARIABLE INCORRECTLY SUBSCRIPTED'
NL-7   'SUBSCRIPT OUT OF RANGE'

'PARENTHESES'
PC-0   'UNMATCHED PARENTHESIS'
PC-1   'INVALID PARENTHESIS NESTING IN I/O LIST'

'PAUSE, STOP STATEMENTS'
PS-0   'OPERATOR MESSAGES NOT ALLOWED:SIMPLE STOP ASSUMED FOR STOP,
        CONTINUE ASSUMED FOR PAUSE'

'RETURN STATEMENT'
RE-1   'RETURN I, WHERE I IS OUT OF RANGE OR UNDEFINED'
RE-2   'MULTIPLE RETURN NOT VALID IN FUNCTION SUBPROGRAM'
RE-3   'VARIABLE IS NOT A SIMPLE INTEGER'
RE-4   'A MULTIPLE RETURN IS NOT VALID IN THE MAIN PROGRAM'

'ARITHMETIC AND LOGICAL STATEMENT FUNCTIONS'
        PROBABLE CAUSE OF SF ERRORS - VARIABLE ON LEFT OF = WAS NOT DIMENSIONED
SF-1   'A PREVIOUSLY REFERENCED STATEMENT NUMBER APPEARS ON A STATEMENT
        FUNCTION DEFINITION'
SF-2   'STATEMENT FUNCTION IS THE OBJECT OF A LOGICAL IF STATEMENT'

SF-3   'RECURSIVE STATEMENT FUNCTION DEFINITION:NAME APPEARS ON BOTH SIDES OF
        EQUAL SIGN.LIKELY CAUSE:VARIABLE NOT DIMENSIONED'
SF-4   'A STATEMENT FUNCTION DEFINITION APPEARS AFTER THE FIRST EXECUTABLE
        STATEMENT'
SF-5   'ILLEGAL USE OF A STATEMENT FUNCTION NAME'

'SUBPROGRAMS'
SR-0   'MISSING SUBPROGRAM'
SR-1   'SUBPROGRAM REDEFINES A CONSTANT,EXPRESSION,DO-PARAMETER OR ASSIGNED
        GOTO INDEX'
SR-2   'THE SUBPROGRAM WAS ASSIGNED DIFFERENT TYPES IN DIFFERENT PROGRAM
        SEGMENTS'
SR-3   'ATTEMPT TO USE A SUBPROGRAM RECURSIVELY'
SR-4   'INVALID TYPE OF ARGUMENT IN REFERENCE TO A SUBPROGRAM'
SR-5   'WRONG NUMBER OF ARGUMENTS IN A REFERENCE TO A SUBPROGRAM'
SR-6   'A SUBPROGRAM WAS PREVIOUSLY DEFINED. THE FIRST DEFINITION IS USED'
SR-7   'NO MAIN PROGRAM'
SR-8   'ILLEGAL OR MISSING SUBPROGRAM NAME'
SR-9   'LIBRARY PROGRAM WAS NOT ASSIGNED THE CORRECT TYPE'
SR-A   'METHOD FOR ENTERING SUBPROGRAM PRODUCES UNDEFINED VALUE FOR
        CALL-BY-LOCATION PARAMETER'

'SUBSCRIPTS'
SS-0   'ZERO SUBSCRIPT OR DIMENSION NOT ALLOWED'
SS-1   'ARRAY SUBSCRIPT EXCEEDS DIMENSION'
SS-2   'INVALID SUBSCRIPT FORM'
SS-3   'SUBSCRIPT IS OUT OF RANGE'

'STATEMENTS AND STATEMENT NUMBERS'
ST-0   'MISSING STATEMENT NUMBER'
ST-1   'STATEMENT NUMBER GREATER THAN 99999'
ST-2   'STATEMENT NUMBER HAS ALREADY BEEN DEFINED'
ST-3   'UNDECODABLE STATEMENT'
ST-4   'UNNUMBERED EXECUTABLE STATEMENT FOLLOWS A TRANSFER'
ST-5   'STATEMENT NUMBER IN A TRANSFER IS A NON-EXECUTABLE STATEMENT'
ST-6   'ONLY CALL STATEMENTS MAY CONTAIN STATEMENT NUMBER ARGUMENTS'
ST-7   'STATEMENT SPECIFIED IN A TRANSFER STATEMENT IS A FORMAT STATEMENT'
ST-8   'MISSING FORMAT STATEMENT'
ST-9   'SPECIFICATION STATEMENT DOES NOT PRECEDE STATEMENT FUNCTION DEFINITIONS
        OR EXECUTABLE STATEMENTS'
ST-A   'UNREFERENCED STATEMENT FOLLOWS A TRANSFER'

'SUBSCRIPTED VARIABLES'
SV-0   'THE WRONG NUMBER OF SUBSCRIPTS WERE SPECIFIED FOR A VARIABLE'
SV-1   'AN ARRAY OR SUBPROGRAM NAME IS USED INCORRECTLY WITHOUT A LIST'
SV-2   'MORE THAN 7 DIMENSIONS ARE NOT ALLOWED'
SV-3   'DIMENSION OR SUBSCRIPT TOO LARGE (MAXIMUM 10**8-1)'
SV-4   'A VARIABLE USED WITH VARIABLE DIMENSIONS IS NOT A SUBPROGRAM PARAMETER'
SV-5   'A VARIABLE DIMENSION IS NOT ONE OF SIMPLE INTEGER VARIABLE,SUBPROGRAM
        PARAMETER,IN COMMON'

'SYNTAX ERRORS'
SX-0   'MISSING OPERATOR'
SX-1   'EXPECTING OPERATOR'
SX-2   'EXPECTING SYMBOL'
SX-3   'EXPECTING SYMBOL OR OPERATOR'
SX-4   'EXPECTING CONSTANT'
SX-5   'EXPECTING SYMBOL OR CONSTANT'
SX-6   'EXPECTING STATEMENT NUMBER'
SX-7   'EXPECTING SIMPLE INTEGER VARIABLE'
SX-8   'EXPECTING SIMPLE INTEGER VARIABLE OR CONSTANT'
SX-9   'ILLEGAL SEQUENCE OF OPERATORS IN EXPRESSION'
SX-A   'EXPECTING END-OF-STATEMENT'

'TYPE STATEMENTS'
TY-0   'THE VARIABLE HAS ALREADY BEEN EXPLICITLY TYPED'
TY-1   'THE LENGTH OF THE EQUIVALENCED VARIABLE MAY NOT BE CHANGED.
        REMEDY: INTERCHANGE TYPE AND EQUIVALENCE STATEMENTS'

'I/O OPERATIONS'
UN-0   'CONTROL CARD ENCOUNTERED ON UNIT 5 AT EXECUTION.
        PROBABLE CAUSE:MISSING DATA OR INCORRECT FORMAT'
UN-1   'END OF FILE ENCOUNTERED (IBM CODE IHC217)'
UN-2   'I/O ERROR (IBM CODE IHC218)'
UN-3   'NO DD STATEMENT WAS SUPPLIED (IBM CODE IHC219)'
UN-4   'REWIND,ENDFILE,BACKSPACE REFERENCES UNIT 5, 6 OR 7'
UN-5   'ATTEMPT TO READ ON UNIT 5 AFTER IT HAS HAD END-OF-FILE'
UN-6   'AN INVALID VARIABLE UNIT NUMBER WAS DETECTED (IBM CODE IHC220)'
UN-7   'PAGE-LIMIT EXCEEDED'
UN-8   'ATTEMPT TO DO DIRECT ACCESS I/O ON A SEQUENTIAL FILE OR VICE VERSA.
        POSSIBLE MISSING DEFINE FILE STATEMENT (IBM CODE IHC231)'
UN-9   'WRITE REFERENCES 5 OR READ REFERENCES 6 OR 7'
UN-A   'DEFINE FILE REFERENCES A UNIT PREVIOUSLY USED FOR SEQUENTIAL I/O (IBM
        CODE IHC235)'
UN-B   'RECORD SIZE FOR UNIT EXCEEDS 32767,OR DIFFERS FROM DD STATEMENT
        SPECIFICATION (IBM CODES IHC233,IHC237)'
UN-C   'FOR DIRECT ACCESS I/O THE RELATIVE RECORD POSITION IS NEGATIVE,ZERO,OR
        TOO LARGE (IBM CODE IHC232)'
UN-D   'AN ATTEMPT WAS MADE TO READ MORE INFORMATION THAN LOGICAL RECORD
        CONTAINS (IBM CODE IHC236)'
UN-E   'FORMATTED LINE EXCEEDS BUFFER LENGTH (IBM CODE IHC212)'
UN-F   'I/O ERROR - SEARCHING LIBRARY DIRECTORY'
UN-G   'I/O ERROR - READING LIBRARY'
UN-H   'ATTEMPT TO DEFINE THE OBJECT ERROR FILE AS A DIRECT ACCESS FILE
        (IBM CODE IHC234)'
UN-I   'RECFM IS NOT V(B)S FOR I/O WITHOUT FORMAT CONTROL " (IBM CODE IHC214)'
UN-J   'MISSING DD CARD FOR WATLIB.NO LIBRARY ASSUMED'
UN-K   'ATTEMPT TO READ OR WRITE PAST THE END OF CHARACTER VARIABLE BUFFER'
UN-L   'ATTEMPT TO READ ON AN UNCREATED DIRECT ACCESS FILE (IHC236)'

'UNDEFINED VARIABLES'
UV-0   'VARIABLE IS UNDEFINED'
UV-3   'SUBSCRIPT IS UNDEFINED'
UV-4   'SUBPROGRAM IS UNDEFINED'
UV-5   'ARGUMENT IS UNDEFINED'
UV-6   'UNDECODABLE CHARACTERS IN VARIABLE FORMAT'

'VARIABLE NAMES'
VA-0   'A NAME IS TOO LONG.IT HAS BEEN TRUNCATED TO SIX CHARACTERS'
VA-1   'ATTEMPT TO USE AN ASSIGNED OR INITIALIZED VARIABLE OR DO-PARAMETER IN A
        SPECIFICATION STATEMENT'
VA-2   'ILLEGAL USE OF A SUBROUTINE NAME'
VA-3   'ILLEGAL USE OF A VARIABLE NAME'
VA-4   'ATTEMPT TO USE THE PREVIOUSLY DEFINED NAME AS A FUNCTION OR AN ARRAY'
VA-5   'ATTEMPT TO USE A PREVIOUSLY DEFINED NAME AS A SUBROUTINE'
VA-6   'ATTEMPT TO USE A PREVIOUSLY DEFINED NAME AS A SUBPROGRAM'
VA-7   'ATTEMPT TO USE A PREVIOUSLY DEFINED NAME AS A COMMON BLOCK'
VA-8   'ATTEMPT TO USE A FUNCTION NAME AS A VARIABLE'
VA-9   'ATTEMPT TO USE A PREVIOUSLY DEFINED NAME AS A VARIABLE'
VA-A   'ILLEGAL USE OF A PREVIOUSLY DEFINED NAME'

'EXTERNAL STATEMENT'
XT-0   'A VARIABLE HAS ALREADY APPEARED IN AN EXTERNAL STATEMENT'

ANSWERS TO SELECTED EXERCISES

There are several acceptable answers to many of the exercises. The one shown here is sometimes "better" than other possibilities, but only occasionally is the criterion of "goodness" unambiguous. In other cases there are several equally "good" answers; for instance, it makes no difference whether one writes $A = B + C$ or $A = C + B$. In short, the answers given here are correct but not ordinarily *uniquely* correct. If another answer can be shown to be equivalent, it must be accepted unless other criteria have been stated.

CHAPTER 1

Section 1.4 (page 6)

1 256.   2.56 $-43000.$ $1.0E+12$ $4.92E-7$ -10.0
$-1.E-16$

3 87, 654.3 (comma not permitted); $+987$ (no decimal point); $9.2E+98$ (too large in most versions); $7E-9.3$ (decimal point not permitted in exponent).

5 Yes.

6 $-234.$ (decimal point not permitted); 23,400 (comma not permitted); 1E12 (E not permitted); 100000000000 (too large in most versions).

Section 1.5 (page 7)

1 Integer: I, IJK, LARGE, KAPPA, IBM360. Real: G, GAMMA, BTO7TH, ZCUBED, B6700, DELTA, EPSILN, A1P4, AONEP4, ALGOL, SNOBOL. Unacceptable: GAMMA421 (too many characters); J79-1 ($-$ not permitted); R(2)19 (parentheses not permitted); ZSQUARED (too many characters); 12AT7 (does not begin with a letter); 2N173 (does not begin with a letter); CDC6600 (too many characters); S/360 (/ not allowed); EPSILON (too many characters); A1.4 (decimal point not permitted); A1POINT4 (too many characters); FORTRAN (too many characters); PL/1 (/ not allowed).

Section 1.6 (pages 10–11)

1 a. X + Y**3
   d. A + B/C
   f. A + B/(C + D)
   h. ((A + B)/(C + D))**2 + X**2
   j. 1.0 + X + X**2/2.0 + X**3/6.0
   k. (X/Y)**(G − 1.0)
2 b. (X + 2.0)/(Y + 4.0). Constants may be written in any other
      equivalent form, such as (X + 2.)/(Y + 4.).
   e. ((X + A + 3.14)/(2.0*Z))**2
   g. (X/Y)**(R − 1.0)
   j. A + X*(B + X*(C + D*X))

Section 1.8 (pages 13–15)

1 a. 13.0, real.
   b. zero, real.
   e. 4, integer.
   f. 4.0, real
   k. 1.3333332, real.
   n. 8.0, real (might be 7.9999999 or 8.0000001).
   o. 5, integer.
3 a. DELTA = BETA + 2.0
   c. C = SQRT (A**2 + B**2) or
      C = SQRT (A*A + B*B)
   d. R = 1.414214
   g. Y = COS(2.0*X)*SQRT(X/2.0)
   h. G = G + 2.0
4 a. AREA = 2.0*P*R*SIN(3.141593/P)
   c. ARC = 2.0*SQRT(Y**2 + 1.333333*X**2)
   e. S = −COS(X)**(P + 1.0)/(P + 1.0)
   f. G = 0.5*ALOG((1.0 + SIN(X))/(1.0 − SIN(X)))
      Preferably written as two statements to avoid computing the sine
      twice:
      S = SIN(X)
      G = 0.5*ALOG((1.0 + S)/(1.0 − S))
   i. E = X*ATAN(X/A) − (A/2.0)*ALOG(A**2 + X**2)
   l. Q = (2./(3.141593*X))**0.5*SIN(X)
      Since $(2/\pi)^{1/2}(1/X)^{1/2} = \sqrt{2/\pi} / \sqrt{X} = 0.7978846/\sqrt{X}$, this can be
      written more compactly and thus requires less time in the object
      program:
      Q = 0.7978846/SQRT(X)*SIN(X)
   n. Y = 2.506628*X**(X + 1.0)*EXP(−X)
7 S = (A + B + C) / 2.0
   AREA = SQRT(S*(S − A)*(S − B)*(S − C))
8 PN = (XLMBDA/XMU)**N * (1.0 − XLMBDA/XMU)

Section 1.9 (pages 18–19)

1
```
      READ (5, 10) A, B, C
   10 FORMAT (8F10.0)
      F = (1.0 + A) / (1.0 + B/(C + 6.0))
      WRITE (6, 20) A, B, C, F
   20 FORMAT (1P8E15.6)
```

```
4       READ (5, 10) A, B, C
  10    FORMAT (8F10.0)
        RADICL = SQRT(B**2 - 4.0*A*C)
        X1 = (-B + RADICL) / (2.0 * A)
        X2 = (-B - RADICL) / (2.0 * A)
        WRITE (6, 20) A, B, C, X1, X2
  20    FORMAT (1P8E15.6)

6       READ (5, 10) A, E, H, P
  10    FORMAT (8F10.0)
        X = E * H * P / (SIN(A) * (H**4/16.0 + H**2*P**2))
        WRITE (6, 20) A, E, H, P, X
  20    FORMAT (1P8E15.6)

7       READ (5, 10) A, X, S
  10    FORMAT (8F10.0)
        Y = SQRT(X**2 - A**2)
        Z = X*S/2.0  - (A**2/2.0) * ALOG(ABS(X + S))
        WRITE (6, 20) A, X, S, Y, Z
  20    FORMAT (1P8E15.6)

9(7)    READ (5, 10) A, B, C,
  10    FORMAT (8F10.0)
        S = (A + B + C) / 2.0
        AREA = SQRT(S*(S-A)*(S-B)*(S-C))
        WRITE (6, 20) A, B, C, S, AREA
  20    FORMAT (1P8E15.6)

9(8)    READ (5, 10) XLMBDA, XMU
  10    FORMAT (8F10.0)
        PN = (XLMBDA/XMU)**N * (1.0 - XLMBDA/XMU)
        WRITE (6, 20) XLMBDA, XMU, PN
  20    FORMAT (1P8E15.6)
```

CHAPTER 2

1 a. Using arithmetic IF:

```
        IF (A - B) 10, 10, 20
  10    X = 56.9
        GO TO 30
  20    X = 16.9
  30
```

Using logical IF:

```
X = 56.9
IF (A .GT. B) X = 16.9
```

or:

```
        IF ( A .GT. B ) GO TO 100
        X = 56.9
        GO TO 110
  100   X = 16.9
  110
```

c. Using arithmetic IF:

```
IF ( RHO + THETA - 1.0E-6 ) 156, 762, 762
```

Using logical IF:

```
IF ( RHO + THETA .LT. 1.0E-6 ) GO TO 156
GO TO 762
```

d. Using arithmetic IF:
```
      IF (X-Y) 11, 11, 12
11    BIG = Y
      GO TO 13
12    BIG = X
13
```

Using logical IF:
```
BIG = X
IF ( Y .GT. X ) BIG = Y
```

g.
```
400   IF ( THETA - 6.283186 ) 402, 401, 401
401   THETA = THETA - 6.283186
      GO TO 400
402
```

h.
```
IF ( G .LT. 0.0 .AND. H .LT. 0.0 ) SIGNS = -1
IF ( G .GT. 0.0 .AND. H .GT. 0.0 ) SIGNS = +1
IF ( G*H .LT. 0.0 ) SIGNS = 0
```

j. `IF (A .LT. 0.0 .AND. B .GT. 0.0 .OR. C .EQ. 0.0)OMEGA = COS(X+1.2)`

l. `GO TO (250, 250, 251, 252, 252, 252, 251, 250), N`

n.
```
IF ( 0.999 .LE. X .AND. X .LE. 1.001 ) STOP
GO TO 639
```
```
IF ( ABS(X - 1.000) .LE. 0.001 ) STOP
GO TO 639
```

o. `IF (ABS(XREAL) .LT. 1.0 .AND. ABS(XIMAG) .LT. 1.0) SQUARE = 1`

2 a.
```
      READ (5, 20) ANNERN
20    FORMAT (F10.0)
      IF ( ANNERN .LE. 2000.00 ) TAX = 0.0
      IF ( ANNERN .GT. 2000.00 .AND. ANNERN .LE. 5000.00 )
1     TAX = 0.02 * (ANNERN - 2000.00)
      IF ( ANNERN .GT. 5000.00 ) TAX = 60.00 + 0.05 * (ANNERN - 5000.00)
      WRITE (6, 30) ANNERN, TAX
30    FORMAT (1P2E15.6)
      STOP
      END
```

c.
```
      X = 1.0
60    Y = 16.7*X + 9.2*X**2 - 1.02*X**3
      WRITE (6, 70) X, Y
70    FORMAT (1P2E15.6)
      IF ( X .GE. 9.9 ) STOP
      X = X + 0.1
      GO TO 60
      END
```

d.
```
      I = 10
60    X = I
      X = X/10.0
      Y = 16.7*X + 9.2*X**2 - 1.02*X**3
      WRITE (6, 70)
70    FORMAT (1P2E15.6)
      IF ( I .EQ. 99 ) STOP
      I = I + 1
      GO TO 60
      END
```

CHAPTER 3

1 a. (2.0, 4.0)
   d. (5.0, 16.0)
   g. 24.0
2 a. Yes
   c. Yes
   e. Yes
   f. Yes
3 a. Yes
   d. Yes
   f. No
   h. No
   j. Yes
   l. Yes
   n. Yes
   p. Yes
   s. Yes

6
```
      COMPLEX A, B, C, D, E, F, DENOM
      A = CMPLX(2.0, 3.0)
      B = CMPLX(4.0, -2.0)
      C = CMPLX(5.0, -3.0)
      D = CMPLX(4.0, 1.0)
      E = CMPLX(-2.0, 3.0)
      F = CMPLX(2.0, 13.0)
      DENOM = A*E - B*D
      X = (E*F - B*C) / DENOM
      Y = (A*F - C*D) / DENOM
      WRITE (6, 10) X, Y
   10 FORMAT (1P8E15.6)
      STOP
      END
```

8
```
      COMPLEX Z, EXPON
   10 READ (5, 20) Z
   20 FORMAT (2F10.0)
      IF ( REAL(Z) .EQ. 0.0 ) STOP
      EXPON = CEXP(Z)
      WRITE (6, 30) Z, EXPON
   30 FORMAT (1P4E15.6)
      GO TO 10
      END
```

12
```
      COMPLEX A, C, Z
   10 READ (5, 20) Z, C
   20 FORMAT (4F10.0)
      IF ( CABS(Z) .EQ. 0.0 ) STOP
      A = CEXP(C*CLOG(Z))
      TEST = EXP(3.141593/2.0)
      WRITE (6, 30) Z, C, A, TEST
   30 FORMAT (1P7E15.6)
      GO TO 10
      END
```

```
1  a. DIMENSION A(10)
      PROD = A(1) * A(2)

   b. DIMENSION A(10)
      A(3) = ( A(1) + A(3) + A(5) ) / 3.0

   c. DIMENSION A(10)
      IF ( A(10) .LT. 0.0 ) A(10) = -A(10)

      or:
      DIMENSION A(10)
      A(10) = ABS(A(10))

   d.    DIMENSION A(10)
         I = 1
     120 A(I) = ABS(A(I))
         I = I + 1
         IF ( I .LE. 10 ) GO TO 120

3  a. DIMENSION XYZ2(3, 4)
      RST = XYZ2(1,3) + XYZ2(2,3) + XYZ2(3,3)

   b. DIMENSION XYZ2(3, 4)
      XYZ2(1, 1) = XYZ2(2, 1)
      XYZ2(1, 2) = XYZ2(2, 2)
      XYZ2(1, 3) = XYZ2(2, 3)
      XYZ2(1, 4) = XYZ2(2, 4)

   c.    DIMENSION XYZ2 (3, 4)
         J = 1
      70 XYZ2(3, J) = XYZ2(1, J) + XYZ2(2, J)
         J = J +1
         IF ( J .LE. 4 ) GO TO 70

5  a. DIMENSION PUPILS (2, 12, 5)
      D1 = PUPILS (1, 5, 2) + PUPILS (2, 5, 2)

   b.    DIMENSION PUPILS (2, 12, 5)
         I = 1
         E1971 = 0.0
      10 E1971 = E1971 + PUPILS (1, I, 4) + PUPILS (2, I, 4)
         I = I + 1
         IF ( I .LE. 12 ) GO TO 10

   c. DIMENSION PUPILS (2, 12, 5)
      BIG = PUPILS (1, 12, 5)
      IF ( PUPILS(2,12,5) .GT. PUPILS(1,12,5) ) BIG = PUPILS(2,12,5)

   d.    DIMENSION PUPILS (2, 12, 5), SUM71(12)
         I = 1
      20 SUM71(I) = PUPILS (1, I, 4) + PUPILS (2, I, 4)
         I = I + 1
         IF ( I .LE. 12 ) GO TO 20

7  DIMENSION X(3)
   DIST = SQRT ( X(1)**2 + X(2)**2 + X(3)**2 )

9  DIMENSION A(2,2), B(2,2), C(2,2)
   C(1,1) = A(1,1)*B(1,1) + A(1,2)*B(2,1)
   C(1,2) = A(1,1)*B(1,2) + A(1,2)*B(2,2)
   C(2,1) = A(2,1)*B(1,1) + A(2,2)*B(2,1)
   C(2,2) = A(2,1)*B(1,2) + A(2,2)*B(2,2)
```

```
11       DIMENSION A(30), B(30)
         I = 1
         D = 0.0
   450   D = D + (A(I) - B(I))**2
         I = I +1
         IF ( I .LE. 30 ) GO TO 450
         D = SQRT(D)

12       DIMENSION X(50), DX(49)
         I = 1
    10   DX(I) = X(I+1) - X(I)
         I = I + 1
         IF ( I .LE. 49 ) GO TO 10

15   DIMENSION Y(50)
     S = Y(I) + U*(Y(I+1) - Y(I-1))/2.0
    1    + (U**2/2.0) * (Y(I+1) - 2.0*Y(I) + Y(I-1))

17       DIMENSION A(7), B(7)
    20   FORMAT (7F10.0)
         READ (5, 20) A
         READ (5, 20) B
         I = 1
         SUM = 0.0
    30   SUM = SUM + A(I)*B(I)
         I = I + 1
         IF ( I .LE. 7 ) GO TO 30
         ANORM = SQRT(SUM)
         WRITE (6, 40) ANORM
    40   FORMAT (1PE20.7)

19   Either add:
     DOUBLE PRECISION A, B

     or change to:
     DOUBLE PRECISION A(30), B(30)

21       COMPLEX COMPLX(30)
         I = 1
         SUMABS = 0.0
    80   SUMABS = SUMABS + CABS(COMPLX(I))
         I = I + 1
         IF ( I .LE. 30 ) GO TO 80

23       LOGICAL TRUTH(40)
         INTEGER TRUE, FALSE
         I = 1
         TRUE = 0
         FALSE = 0
    60   IF ( TRUTH(I) .EQ. .TRUE. ) TRUE = TRUE + 1
         IF ( TRUTH(I) .EQ. .FALSE. ) FALSE = FALSE + 1
         I = I + 1
         IF ( I .LE. 40 ) GO TO 60

26       DIMENSION U(14), V(14)
         I = 1
         SUM = 0.0
    10   SUM = SUM + (U(I) - V(I))**2
         I = I + 1
         IF ( I .LE. 14 ) GO TO 10
         DENOM = N*(N**2 - 1)
         RHO = 1.0 - 6.0 * SUM / DENOM
```

```
 1      DIMENSION A(30), B(30)
        D = 0.0
        DO 23 I = 1, 30
   23   D = D + (A(I) - B(I))**2
        D = SQRT(D)


 4      DIMENSION M(20)
        DO 92 I = 1, 20
   92   M(I) = I * M(I)


 5      DIMENSION R(40), S(40), T(40)
        DO 3 I = 1, M
    3   T(I) = R(I) + S(I)


 7      DIMENSION F(50)
        MM1 = M - 1
        DO 692 I = 2, MM1
  692   F(I) = ( F(I-1) + F(I) + F(I+1) ) / 3.0


 8      DIMENSION B(50)
        BIGB = B(1)
        NBIGB = 1
        DO 40 I = 2, 50
           IF ( BIGB .GE. B(I) ) GO TO 40
           BIGB = B(I)
           NBIGB = I
   40   CONTINUE


10      DIMENSION A(15, 15), X(15), B(15)
        DO 60 I = 1, 15
           B(I) = 0.0
           DO 50 J = 1, 15
              B(I) = B(I) + A(I, J) * X(J)
   50      CONTINUE
   60   CONTINUE


12      DIMENSION RST(20, 20)
        DPROD = RST(1, 1)
        DO 1 I = 2, 20
           DPROD = DPROD * RST(I, I)
    1   CONTINUE


13      DO 80 I = 100, 300
           X = I
           X = X/100.0
           Y = 41.298*SQRT(1.0 + X**2) + X**0.3333333 * EXP(X)
           WRITE (6, 70) X, Y
   70      FORMAT (1P2E15.6)
   80   CONTINUE


15 a.   DIMENSION A(100, 100), B(100), X(100)
        X(1) = B(1) / A(1, 1)
        DO 50 I = 2, 100
           SUM = 0.0
           ILESS1 = I - 1
           DO 40 J = 1, ILESS1
              SUM = SUM + A(I, J) * X(J)
   40      CONTINUE
           X(I) = (B(I) - SUM) / A(I, I)
   50   CONTINUE
```

b.
```
      DIMENSION A(5050), B(100), X(100)
      X(1) = B(1) / A(1)
      K = 1
      DO 150 I = 2, 100
         SUM = 0.0
         ILESS1 = I - 1
         DO 140 J = 1, ILESS1
            L = J + K
            SUM = SUM + A(L) * X(J)
  140    CONTINUE
         K = K + I
         X(I) = (B(I) - SUM) / A(K)
  150 CONTINUE
```

24
```
      REAL NFACT, XFACT, NXFACT
      INTEGER N, X
      NFACT = 1.0
      DO 10 I = 2, N
         FI = I
         NFACT = NFACT * FI
   10 CONTINUE
      XFACT = 1.0
      DO 20 I = 2, X
         FI = I
         XFACT = XFACT * FI
   20 CONTINUE
      NXFACT = 1.0
      NMX = N - X
      DO 30 I = 1, NMX
         FI = I
         NXFACT = NXFACT * FI
   30 CONTINUE
      B = NFACT / (XFACT * NXFACT) * P**X * (1.0 - P)**(N-X)
```

31 a.
```
      I = I1 - 1
    6 J = J1 - 1
    7 IF ( I .EQ. I1 .AND. J .EQ. J1 ) GO TO 9
      IF ( I .LT. 1 .OR. I .GT. 8 .OR. J .LT. 1 .OR. J .GT. 8 ) GO TO 9
      IF ( BOARD(I,J) .EQ. 0 ) WRITE (6, 8) I, J
    8 FORMAT (2I5)
    9 J = J + 1
      IF (J .LE. J1 + 1 ) GO TO 7
      I = I + 1
      IF ( I .LE. I1 + 1 ) GO TO 6
```

c.
```
      IF ( I1 .EQ. I2 ) GO TO 16
      IF ( J1 .EQ. J2 ) GO TO 17
      LEGAL = .FALSE.
      GO TO 15
   16 J = MIN0(J1, J2) + 1
      LIMIT = MAX0(J1, J2)
      IF ( J + 1 .EQ. LIMIT ) GO TO 18
   20 IF ( BOARD (I1, J) .NE. 0 ) GO TO 19
      IF ( J + 1 .EQ. LIMIT ) GO TO 18
      J = J + 1
      GO TO 20
   17 I = MIN0(I1, I2) + 1
      LIMIT = MAX0(I1, I2)
      IF ( I + 1 .EQ. LIMIT ) GO TO 18
   21 IF ( BOARD(I, J1) .NE. 0 ) GO TO 19
      IF ( I + 1 .EQ. LIMIT ) GO TO 18
      I = I + 1
      GO TO 21
   18 MOVE = .TRUE.
      GO TO 15
   19 MOVE = .FALSE.
   15
```

```
e.      INTEGER WPIECE, PIECE, VALUE(6)
        VALUE(1) = 1
        VALUE(2) = 3
        VALUE(3) = 3
        VALUE(4) = 5
        VALUE(5) = 10
        VALUE(6) = 0
        DO 60 I = 1, 8
           DO 50 J = 1, 8
              PIECE = BOARD(I, J)
              IF ( PIECE .GT. 0 ) WPIECE = WPIECE + VALUE(PIECE)
  50       CONTINUE
  60    CONTINUE
```

CHAPTER 6

2 a. M= 12X= 407.8Y= -32.8

3   READ (5, 500) BOS, EWR, PHX, DCA
  500 FORMAT (4F8.0)

6   READ (5, 600) LAX, JFK, PDX, SFO
  600 FORMAT (2I3, 2E14.7)

7 a. FORMAT (2I7, 2F8.2)

   b. FORMAT (2I7, 2F6.0)

   c. FORMAT (I6, I8, 2E13.5)

   d. FORMAT (I6, I8, 1P2E12.4)

   e. FORMAT (3H I=, I6, 4H J=, I6, 4H R=, F6.1, 4H S=, F6.1)

   f. FORMAT (3H I=, I6/3H J=, I6/3H R=, F6.1/3H S=, F6.1)

9   READ (5, 90) N, (DATA(I), I = 1, N)
  90 FORMAT (I2, 10F7.0)

11 a. One data card will be read. It should have seven numbers
       punched in it, with four columns for each number; if decimal
       points are not punched, the numbers will be taken to be integers
       and converted to real form. The first of the numbers should
       begin in column 1.
   b. One data card will be read. It should have a two-digit integer
       punched in columns 1–2, and a maximum of 10 four-digit
       numbers punched in the columns following. There should be as
       many numbers as the value of the integer in columns 1–2.
   c. Two cards will be read. The first should contain an integer in
       columns 1–2. The second should contain as many four-digit
       numbers as the value of the integer in the first card.
   d. $N + 1$ cards will be read. The first should contain an integer in
       columns 1–2. There should be as many cards following as the
       value of this integer, each containing a four-digit number in
       columns 1–4.

13   WRITE (6, 40) A, B, X, Z
  40 FORMAT (2F12.4, 2E20.8)

```
15      WRITE (6, 60) ((PHL(I,J), J = 1,4), I = 1,10)
  60    FORMAT (11H1MATRIX PHL///(1P4E20.7)

17 10   FORMAT (2I2, 1PE20.7)
        DO 14 I = 1, M
          DO 13 J = 1, N
            WRITE (7, 10) I, J, STL(I, J)
  13      CONTINUE
  14    CONTINUE

18      DIMENSION MONTH(12)
        READ (5, 90) (MONTH(I), I = 1, 12)
  90    FORMAT (12A3)
         .
         .

         .
        WRITE (6, 100) MONTH(I)
 100    FORMAT (1H , A3)

20  a. (10F10.2)

    b. (1P5E20.6)

    c. (F10.2//(1P3E20.6))

24      DIMENSION G(48, 80)
        INTEGER A
        DATA BLANK, DOT, XPRINT/1H , 1H., 1HX/
        DO 40 I = 1, 48
        DO 40 J = 1, 80
  40    G(I, J) = BLANK
        DO 50 I = 1, 48
  50    G(I, 40) = DOT
        DO 60 J = 1, 80
  60    G(24, J) = DOT
        DO 70 A = 9, 360, 9
        T = A
        T = T/(180.0/3.141593)
        X = COS(T)
        Y = SIN(T)
        I = 6.0*(Y+4.0) + 0.5
        J = 10.0*(X+4.0) + 0.5
  70    G(I, J) = XPRINT
        DO 80 K = 1, 48
          I = 49 - K
          WRITE (6, 90) (G(I, J), J = 1, 80)
  80    CONTINUE
  90    FORMAT (1H , 80A1)
        STOP
        END
```

CHAPTER 7

```
1 DENOM(X) = X**2 + SQRT(1.0 + 2.0*X + 3.0*X**2)
  ALPHA = (6.9 + Y) / DENOM(Y)
  BETA = (2.1*Z + Z**4) / DENOM(Z)
  GAMMA = SIN(Y) / DENOM(Y**2)
  DELTA = 1.0 / DENOM(SIN(Y))

3 LOGICAL EXOR, A, B, C, ANS1, ANS2
  EXOR(A, B) = A .AND. .NOT. B .OR. .NOT. A .AND. B
  ANS1 = EXOR(EXOR(A, B), C)
  ANS2 = EXOR(A, EXOR(B, C))
```

```
5        LOGICAL A(40), B(40), C(41), K, SUM, CARRY
         C(1) = SUM(A(1), B(1), .FALSE.)
         K = CARRY(A(1), B(1), .FALSE.)
         DO 20 I = 2, N
            C(I) = SUM(A(I), B(I), K)
            K = CARRY(A(I), B(I), K)
   20    CONTINUE
         C(N+1) = K

6        FUNCTION Y(X)
         IF (X) 10, 11, 12
   10    Y = 1.0 + SQRT(1.0 + X*X)
         RETURN
   11    Y = 0.0
         RETURN
   12    Y = 1.0 - SQRT(1.0 + X*X)
         RETURN
         END


         F = 2.0 + Y(A + Z)
         G = (Y(X(K)) + Y(X(K+1))) / 2.0
         H = Y(COS(6.283186*X)) + SQRT(1.0 + Y(6.283186*X))

10       FUNCTION SUMABS(A, M, N)
         DIMENSION A(M, N)
         SUMABS = 0.0
         DO 30 I = 1, M
            DO 20 J = 1, N
               SUMABS = SUMABS + ABS(A(I, J))
   20       CONTINUE
   30    CONTINUE
         RETURN
         END

12       SUBROUTINE AVERNZ(A, N, AVER, NZ)
         DIMENSION A(50)
         AVER = 0.0
         NZ = 0
         DO 10 I = 1, N
            AVER = AVER + A(I)
            IF ( A(I) .EQ. 0.0 ) NZ = NZ + 1
   10    CONTINUE
         AN = N
         AVER = AVER / AN
         RETURN
         END

         CALL AVERNZ(ZETA, 20, ZMEAN, NZCNT)

16  a. A(1)   A(2)   A(3)
          B(1)   B(2)   B(3)   B(4)

    b.                   C(1,1)  C(2,1)  C(1,2)  C(2,2)  C(1,3)  C(2,3)
        D(1,1)  D(2,1)  D(3,1)  D(1,2)  D(2,2)  D(3,2)

17  a. C(1)   C(1)   C(2)   C(2)   C(3)   C(3)
       I(1)   I(2)   R(1)   R(2)   R(3)   R(4)

    b. D(1)   D(1)   D(2)   D(2)   D(3)   D(3)   D(4)   D(4)
       R1            R2     I(1)   I(2)   I(3)   I(4)   I(5)

19  a. DATA A, C, (STRING(I), I = 1, 23)/21.9, (1.0, 2.0), 23*2.0/

    b. DATA (NUMBER(I), I = 1, 4)/3HONE, 3HTWO, 5HTHREE, 4HFOUR/
```

INDEX

Blocking, of records, 142, 143, 167
Bowling scoring exercise, 166, 167
Box filling exercise, 118
Braun, Christine, 225
Breakage exercise, 250
Bridge playing exercise, 250
Bubble chamber exercise, 50
Bubble sorting exercise, 117
Buffer, 142, 143, 206, 234
Built-in function, 11, 43, 169, 170
Burroughs Corporation, 189
  6000 Series, 54, 159
Buxton, John N., 227
Byte, 54

California Computer Products, 148,
  149
CALL, 174, 234, 251
Call by name, 238
Call by value, 238
Calling program, 173
Capital letter, 21
Card, 16, 17, 20, 126, 137, 143
  column, 20
  punch, 44, 137, 223, 229
  reader, 137
Carr, John W., III, 249
Carriage control, 57, 58, 66, 74,
  130, 136, 143, 148
Central processing unit, 99, 167,
  202
Checkerboard exercise, 51
Checking, data validity, 105, 108,
  113, 138, 221-223
Checkout, program, 3, 27, 47, 99,
  169, 222, 223, 231, 253, 254
Chess exercise, 121-123, 163, 164,
  250
Churchman, C. West, 119
Cipher exercise, 166
Circle, flowchart, 33
Clearing, of array, 96, 108
Closed function, 170
Clock, CPU, 167
CMPLX, 63, 65, 66, 67, 247
COBOL, 166
CODE, 222
Coding form, 20, 23
Coefficient of correlation example,
  81-88, 92
Column, card, 16, 20
  of array, 77
Column design example, 38-42, 96
Comment, 20, 23, 36, 151, 226, 235
COMMON, 79, 176-180, 184, 185
Comparison, 32, 61, 244
Compiler, 4, 22, 25, 45, 99, 172,
  179, 202, 231-242, 253, 254

Compilogram, 189
Complex, constant, 63
  expression, 63, 64, 243, 244
  function, 63, 76, 245-247
  input and output, 64, 131
  variable, 5, 53, 178
COMPLEX, 53, 63, 65, 78, 80
COMPLEX*16, 64
Compression, of data, exercise, 117,
  118, 206
Computed GO TO, 31, 33, 227
Computer Synectics, Inc., 231
Computers and Automation, 249
Compound condition, 32, 227
COMPUTRA, 149
Condition, 32, 227
Connor, Ursula, 198
Console, computer, 19
  time-sharing, 4, 20, 27, 151, 198
Constant, 4, 240
  complex, 63
  double precision, 54
  integer, 4
  logical, 68
  real, 4, 5
Continuation, statement, 20, 37, 58,
  228
CONTINUE, 98, 99, 100, 227, 241
Control Data Corporation, 62, 159,
  234
Convergence, of Gauss-Seidel method,
  107, 112, 119, 121
  of Newton-Raphson method, 43, 47
Conversational Software System, 198
Conversion, of data types, 12, 235
Core-resident compiler, 254
Correlation coefficient example,
  81-88, 92
Cosine function, complex, 63, 245
  double precision, 245
  real, 11, 245
CPU, see Central Processing Unit
Cramer's rule, 75, 78
Creation date, of file, 143
Cress, Paul, 254
Current flow example, 35
Cycloid exercise, 15
Cylinder, disk, 206

D field descriptor, 55, 127, 129
Damped oscillation example, 105-107
DATA, 180, 181
Data base exercise, 168, 250
Data compression exercise, 117, 118,
  206
Data Definition, 25, 142, 143, 159,
  234
Data organization, 136

Data set, 136, 139, 141, 151, 158, 204
Data set reference number, 137, 139, 141
Data validation, 105, 108, 113, 221-223
Datamation, 231, 241, 254
Date, file creation, 143
DD, 25, 142, 159, 234
Debugging, see Checkout
Decimal places, 18
Decimal point, 5, 17, 37, 41, 85, 127, 128
Decision, 33, 38, 70
Deck of cards, 22, 137, 163, 221
Declaration, see Specification
DECODE, 222
Default, of input and output characteristics, 137, 142, 158, 204
DEFINE FILE, 139-141
Definite integral example, 90, 103, 104
Definition, of statement function, 170, 171
  of FUNCTION, 172
Delay, access, 141
Delimiter, 61, 202
De Moivre's formula, 63
Desk calculator simulation exercise, 249
Desk checking, 47
Diagnostic checking, 45, 46, 202, 222, 253, 254
Diamond, flowchart, 33
Digital clock, 167
Dijkstra, Edsger W., 227
Dimension, 77, 222
DIMENSION, 79, 80, 81, 85, 86, 93, 126, 172, 177, 179, 221
Direct access data set, 137, 140, 168
Direction cosine exercise, 90
Dirksen, Paul, 254
Disk, magnetic, 136, 137, 139, 141, 143, 150, 151, 156-159, 185, 206
Division, 7, 10, 240, 243
DO, flowchart symbol, 108, 109
  statement, 32, 93-123, 227, 228, 240, 241, 243, 254
Documentation, 3, 225-229, 240
Dollar sign, 6, 165
Dorn, William S., 225
Double precision, constant, 54
  expression, 54, 55, 64, 85, 243, 244
  function, 55, 245-247
  input and output, 55, 127, 129
  variable, 5, 53, 54, 85, 178

DOUBLE PRECISION, 53, 60, 61, 78, 80, 236, 241
Double spacing, 57, 58, 130
Draft lottery exercise, 119, 120, 163, 167
Drum, magnetic, 143
Dummy variable, 171, 172, 173

E field descriptor, 17, 18, 127, 128
Economic order quantity example, 21-27
Editing program, 20, 200-210, 229
Efficiency of program execution, 127, 138, 139, 167, 210, 231-242, 253, 254
EJECT, 226
Electrocardiograph exercise, 166, 167
Element, of array, 77
  successor rule, 177, 178
END, 19, 20, 23, 172
END FILE, 137, 138, 151, 236
END option on READ, 138
Endless loop, 46
ENTRY, 218
Environment, time-sharing, 200
EQ, 32, 68, 244
Equal sign, 12
Equation, quadratic, 75, 182-188
  simultaneous, 75, 78, 105-114, 116, 119, 121, 150-159, 163, 172
EQUIVALENCE, 176-180, 235, 241
ERR option on READ, 138
Error message, 45, 46, 138
  WATFOR, 255-260
  WATFIV, 261-267
Error routine, 139
Error, data, 2, 105, 108, 113, 138, 221-223
  program, 42-48, 169, 202, 253-261
  relative, 79
  rounding, 54, 78
  transmission, 210
  truncation, 55
Exclusive OR exercise, 194
EXEC, 25, 204, 216
EXEC 8, 159
Executable statement, 34, 80, 181
Execution, program, 22, 25, 26, 127, 138, 139, 167, 204, 210, 231-242, 253, 254
Executive language, 204, 216
Exit, of DO, 95
Exponent, of number, 5, 6, 18, 37, 128
Exponential function, complex, 63, 64, 75, 245
  double precision, 245
  real, 11, 245

Magnetic, disk, 136, 137, 139, 141,
    143, 150, 151, 156-159, 185, 206
  drum, 143
  tape, 136, 137, 138, 150, 151,
    156-159
Magnitude, 5
Maintenance, program, 3, 225
Management information system
    exercise, 250
Master Control Program, 159
Matrix multiplication exercise, 90,
    115
McCracken, Daniel D., 76, 166, 188,
    198, 221, 225
Mean, 15, 81-88
Medium, data, 143
Memory protection, 112
Minus sign, 5, 7, 128
Mixed expression, 9, 12, 48, 61, 64,
    95, 235, 236, 243, 244
Multiplexor, 198
Multiplication, 7, 236, 240, 243
Musical transposition exercise, 249

Name, of function, 170-177
  of variable, 6, 17, 21, 36, 53,
    176, 228
NAMELIST, 134-136
National CSS, Inc., 142, 158, 198,
    206, 208
NE, 32, 68, 244
Negative subscript, 80, 104, 221
Nested DOs, 96, 98, 99, 127, 241
Newton-Raphson method, 42-48
Nonexecutable statement, 34, 80, 181
Nonnumerical data, 121, 187,
    206-220, 222
Normal exit, of DO, 95
NOT, 32, 33, 68, 227
NOVAR Corporation, 198
Null line, 200, 210
Null statement, 25, 26
Numerical analysis, 2
Numerical integration example, 90,
    103, 104

Object program, 4, 19, 22, 23, 27,
    138, 180, 185, 204, 231-242,
    253, 254
Object-time FORMAT, 132-134, 241
Open function, 170
Operating instructions, 225
Operating system, 19, 21, 24, 25,
    126, 137, 141-144, 159, 231,
    253, 254
Operation, 243, 244
  arithmetic, 7-10, 187
  complex, 63

Operation, double precision, 54
  integer, 7-10
  logical, 32, 68, 227
  real, 7-10
  relational, 32, 68
  symbol, 7, 20, 32, 187
Optimization, program, 231-242, 254
OR, 32, 68, 194, 227, 240
Organick, Elliott I., 85, 99, 100,
    108
Organization, of data, 136
OS/360, 25, 26, 142, 143, 159, 234
Outer DO, 96
Out-of-range subscript, 80, 81, 112,
    221
Output, 15-18, 33, 125-167, 225,
    233, 234, 253
  alphanumeric, 129
  complex, 64, 131
  double precision, 55, 127, 129
  FUNCTION, 174
  integer, 17, 127, 128
  logical, 70, 129
  real, 127-129
  SUBROUTINE, 174
  unformatted, 139, 150, 151,
    156-159, 167, 233
  unit, 17, 125, 137
Oval, flowchart, 33

Packing, of data, exercise, 117,
    118, 206
Padding, of data, 131
Page counting, 183
Paging, 241
Parallel operation of arithmetic
    units, exercise, 121
Parallelogram, flowchart, 33
Parentheses, 8, 9, 10, 11, 12, 30,
    63, 68, 70, 72, 127, 131, 228,
    239
Parity checking, 138
Password, 198
PAUSE, 19, 98
Period, 32
Physical record, 142, 143
Pi, 61, 76, 118, 252
PICTURE exercise, 166
Pipe temperature example, 148, 150,
    154, 155
PL/I, 227
Plus sign, 5, 7, 16, 128
Poisson distribution exercise, 119
Polish notation, 186
Precision, 5, 39, 85
PRINT, 137
Printer, 17, 57, 137, 142
Processor, see Compiler

This index was prepared using the Fortran program

shown on pages 218-220, run on the time-sharing

services of National CSS, Inc., Stamford, Conn.

FORTRAN STATEMENT PUNCTUATION SAMPLES

Page numbers refer to text discussions of the statements.
Blanks are ignored except within Hollerith fields; statement
spacing is otherwise at the discretion of the programmer.

Page	Statement sample
12	ZCUBED = Z ** 3
12	ROOT1 = (-B + SQRT(B**2 - 4.*A*C)) / (2.0 * A)
78	X(K) = (RIGHT(K) - SUM) / D(K, K)
68	SWITCH = .TRUE.
68	LOGIC1 = LOGIC2 .OR. (A .NE. B)
170	ROOT2(A, B, C) = (-B - SQRT(B**2 - 4.0*A*C)) / (2.0*A)
137	BACKSPACE 7
175	CALL MATMPY (A, BMATRX, RESULT, 6, M, 10)
178	COMMON ABC, IJK, C, G1H2Q3(100)
180	COMMON /BLOCK1/CAT, I91/BLOCK2/DOG, HORSE, I284/
53	COMPLEX PHASE, J, CPX, W2, C2(20)
98	CONTINUE
181	DATA A/12.0/, N1, N2, N3, N4/2, 3*19/
181	DATA CPX/(1.0, 2.0)/, LOGIC1, LOGIC2/.TRUE., .FALSE./
181	DATA DP/1.234D-05/, LITERL/4HABCD/, QUOTE/'WXYZ'/
181	DATA ARRAY(1), ARRAY(2), ARRAY(3)/3.4, -6.22, 9.0/
79	DIMENSION AA(2,10,6), ARRAY(10), K12(50, 2), FORMT(8)
93	DO 80 I = 1, 100
93	DO 200 KLM = 2, NPLUS1, 3
53	DOUBLE PRECISION DP, D(10, 10), XSQ, DENOM8, X(10)
20	END
138	END FILE 7
176	EQUIVALENCE (ABC, BCD), (X, Y, Z), (C2(1), D(20))
181	EXTERNAL SIN, SQRT, MYOWN
127	FORMAT (I6, 4F6.0, E12.4, 5L1, D20.16)
127	FORMAT (1X, 1P8E15.6)
130	FORMAT (1H1, 28HHEADING LINE AND PAGE NUMBER, 10X, I3)
130	FORMAT ('1', 'HEADING LINE AND PAGE NUMBER', 10X, I3)
131	FORMAT (1X, 4(F8.2, F9.3), 1PG12.6/I4, F5.1)
172	FUNCTION BESSEL (X, N)
29	GO TO 300
31	GO TO (200, 100, 80, 300), KPOINT
30	IF (ABS(XNEW - 100.0) - 0.001) 50, 50, 100
32	IF (Q2 .GT. Q1) BIGGER = Q2
32	IF ((RESID .LT. TOLER) .OR. (ITER .GT. 20)) GO TO 70
53	IMPLICIT COMPLEX(E), INTEGER(F, S-V)
53	INTEGER ABC, BCD, J79, LITERL
174	INTEGER FUNCTION FACTRL (N)
53	LOGICAL SWITCH, LOGIC1, LOGIC2, TICTAC(3, 3)
19	PAUSE
137	PRINT 8000, A, B, C, RLS
137	PUNCH 27, DELTA, EPSLON, RMN
137	READ 707, X, Y, D(2, 7), RFK
139	READ (12) ARRAY1, ARRAY2
16	READ (5, 500) I, J, ABC, DEF
132	READ (5, FORMT) L, M, N, GHI
138	READ (4, 400, END=950, ERR=150) A, B, C
53	REAL IJK, MAJOR(2,4,8), G123, W, Y, Z, RIGHT(10), QUOTE
173	RETURN
138	REWIND 12
19	STOP
174	SUBROUTINE MATADD (AMATRX, BMATRX, CMATRX, M, N)
139	WRITE (12) ARRAY1, ARRAY2
17	WRITE (6, 300) A, B, C, I, J, K
127	WRITE (6, 200) ((ARRAY(J, K), K = 1, N), J = 2, 8)